Digital Religion

"*Digital Religion* is a watershed publication that documents and defines the field, one that will quickly establish itself as an essential teaching text and reference volume. It deftly balances more theoretical overviews with specific case studies rich in needed context and detail. Through its inclusion of work on Buddhist, Hindu, and other non-Western traditions, the book succeeds in the essential goal of providing genuinely global coverage of digital religion."

Charles Ess, *University of Oslo, Norway*

"Digital religion is evolving quickly from its creation. This network of scholars analyze in depth how people are finding their spiritual selves and community online."

Barry Wellman, *University of Toronto, Canada*

Digital Religion offers a critical and systematic survey of the study of religion and new media. It covers religious engagement with a wide range of new media forms, highlighting examples from all five of the major world religions and other new religious movements. From cell phones and video games to blogs and Second Life, this book:

- provides a detailed review of issues related to religious authority, authenticity, community, identity, and ritual online
- includes a series of case studies to illustrate and elucidate thematic explorations
- considers the theoretical, ethical, and theological issues raised.

Drawing together the work of leading international experts from key disciplinary perspectives, *Digital Religion* is invaluable for scholars and students wanting to develop a deeper understanding of the field.

Heidi A. Campbell is Associate Professor of Communication at Texas A&M University, USA. Her books include *Exploring Religious Community Online* (2005) and *When Religion Meets New Media* (2010).

Digital Religion

Understanding Religious Practice in
New Media Worlds

Edited by
Heidi A. Campbell

LONDON AND NEW YORK

First published in 2013
by Routledge
2 Park Square, Milton Park, Abingdon, Oxon OX14 4RN

Simultaneously published in the USA and Canada
by Routledge
711 Third Avenue, New York, NY 10017

Routledge is an imprint of the Taylor & Francis Group, an informa business

© 2013 Heidi A. Campbell for selection and editorial matter; individual contributors, their contributions

The right of Heidi A. Campbell to be identified as the author of the editorial material, and of the authors for their individual chapters, has been asserted in accordance with sections 77 and 78 of the Copyright, Designs and Patents Act 1988.

All rights reserved. No part of this book may be reprinted or reproduced or utilized in any form or by any electronic, mechanical, or other means, now known or hereafter invented, including photocopying and recording, or in any information storage or retrieval system, without permission in writing from the publishers.

Trademark notice: Product or corporate names may be trademarks or registered trademarks, and are used only for identification and explanation without intent to infringe.

British Library Cataloguing in Publication Data
A catalogue record for this book is available from the British Library

Library of Congress Cataloging in Publication Data
Digital religion: understanding religious practice in new media worlds / edited by Heidi A. Campbell.
p. cm.
Includes index.
1. Mass media in religion. 2. Mass media–Religious aspects. 3. Digital media.
I. Campbell, Heidi, 1970–
BL638.D54 2012
201'.7–dc23
2012015446

ISBN: 978-0-415-67610-6 (hbk)
ISBN: 978-0-415-67611-3 (pbk)
ISBN: 978-0-203-08486-1 (ebk)

Typeset in Bembo
by Taylor & Francis Books

Printed and bound in Great Britain by the MPG Books Group

Contents

	List of contributors	viii
1	Introduction: The rise of the study of digital religion HEIDI A. CAMPBELL	1

PART I
Themes in the study of religion and new media — 23

2	Ritual CHRISTOPHER HELLAND	25
3	Identity MIA LÖVHEIM	41
4	Community HEIDI A. CAMPBELL	57
5	Authority PAULINE HOPE CHEONG	72
6	Authenticity KERSTIN RADDE-ANTWEILER	88
7	Religion GREGORY PRICE GRIEVE	104

PART II
Thematic case studies — 119

Ritual

8	Hindu worship online and offline HEINZ SCHEIFINGER	121
9	Virtual Buddhism: Buddhist ritual in Second Life LOUISE CONNELLY	128

Identity

10 Playing Muslim hero: Construction of identity in video games 136
VIT SISLER

11 Digital storytelling and collective religious identity in a moderate to progressive youth group 147
LYNN SCHOFIELD CLARK AND JILL DIERBERG

Community

12 Charting frontiers of online religious communities: The case of Chabad Jews 155
OREN GOLAN

13 Considering religious community through online churches 164
TIM HUTCHINGS

Authority

14 The kosher cell phone in ultra-Orthodox society: A technological ghetto within the global village? 173
TSURIEL RASHI

15 Formation of a religious Technorati: Negotiations of authority among Australian emerging church blogs 182
PAUL EMERSON TEUSNER

Authenticity

16 Alt-Muslim: Muslims and modernity's discontents 190
NABIL ECHCHAIBI

17 You are what you install: Religious authenticity and identity in mobile apps 199
RACHEL WAGNER

Religion

18 Japanese new religions online: Hikari no Wa and "net religion" 207
ERICA BAFFELLI

19 "'Go online!' said my guardian angel": The Internet as a platform for religious negotiation 215
NADJA MICZEK

PART III
Reflections on studying religion and new media 223

20 Theoretical frameworks for approaching religion and new media 225
KNUT LUNDBY

21	Ethical issues in the study of religion and new media MARK D. JOHNS	238
22	Theology and the new media STEPHEN GARNER	251
23	Concluding thoughts: Imagining the religious in and through the digital STEWART M. HOOVER	266

Index   269

List of contributors

Erica Baffelli is Lecturer in Asian Religions at the University of Otago, New Zealand. Her research interest lies primarily in the interaction between Japanese "new religions" and media. In 2010 she co-edited, with Ian Reader and Birgit Staemmler, the volume *Japanese Religions on the Internet: Innovation, Representation and Authority* (Routledge Research in Religion, Media and Culture Series).

Heidi A. Campbell is Associate Professor of Communication at Texas A&M University, USA, where she teaches in media studies. She has researched and published extensively on themes related to religion and the Internet for over fifteen years, focusing on the behaviors of online religious communities as well as comparative work on Jewish, Muslim, and Christian groups' use and perception of new media forms. She is the author of *Exploring Religious Community Online* (Peter Lang, 2005), *When Religion Meets New Media* (Routledge, 2010) and more than 30 articles and book chapters on issues related to new media, religion, and digital culture.

Pauline Hope Cheong is Associate Professor at the Hugh Downs School of Human Communication, Arizona State University, USA. Her published studies have examined the sociocultural implications of media among minority and marginal communities, including how religious leaders negotiate their authority and influence amidst technology-related changes in their work. www.paulinehopecheong.com

Lynn Schofield Clark is Associate Professor and Director of the Estlow International Center for Journalism and New Media at the University of Denver's Department of Media, Film, and Journalism Studies, USA. Clark is author, co-author, or editor of five books and more than 50 articles, book chapters, and essays on the role of media in social and cultural change.

Louise Connelly recently submitted her PhD to the University of Edinburgh, UK. Her research interests include early Buddhism; material and visual culture; and Buddhist religious communities and identity online, specifically within blogs and Second Life. Her recently published work focuses on Buddhist religious practice and aesthetics in Second Life.

List of contributors ix

Jill Dierberg is a Doctoral Candidate at the University of Denver, USA. Her dissertation research focuses on the reception of Stephen Colbert's television persona among persons and communities of faith. She is currently adjunct faculty in Religion and Media at Carthage College.

Nabil Echchaibi is Assistant Professor of Mass Communication, University of Colorado Boulder, USA. His research expertise is in diasporic media and Islam and the media. His research has appeared in *International Communication Gazette*, *Journal of Intercultural Studies*, *Journal of Arab and Muslim Media Research*, and *Nations and Nationalism*. He is also author of *Voicing Diasporas: Ethnic Radio in Paris and Berlin Between Culture and Renewal* (Lexington Books, 2011).

Paul Emerson Teusner is a recent PhD Graduate from the School of Media and Communication at RMIT University, Australia. His current research interests lie in the use of mobile technologies and cloud computing among young Australians as they develop cultural, gender, social, and economic identities.

Stephen Garner is Lecturer in Practical Theology in the School of Theology, University of Auckland, New Zealand. He holds an MSc in computer science and a PhD in theology and has worked in a variety of information technology-related fields. He currently teaches in theological ethics, public and contextual theology, science and religion, religion and popular culture, and spirituality. His research interests focus particularly on the interaction of technology, theology, and popular culture, and his PhD dissertation was titled "Transhumanism and the imago Dei: narratives of apprehension and hope."

Oren Golan is Lecturer in the Faculty of Education at the University of Haifa, Israel. He received his PhD in sociology and social anthropology from the Hebrew University in Jerusalem (available on his blog: http://cyber-youth.blogspot.com), was recipient of a Fulbright scholarship, and in 2009/10 was a postdoctoral scholar at NYU's Center for Religion and Media. Golan's research interests include: Internet and new media studies, the sociology of youth, social and ethnographic aspects of Israeli society, informal education, social trust, friendship, entrepreneurship, and – of late – online religion in the US and Israel.

Gregory Price Grieve is Associate Professor of Religious Studies and the Director of MERGE: A Network for Interdisciplinary and Collaborative Scholarship at the University of North Carolina at Greensboro, USA. He researches and teaches in the intersection of Asian religions, digital media, and postmodern and pluralistic approaches to the study of religion. He is the author of numerous articles, the monograph *Retheorizing Religion in Nepal* and the co-editor of the volume *Historicizing Tradition in the Study of Religion*. He is currently working on a book titled *Empty Worlds: Buddhism, Virtual Reality, and Liquid Modern Religion*, which analyzes Second Life's Zen

Buddhist cluster to comprehend the early efforts of practitioners to reshape religious practices on the virtual frontier.

Christopher Helland is Associate Professor of Sociology of Religion, Dalhousie University, Canada. Helland's research focuses on the impact of the Internet on a variety of religious traditions and diaspora communities, with a special interest in Hinduism and new religious movements such as pre-millennial, apocalyptic movements and UFO-based religious groups. He is the author of the forthcoming book *Internet Communion and Virtual Faith* (Oxford University Press) and articles appearing in the *Journal of Computer Mediated Communication*, *Religious Studies Review*, *Religion*, *Religion on the Internet* (JAI, 2000), and *Religion Online* (Routledge, 2004).

Stewart M. Hoover is Professor of Media Studies and Religious Studies at the University of Colorado Boulder, USA, and Director of the Center for Media, Religion, and Culture. His research focuses on qualitative studies of media audiences, looking at questions of communication and culture, and the implications of media technology for religious meaning-making. He is author of five books, including *Religion in the Media Age* (Routledge, 2006), and co-editor of five books, including *Fundamentalisms and the Media* (Continuum, 2007). He currently heads a Ford Foundation–funded research project entitled "Finding Religion in the Media," exploring the extent to which religious belief, practice, and action are generated in the media sphere, with special attention given to digital media and religion.

Tim Hutchings completed his PhD, examining five online churches, at Durham University, UK, in 2010. His current research explores the role of new media in religious recruitment and disaffiliation. His work has been published in the *Australian Religious Studies Review*, *Online – Heidelberg Journal of Religions on the Internet*, and the *Expository Times*.

Mark D. Johns is Associate Professor of Communication Studies at Luther College in Decorah, Iowa, USA, where he teaches courses in media and Internet studies. He is the author of *Our Context: Exploring Our Congregation and Community* (Fortress, 2002), as well as co-editor of *Online Social Research: Methods, Issues, and Ethics* (Peter Lang, 2004) and *Social Media Campaigns: Methods and Issues* (Peter Lang, forthcoming).

Mia Lövheim is Professor of Sociology of Religion, University of Uppsala, Sweden. Lövheim's research focuses on youth, gender, and identity and the Internet. Her work has appeared in a number of journals, such as *Nordicom Review* and *Online – Heidelberg Journal of Religions on the Internet*, and as noted book chapters in *Mediating Religion* (Continuum, 2003), *Religion Online* (Routledge, 2004), *Religion in Cyberspace* (Routledge, 2005), and *Everyday Religion* (Oxford University Press, 2007).

Knut Lundby is Professor of Media Studies, Department of Media and Communication, University of Oslo, Norway. He holds a doctoral degree in sociology of religion. Among his books are *Mediatization: Concept, Changes, Consequences* (ed., Peter Lang, 2009) and *Rethinking Media, Religion, and Culture* (ed. with Stewart M. Hoover, Sage, 1997).

Nadja Miczek is a Postdoctoral Researcher at the Institute of Religious Studies at the University of Lucerne, Switzerland. She received her master's degree in religious studies and finished her doctoral thesis in 2009. She conducted her doctoral research as a fellow of the Collaborative Research Center 619 "Ritual Dynamics" at the University of Heidelberg.

Kerstin Radde-Antweiler is a Lecturer in Religious Studies, University of Bremen, Germany. Her research focuses on Pagan and Christian rituals in online environments, especially Second Life. She has published articles in *Online – Heidelberg Journal of Religions on the Internet*, *Masaryk University Journal of Law and Technology*, *Journal of Ritual Studies*, and *Ritual Matters* (Routledge, 2010).

Tsuriel Rashi is the Head of the Mass Communication Department at Lifshitz College of Education in Jerusalem, Israel, and a Lecturer at Bar Ilan University's School of Communication, serving as the academic advisor for communication graduate students. His research fields of interest and publication are Judaism and communication, Jewish law, philosophy, and media ethics.

Heinz Scheifinger is Lecturer in Sociology-Anthropology at the University of Brunei Darussalam, Brunei. His primary research interest concerns the relationship between Hinduism and the Internet and he has published a number of articles on this topic. These include "Researching Religion on the WWW: Identifying an Object of Study for Hinduism" in *Methodological Innovations Online* (2008) and "Internet Threats to Hindu Authority: *Puja* Ordering Websites and the *Kalighat* Temple" in *Asian Journal of Social Science* (2010).

Vit Sisler is Assistant Professor of New Media at the Faculty of Arts at Charles University in Prague, Czech Republic. His research deals with the relation between Islam and digital media, and the topic of educational and political video games. He was a visiting Fulbright scholar at Northwestern University in 2008–9.

Rachel Wagner is Associate Professor of Religion at Ithaca College, USA. Her research expertise is in religion in popular culture and the nature of religion in virtual reality. She is author of *Godwired: Religion, Ritual and Virtual Reality* (Routledge, 2011).

1 Introduction

The rise of the study of digital religion

Heidi A. Campbell

This volume revolves around a seemingly simple question: What is "digital religion"? In the last several decades we have seen significant changes take place in the ways communication technology is influencing how people practice religion. Take for example the birth and evolution of cyberchurches, from broadcast-style web forums to virtual interactive worship environments. Early cyberchurch entities were often websites set up by independent groups seeking to replicate or mirror some feature of church life online through their design or the resources they offered, such as a scriptorium page of religious texts or a place to leave prayer requests (for example the Virtual Church of the Blind Chihuahua, www.dogchurch.org). Then cyberchurches emerged which tried to emulate aspects of offline church services online by using technologies such as IRC, podcasts or RealAudio players to offer sermons, singing, and limited engagement between congregants (for example, First Church in Cyberspace). With the rise of the virtual world many groups are embracing technologies such as Second Life to create an online worship experience that offers an interactive worship via avatars (for example the Anglican Cathedral in Second Life, or the Church of Fools). Now we see the Internet becoming a tool to extend a church's offline ministry into online spaces. For instance, we see the rise of Internet campuses within many multisite churches, and webcasting of services via iPhone and Facebook apps (for example LifeChurch.tv) becoming common. Thus, rather then being an alternative social space for a few, digital technology becomes an important platform extending and altering religious practice for many.

Yet, while there have been radical changes in communication technology, the terms or frames used to describe these changes and how religion is conceived of within digital culture have not always kept up. The term "digital religion" is used and defined here in order to fill this void, by giving us a new frame for articulating the evolution of religious practice online, as seen in the most recent manifestations of cyberchurches, which are linked to online and offline contexts simultaneously. "Digital religion" does not simply refer to religion as it is performed and articulated online, but points to how digital media and spaces are shaping and being shaped by religious practice. As a concept it allows us to talk about the current state of religion in relation to digital artifacts and the culture in which it is situated. The chapters in this volume address in different ways the context and performance of digital religion in the twenty-first century, so that we can take stock of how religious practice has been described, approached, and changed in the last few decades.

Cyber, online, and/or digital religion

In order to understand what is unique about "digital religion" as a conceptual lens, we must first investigate how it relates and compares to previous terminology used to describe religious engagement with the Internet. In the mid- to late 1990s "cyber-religion" surfaced as a way to describe the importing of religion to the new frontier of cyberspace, or the not-so-real world created by virtual reality technologies. Initially this metaphorical framing evoked mythical utopian and dystopian images of religion, where religious practice could be freed from traditional constraints and patterns so it could be re-envisioned beyond the screen. "Cyber-religion" was used by some to suggest new kinds of religious community and ritual, and suggested a new alliance was emerging between computer technology and religion as people experimented with bringing their spiritual lives into cyberspace (Bauwens 1996). Over the next decade scholars defined and applied the term "cyber-religion" to a variety of contexts. Dawson used it to specifically identify "those religious organizations or groups which exist only in cyberspace" (2000: 29). Brasher in *Give Me that Online Religion* (2001) uses cyber-religion as a broad concept, one that could refer both to "the presence of religious organization and religious activities in cyberspace" (p. 9) or could encompass the notion of "the gradual emergence of new, electronically inspired religious practice and ideas" (p. 30). Hojsgaard's (2005) thoughtful reflection on cyber-religion as a theoretical concept concluded it was a term "whose contents reflect the main features of postmodern cyberculture ... a solid opposition to traditionally structured religious institutions" and yet as "a phenomenon that addresses the same type of ontological and metaphysical questions that religious institutions and traditions have usually done" (p. 62). Thus the concept of cyber-religion provided a way to explore and call into question traditional assumptions and understandings of religion as it engaged with new cultural and technological contexts. However, due to cyber-religion being an amorphous and broad concept, and the fact that its links to concepts of cyberspace and virtuality often evoked assumptions that it was based on an incomplete or somehow false form of religiosity, meant there were limits to its usefulness.

In an attempt to distinguish the different forms of religion emerging online, Helland (2000) offered another conceptual framing. He presented the categories of "religion online" and "online religion" in order to differentiate religious uses of the Internet on the basis of whether information and rituals are largely based on offline sources and practices or on forms arising from the practicing of religion online. Religion online was lauded for empowering its members to re-form rituals and bypass traditional systems of legitimation or recognized gatekeepers, and the opportunities it provided to transcend normal limits of time, space, and geography. Online religion represented how the fluid and flexible nature of the Internet allowed new forms of religiosity and lived religious practices online. Though much less common than the occurrence of religion online, online religion demonstrated how the Internet offered a new social landscape for imaging the spiritual contemporary society. These initial categories helped scholars distinguish the type of practice they were studying and the motivations of a given user community. These framing concepts played an important role in many studies of religion and the Internet, allowing scholars to talk in more concrete terms about the traits of Internet-based religiosity (Kawabata and Tamura 2007) and the extent to which traditional religious practices and community could be transported or replicated online (Howard 2010), as well as debate the relationship or overlapping nature of the framings of religious expression and activity online (Young 2004). Helland has gone on to critique his categories as theoretical endpoints in and of themselves, and even to reformulate them in his own work by acknowledging that the separation between religion online and offline is becoming increasingly blurred and blended (see Helland 2007). Yet the distinction between religion online and online religion still serves as an important tool for mapping nuances and different strategies employed by religious groups and users in their online activities.

In the last few years a new term has emerged to describe religious practice online, that of "digital religion." It has been used as the title of a number of conferences (for example the International Conference on Digital Religion at the University of Colorado Boulder, January 2012; and the Digital Religion Symposium at the Donner Institute in Turku, Finland, June 2012), research initiatives (for example the Digital Religion: Knowledge, Politics and Practice project run by the Center for Religion and Media at New York University), and book projects. Cheong, Fisher-Nielsen, Gelfgren and Ess in their 2012 edited collection *Digital Religion, Social Media and Culture* draw together a range of studies which reflect the complex relationship emerging between digital media and contemporary religiosity in a Web 2.0 world. Stewart Hoover (2012) suggests in his foreword to this collection that the study of religion and new media has moved on from simply exploring the "digitalization of religion" – which considers how digital media force religious groups and practitioners to adapt to altering notions of religious tradition, authority, or authenticity – to consider at a deeper level "the actual contribution 'the digital' is making to 'the religious'" (p. ix). In other words, digital religion is religion that is constituted in new ways through digital media and cultures. Hoover highlights that this may lead to a new understanding of religion, one that is rooted in unique understandings and experiences of mediation of meaning via digital technology. This recognizes that the reformulation of existing religious practices has both online and offline implications. It also means digital culture negotiates our understandings of religious practice in ways that can lead to new experiences, authenticity, and spiritual reflexivity.

Based on this I suggest that the term "digital religion" describes the technological and cultural space that is evoked when we talk about how online and offline religious spheres have become blended or integrated. We can think of digital religion as a bridge that connects and extends online religious practices and spaces into offline religious contexts, and vice versa. This merging of new and established notions of religious practice means digital religion is imprinted by both the traits of online culture (such as interactivity, convergence, and audience-generated content) and traditional religion (such as patterns of belief and ritual tied to historically grounded communities). This echoes assertions made by Hoover and Echchaibi (2012) that discussion of "the religious digital" requires a recentering of our attention on the shape of religion in light of the digital. They suggest that when lived religious practice and digital culture meet a "third space" emerges, a hybridized and fluid context requiring new logics and evoking unique forms of meaning-making. Digital religion as a concept acknowledges not only how the unique character of digital technology and culture shapes religious practice and beliefs, but also how religions seek to culture new media contexts with established ways of being and convictions about the nature of reality and the larger world.

Gregory Price Grieve similarly argues in this volume that digital religion represents a distinct cultural sphere of religious practice that is unique but not dichotomous with other forms of religion. This understanding of digital religion helps scholars push past previous discourses that simply look at religion online as an innovation occurring in a unique media space to consider how religious practice online is a vital expression of the religious in contemporary culture. Digital religion points to a different understanding of religion online and offline, one that is informed by the social structures and cultural practice of life in a technological and information-saturated society. It is with this recognition that this collection, *Digital Religion: Understanding Religious Practice in New Media Worlds*, emerges, seeking to offer a nuanced reflection on how religion is taking place in a digital environment, and becomes informed by the key characteristics and ideology of new media, which can alter not only practice but the meaning-making process itself. *Digital Religion* is situated within a growing scholarly literature on religious engagement online, spanning three decades. This introduction frames not only this collection, but provides an overview of the birth and development of this area of scholarly inquiry in order to contextualize both the state of the field and the contribution this volume seeks to make to it.

Religion and new media studies: a new scholarly subfield

Over the past decade and a half my scholarship on religion and new media has been motivated by three aims. First, I have sought to produce work that provides an apologetic for this new subfield of inquiry, highlighting how the study of religion and new media is not only a vibrant and valid area of scholarly interdisciplinary investigation within Internet studies, but offers potential broader cultural insights into the social practices emerging within new media culture. Second, I have sought to provide a map to other scholars of key research

Introduction 5

themes and questions currently covered in this area, which offers a clear overview of the parameters of the subfield or what can truly be claimed about how the Internet and other digital technologies are shaping religious communities and practice. Third, I have endeavored to carve out a space where interdisciplinary inquiry and interaction could occur for scholars and students, drawing together the work of scholars in various disciplines and cultural contexts in order to demonstrate what each has to offer in relation to the shared questions and concerns emerging about religion and new media. This introduction offers an overview of these endeavors and situates the role *Digital Religion* plays in this vibrant and growing subfield.

An apologetic for a new subfield

Important to the framing of the study of religion and the Internet as a new subfield within Internet studies, and media, religion, and culture studies has been scholarly work documenting and categorizing the rise of religious practice online. Scholars have noted examples of people practicing and bringing their religious practice online as early as the mid-1980s, when computer hobbyists, governmental researchers, and individuals with early Internetworking connections brought their spirituality into online discussion forums (Ciolek 2004). Rheingold (1993) documents the rise of religious discourse in bulletin board systems (BBSs) in a "create your own religion" thread on the CommuniTree discussion forum. During this same period online religious discussion surfaced on Usenet. It was a time when religious computer enthusiasts began to explore "ways to use this new means of communication to express their religious interests" (Lochhead 1997: 46). Also in 1984 Usenet began to be split into a number of specialized hierarchies, such as "alt.philosophy" and "soc.culture," to accommodate the growing number of special interest network users. This included such hierarchies as "alt.religion," "soc.religion," and "talk.religion." Helland (2007), for instance, documented how tensions in the general religion discussion forums led to the need to establish specialized religious discussion forums, and the creation of the first religion-specific online community, "net.religion.jewish," a discussion forum on Judaism and Jewish spirituality online.

In the early to mid-1990s, the Internet was a heavily text-based medium, so we see most of the religious interaction online taking place on bulletin boards, newsgroups, and e-mail lists, spaces where people would come together to discuss religious topics or form religious communities online. For example Ecunet, an ecumenical Christian e-mail listserve (www.ecunet.org), became a very active e-mail-based group seeking to build a conversational Christian community across denominational lines (see Farrington 1993). The rise of websites in the 1990s led to numerous religious websites and even the establishment of various virtual churches and temples. For example the First Church of Cyberspace (www.godweb.org), was established by American Presbyterians in 1992 as the first virtual non-denominational online church, which ran weekly services via a chat forum for over a decade. A key moment came in 1996, when the *Time* magazine cover story "Finding God on the web" (Chama 1996) documented the impact dozens of religious websites were having on various religious groups, from reviving ancient religions such as the worship of Thor and invigorating minority religions such as the Zoroastrian cybertemple (www.zarathushtra.com), to providing new outreach and proselytizing opportunities such as the website Monastery of Christ in the Desert (www.christdesert.org) and creating new forms of religious practice such as the Virtual Memorial Garden tribute to people and pets (www.catless.ncl.ac.uk/VMG).

In the 1990s many religious traditions migrated online through various users and institutional practices. Buddhists began to experiment with bringing traditional religious practices such as sangha and dharma combat online, and the Dalai Lama's monastery in New York even performed a ritual to sanctify cyberspace for such practices (Zaleski 1997). This raised concerns about the extent to which the Internet could serve as a sacred space for religious ritual. This was further complicated by the rise of pilgrimage sites such as Virtual Jerusalem (www.virtualjerusalem.com) that provided not just access to religious goods and information, such as where to find kosher products online or times for shabbat services in different parts of the world, but allowed you via a webcam and e-mail service to partake in the ritual of placing prayers in the Western Wall in Jerusalem. By the late 1990s, multitudes of different religious online groups and resources began to surface. These were often created by religious individuals rather than institutions, leading to discussion about whether the Internet promotes individualized spirituality over communal affiliations. For instance, sites such as Beliefnet (www.beliefnet.com) sought to create a "multi-faith e-community" offering e-devotionals and access to sacred texts from different faith traditions, allowing individual to "pic-n-mix" between different religious traditions and sources. Online religious communities also continued to rise in popularity, some focused around theological discussion or religious study, others offering prayer and support, and others seeking to provide common ground for affirming religious identity.

By the early 2000s a debate emerged amongst religious leaders about how religion online, especially individualized information seeking and engagement, was changing religious culture. Clergy and religious leaders reflected on the extent to which they needed to adapt: did they need to take control of the Internet and culture in a way that would take back some of the authority they saw as being undermined by Internet practice? Within Internet studies, debates arose regarding whether Internet practice encouraged diversity of religious dialogue and provided a place where users could build bridges, or were people actually gravitating to the same groups online as offline, and building religious ghettos and stereotypes? Another question was whether the Internet was a tool for individual empowerment, and was this going to be a good thing for religion and even political and social culture, or a threat to offline authority? In the 2000s many religious congregations were beginning to see the importance of having a presence online, of being able to connect to spiritual information seekers online. Many religious traditions saw not only the importance of offering an online presence, but also how the Internet could extend their mission and outreach, with things like online fatwa sites (a fatwa is a juristic ruling concerning Islamic law), and bringing official and unofficial religious leaders together to answer questions generated from religious dialogue online.

This study of religion and the Internet emerged alongside a growing scholarly interest in the Internet as an important object and space for study. In many respects the field of Internet studies is still a relatively new research field, trying to solidify its own identity and contribution to our understanding of digital technologies and culture. It was only in 2005 that Nancy Baym posed the question, "Is 'Internet Research' a Virtual Field, a Proto-Discipline, or Something Else?" as guest editor of a special issue of the journal *The Information Society* (volume 21, issue 4). This issue brought together a variety of scholars to reflect on the extent to which Internet studies could be seen as its own unique field, and how an area of study which transcends multiple disciplines, methods, and theoretical approaches could come together to represent a cohesive scholarly conversation. The works in this collection concluded that Internet studies was indeed gathering a corpus of data, beginning to develop unique methods and approaches, and collecting some common findings about the impact of the Internet and other digital technologies on a variety of social and cultural contexts. Indeed Ron Rice (2005) in his article provided an overview of core research themes frequently investigated by scholars, including issues of community formation, online communication, users' patterns and processes, role and process in e-organizations, and digital media and culture. This special issue also noted that there remained considerable gaps in Internet scholarship, and one of the areas highlighted was the study of religion.

In an article entitled "Making Space for Religion in Internet Studies," I argued that religious practice and user communities needed to be given more scholarly attention (Campbell 2005a). This was not just because religious engagement online is an interesting phenomenon in and of itself, nor that it was an increasingly popular use of the Internet, but also because religion is an important part of contemporary life for many people within an information society. I suggested that paying attention to how scholars of religion and the Internet approach questions of authority, identity construction, and community online could provide important methods and analysis that would benefit the wider field of Internet studies. This article made an important declarative statement within the field of Internet studies, drawing attention to the contribution the study of religion could make to our understanding of computer-mediated communication within a global information culture. It is based on this work that scholars began to speak of religion and the Internet not just as unique phenomenon worthy of attention, but also as an important space for understanding the complexities and characteristics of digital and new media culture.

This scholarly apologetic, highlighting the importance of studying religion within digital culture, has been extended through my work in a variety of disciplines, which seeks to demonstrate how the study of digital religion illuminates the larger impact the Internet is having on society (Campbell 2005b, 2007). Thus a significant portion my scholarly work has been dedicated to establishing and validating the study of new media, religion, and digital culture as an important new subfield.

A map of the scholarship

Vital to making the case for the importance and validity of this new subfield has been my work seeking to map the variety of subjects, approaches, and questions scholars have engaged with in their study of religion and the Internet (Campbell 2003b, 2005c, 2006, 2011). I have sought to spotlight key questions of how religious community, identity, ritual, and authority are being informed by new media technologies and cultures, and the different approaches taken to the subject. Through these efforts I have sought to offer a number of critical literature reviews mapping the range of topics covered in this growing area of academic inquiry. In these works I have endeavored to provide a guide to key articles and books published on religion and the Internet since the 1990s.

When the literature is viewed as a whole one can see that the approaches taken seem to closely match the categories offered by Hojsgaard and Warburg (2005a) when they describe the development of the academic study of religion and the Internet in terms of three waves of research. In their assessment, the first wave of research focused on the new, extraordinary aspects of cyberspace in which religion "could (and probably would) do almost anything" (p. 8). Internet scholars sought to document and describe these new online phenomena while trying to weigh utopian and dystopian discourses about how the Internet would save or ruin the world as we knew it. Early text on religion and the Internet tended to offer a broad or general survey of religious engagement with the Internet and offer reflections on their potential religious or cultural implications (for example Zaleski 1997; Brasher 2001), positive reflections on how the Internet may reconnect people with spirituality in postmodern society (for example Cobb 1998; Wertheim 1999), or critical analysis of the ethical challenges posed by digital technology (Houston 1998; Wolf 2003). While many of these texts have now become dated due to the quickly evolving nature of technology, they provided important early documentation of the rise of different forms of religion online. These works also pointed to important questions beginning to emerge through this research, such as the nature of religious rituals and community online.

Hojsgaard and Warburg (2005a) noted that the second wave of research focused on a "more realistic perspective," in which it was understood that it was not just the technology but also people who were generating these new forms of religious expression online. They observed how scholars attempted to provide categorizations and typologies to understand common trends within Internet practice. This type of work is easily seen in the three most cited scholarly books on religion and Internet studies, all representing edited collections drawn from different conferences highlighting various studies of religion online. *Religion on the Internet: Research Prospects and Promises* (Hadden and Cowan 2000) was important as the first collection seeking to identify early issues being explored by scholars concerning the impact of the Internet on religious groups and culture, though often reflecting the utopian or dystopian paradigms characteristic of early discussions of the Internet. Dawson and Cowan's *Religion Online* (2004) presented a more diverse and sophisticated collection of studies. Hojsgaard and Warburg's (2005b) *Religion and Cyberspace* presented papers from a 2001 international conference on "Religious Encounters with Digital Networks," held at the University of Copenhagen. Both volumes sought to identify common questions and forms of methodology scholars were employing in this area of study. While all three are valuable works, they represent disparate collections of studies seeking to identify key scholarly studies and their findings, rather than cohesive commentaries on how religious groups and practices as a whole are being shaped by Internet technology and culture. Here questions of religious identity and authenticity of religious practice online began to surface as key concerns for researchers.

According to Hojsgaard and Warburg (2005a), the third wave was only beginning to surface in the mid-2000s as a "bricolage of scholarship coming from different backgrounds" (p. 9). Third-wave research was characterized by a turn towards theoretical and interpretative research, where scholars sought to identify methods and tools for analyzing data and assessing findings in light of larger theoretical frameworks. In this era, the study of previous questions related to ritual, community, and identity were explored in more detail, to look at how the embeddedness of the Internet in everyday life was influencing religious digital practice. Scholars sought to draw conclusions about how examples of religion online – such as religious rituals (for example Helland 2007; Krueger 2004), community (for example Cheong and Poon 2009; Campbell 2010), and identity (for example Lövheim 2006; Cowan 2005) – were impacting religious communities and organizations as well as mirroring practices in a broader offline context. New research themes were noted – such as how the Internet challenged established religious authorities (for example Barker 2005), empowered new religious leaders (for example Campbell and Golan 2011), and provided new opportunities for traditional leaders to re-assert influence online (for example Barzalai-Nahon and Barzalai 2005) – were given significant attention. We also see the beginnings of theoretical and methodological frameworks, as some scholars seek to provide systematic interpretive tools for analyzing offline religious communities' negotiation patterns with new media (Campbell 2010) and gaining nuanced understanding of authority negotiations online (Campbell 2007).

These three waves – the descriptive, the categorical, and the theoretical – have become an important typology, used as a tool and applied by various researchers, including those in this book, to describe the progression and development of research in religion and Internet studies. The metaphor of waves is often used to describe how research methods and approaches to various research questions have matured over time, as our knowledge of the implications of Internet technologies on various social and cultural processes has increased.

Some scholars are also beginning to suggest that a fourth wave of research into religion online is emerging, offering further refinement and development of methodological approaches, as well as the creation of typologies for categorization and interpretation (Campbell and Lövheim 2011). This is seen in new methodological models being offered to assist scholars, such as those provided in a study of religious ritual in virtual world environments (Grieve 2010). This current wave of research also seeks to provide a basis for longitudinal studies on the relationship between religions in online contexts. This requires a careful study of "the social and institutional implications of practicing religion online; and what impact, if any, this will have on the construction of identity, community, authority and authenticity in wider culture" (Campbell and Lövheim 2011: 11). It is in this current wave of research that this volume seeks to make an important contribution.

Creating space and bridging interdisciplinary inquiry

Over the past decade and a half my research program has also sought to offer a thematic analysis of the study of religion and the Internet for scholarly audiences in specific disciplines, including sociology (Campbell 2003a), media studies (Campbell 2005b, 2005c), religious studies (Campbell 2012), and psychology (Campbell and Connelly 2012). This aim has been further solidified in an article published in the *Journal of the American Academy of Religion* in which I argue that one cannot fully understand contemporary religiosity without understanding the traits of religious practice online and how they reflect larger trends in religious beliefs and practices offline (Campbell 2012). The interdisciplinary study of religion and the Internet highlights the growing recognition that new media has become embedded in our everyday lives and a common platform for spiritual engagement.

In an era marked by social media we see that religious self-expression and representation has become an accepted part of religious identity and practice. Through the network Jesus has his own Facebook page, the Buddha tweets, and you can download a variety of religious mobile phone apps that can help you pray towards Mecca or connect with the Pope. We also see religious groups leveraging the advantages of social media but seeking to avoid the problematic moral content it can relay, creating religiously framed versions of various social media applications for their specific communities, such as GodTube.com, a Christian-filtered version of YouTube, and Salamworld.com and MillatFacebook (www.mymfb.com), Muslim versions of Facebook. So as new media have become infused into our daily patterns, technology helps extend our abilities to integrate spirituality into our everyday lives in new ways. These new social media opportunities continue to raise a number of core questions related to religious practice online and digital environments of interest to scholars in a variety of disciplines, including area studies, communication, human–computer interaction, philosophy, political science, religious studies, sociology, and theology, to name just a few. While coming from different theoretical and methodological perspectives, scholars often raise similar or overlapping questions. For example, how is religious practice being transferred and transformed online? How does the way religious individuals leverage new media enable them to perform or constitute their religious selves online? What are the social and cultural implications of such moves? How are religious institutions and globalized cultures responding to or being impacted by such developments? Are religious authorities undermined due to religious practice online, or can they leverage new media to maintain influence in their communities? Questions such as these, along with the range of religious practice online, continued to evoke interest and debates among both scholars and practitioners, leading to vibrant scholarly conversation.

Over the past decade we have seen increasing interest in researching the role religion plays in online and digital contexts. This is illustrated by a number of scholarly initiatives, including the study of ritual online spearheaded by the Ritual Dynamics Project at the University of Heidelberg, explorations of the role digital media plays in religious social and political transformations by New York University's Center for Religion and Media, and investigation into where in the digital media realm religion is found as part of the current work of the Center for Media, Religion, and Culture at the University of Colorado. Such initiatives highlight the growing interest in digital religion from various disciplinary areas. Over the past few years I have similarly been working to create an online resource center for scholars studying religion and digital culture within a variety of contexts. This has involved pulling together a network of scholars in media studies, religious studies, and sociology of religion to help think through the state of research, and to identify notable gaps in current scholarship and what is needed to help this area further develop. In the course of putting together the Network for New Media, Religion and Digital Culture Studies (digitalreligion.tamu.edu), which was officially launched in early 2012, and of working with the advisory board of established scholars in this research area, it quickly became evident that, while a growing literature has emerged in the past decade, few cohesive or comprehensive survey texts exist which provide a clear overview of this emerging field and are targeted at both scholars and students. Based on this, the advisory board and I saw the need for a text providing a clear and thorough overview of the variety of forms of religious use of new media and a rigorous analysis of key questions raised by religion online. Based on efforts to offer a scholarly apologetic, a map, and an interdisciplinary frame for the study of religion and new media, *Digital Religion: Understanding Religious Practice in New Media Worlds* seeks to provide a full overview of the terrain of this subfield, and the direction in which it is currently moving.

An overview of *Digital Religion*

Digital Religion seeks to provide a critical survey of the study of new media, religion, and digital culture for both students and scholars new to this area, by introducing them to the central areas of research inquiry emerging from fifteen years of scholarship on religion and the Internet. It does this through a detailed review of major themes in the study of religion and the Internet, and by reflecting on how these apply to the broader study of religion and new media. Through my previous scholarly literature reviews and conversations with members of the Network for New Media, Religion and Digital Culture Studies, a number of key research areas and questions were identified, including how new media shapes our understanding of authority, authenticity, community, identity, and ritual, and even our notion of how religion is defined. Thus the text offers critical literature reviews of each of these core themes, written by recognized experts in the study of religion and the Internet whose work has helped pioneer and define these areas of inquiry. These essays seek to map how each of these research topics has emerged and is currently developing so that readers are provided with a fuller understanding of how religion online relates to and influences religious culture as a whole.

These themes of authority, authenticity, community, identity, ritual, and religion are further explored through focused research case studies linked to each of these themes. Case studies are written by both established and emerging scholars doing significant work in this field; these works demonstrate how different religious traditions are engaging with a variety of new media forms (blogs, cell phones, Second Life, video games, websites, etc.) and how focused studies can illuminate larger themes and research questions in the subfield, when presented in a systematic format. *Digital Religion* is also the first systematic, structured, and analytical review of research on religion and the Internet addressing all five of the major world religions (Buddhism, Christianity, Hinduism, Islam, and Judaism), as well as select new religious movements. *Digital Religion* thus offers a comprehensive survey of the variety of technologies, religious contexts, and core questions explored within this unique subfield of scholarship.

Digital Religion starts with a survey of themes in the study of religion and new media. Part I offers six thematic chapters providing an overview of key research topics within the study of religion and the Internet in the past 15 years. Each chapter corresponds with two case studies, found in Part II, which explore these themes through concrete examples illustrating the different approaches taken to these core topics. Chapter 2 begins with the theme of ritual. Christopher Helland outlines how religious practices have been transported online and discusses the implications of ritualized behaviors in online religious environments. Ritual, he suggests, is part of the cultural meaning-making system, such that it can be both a religious and secular act. This means that ritual plays an important role in the human experience, and so considering ritual online becomes essential for understanding how people culture online environments with familiar patterns of practice to incorporate them into their systems of meaning-making. He argues that the study of online ritual has challenged scholars to carefully consider what it means to "do" religion and even to "be" religious in a digital realm. Looking at how and why various religious groups practice religious rituals online can help point towards a broader understanding of what constitutes religion in a digital world.

This overview of ritual online is paired with two case studies of Asian religions' ritual practice online. Buddhism and Hinduism online have until recently been little studied within religion and Internet studies, and so these chapters offer an important contribution, illustrating this emerging work and how it extends our understanding of religious ritual online. In "Hindu Worship Online and Offline," Heinz Scheifinger explores how *puja*, the ritualistic worship of a Hindu deity, has been performed online, and compares this with traditional *puja* rituals that necessitate fully embodied interaction. He carefully considers the extent to which a *puja* conducted online can constitute a valid form of religious expression and the debates that such online ritual can raise for offline Hindu communities. Louise Connelly investigates Buddhist rituals in virtual worlds in her case study, "Virtual Buddhism: Buddhist ritual in Second Life." Specifically, she focuses on Buddhist meditation as a ritual which incorporates material objects and the use of both voice and text, and the negotiation process between offline and online ritual. She suggests the practice of Buddhism online has ramifications for Buddhist doctrine and practice both offline and online, which are in need of further exploration.

In Chapter 3, "Identity," Mia Lövheim investigates how the Internet has been framed as a site of identity construction, negotiation, and performance, offering unique opportunities and challenges for individuals and religious groups. Within the study of identity a key concern is how individuals link their online and offline identities in the ways in which they use digital media. Lövheim suggests that scholars need to contextualize claims about religious identity on the Internet within broader understandings of the processes of social and cultural transformation at work within late modern society. She concludes that scholarship demonstrates that religious identity online is not that different nor completely disconnected from religious identity in everyday offline life. This means that, while the Internet enhances the possibility that individuals may practice religion outside institutional contexts, digital media also provide a space for anchoring one's religious identity and helping one connect the online and offline in order to find and negotiate personal meaning in everyday life.

To further consider the possibilities and challenges new media offers religious individuals in their construction of identity, two case studies are presented which explore how different digital mediums provide opportunities for re-presenting religious identity online. Vit Sisler, in "Playing Muslim hero: Construction of identity in video games," analyzes how contemporary Islamic video games can offer players a new virtual representation of Muslim identity, as hero rather than victim or villain, as is often seen in popular digital game narratives. Through an analysis of recent games produced in the Arab world he explores how religious identity can be understood, defined, and performed via new media. He suggests that, while one cannot assume that Muslim-created video games which offer alternative Muslim identities will cause an ontological shift for the gamer, such narratives are worth exploring to consider the potential implications they have for religious identification.

14 Heidi A. Campbell

In "Digital storytelling and collective religious identity in a moderate to progressive youth group," Lynn Schofield Clark and Jill Dierberg consider religious identity construction through digital storytelling. They suggest that digital media, especially video, offer new means for religious groups to construct their religious identities, as video sharing sites offer enhanced means of social interaction and public self-representation. They conclude that "the digital storytelling process enabled young people to write themselves, and their community, into being in a way that was fresh and meaningful for them" (p. 148). Thus new media forms offer a platform for the public performance and reimaging of religious identities which can help shape individual and communal narratives in a new public space.

Chapter 4 addresses the theme of community. I offer an overview of the rise of groups online and how they began to be viewed as communities. The emergence of online communities created both new possibilities for social interaction and challenged traditional notions of community for many religious groups. I suggest the exploration of online communities through the lens of social networks, which presents community in terms of fluid social interactions rather than notions of shared geography and familial ties, and highlights a distinctive understanding of how community is lived out online and offline in contemporary society. Thus the careful study of community online points to a shift in the conception of how community is formed and how it functions in new media culture.

The implications of an online community functioning as a network of loosely bounded social relations that may challenge the beliefs of and relationship to traditional religious communities are explored in relation to Jewish ultra-Orthodox and Christian communities online. In "Charting frontiers of online religious communities: The case of Chabad Jews," Oren Golan considers how new media culture and the spiritual marketplace of the Internet offer contemporary religious communities opportunities to enlist new members and expand their influence. By looking at the Chabad, a Jewish ultra-Orthodox community which has had an Internet presence since the 1980s, he shows how online groups can help a religious community consolidate its transnational religious identity while simultaneously challenging traditional community boundaries and patterns. In "Considering religious community through online churches," Tim Hutchings explores two online Christian churches, St Pixels and Life Church, that use digital media platforms for worship, conversation, and proselytization. He shows the different understandings and patterns of "community" fostered in each group, and how these strategies have implications for local offline churches within this tradition. Both case studies demonstrate that the question of community online does not simply concern how community is lived out online, but also how these practices connect to and have implications for offline religious communities and institutions.

In Chapter 5, "Authority," Pauline Cheong provides an analysis of recent studies examining the implications of the Internet for religious authority. Her review highlights early framings of the Internet as a decentralized space lacking hierarchical control, suggesting that traditional religious authority would be disrupted or undermined by digital technologies. Such studies suggested that the Internet might facilitate changes in the personal and organizational structures by which religious leaders operate, requiring religious leaders to negotiate such tensions and more tightly manage their online representations. Yet other studies have shown that religious authorities are developing strategies online that enable them to regain their legitimacy in and oversight of the religious sphere. Thus she proposes that the Internet highlights paradoxes regarding authority online, suggesting it can simultaneously empower and challenge new and traditional forms of religious authority.

These tensions and possibilities created by the Internet in relation to the enactment of religious authority are explored through discourses surrounding the creation of the kosher cell phone in Israel and the role played by Australian emerging church bloggers as religious authority figures. In "The kosher cell phone in ultra-orthodox society: A technological ghetto within the global village?" Tsuriel Rashi investigates the rhetoric generated by rabbis of several Israeli Jewish ultra-Orthodox communities when they declared a ban against cell phone companies between 2004 and 2007. The ban represented an attempt by religious leaders to assert control over this technology, which they viewed as allowing secular and sinful content into their closed community. Identifying arguments voiced by community members against uncensored cell phone use highlights key concerns established offline religious authorities have regarding how new media technologies may allow users to bypass traditional community gatekeepers and boundaries. Investigating how the Internet may give rise to new classes of religious authority, Paul Teusner considers the extent to which institutional religious authority is reflected, reinforced, or challenged in online settings of social interaction. His case study, "Formation of a religious technorati: Negotiations of authority among Australian emerging church blogs," provides a discursive analysis of Australian religious bloggers, showing how religious authority is enacted in the online blogosphere. He suggests that, rather than challenge traditional religious authorities, religious bloggers that emerge as recognized religious authorities may simply mirror the attributes and pattern of traditional religious leaders. Thus these case studies highlight the paradox of the Internet as a platform that simultaneously affirms and undermines religious authority.

Chapter 6 explores the theme of authenticity. Kerstin Radde-Antweiler investigates the distinction between online and offline, and debates about what is considered the real and the virtual in Internet contexts. She approaches this analytical distinction by considering whether people's digital experiences and bodies (i.e. one's textual body or avatar), can be considered authentic or real, and the extent to which the Internet or "cyberspace" can be considered a "real" place that can function as a sacred space. In highlighting these debates over what constitutes the "real" versus the "virtual" online she concludes that a binary view of the online space or body seen as either authentic or as mere simulation is problematic, as such judgments are often made without face-to-face contact, so "the Internet requires different criteria for judging whether other users are trustworthy" or credible (p. 98).

Issues of what can be considered or judged to be authentic online are explored in more detail through two case studies looking at how new media can be used to present one's religious identity online. Nabil Echchaibi explores how an online forum for progressive Muslims can act as a transformative space for presenting a new Muslim identity. In "Alt-Muslim: Muslims and modernity's discontents" he examines the site's attempt to function as an alternative to conventional authority in Islam and the veracity of its claims that it creates a counterculture for Muslims around the world. In "You are what you install: Religious authenticity and identity in mobile apps," Rachel Wagner reflects on how religious mobile applications offer individuals new opportunities to engage in religious bricolage, as the personalization of one's mobile devices becomes an act of religious identity construction and presentation. Yet such acts raise questions of authenticity. In other words, to what extent does one's selection of religious apps represent an actual and cohesive religious identity, or does app selection more accurately reflect an individualized religious identity that works against a fixed notion of religious identity or authority? Both these case studies reflect on the extent to which the Internet provides online resources that build new forms of religious identity which may be seen as inauthentic because they encourage personalized over traditional or institutional religious identities.

In Chapter 7, Gregory Price Grieve tackles the theme of religion, considering how religion can be understood in relation to the digital realm, and to what extent the category "digital religion" exists and can be defined. He argues that "religion" is a complex concept with many different interpretations, and offers a thoughtful investigation into what he sees as the essential features of religion (worldview myths, rituals with mythic significance, and faith or beliefs) in order to reflect on how those features are translated or lived out when applied to digital media. After discussing the unique aspects of digital media he argues that digital religion, or religion that is lived out and practiced online, offers a workaround, providing religious Internet users with dynamic opportunities to navigate the problems created by the fluid nature of "liquid modern life," which challenges previous definitions of religion and traditional patterns of religiosity. His overview of how digital religion has been studied illuminates the complexity of studying religion and how traditional definitions may need renegotiation in relation to new media contexts.

The complexity of studying and defining religion in new media worlds is then explored in relation to the engagement of new religious movements (NRMs) with the Internet. In "Japanese new religions online: Hikari no Wa and 'net religion,'" Erica Baffelli discusses the use made by Aum Shinrikyô, a Japanese NRM, of the Internet. Through this study she demonstrates how a group's understanding of religion and the role of religious leaders are negotiated online when the incorporation of digital media, such as websites and social networking services, inform and extend the practices of a community. Nadja Miczek details the meaning New Age practitioners attribute to their Internet use in "'Go online! said my guardian angel': The Internet as a platform of religious negotiation." She argues that New Age practitioners actively go online to present their religiosity because of the unique opportunities the Internet provides for creating a personalized assemblage of their spiritual beliefs. She suggests this shows that the Internet offers an important opportunity for users to make visible their people's religiosity, since modern media usage allows them to create unique, dynamic presentations of traditional religious beliefs and formations. Both case studies highlight the freedom of and new opportunities for expression that the Internet offers, allowing NRMs flexibility to present unique religious patterns and meanings to the public.

In the final part of the book, "Reflections on studying religion and new media," three chapters highlight several key research themes concerned with how religion and new media are approached and investigated. In Chapter 20, "Theoretical frameworks for approaching religion and new media," Knut Lundby surveys the dominant theoretical approaches commonly used in the study and evaluation of new media. These include five dominant approaches to religion in new media: technological determinism, as seen in the work of Marshall McLuhan; mediatization of religion, developed by Stig Hjarvard; mediation of meaning, as discussed by Stewart Hoover; mediation of sacred forms, highlighted by the work of Gordon Lynch; and the social shaping of technology approach, developed by me. His survey addresses how these theories have been employed in the study of media and religion generally and how they have begun to be applied to the study of new media in relation to religion.

In Chapter 21, "Ethical issues in the study of religion and new media," Mark Johns provides an overview of key ethical issues which arise when conducting research in new media contexts. He details the ethical challenges encountered in studying questions such as identity, community, and authority online, and notes that key methodological issues must be considered by those wanting to pursue research of religion on the Internet.

Then, in Chapter 22, "Theology and the new media," Stephen Garner considers what theological discourses and approaches add to the study of religion and new media, an area which has previously been dominated primarily by religious studies, sociology, and media studies approaches. He addresses the question of how theology can influence thinking in the technological age, on what role it can or should play in informing and interpreting religious negotiation with new media.

Finally, in Chapter 23, Stewart Hoover reflects on the common questions and issues raised within this volume, and the different frames used by scholars and practitioners to respond to the "changed realities resulting from the digitalization of religion and spirituality" (p. 266).

Together these essays seek to contribute to a new wave of research, which expands previous conversations, looking primarily at the Internet alone as the site where digital religion occurs, to include reflection on other digital spaces and technologies. It also seeks to consider how this new, digitally mediated context creates not only new spaces for religiosity to be constituted but a lens for meaning-making that may transform our conversations about what it means to be religious in a digital, mobile, augmented reality.

Acknowledgments

The aim of this book project has been to help build and resource this vibrant and emerging subfield of research within Internet studies and growing area of interdisciplinary investigation in the study of media, religion, and culture. This volume would not have been possible if it were not for the support of a number of crucial groups. First I wish to thank a number of key scholars and mentors whose feedback and interactions over the past decade have informed my thinking on new media and religion, namely Clifford Christians, Charles Ess, Lorne Dawson, Stewart Hoover, Knut Lundby, and Barry Wellman. I am also grateful for the support of the advisory board of the newly formed Network for New Media, Religion and Digital Culture Studies, whose scholarship and encouragement have inspired this project: Erica Baffelli, Pauline Hope Cheong, Lynn Schofield Clark, Nabil Echchaibi, Gregory Price Grieve, Christopher Helland, Mia Lövheim, and Kerstin Radde-Antweiler.

The contributions in this book have benefited from the attentive eyes and editorial assistance of Rebecca Bennett, Michelle Osbourn, Emma Griffith, Judy Webster, and Brian Altenhofen, who reviewed the initial manuscript and provided valuable feedback on its readability. I am also indebted to Chris Helland, Greg Grieve, and Louise Connelly for their thoughtful comments on the drafts of key chapters, organization of this collection, and insights into what is unique about the notion of "digital religion." I also wish to thank my Comm 460 Class "Religion and Digital Culture" from Fall of 2011 at Texas A&M University, who read and discussed the first full draft of the book, offering useful feedback on the book's organization and content, and raising important questions regarding the future of religion in a digital age. Furthermore I am grateful for the support of TAMU's Glasscock Center for Humanities Research, the Religious Studies Interdisciplinary Program, and members of the Religion and Culture Working Group who helped sponsor the Digital Religion symposium in the fall of 2011 at which several of these chapters received their first public reading and audience.

This book would also not have been possible without the excellent editorial staff at Routledge, especially Lesley Riddle and Katherine Ong, whose patience and guidance helped bring the book to fruition. Finally I am grateful for the support of family and friendship networks who have cheered me on over the course of this project, especially Sarah Brooks, John and Vivian Campbell, Kathy DiSanto, Heather and Robb Elmatti, Kate Carte Engle, Srivi Ramasubramanian, Rick and Suzanne Ousley, Iris Villareal, Cara Wallis, and Emily Zechman.

References

Barker, E. (2005) "Crossing the Boundary: New Challenges to Religious Authority and Control as a Consequence of Access to the Internet," in M. Hojsgaard and M. Warburg (eds) *Religion and Cyberspace*, London: Routledge, 67–85.

Barzilai-Nahon, K. and Barzilai, G. (2005) "Cultured Technology: Internet and Religious Fundamentalism," *The Information Society*, 21(1). Online. Available: www.indiana.edu/~tisj/21/1/ab-barzilai.html (accesssed May 18, 2012).

Bauwens, M. (1996) "Spirituality and Technology," *First Monday*, 1(5). Available: http://firstmonday.org/htbin/cgiwrap/bin/ojs/index.php/fm/article/viewArticle/496/417 (accessed May 18, 2012).

Baym, N. (2005) "Special Issue: ICT Research and Disciplinary Boundaries: Is 'Internet Research' a Virtual Field, a Proto-Discipline, or Something Else?" *The Information Society*, 21(4).

Brasher, B. (2001) *Give Me that Online Religion*, San Francisco: Jossey-Bass.

Campbell, H. (2003a) "Online Communities, Religious," in *Encyclopaedia of Community*, 3, Great Barrington: Berkshire Publications/Sage Reference, 1027–8.

——(2003b) "A Review of Religious Computer-Mediated Communication Research," in S. Marriage and J. Mitchell (eds) *Mediating Religion: Conversations in Media, Culture and Religion*, Edinburgh: T & T Clark/Continuum, 213–28.

——(2005a) "Making Space for Religion in Internet Studies," *The Information Society*, 21(4), 309–15.

——(2005b) "Considering Spiritual Dimensions within Computer-Mediated Communication Studies," *New Media and Society*, 7(1), 111–35.

——(2005c) "Spiritualising the Internet: Uncovering Discourses and Narratives of Religious Internet Usage," *Heidelberg Journal of Religion on the Internet*, 1(1). Online. Available: www.ub.uni-heidelberg.de/archiv/5824 (accessed May 18, 2012).

——(2006) "Religion and the Internet," *Communication Research Trends*, 26(1), 3–24.

——(2007) "Who's Got the Power? Religious Authority and the Internet," *Journal of Computer-Mediated Communication*. Online. Available at: http://jcmc.indiana.edu/vol12/issue3/campbell.html (accessed May 18, 2012).

——(2010) *When Religion Meets New Media*, London: Routledge.

——(2011) "Internet and Religion," in C. Ess and M. Consalvo (eds) *Handbook on Internet Studies*, Oxford: Blackwell, 236–50.

——(2012) "Understanding the Relationship Between Religious Practice Online and Offline in a Networked Society," *Journal of the American Academy of Religion*, 79(1), 1–30.

Campbell, H and Connelly, L. (2012) "Cyber Behavior and Religious Practice on the Internet," in Z. Yeng (ed.) *Encyclopedia of Cyber Behavior*, 1, Hershey, PA: IGI Global, 434–45.

Campbell, H. and Golan, O. (2011) "Creating Digital Enclaves: Negotiation of the Internet amongst Bounded Religious Communities," *Media, Culture & Society*, 33(5), 709–724.

Campbell, H. and Lövheim, M. (2011) "Studying the Online-Offline Connection in Religion Online," *Information, Communication & Society*, 14(8), 1083–96.

Chama, J.R.C. (1996) "Finding God on the Web," *Time*, December 16, 149(1), 52–9.

Cheong, P. and Poon, J. (2009) "Weaving Webs of Faith: Examining Internet Use and Religious Communication Among Chinese Protestant Transmigrants," *Journal of International and Intercultural Communication*, 2(3), 189–207.

Cheong, P.H., Fisher-Nielsen, P., Gelfgren, S. and Ess, C. (2012) *Digital Religion, Social Media and Culture: Perspective, Practices and Futures*, New York: Peter Lang Publishing.

Ciolek, M.T. (2004) "Online Religion: The Internet and Religion," in Hossein Bidgoli (ed.) *The Internet Encyclopedia*, 2, Hoboken, NJ: John Wiley & Sons, 798–811.

Cobb, J. (1998) *Cybergrace: The Search for God in the Digital World*, New York: Crown Publishers.

Cowan, D. (2005) *Cyberhenge: Modern Pagans on the Internet*, Routledge: New York.

Dawson, L. (2000) "Researching Religion in Cyberspace: Issues and Strategies," in J.K. Hadden and D.E. Cowan (eds) *Religion on the Internet: Research Prospects and Promises*, New York: JAI Press, 25–54.

Dawson, L. and Cowan, D. (eds) (2004) *Religion Online: Finding Faith on the Internet*, New York: Routledge.

Farrington, D. (1993) "Ecunet: Our History," in *What is Ecunet?* Online. Available: www.ecunet.org/history.html (accessed March 10, 2006).

Grieve, G.P. (2010) "Virtually Embodying the Field: Silent Online Meditation, Immersion, and the Cardean Ethnographic Method," *Heidelberg Journal of Religions on the Internet*, 4(1). Online. Available: www.online.uni-hd.de (accessed May 18, 2012).

Hadden, J.K. and Cowan, D.E. (eds) (2000) *Religion on the Internet: Research Prospects and Promises*, Amsterdam, London and New York: JAI Press.

Helland, C. (2000) "Online-Religion/Religion-Online and Virtual Communities," in J.K. Hadden and D.E. Cowan (eds) *Religion on the Internet: Research Prospects and Promises*, New York: JAI Press, 205–23.

——(2007) "Diaspora on the Electronic Frontier: Developing Virtual Connections within Sacred Homelands," *Journal of Computer-Mediated Communication*, 12(3). Online. Available: http://jcmc.indiana.edu/vol12/issue3/helland.html (accessed May 18, 2012).

Hojsgaard, M. (2005) "Cyber-Religion: On the Cutting Edge between the Real and the Virtual" in M. Hojsgaard and M. Warburg (eds) *Religion and Cyberspace*, London: Routledge, 50–63.

Hojsgaard, M. and Warburg, M. (2005a) "Introduction: Waves of Research," in M. Hojsgaard & M. Warburg (eds.) *Religion and Cyberspace*, London: Routledge, 1–11.

Hojsgaard, M. and Warburg, M. (eds) (2005b) *Religion and Cyberspace*, London: Routledge.

Hoover, S. (2012) "Foreword: Practice, Autonomy and Authority in the Digitally Religious and Digitally Spiritual," In P.H. Cheong, P. Fisher-Nielsen, S. Gelfgren and C. Ess (eds) *Digital Religion, Social Media and Culture: Perspectives, Practices and Futures*, New York: Peter Lang publishing, vii–xi.

Hoover, S. and Echchaibi, N. (2012) "The 'Third Spaces' of Digital Religion," discussion paper, Boulder, CO: Center for Media, Religion, and Culture, University of Colorado Boulder. Online. Available: http://cmrc.colorado.edu/wp-content/uploads/2012/03/Third-Spaces-Essay-Draft-Final.pdf (accessed May 18, 2012).

Houston, G. (1998) *Virtual Morality*, Leicester: Apollos.

Howard, R.G. (2010) "Enacting a Virtual 'Ekklesia': Online Christian Fundamentalism as Vernacular Religion," *New Media & Society*, 12(5), 729–44.

Kawabata, A. and Tamura, T. (2007) "Online-Religion in Japan: Websites and Religious Counseling from a Comparative Cross-Cultural Perspective," *Journal of Computer-Mediated Communication*, 12(3), article 12. Online. Available: http://jcmc.indiana.edu/vol12/issue3/kawabata.html (accessed May 18, 2012).

Krueger, O. (2004) "The Internet as a Mirror and Distributor of Religious and Ritual Knowledge," *Asian Journal of Social Sciences*, 32(2), 183–97.

Lochhead, D. (1997) *Shifting Realities: Information Technology and the Church*, Geneva: WCC Publications.

Lövheim, M. (2006) "A Space Set Apart? Young People Exploring the Sacred on the Internet," in J. Sumiala-Seppänen, K. Lundby and R. Salokangas (eds) *Implications of the Sacred in (Post)Modern Media*, Göteborg: Nordicom, 255–72.

Rheingold, H. (1993) *The Virtual Community*, New York: Harper Perennial.

Rice, R. (2005) "New Media/Internet Research Topics of the Association of Internet Researchers," *The Information Society*, 21(4), 285–99.

Wertheim, M. (1999) *The Pearly Gates of Cyberspace*, London: Virago.

Wolf, M. (ed.) (2003) *Virtual Morality: Morals, Ethics and New Media*, London: Peter Lang Publishing.

Young, G. (2004) "Reading and Praying Online: The Continuity of Religion Online and Online Religion in Internet Christianity" in L. Dawson and D. Cowan (eds) *Religion Online: Finding Faith on the Internet*, New York: Routledge, 93–106.

Zaleski, J. (1997) *The Soul of Cyberspace: How Technology is Changing our Spiritual Lives*, San Francisco: Harper San Francisco.

Part I

Themes in the study of religion and new media

2 Ritual

Christopher Helland

As Internet technology has developed, people's level of engagement with the online environment has changed significantly. Over the last thirty years, there have been revolutionary changes in the way we go online and the things we can do with this new form of media. Many people using the Internet no longer distinguish between life-online and life-offline – rather, being "online" has become part of their daily life and social existence. Checking e-mail, searching for information, maintaining friendships and social networks are part of the everyday routine for a vast majority of the population. This is having significant impact upon people's religious information-seeking behaviour and also on the way people "do" religion.

With computers and Internet access devices (e.g., iPads and iPods) becoming more powerful and less expensive, combined with an ever-expanding high-speed and wireless network, people continue to assimilate this technology into their activities. Focusing specifically on ritual practice, this chapter will explore some of the key issues surrounding online religious interactions with the sacred through ritualized behaviours. Some of the key questions associated with this new form of online activity are generally focused upon two themes: authenticity and authority. Are online rituals real religious rituals? Can virtual pilgrimage be a real sacred journey? Do you need to be bodily present to be a participant in religious rituals? Do online rituals have efficacy for the faithful or are they too superficial for real spiritual transformations? Can anyone participate, create, or host an online ritual or do you have to be somehow religiously qualified? Do the online rituals even count as real ritual within the tradition? If not, what if people still do them? Can online ritual engagement provide substantial and deep religious meaning or do people "point, click, and surf" their way through cyberspace like virtual tourists, observing but not engaging with the religious activity? These are questions that researchers (both religious and secular) are trying to answer. Through a critical literature review of material that has examined these issues, this chapter offers a summary and an abridged overview of the last fifteen years of research, presenting a synthesis of the common methods, theories, and approaches used for studying rituals on the Internet. Examining online ritual requires a continually evolving field of study, challenging academics to push the boundaries of theoretical frameworks and conceptual understandings of what it means to "do" religion and even "be" religious in a wired world.

Ritual: its form and function

To understand the impact of the Internet and World Wide Web on ritual activity it is important to clearly define the term "ritual". Similar to defining "religion", this is a far more complex task than it would appear. Ritual studies have developed into a multi-disciplinary form of research that examines a wide variety of behaviours associated with the ritualization of activities. Although "ritology" examines a variety of actions, even those of animals, "ritual studies" is a sub-field of "religious studies" and is focused upon personal, cultural, and societal performances that intersect with religious symbols and ideologies (Driver 1990). Definitions are often hotly debated by scholars in this field over a wide range of theoretical concepts, systems of classification, and particular characteristics (Bell 1992).

Early theories examining the role and function of religious ritual were very broad, over-generalized, and functional in their approaches. Similar to defining "religion", early sociologists and anthropologists provided reductionist views often based upon limited fieldwork, biased ethnographies, and presupposed views of the role of religion itself. For example, Emile Durkheim (1995 [1912]) theorized that ritual was a powerful tool for maintaining social cohesion. He argued that when people collectively came together to perform a ritual they moved past the limitations of their own individual (selfish) identity and became collectively united with the group. The ritual activity created a sense of community and group identity that was reinforced over and over through the repetition of the ritual practice. Durkheim believed that the real role and function of ritual was to maintain the society. Through ritual practice, people felt a real sense of belonging and social cohesion; they experienced "collective effervescence" and felt that they were part of something larger and greater than themselves.

Presenting a different view based upon fieldwork, Bronislaw Malinowski (1954) believed that ritual was a mechanism for coping with anxiety and uncertainty. He argued that it was not necessarily a form of irrational behaviour, rather it was a way of dealing with danger and fear when there was no other way to control the outcome of the activity – his classic example was based upon the Trobriand Islanders and their travels in the open ocean. He argued that when the Islanders fished in the lagoon (a calm and safe environment) they did not perform rituals; however, when they practiced deep-sea fishing in canoes (which was a fairly dangerous undertaking) a number of rituals were performed. Malinowski believed that people turned to rituals and magic when they had no other means for dealing with situations that were beyond their control. These are just two cases in the early scholarship examining ritual that highlight some of the controversy surrounding the definition – controversy that still exists today. Both of these theories are right and both of them are wrong. Despite the brilliance of the people that wrote them and the significant contribution they provided to the academic study of ritual, they are wrong because they have attempted to place ritual practices within absolute terms. They have limited and reduced "ritual" down to one function.

As ritual studies developed, a number of scholars were critical of these earlier reductionist views, developing our understanding of the complexity of ritual. Edmund Leach (1968) argued that ritual has a number of different forms and a variety of functions that play out differently in different social contexts. Victor Turner (1969) also challenged these earlier "absolutes" by developing Arnold van Gennep's work on rites of passage to show the amazing levels of complexity occurring when people engage in ritual actions. For Turner, ritual was a dynamic and transformative form of social interaction, facilitated through the exchange of religious symbols. Other scholars, such as Mary Douglas and Clifford Geertz, emphasized the performative and communicative aspects of ritual, further expanding our academic understanding of the complexity of this activity.

Definitions of "ritual" can be broken down into those that look at "what ritual is" and also those that look at "what ritual does", although, as Leach (1968) recognized, sometimes these distinctions are extremely hard to separate out. For example, a definition such as "ritual consists of symbolic actions that represent religious meaning" (McGuire 1997: 16), clearly blends the two. There are a number of possible working definitions of ritual that are useful for examining the complexity of this activity in cyberspace – depending on the focus of the research, these can help or hinder a person's perceptions of online ritual activity. My own definition of ritual has always been a simple one: ritual is purposeful engagement with the sacred (whatever the sacred may be for those involved). This is general enough to recognize individual and personal ritual activities alongside formal rites and group rituals. It also recognizes the fluid nature of "the sacred", which for many people can be something that does not seem "religious" to the outside observer. No definition of ritual will be perfect on all theoretical levels. There is debate over how "purposeful" ritual activity must be for it to be authentic. For example, some people say Christian grace at the dinner table with very little "purposeful engagement"; they just want to do the ritual so that they can eat. However, by participating in the ritual, members of the group are affirming (at least in a performative way) that they accept the ritual activity they are undertaking and maintain the beliefs and practices associated with the ritual.

Ritual can be elaborate, structured, and extremely formal or it can be spontaneous and personally constructed. Through an examination of the variety of forms of ritual activity that exist, it is possible to conclude that religious ritual is an aggregate of performance, media, script, and representation of belief (Kreinath *et al.* 2004). These are basic building blocks or components that make up a ritual – and they impact on each other as they change, develop, or are transformed. The script is the set of rules that are laid out to be followed by the ritual, the words, action, gestures, and symbols that are to be used. The performance is the carrying out of the ritual, the attempt to follow the script.

The media are the mechanisms for communicating and receiving the ritual performance. Last, but not least, are the representations of belief that are embodied through the ritual performance itself: myths, sacred narratives, sacred stories, the belief of the supernatural, or whatever the participants view as sacred.

Assessing the function of ritual or "what it does" is contingent on the social context or setting. It is also important to stress that the participants in the ritual may feel it serves a purpose that is clearly (and perhaps only) linked with the supernatural – while the academic researcher may feel that it fulfills a social role. For the believer, rituals are a means by which supernatural beings and powers can be contacted, influenced, or coerced into helping humans accomplish what they are unable or less likely to achieve without supernatural assistance. This means that there is a level of function within the ritual activity that an "outsider" to the tradition cannot evaluate but is nevertheless true to the participant. Therefore, it is the actively engaged person conducting or participating in the ritual that determines if the ritual has efficacy – if the ritual has achieved the supernatural or spiritual goals that it set out to achieve. On a more social and observable level, ritual is used to teach, form identities, regulate societies, draw a community together, transform the psyche, and enacts faith (Bell 1992; Grimes 1982).

To this end, rituals are multivocalic, in that they "say" a lot of things at one time – they also do a variety of things and they achieve a variety of ends. For example, a funeral ritual can be a highly formalized and prescriptive (required) ritual. For the believers, it is a rite of passage ceremony for the newly deceased. A ritual that will ensure that the soul of the recently departed will go to wherever they believe the soul should go. There will be a script that should be followed, and if the ritual goes well, the people participating will rest assured knowing that they did their part to ensure that the deceased person will be successful in the afterlife. On another level, by participating in the ritual, the members of the community are also affirming and reinforcing their beliefs about the soul, the afterlife, and the role of the living. They are coming together as a community of believers, and part of the script will undoubtedly remind people of their social roles and responsibilities, of the rules and regulations they must all follow if they too wish to be successful in the afterlife. The ritual will also reaffirm their faith at a time when they may need it most. Even if some of the participants do not fully believe what is being espoused during the ritual, they are at least socially accepting it, reinforcing their loyalty to the beliefs and the group of people that maintain them. Social networks will also be reconnected and restructured to help people get on with their lives despite the loss that they must feel. Ritual is a powerful mechanism on both supernatural (sacred) and social (profane) levels.

The distinction between the believers' and the objective observers' perspectives has become an interesting point of conflict as ritual activity has moved online. Insiders believe that the online rituals "work" and they have supernatural efficacy. However, outside observers looking at the same activity have argued that they don't "work" because they have not (or they do not appear to have) fulfilled the "normal" social activities ritual studies scholars have identified as being the "real" benefits or "real" functions of ritual activities. This is one of the key issues that confronted academics when they began to study this activity and it is best highlighted by an example of early scholarship.

Cyberspace as ritual place

When the Internet was still a relatively new technological advancement, online ritual activity was limited to text-based interactions, either in real-time chat or by posting on bulletin boards and listserves. Despite what would seem to be a minimal form of engagement, ritual activities were adapted by religiously enthusiastic people so they could be performed online. When this began to happen, most academics ignored this new activity, believing it to be inauthentic, superficial, and more of a "game" than a real form of religious engagement (Campbell 2005a). Some of the most frequent forms of online ritual were those associated with prayer and prayer requests on bulletin board systems (Helland 2005). Although rarer in its early forms, due to technological constraints and the limited number of people experimenting and using IRC "chat" software, rites and liminal rituals were also conducted online.

In some of the earliest research examining online ritual activity, Stephen O'Leary (1996) recognized that the new environment presented a very unique development in the continued expressions and transformations of religious activity in our contemporary culture. O'Leary argued that within ritual activities there can be "novelty" (new and original components), while at the same time there can be a link with tradition, recognizing that ritual "adapts, mutates, and survives to prosper in a new communicative environment" (O'Leary 1996: 793). People were doing rituals online – but from an academic perspective there were a number of hurdles that would seem to limit or even oppose this form of activity. First and foremost, "cyberspace" is a human and social construction and many people saw virtual reality as being "unreal" space. The people that participate in any form of activity online are constantly "faced with the evidence of its own quality as constructed, as arbitrary, and as artificial" (O'Leary 1996: 804). Despite the environment being an absolute human construction created through computer programs with no "natural" components, people still felt it could become a space that authentically facilitated their sacred ritual activity. One of the first questions O'Leary asked was how this could be done through simple text-based interactions and "chat" software.

His case study involved "Technopagans", a new and unique form of religious community in that it "constituted something close to an actual neopagan congregation, a community of people who gather regularly to worship even though they had never seen each other face to face" (ibid.: 794). By reviewing the transcripts that were left after the rituals had been conducted, it became clear that the group thrived in the online environment. Their membership (although small) had embraced the new technology to the point where they came "to life with the creation of performative rituals that create their virtual reality through text" (ibid.: 797). What was interesting about this early online activity is that the script for the rituals was more than just rules for enacting the ritual; it was the means by which the participants actually created the space in which the ritual could occur. Recognizing the work of J.Z. Smith, O'Leary posited that ritual needs to be geographically located in a communal space and landscape, and it was in the ritual activity itself that the group turned cyberspace into a place where this could occur. In a similar way to "offline" ritual activity in which a neopagan community "casts a circle" or does a ritual activity to create a sacred liminal space, the online community participated in rituals that set apart a special space in the online world. The participants in the ritual did not view cyberspace as being a separate "virtual" reality, rather they viewed the environment as a "theatre of the imagination" where they could use text to create the components they needed for the ritual and the "space" they needed to then engage with the objects they had created. Although this may sound redundant, it was through this performative mechanism that the proper space was conceptualized by the participants as being created (constructed) so that they could do the performative rituals:

> We the members of this full moon circle claim this space
> A space set apart
> A world between worlds
> Our special place to meet with the goddess,
> For the purpose of spiritual growth,
> To promote the fellowship/sisterhood
> In the pagan community,
> And to witness the entrance of others into the Path of the Goddess of the Craft.
> (quoted in O'Leary 1996: 800)

Through "declarative acts" and "performative utterances" the neopagan community affirmed that cyberspace could be sacred space. Drawing upon a number of theoretical frameworks, O'Leary demonstrated that the same mechanisms occur in offline ritual, and the authenticity of the ritual actions and activities is dependent upon the participants' engagement with and acceptance of the ritual activities taking place. The issue was that for many people, including academics, it seemed inauthentic – but as O'Leary demonstrated, so does transubstantiation to those who are not involved in, and accepting of, the ritual. For this small group of neopagans, this was a form of authentic ritual activity and cyberspace was indeed transformed for them into sacred space.

Through "discursive framing strategies" people in these new online environments created places where ritual could occur and through their own construction, shared narratives, and similar vision, they perceived these places to be special, set apart, and even sacred. Not everyone within the neopagan community believed that ritual could take place in this "inorganic" and human (as opposed to natural) space (see Cowan 2005) – but some did, and the ones that did embraced the activity as authentic. Heidi Campbell (2005b) examined the varying levels of perception and engagement religiously motivated people had with regard to the online environment and found that there were several different ways the technology was "framed" and presented by the group to its members. In some cases, the Internet and cyberspace was recognized as a sacramental space suitable for religious use, "a place that can be set apart for 'holy use' enabling people to describe online activities as part of their religious life" (Campbell 2005b: 11). One of the easiest ways to articulate what began to occur online might be the old saying "birds of a feather flock together" – like-minded people gathered together in these online environments to conduct ritual activity. People that did not believe that cyberspace could be ritual space would not participate.

This presented a number of new challenges to traditional religious structures, because people participated in these online groups even if their own church or religious congregation would not. Religious authority plays a key role in determining the rules and regulations associated with people's interactions with the sacred. Religious authority often dictates the symbols that will represent the sacred, how they will be used, who can use them, what benefit people receive from the interaction, etc. In the new online environment, all of these issues become contentious. Individuals have a great deal of freedom in the online environment to experiment, and even develop their own views regarding the role of the Internet in religious ritual life. In most cases, the religious authorities of the church or organization are the "gatekeepers" that control how that organization will utilize Internet technology. It is the people in charge of the group who decide if they need a website, what the website will contain, how it will be developed, and so forth. However, in the contemporary Western society, there is a great deal of individual religiosity or "patchwork" religion, and although the "official" church position may be that online rituals are not authentic, people may choose to disagree.

Kerstin Radde-Antweiler (2006) found that patchwork religion played a significant role in the online religious environments that were developing on the Internet. Although people may be involved in a religious tradition, they often are "clustered" together into a general grouping online (Buddhist, Hindu, Christian, etc.) and they are mixing and incorporating a variety of beliefs and practices that may differ significantly from the orthodoxy (Radde-Antweiler 2008). For the individuals involved, this is not an issue and there is a great deal of syncretism and innovation developing in the online world. This type of activity in turn has led to forms of "patchwork ritual", particularly in personal homepages (Radde-Antweiler 2006) and "individual rituality" (Heidbrink 2007). For the organized religious traditions that maintain strict boundaries concerning their beliefs and practices, this high level of ritual freedom and experimentation does not play out well for them in cyberspace.

One of the key divisions between religious groups that oppose ritual activity on the Internet and groups that have embraced it concerns the perceived legitimacy of the online space as ritual space and the online symbols as authentic manifestations of their sacred objects. As Internet technology has developed and life online has become more "real", this issue has continuously challenged religious groups to clarify, and often defend, their position. The distinctions that exist between those that have embraced online ritual activity and those that oppose it can be seen playing out in a variety of online rituals, one clear example being "virtual" pilgrimage. In this developing form of online ritual activity, Mark MacWilliams (2004) found that the concept of "virtual" was a key factor in determining how people embraced or rejected the Internet as a means of conducting authentic ritual activity. He found an emerging theme, in that people engaged with the medium very differently if they felt that "virtual" meant unreal or illusionary, rather than a real, albeit different, place.

Virtual pilgrimages online

Pilgrimage on the Internet developed rather quickly and has become a very popular form of online activity. Humans have always initiated travel to sacred sites for supernatural purposes and within all the major world religions certain locations are viewed as more sacred or "set apart" than others. This could be for a variety of reasons (where Gautama Buddha was born, where Jesus was crucified, where the remains of the Second Temple still stand, etc.) and religiously motivated people will go to great lengths to experience these places. In some traditions, pilgrimage is mandatory (e.g., the *Hajj*), in others it is highly auspicious and beneficial but not required (e.g., Mount Kailash). When the web was still a relatively new development, MacWilliams (2004) found that people were starting to use it to facilitate this activity – yet significant questions arose in conjunction with this technological development: is online pilgrimage a real form of pilgrimage, and if it is do people receive the same supernatural "benefits" from undertaking this activity that they would if they travelled to the "real" site?

Through a detailed analysis of Croagh Patrick, MacWilliams addressed these questions, focusing in on the types of experiences people had when they went online to various websites associated with Croagh Patrick, compared to reports from people that had been to the physical sacred site. One of the key issues that surfaced was the importance, or lack thereof, of physically as opposed to "virtually" travelling to the site. For theorists such as Victor Turner, pilgrimage takes place on foot as a physical journey from a familiar or everyday place to a faraway place that is sacred and often miraculous (Turner 1974). If Turner's theory regarding this form of ritual holds true, then no one can conduct a virtual pilgrimage.

The problem was, as MacWilliams demonstrated, people were. To begin to place this form of online ritual activity in context, MacWilliams looked to other theories that explored pilgrimage on more than just a physical level, recognizing the spiritual component of the journey – which in some cases is more metaphorical than physical. These "metaphorical" pilgrimages (such as the Stations of the Cross as a representation of the Way of the Cross) can be as spiritually powerful and real to believers as actual ones (MacWilliams

2004: 224). Recognizing what J.Z. Smith calls "relations of equivalence", it becomes clear that there is a symbolic substitution occurring online where the virtual space simulates the representation of sacred space to the point where genuine ritual experience can occur. This is nothing new, when we consider shamanic experiences and "vision quests", where the person experiencing the event is not bodily present but rather deeply engaged in a different, but authentic reality. A good example of blending of the virtual and the physical form in popular culture can be seen in the last instalment of the Harry Potter series, where Harry has a near-death experience in which he is able to talk with his recently departed mentor Professor Dumbledore, receiving advice and reviewing events and outcomes. Potter asks if the experience he is having is real or just in his head. His mentor tells him that of course it is all in his head but that does not mean it is not real (Rowling 2007: 579).

In this case, the "virtual" is still authentic and representative of a physical place but the bodily connection occurring with the site has been altered. The "cyberpilgrims travel electronically through the same mythic imaginaire that is architecturalized in situ in the 'real' pilgrimages" (MacWilliams 2004: 227). The sacred site is recreated and represented in a conservative way on the website, which allows for an authentic representation of offline events – people can see every step of the physical journey, even hear the ambient sounds, but their connection to the material site plays out through a computer screen. Through this deep visual connection with the physical place, people can navigate their "telepresence" into a liminal space where they feel an authentic connection with the sacred site. As MacWilliams found, for some, this does become a form of online ritual activity, but for others there is not a strong enough connection to the physical site and the ritual activity associated with that place – despite the amazing complexity of the website (see Hill-Smith 2011).

Ritual engagement in virtual worlds

In an attempt to make virtual connections with sacred sites more authentic and Internet rituals more genuine, a number of religiously motivated computer developers created websites to facilitate more interactive forms of ritual activity. Examples can be seen at Lourdes France (www.lourdes-france.org), where people can log on and experience all the aspects of a cyberpilgrimage, including images, recordings, 3D representations, and real-time 24/7 live video feeds from 13 webcams. The virtual pilgrim can also connect with the real place by submitting a prayer petition that will be placed within the sacred grotto and read during a special service. The Western Wall in Jerusalem is also "wired", allowing for people to view the sacred site 24/7 (www.aish.com/w). They can also submit prayer requests that will be printed and then placed within a crevice in the wall itself. In these two examples, the person visiting the website has more than just a virtual connection, they are participating in a form of "long-distanced" ritual practice that is facilitated by the Internet. They have connected with the sacred site, conducted a ritual (in this case a prayer request), and left tangible proof of their visit. The participant is not just watching a computer screen to view the activity; they are entering a liminal space, betwixt and between, where they manipulate the actual environment by leaving tangible proof of their ritual activity.

Along with developing connections to "real" sacred sites and temples, religiously motivated computer programmers have also taken advantage of new technological developments to recreate sacred sites within cyberspace itself. Virtual worlds and 3D online environments were very new and dynamic when they first appeared in 1995, being built at the cutting edge of Internet programming. However, with the ever-developing technology associated with online gaming, they are becoming common and "everyday" for millions upon millions of computer users. Within these new virtual reality environments, there have been magnificent recreations of a number of sacred and religious sites (Radde-Antweiler 2008), and people have begun to go online to participate in ritual activities. In a similar fashion to what Stephen O'Leary first noticed in text-based online ritual, people are turning this more tangible version of cyberspace into sacred space through their ritual activities. Although some theories would argue that the detailed 3D recreation of the sacred site creates the liminal place for people to experience, I would argue that it is not because of the digital architecture that they are "set apart" but rather because of the ritual activity that people are conducting (see Jacobs 2007). As J.Z. Smith argues, "there is nothing that is inherently sacred or profane. These are not substantive categories, but rather they are situational or relational categories, mobile boundaries, which shift according to the map being drawn" (Smith 1980: 115). Although there are magnificently recreated sacred architectural spaces in virtual reality worlds, they have no inherent "sacredness" until they become utilized for their original function, which is purposeful engagement with the sacred. It is through the ritual action itself that the space becomes an environment for engaging with the sacred and is therefore regarded as sacred by the participants.

This is the point of division for those that accept online ritual as being authentic and those that reject it. In the offline world, people "know" the general rules and regulations associated with the religious and sacred spaces of their communities. They have a general idea of how to behave at a sacred site, what rules to follow, and some basic behavioural guidelines. The online virtual environment is a fairly new social space and in many ways it has not developed a "cultural memory" that the majority of people in the environment subscribe to – despite recreating the symbols and the architecture online. For example, in Second Life there are amazing recreations of sacred churches; however, the behaviour of many online avatars is anything but sacred or respectful in these environments. There is no collective "ritual memory" that grounds people's behaviour and orients them toward the sacredness of the events occurring. Ritual memory is developing in places like Second Life, where regular ritual events are held based upon rules and regulations, but the participants must prescribe the area and impose restrictions on the liminality itself, enforcing the sacredness of the event by booting and blocking people that are disruptive.

Online ritual – getting it "rite"

There are several factors that influence whether online ritual will be accepted as an authentic ritual practice and they are highlighted in the ritual transfer theory developed at the University of Heidelberg (Langer *et al.* 2006). Recognizing that rituals are dynamic and ever-changing, a framework was developed for assessing the different components that would be altered or transformed when a ritual is transferred into new media. The adapting and changing process can be described by the three heuristic components of transformation, invention, and exclusion (Miczek 2008). Transformation is the process of shaping or reshaping a ritual that already exists, changing its content or structure in certain ways so it can be facilitated online. For this process to proceed, there may need to be innovation within the ritual based upon the new media environment, and new aspects may have be invented to allow for the ritual to work in cyberspace. The final element is exclusion, since certain things inevitably have to be left out of the ritual activity in order for it to take place online. When these three forces act upon the ritual, the people participating are then left with a different ritual than they have previously participated in and they have to decide if the ritual "works" or if it has failed. For many people, the exclusion of a real body is too much of a change and they will not participate, for others it may be the lack of nature, the taste of the wine, or the meal after the ceremony. In any case, the ritual transfer process will fail if these three forces somehow destabilize the ritual to the point that people will not recognize it as an authentic ritual activity. For other participants, the changes and transformations that occur to "bring" the ritual online will be seen as being within a margin of acceptability and they will view the ritual as authentic.

This theory is helpful in highlighting the changes that occur in rituals as they are adapted to function in the online environment, and there are a number of ways researchers are examining the impact this has upon religion in our society. As this scholarship has developed, there has been a divergence between those that are exploring the effects of online religious and ritual activity on "offline" religious participation and those that are studying the virtual world, examining new forms of religious expression and ritual engagement in places like Second Life and in online gaming environments such as EverQuest. This developing scholarship has highlighted the complexity of this ritual activity and also the role religion continues to have within our contemporary culture. What this vast array of ritual and Internet-related activity demonstrates is that ritual activities and performance are not static. They are constantly being changed and adapted so that they can be engaged in and experienced within the contemporary environment. Ritual is woven into our culture's meaning-making systems, and now that life online has just become part of the way our culture functions, it clearly demonstrates that "ritual cannot be divorced from the changing pattern which is society" (Grimes 1982: 151).

To try and sort out the vast amount of online religious activity, it is important to examine the type of rituals people are engaging in. Are people going online to participate in a rite or liminal ritual (such as an initiation into an online coven or a wedding ceremony) or are they getting information from web sources so that they can perform a magic ritual at their home altar? In some cases the computer *becomes* part of the sacred space and in other situations it acts as a *portal, conduit, or tool to connect with* the sacred. Nadja Miczek (2008) and Simone Heidbrink (2007) recognize a distinction between "rituals online" and "online rituals", arguing that "online rituals" are those that are performed in virtual space while "rituals online" refers to prescripts, ritual texts, and material about ritual that can be found on websites.

This distinction highlights the two powerful and distinct capacities of the World Wide Web. The first has to do with data. Information stored on computers that are connected to the web can be accessed by any computer that is also connected to the system. For example, you can search ancient Tibetan manuscripts at the Library of Tibetan Works and Archives (www.ltwa.net/library), view illuminated Islamic manuscripts at the University of Michigan (www.lib.umich.edu), and browse through the Secret Archives of the Vatican (asv.vatican.va) without having to leave the comforts of home. The web is a massive data storage device that can be searched, and is easily accessed and explored through hyperlinks. Ritual scripts, ancient texts, magical spells, and "how-to" instructions are available for everything from Eucharist celebrations to *puja* ceremonies. The second important aspect of the web is that it is a powerful social networking tool. Everyone reading this chapter is familiar with Facebook – yet that is only one manifestation of the web's social networking abilities. "Web 2.0" heavily expands upon the social dimension of this medium, promoting openness, interaction, and virtual community – allowing the "end user" the ability to contribute to the online environment. Web 2.0 is a social space, where people interact, converse, and work with each other in a variety of different ways.

This creates an interesting paradox for people studying ritual activity and the Internet. Since ritual is performative, engaging, and often involves an audience (Grimes 1982), it is Web 2.0 environments that allow for "online ritual". However, when people "do" religion they often participate in activities which involve an engagement with the sacred facilitated by a religious specialist or intermediary. In the offline world, this happens when a person is a member of the audience, observing the ritual as a congregant. However, in the online world, the participant may be at home – receiving the information through the computer and acting very much in private. The people providing the website may not even know that someone is using their religious or ritual information. This is a form of religion online (Helland 2000, 2005), and the computer is being used for one-to-many communication – much like preaching from the mountaintop to the people below. However, for many people, sitting at the foot of the mountain (or at the feet of the guru) and receiving their teachings is a powerful form of religious engagement. It is a one-way flow of information (and does not reflect a Web 2.0 form of interactivity), but people are "doing" religion this way, and as the technology continues to develop this is becoming much more common. The difficult question concerns when this type of "information reception" becomes an online ritual activity. It is a grey area, but examples of this can be seen with Christian evangelists using websites to broadcast their sermons and connect with viewers that they cannot reach by television or in person (e.g., www.saddleback.com). Other cases include the Vatican's YouTube channel (www.youtube.com/user/vatican), the Dalai Lama's website (www.dalailama.com), and even personal Wiccan homepages providing spells, information, and video clips for people to practice magic offline.

Concluding observations

Online ritual is not representative of some form of extraordinary activity – rather it shows "ordinary" religious engagement in an extraordinary environment. Online ritual makes it clear that religion and religious practices are not going to disappear with the continued developments of science and technology. Ritual is woven into the cultural meaning-making system and, although many people in our contemporary world are not explicitly religious, ritual continues to play a significant role on a number of different social, personal, and institutional levels. This challenges us to explore new forms of online religious engagement, patchwork forms of religious participation, and patchwork ritual structure as very authentic and very real forms of religious activity in our wired world.

Ron Grimes (2006) reviewed much of the current scholarship exploring the relationship between new media and ritual and found that there were a variety of ways the Internet could impact and influence this activity. Some key examples include: rites being presented over the Internet (on YouTube, for example); online rituals that people view and participate in "live"; rituals conducted in virtual reality environments; rituals and myths that people participate in during online gaming; magical rites in which the media device has become a fetish or icon; ritual activity that incorporates the computer as part of the altar space; ritual objects that are delivered "online"; and cases where the ritual uses the computer as a tool around which its activities are built (Grimes 2006: 3–13). In some of these situations, people are using the Internet as a mechanism to help facilitate the ritual – they may not be doing anything "online" – yet in other cases they are engaging in ritual in cyberspace itself. Changes in the way a ritual is presented, the way the rules are developed or changed, how people engage with the activity, and even the beliefs about where it can take place then impact upon what ritual "does" for both individuals and religious communities.

Online rituals also pose distinct challenges for scholars studying this activity. One key issue concerns definitions and theories of ritual that were developed before the creation of this form of new media. Many theoretical ritual studies frameworks identify key social and cultural functions of ritual within society – yet some of these functions are not "satisfied" with online ritual practices. However, people are doing the rituals online and the participants are testifying to their efficacy. Instead of dismissing this activity as being inauthentic or superficial, scholars need to explore it in greater depth. This area of study has the potential to shed light not only on ritual and its continuing role but also upon the relationship between technology and society, the social construction of belief, the boundary construction of the sacred, and symbolic substitution and representation.

Recommended reading

Helland, C. (2005) 'Online Religion as Lived Religion: Methodological Issues in the Study of Religious Participation on the Internet', *Online – Heidelberg Journal of Religions on the Internet*, 1(1). Online. Available: http://archiv.ub.uni-heidelberg.de/volltextserver/volltexte/2005/5823/pdf/Helland3a.pdf (accessed 1 June 2011).

Helland examines the limitations of the online-religion/religion-online framework in relation to ritual practices, developing the framework through an examination of various forms of online ritual activity.

MacWilliams, M. (2006) 'Techno-Ritualization: The Gohonzon Controversy on the Internet', *Online – Heidelberg Journal of Religions on the Internet*, 2(1). Online. Available: http://archiv.ub.uni-heidelberg.de/volltextserver/volltexte/2006/6959/pdf/Aufsatz_MacWilliams.pdf (accessed 1 June 2011).

Through a detailed study of Nichiren Buddhism, Soka Gakkai International (SGI), and the American Nichiren Buddhist Independent Movement, MacWilliams examines the controversy over ritual practice and authenticity of the sacred when the Gohonzon is produced online and made accessible through the Internet.

Miczek, N. (2008) 'Online Rituals in Virtual Worlds: Christian Online Services between Dynamics and Stability', *Online – Heidelberg Journal of Religions on the Internet*, 3(1). Online. Available: http://archiv.ub.uni-heidelberg.de/volltextserver/volltexte/2008/8293/pdf/nadja.pdf (accessed 1 June 2010).

Miczek examines two forms of online Christian ritual activity to develop the ritual transfer theory. Her work highlights the changing processes that occur when ritual is transferred into cyberspace.

O'Leary, Stephen (1996) 'Cyberspace as Sacred Space: Communicating Religion on Computer Networks', *Journal of the American Academy of Religion*, 64(4): 781–807.

In this foundational examination of the development of online ritual activity, O'Leary draws upon the work of Walter Ong to highlight the transformations that have occurred in communications through the Internet, demonstrating how this may be conducive to the development of online ritual activities.

References

Bell, C. (1992) *Ritual Theory, Ritual Practice*, New York: Oxford University Press.
Campbell, H. (2005a) 'Making Space for Religion in Internet Studies', *The Information Society*, 21(4): 309–15.
Campbell, H. (2005b) 'Spiritualising the Internet: Uncovering Discourse and Narratives of Religious Internet Usage', *Online – Heidelberg Journal of Religions on the Internet*, 1(1). Online. Available: http://archiv.ub.uni-heidelberg.de/volltextserver/volltexte/2005/5824/pdf/Campbell4a.pdf (accessed 1 June 2011).

Cowan, D.E. (2005) *Cyberhenge: Modern Pagans on the Internet*, New York: Routledge.

Driver, T. (1990) *The Magic of Ritual: Our Need for Liberating Rites that Transform Our Lives and Our Communities*, Toronto: Harper Collins.

Durkheim, E., trans. Fields, K. (1995 [1912]) *The Elementary Forms of Religious Life*, New York: Free Press.

Grimes, R. (1982) *Beginnings in Ritual Studies*, Washington, DC: University Press of America.

Grimes, R. (2006) *Rite Out of Place: Ritual, Media, and the Arts*, New York: Oxford University Press.

Heidbrink, S. (2007) 'Exploring the Religious Frameworks of the Digital Realm: Offline-Online-Offline Transfers of Ritual Performance', *Masaryk University Journal of Law and Technology*, 1(2). Online. Available: www.digitalislam.eu/article.do?articleId=1703 (accessed 1 June 2011).

Helland, C. (2000) 'Online-Religion/Religion-Online and Virtual Communities', in J. Hadden and D. Cowan (eds) Religion on the Internet: Research Prospects and Promises, New York: JAI Press, 205–23.

Helland, C. (2005) 'Online Religion as Lived Religion: Methodological Issues in the Study of Religious Participation on the Internet', *Online – Heidelberg Journal of Religions on the Internet*, 1(1). Online. Available: http://archiv.ub.uni-heidelberg.de/volltextserver/volltexte/2005/5823/pdf/Helland3a.pdf (accessed 1 June 2011).

Hill-Smith, C. (2011) 'Cyberpilgrimage: The (Virtual) Reality of Online Pilgrimage Experience', *Religion Compass*, 5(6): 236–46.

Jacobs, S. (2007) 'Virtually Sacred: The Performance of Asynchronous Cyber-Rituals in Online Spaces', *Journal of Computer-Mediated Communication*, 12(3). Online. Available: http://jcmc.indiana.edu/vol12/issue3/jacobs.html (accessed 1 June 2011).

Kreinath, J., Hartung, C., and Deschner, A. (eds) (2004). *The Dynamics of Changing Rituals: The Transformation of Religious Rituals Within Their Social and Cultural Context*, New York: Peter Lang.

Langer, R., Lüddeckens, D., Radde, K., and Snoek, J. (2006): 'Transfer of Ritual', *Journal of Ritual Studies*, 20(1): 1–20.

Leach, E. (1968) 'Ritual', in S. Hugh-Jones and J. Laidlaw (eds) *The Essential Edmund Leach*, New Haven, CT: Yale University Press, 165–73.

McGuire, M. (1997) *Religion: The Social Context*, Belmont, CA: Wadsworth Publishing.

MacWilliams, M. (2004) 'Virtual Pilgrimage to Ireland's Croagh Patrick', in L. Dawson and D. Cowan (eds) *Religion Online: Finding Faith on the Internet*, New York: Routledge, 223–38.

Malinowski, B. (1954) *Magic, Science and Religion and Other Essays*, Garden City, NY: Doubleday.

Miczek, N. (2008) 'Online Rituals in Virtual Worlds: Christian Online Services between Dynamics and Stability', *Online – Heidelberg Journal of Religions on the Internet*, 3(1). Online. Available: http://archiv.ub.uni-heidelberg.de/volltextserver/volltexte/2008/8293/pdf/nadja.pdf (accessed 1 June 2011).

O'Leary, S. (1996) 'Cyberspace as Sacred Space: Communicating Religion on Computer Networks', *Journal of the American Academy of Religion*, 64(4): 781–808.

Radde-Antweiler, K. (2006) 'Rituals-Online: Transferring and Designing Rituals', *Online – Heidelberg Journal of Religion on the Internet*, 2(1). Online. Available: http://archiv.ub.uni-heidelberg.de/volltextserver/volltexte/2006/6957/pdf/Aufsatz_Radde_Antweiler.pdf (accessed 1 June 2011).

Radde-Antweiler, K, (2008) 'Virtual Religion: An Approach to a Religious and Ritual Topography of Second Life', *Online – Heidelberg Journal of Religion on the Internet*, 3(1). Online. Available: http://archiv.ub.uni-heidelberg.de/volltextserver/volltexte/2008/8294/pdf/Radde.pdf (accessed 1 June 2011).

Rowling, J.K. (2007) *Harry Potter and the Deathly Hallows*, London: Bloomsbury.
Smith, J.Z. (1980) 'The Bare Facts of Ritual', *History of Religions*, 20(1/2): 112–27.
Turner, V. (1969) *Structure and Anti-Structure*, London: Routledge.
Turner, V. (1974) *Dramas, Fields and Metaphors: Symbolic Action in Human Society*, London: Cornell University Press.

3 Identity

Mia Lövheim

The implications of digital media for the formation and presentation of identity have been a significant issue since the beginning of research into social and cultural implications of new media (cf. Kitchin 1998). Religion has been considered a core dimension of individual and collective identity through the transmission of religious narratives, enacting of rituals and framing of individual belief and practice since pre-modern societies (Durkheim 1995). The social and cultural processes shaping modern society, including the increasing mediation of self-representation and social interaction, challenge the traditional role of religion in the formation of identity. Thus, the question of how identity has been conceptualized and studied in research on religion and the Internet highlights crucial issues for understanding how new media technology transforms religion in contemporary society.

This chapter deals with the question of how possibilities and affordances for social interaction and self-presentation in Internet-based communication shape the formation and presentation of identity. We begin with an overview of main trends and issues in studies of the Internet as a site for exploring and representing identity, followed by a review of how these questions have been addressed in studies of identity and religion on the Internet during the past 15 years. A key theme concerns relations between the offline context in which individuals live their everyday life and the ways in which they use digital media. This implies contextualizing expressions of religious identity on the Internet within broader processes of social and cultural transformation in late modern society. Thus, this chapter discusses the following key questions: How do the conditions for forming and presenting identity in digital media differ from face-to-face settings? How do individuals handle this situation given their various social and cultural contexts and resources? How do expressions of religious identity online relate to transformations of religious identity in the physical social world?

Understanding identity in the age of the Internet

Sherry Turkle's (1995) book, *Life on the Screen*, highlighted important aspects of how digital media shapes people's expressions of identity. On one level, the computer can be seen as a tool for organizing personal life, work and communication with others. It also acts as a mirror of how we spend our time or prioritize our commitments, as well as providing new ways of conceptualizing and expressing the self, through the use of digital texts, images, sound and links. Turkle also stressed how computers opened up a new social world for people. Thus, she argued, the Internet was a social and technological infrastructure not just for organizing, expressing and reflecting on life but also for living life. Today, with the convergence of the Internet, mobile phone and satellite technology and the personalization of digital media, this experience is even more enhanced.

Turkle's work highlights some important aspects of identity. On a general level, 'identity' refers to the process by which an individual develops the capacity to grasp the meaning of situations in everyday life and their own position in relation to them (Hewitt 2000: 79). In this process, the individual forms a personal identity or a self. The 'self' refers to the individual's experience of herself as a separate, unique person and a subject capable of acting in a situation. The experience of self is also situated in particular contexts of social interaction (Goffman 1959). This refers to a second dimension of identity, concerning the location of the individual in relation to meanings, practices and positions that organize social life. Each situation of social interaction presents certain possibilities for individuals to announce what position they intend to assume in order to act in the situation (cf. Hall 1996). Whether or not the individual can enact this intention is conditioned by the responses of other people, which confirm or question the individual's assumed position.

Digital communication, anonymity and disembodiment

In everyday face-to-face interactions, our bodies, voice and gestures provide markers by which we represent a self, and signal intentions and positions in a situation. These are also cues we rely on in order to relate to others and determine their actions. In early forms of computer-mediated communication (CMC), interaction was primarily text-based, so written text or coded commands became the primary means for managing and forming impressions of one's own and others' identities. In email lists and news groups, identity was established or concealed by, for example, a user's name or signature, as well as language style and history of previous posts online (Donath 1999). Early personal home pages also reflected their makers' identities through the form, content, images and other symbols selected (Chandler 1998). Thus language or design choices made by Internet users reflected and presented their interests, skills, experiences and social networks online.

As noted by Baym (2006), in this early phase, most research focused on how the perceived anonymity of 'disembodied' online interaction challenged previous conceptions of identity. This offered new possibilities for challenging and playing with constraints of social status and power in offline settings (Kollock and Smith 1999: 9; Kitchin 1998: 78–86). This work was primarily theoretical, drawing on concepts of 'multiple' or 'fluid' identities inspired by discussions of a cultural shift from modernity to postmodernity (Bauman 1996). This research asserted that experiments and play with identity enabled in online interaction were indicative of a social and cultural shift in the construction of identity.

Analysis and empirical studies from this period often focused on online representations of identity. Most attention was given to uses of MUDs (multi-user domains or dimensions): online games or social worlds and the identity play that these enabled through the choice of different characters or personas (Turkle 1995) or experiments with online gender swapping (Reid 1999). While some researchers described the Internet as a new space or 'social laboratory for experimenting with the constructions and reconstructions of self that characterize postmodern life' (Turkle 1995: 179), others discussed the risks of deceit and aggressive or risky behavior online (Donath 1999; Reid 1999).

At the same time, studies of online identity showed that few people actually engaged in the exotic kind of identity experiments described by many CMC enthusiasts, while email and instant messaging were more common and mundane uses of the Internet (Parks and Roberts 1998). Research exploring interaction in news groups or email lists found that identity categories of race and gender were not erased by CMC, but rather the limitations of physical cues online might even enhance the assignment of stereotypical identities to others (O'Brien 1999; Burkhalter 1999). On a similar note, these studies showed how the anonymity of online communication allowed people to be more honest and open about themselves than in offline settings (McKenna and Bargh 2000; Henderson and Gilding 2004).

As Internet use became more widespread during the late 1990s, research came to focus on common uses of the Internet, developing a critical analytical approach toward the claims of early studies. Nancy Baym's work on selves constructed in online fan groups demonstrated the significance of norms and values developed among participants for establishing appropriate self-representations and behavior. Attention was also given to different varieties of online identity and how these were contextualized in offline social contexts (Markham 1998: 20, 85). These studies built on research showing that in most forms of CMC 'people are corresponding with people they also know offline and building on their offline social networks' (Baym 2006: 43; Miller and Slater 2000).

James Slevin's (2000) and Sonia Livingstone's (2002) work is indicative of the empirical and theoretical shift of this period. Slevin discusses how the Internet can enhance individuals' ability to handle the ambiguous experience of increased amounts of information, plurality of lifestyle choices and a heightened awareness of contingency and uncertainty in late modern society. Through the concept of 'arenas of circulation' (2000: 82), Slevin argues that such 'arenas' should be approached as socially structured contexts in which individuals live everyday life in ways which require resources such as computer skills and access (2000: 177–9). Livingstone discusses young people's new media use in connection with changes in the contexts that remain crucial for forming personal and social identity – family life and leisure. Here issues of computer access, the nature of domestic practices surrounding new media use and the institutional context within which society regulates and promotes media use among youth are brought to the fore (Livingstone 2002: 241). This work shows how research shifted from a fascination with 'disembodied' experiences and expressions of identity online, to how the Internet is embedded in everyday life. It also shows how location within the larger context of sociology and media studies enriched studies of identity online.

Social networks, participation and convergence

The developments of new mobile devices and social software during the second part of the 2000s meant new opportunities for Internet users to become producers rather than simply users of content produced for them by social, political and cultural institutions and commercial companies (Bruns 2008: 13–15). This development is further enhanced through the increased convergence of digital media, which make content more easily and rapidly shared, recombined and modified. The development of 'personal digital media' (Lüders 2007) for mediated interaction enhances the ubiquity of digital media in everyday life, blurring the boundaries of on- and offline contexts and practices (Lievrouw and Livingstone 2002).

Here several themes emerge as salient for further research on identity formation online. The first concerns self-representations in blogs and amateur videos presented and shared through web cameras and on sites such as YouTube. These web applications provide new genres in which individual self-performance is combined with interactivity through links and comments (cf. Miller and Shepherd 2004). A related theme is the widespread use of social networking sites such as Facebook for self-presentation and social interaction. danah boyd's (2007) study of young people's use of social network sites argues that these provide important spaces for identity outside the control of parents and school. At the same time, the properties of these sites alter relations between the individual and her 'audience' in ways that may have unintended consequences. A third theme concerns self-representation and social interaction in online computer games. Game studies have focused on the identity positions offered and structured within games, as well as the skills and learning developed in game play, in spite of popular media's focus on the dangers of online gaming (Linderoth *et al.* 2004). Among these are abilities to handle experiences of chance, risk and contingency in a society where security is upheld by sophisticated yet opaque systems of digital technology and expert knowledge (DeNicola 2006).

The possibilities for and implications of using the Internet for self-representation, social sharing, entertainment and play have also raised new issues, such as changes in understandings of authentic identity. New media genres enable individuals to present texts and images of private moments and reflections in a public setting, which enhances expectations of openness and intimacy. At the same time, they enhance users' ability to monitor and edit self-representations, which gives them a perception of having greater control over the representation of identity. Thus, the 'authentic self' represented through digital media becomes simultaneously more 'real' and more 'edited' than in face-to-face settings (Lüders 2007).

Another issue concerns the consequences of being constantly connected and available online (Clark 2005). As danah boyd (2007) has argued, the ubiquity, mobility and interactivity of new social media enhance searchability, persistence and replicability and make individual self-representations available to known and 'invisible' audiences that stretch across time and place. These characteristics also open up unprecedented possibilities for surveillance of, for example, religious minorities in public places (Andrejevic 2007). Other scholars argue that new media open new spaces (Senft 2008) for personal as well as public negotiations of identities, values and norms. The information sharing and collaborative work taking place in online fan communities, on YouTube and in online games, or through digital storytelling (Lundby 2008), can also be seen as indicative of a 'participatory culture' (Jenkins 2006) that calls for new perspectives on literacy, learning and collective forms of meaning-making.

Identity in research on religion and the Internet

Following the expansion of the Internet outside the computer industry and universities in the mid-1990s, religious and spiritual information on the Internet rapidly increased. With the development of more user-friendly Internet technology, individual users created their own websites presenting their religious beliefs. As in the study of religious community, three waves or phases of research on religion, identity and digital media can be identified (cf. Højsgaard and Warburg 2005).

First wave: plurality and experiments

The first studies of CMC and religious identity formation appeared in the mid-1990s. Following trends in the broader field of Internet studies, the first phase of research was characterized by a fascination with the possibilities for experimenting with reconstruction of traditional forms of religious identity. Research in this phase displays two salient trends. The first is characterized by wide-ranging, descriptive explorations of the plurality of religious symbols, narratives and forms of interaction online, providing a virtual 'spiritual marketplace' where individuals might pick-and-mix their religious identities. Jeff Zaleski's (1997) overview of how major world religions use Internet technology serves as one such example. However, it was the flourishing of popular or unofficial forms of religion as well as the possibilities of exploring and expressing religious identities outside the control of organized religious institutions that mostly captured scholarly interest. As noted by Helland (2004: 30, 33), the possibility to choose, form and express one's own religious identity challenged the role of religious communities in the formation and control of religious identity. The second trend explored how 'disembodied' communication online would enable more fluid and multiple forms of religious identity, illustrated in this quote from Stephen O'Leary and Brenda Brasher:

> reduction in the importance assigned to the biological components of individual identity in cybernetic communicative acts opens a space where a rare form of creative identity play across the bodily signs of sex and race can occur and new formations of identity can be explored.
>
> (1996: 260)

The empirical grounding for these claims about the transformative power of cyberspace was, however, rather thin. Most studies were based on the researchers' own explorations of the Internet (cf. Brasher 2001) or the on identities expressed in small groups of neopagans using online conference or news groups (O'Leary 2004).

Second wave: critical empirical studies

Dawson's 2000 review of research on religion in cyberspace marked a turn toward a second phase in research on identity, religion and the Internet. His critical examination, drawing on broader findings within Internet studies, concludes that 'the influence of alternative identity formations on the practice of religion is minimal and speculative at present' (2000: 37). Still, he argues, the possibilities introduced by digital communication challenge the way religious identities have traditionally been formed. This relates in particular to the role of the local community in consolidation and integration of religious identities. Dawson ends his review arguing that studies of religious identity online need to be anchored in broader sociological issues raised by the Internet and in theories of ongoing transformation of religious experiences and practices. This call for more empirical studies and for theoretical framing provided the core issues for this phase of research.

The turn of the millennium saw the emergence of more empirical studies of religious identity on the Internet, such as the Pew Internet and American Life Project's survey of how Americans pursue religion online (Larsen 2004). This survey showed the most popular religious activities, such as information seeking or exchanging prayer requests and advice through email, were individually oriented. Further, the study identified varieties of online religious identities based on religious devotion, history and affiliation, and argued that the majority of 'religious surfers' were also active in offline religious settings, using the Internet to enhance commitments to such beliefs and communities. 'Religious outsiders', meanwhile, use the Internet to find others sharing similar religious interests or experiences of discrimination. The findings of this study, showing how people tend to interact online within already established offline social networks, rather than with strangers, or explore new interests online, have been confirmed in later research (Hoover et al. 2004; Lövheim 2008).

After 2000, studies of religious identity mainly focused on the experiences of individuals for whom issues of identity formation appear particularly crucial, such as young people and members of Western religious minority groups. Berger and Ezzy's interviews with young Australian and American witches (2009; cf. Cowan 2005) show that, for individuals attracted to religions such as paganism and witchcraft – characterized by innovation, eclecticism and individual or solitary practice – the Internet provides ample possibilities for exploring one's own version of religion. For religious minority groups, the social risks of practicing their religion in public further adds to the significance of the Internet as an arena to express religious identities. Similar patterns were noted in studies of young Muslim men and women who interact in transnational or diaspora online religious communities (Schmidt 2006). Here the Internet helps users establish connections with believers across different contexts, and also helps in handling tensions within diasporic situations. Online, young Muslims can find resources for exploring religious identities through perceived authentic sources of Islam, rather than practices and norms formed by particular local and ethnic cultures. Websites and discussion groups also become sites for expressing how these identities can be combined with the values of secular, Western youth culture.

Cowan (2005: 176) describes three varieties of online performance of identities. While for some individuals online religious identity is a 'mask' or performance that is primarily presented online, others use the web more as an additional venue for their religious identity and integrate religious elements as part of their identities. Still others use the Internet to present themselves as spiritual experts or guides for others, in this way claiming an authoritative position. The fact that these online 'instant experts' may bypass traditional authorities or commercialize knowledge recirculated from the wider religious community often creates tensions with the traditional process of collective identity formation (cf. Lövheim 2004).

This discussion makes an important contribution to research focusing on individual uses and expressions of religious identity online. By placing online resources on a trajectory from internal identity formation to external, interactional identity presentation, Cowan shows how the performance of religious identity online is a process of negotiation and co-construction (2005: 155–91). Thus, the individualized character of online religious identities should not be overemphasized (Cowan 2005: 35; Aupers and Houtman 2010). The Internet makes visible and provides a discursive and social infrastructure – that is, sacred texts, a shared set of ideas and forum for discussion, rituals and transmission – which sustains as well as forms these religious identities.

A second trend during this phase concerns how researchers engaged in critical discussions of the relation between online expressions of religious identity and individuals' offline experiences. As pointed out by Lövheim and Linderman (2005), even in a 'disembodied' context like the Internet, identity is a process set in and structured by social interaction. My studies of Swedish youth discussing religion on early forms of social network sites (Lövheim 2004) are examples of this trend. Here I showed how expressions of individual religious identity were structured by social and discursive factors online as well as offline. The range of and relations between various religious discourses in an online forum, the norms of social interaction and the individuals' skills in using digital media all structure the experience of the Internet as an arena for religious identity formation (cf. Lövheim 2006, 2007). Furthermore, conceptions of a particular religious identity in the offline society and culture play a crucial part (cf. Cowan 2005: 173).

In sum, research in this phase moved from speculations about the acting out of multiple or new religious identities online, to studying uses of new media to perform identity in everyday offline life. As noted by Dawson and Cowan (2004: 2), religious identity expressed online illustrates two important consequences of the Internet: a crisis of authority and a crisis of authenticity between religious identity performed offline and online. These tensions link to the control of religious identity formation anticipated in earlier research, but also show how authority, control and belonging become reconstructed and negotiated rather than dismissed online. Furthermore, research during this period showed how online contexts generate discursive and social infrastructures for religious identity formation. In this way, it introduced two themes that set the agenda for the third phase of research: the use of new media as it is integrated with individuals' everyday life and identity, and religious life online as an integrated part of transformations of religion in wider society and culture.

Third wave: religious identities online as integrated into everyday life

As described above, the integration of digital media into everyday life and existing social networks, and the convergence of media forms also meant the emergence of new individual uses of the Internet for forming and representing religious identities. Research during the last few years has, for example, explored uses of blogs and podcasts as religious practice (Cheong *et al.* 2008; Teusner 2010) and religious behavior in computer games (Feltmate 2010).

Even though the technology has developed to provide more sophisticated tools for self-expression and social interaction, the questions pursued during the second phase largely remain. It is difficult to characterize the current phase of research, but a few salient themes can be discerned. The first concerns how new developments enhance individuals' capacity to become producers of religious narratives and take part in assessing and controlling religious practice. Cheong's work on blogs related to Christianity (Cheong *et al.* 2008) and Teusner's work on the digital networks of the emerging church movement in Australia (2010) brings out this personalization of religion through digital media. As these studies show, blogs and podcasts are used as a means of chronicling and reflecting on one's spiritual journey. This does not mean blogs are not used for communication with others, but rather that the content communicated is primarily personal religious experience and emotions (Cheong *et al.* 2008: 115).

A related theme concerns how religious individuals using digital media take part in the reshaping of technology to fit their values and lifestyle. This is striking in studies of uses of the 'kosher' cell phone (Campbell 2010). It can also be seen in how young people use the genre of digital storytelling in producing stories of faith in the context of religious institutions. Kaare and Lundby (2008) show how this process involves negotiations of different ideals and conceptions of, for example, what is considered authentic – in the genre, in contemporary youth culture and within the collective traditions of the national church of Norway.

Another theme is how digital media enable individuals to integrate religious aspects of their identity into other spheres of everyday life and to mediate between traditional and/or culturally specific values, identities and norms, and those promoted by a global neoliberal consumer culture. Research in the third phase has seen a growing number of studies of Muslim identity online. With regard to the theme of the individual as a producer of religion, several studies focus on the enhanced plurality of advice for practicing Islam in daily life offered by online fatwa sites (Bunt 2009). Piela's (2011) work on representations of identity on Muslim matchmaking sites shows how Muslim men and women negotiate traditional gender conceptions, roles and practices in online interactions. Studies of cyber-pūjā (Karapanagiotis 2010; see also Helland 2007) explore how Hindu devotees form new ritual practices to ensure the spatial and mental purity required for the ritual in an online setting. These examples all show a concern with personal reflections, practices and settings of the individual's religious life. They also show how individuals use digital media to handle intersecting and blurry boundaries of the sacred and profane as religion is lived out in everyday life. Furthermore, through bringing these issues into new settings of social interaction characterized by a wider circulation, searchability and the intersection of various audiences, digital media can also provide new spaces for collective reflections on religious and moral values.

The focus on continuity and connection between how individuals express and enact their religious identity in online and offline settings has contributed to a gradual shift from studying people's engagement with religion on the Internet as an activity separated from other arenas of their everyday life. Survey studies, such as Hoover, Clark and Rainie (2004) and Lövheim (2008), confirm that for large groups of the population, particularly those not already committed to religious beliefs, the Internet may not be the main context for encounters with religion in everyday life. Further, personal religious practices and expressions of religious identity through digital media are performed in interaction with uses of conventional media, and within the social networks of friends, family, school and the workplace. This might mean that although individual or personal performances of religion dominate online, we see fewer studies focusing on religious identity in this context. As digital media are becoming more integrated and naturalized in individual everyday life, studies of religious identity online increasingly become integrated into studies of religion in everyday life. Through this process, findings on how religious identities are formed and expressed through digital media also contribute to our understanding of the transformations of religious identity in contemporary society.

Religious identity in late modern society

Hoover, Clark and Rainie (2004: 20) argue that the most significant impact of the Internet lies in augmenting a development in which individuals come to exercise more autonomy in relation to formal authorities and institutions in matters of faith. Research so far seems to confirm the tendency that uses of the Internet for religious identity formation as well as expressions of religious identity through digital media are primarily individual and personal. As this chapter has shown, there has also been a growing conviction in research that religion online does not represent a new or other form of religion than that enacted offline, but rather develops alongside it. This complicates any simplistic interpretation of how digital media are related to religious and social transformation. It further underlines what was pointed out in the introduction to the chapter: that in order to assess the relation between religious identity and digital media we need to contextualize this question within theories of transformations of identity and religious identity in late modernity.

As pointed out by sociologists Anthony Giddens (1991) and Zygmunt Bauman (1996), the process of forming identity in late modern society is marked by enhanced plurality, uncertainty and reflexivity. Put simply, in pre-modern society the individual's identity was largely defined by geographical locality and tradition (Giddens 1991: 14–20). The 'disembedding' of social life from these settings and the constant influx of new information creates a situation characterized by 'intrinsic reflexivity' in which evaluation and reconstruction of practices and meanings become the basis for identities and social relations. For the individual, Giddens writes, this means that the formation of identity becomes a reflexive project of sustaining a 'coherent, yet continuously revised' biography of self (1991: 5).

Nancy Ammerman (2003) has applied a similar perspective in her understanding of religious identities in contemporary society. She describes religious identities as 'autobiographical narratives' in which past and present experiences relating to 'religious narratives' are interconnected. Religious narratives are publicly constructed and shared narratives that assign meaning to individuals' everyday experiences by connecting them to transcendent or sacred actors, ideas, institutions and experiences (Ammerman 2003: 213, 217). This relates to the understanding permeating much of modern sociology of religion that, following the social differentiation and cultural plurality of modernization, religious identity has gone from being a 'given' to becoming a 'choice' (Berger 1999). This choice concerns whether to be religious but also whether or to what extent one's religion should be based in a collectivity and play a primary or secondary role in one's identity and lifestyle.

Ammerman's focus is primarily on the role played by religious institutions in this process, although she points out that in contemporary society religious narratives are also mediated through other contexts and actors. In late modern society, religious symbols and narratives increasingly become part of and shaped by mass media, popular culture and the commercial market (Hoover 2006).

While this situation on the one hand enhances the significance of individual preferences and choices, individual choices are also structured by factors such as access to media, gender, race and class (Clark 2003: 231).

Scholars using the concept of 'performance' start out from an understanding of identity as articulated in certain situations and through certain symbols, but focus precisely on the tensions between agency and the underlying social and cultural norms of a certain identity position. Performance theory, inspired by the work of Judith Butler (1997) thus opens up the possibility of analyzing identity as neither 'given' by a particular context nor 'constructed' through the choices of an individual, but instead as performed or *enacted* in a certain situation through particular social rituals as well as forms of expression. These rituals and forms express a range of different subject positions that are structured and conditioned by powerful discourses. However, the various ways in which they are enacted also challenge, by making visible ambivalences, absurdities and cracks between the actual performance and that which it is supposed to enact. As we have seen above, the conceptualization of the self as a story or performance, represented and enacted through social interaction and particular forms of expression, is further enhanced by the characteristics and experiences of new, digital media.

The future of identity in a new media age

In his outline of issues for studies of religion in cyberspace, Dawson (2000) poses the question of what a 'thoroughly mediated social life' might mean for the function of religion in consolidating individual identity and integrating the individual within a larger social context. A decade of research later, this complex question remains salient; however, on the basis of this research review, two attempts to answer it can be outlined. Both answers rest on the understanding that digital media and their increased use for self-expression, self-reflection and social interaction enhance personal or individual expressions of religion. The difference lies in the interpretation of the consequences of this development for religious identities. The first approach, prominent primarily in the first phases of research, is that such a 'thoroughly mediated social life' weakens religion as a resource for the construction of identity. Religion loses its plausibility and thus ability to provide trust and meaning, as well as to motivate certain values and lifestyles, social engagement and a sense of belonging or community. This interpretation often rests on a normative understanding of the character of 'authentic' religious identities and of the relation between religion and media, where media are seen as secularizing society and religion is seen as losing its authenticity when mediated (Hoover 2006).

The other approach is that digital media provide the infrastructure for religious identities in tune with modern, highly technological and globalized societies. Aupers and Houtman argue that 'we are witnessing a relocation of the sacred to the subjective world of the individual and the world of technological objects; a sacralization of the self and the digital' (2010: 25). Furthermore, these new manifestations of religion should not be disregarded as individualistic or marginal. Rather, they are deeply indicative of the cultural tensions and logic of modernization that shape religion in late modern society.

In sum, religious identities online show us that religious identity online is not that different from religious identity in everyday offline life. Religious identities in contemporary society are performed and mediated; in a different way from previous societies, they call for constant revision and continuous performance in known and unknown social settings, of which some are digital and others are physically located. Religious identities online also show us how contemporary religious identities are formed around the individual autobiography rather than geographical place or a particular religious affiliation. The Internet enhances the possibility of individually practiced religion, but digital media also make visible and provide a new form of social infrastructure for the individual's religion: a network of local communities, technological devices and software applications, and geographically close or remote friends and family members. This shows that religious identity in modern society is still a social thing, deeply anchored in the social situations and relations individuals want and need to stay connected to in order to find meaning and act in everyday life.

Developments in new technologies and patterns of use prompt new questions concerning the blurring of boundaries between private and public, facts and fiction, trust and risk, surveillance and participation in contemporary society. These questions and the ethical and moral dilemmas they raise also need to be addressed in research about religion online. As argued by Dawson (2000), scholars of religion and the Internet need to contextualize their research within the broader field of studies of new media. However, as this chapter illustrates, in a modern, digital society, religion remains a significant locus for understanding the new ways of forming and presenting identity in contemporary life.

Recommended reading

Lövheim, M. (2004) 'Young people, religious identity, and the Internet,' in L. L. Dawson and E. D. Cowan (eds) *Religion Online: Finding Faith on the Internet*, New York: Routledge, 59–74.

This study offers a comprehensive discussion of the role of the Internet in processes of identity formation among young people from different religious backgrounds.

Slevin, J. (2000). *The Internet and Society*, Cambridge, UK: Polity Press.

The first significant attempt to develop an analytical framework in which the individual's engagement with new media is situated in the context of identity in late modern society and the socially structured contexts of everyday offline life.

Smith, M. A. and Kollock, P. (eds) *Communities in Cyberspace,* London: Routledge.

Part Two, on identity, presents key ideas about how the Internet changes conditions for forming and presenting identity in social interaction, and discusses possibilities as well as offering critical insights on the implications of these conditions.

Turkle, S. (1995) *Life on the Screen: Identity in the Age of the Internet*, New York, NY: Touchstone.

This book established the theme of how the entry of digital media into everyday life would affect identity, and has remained a key text in discussions of these issues ever since.

References

Ammerman, N. T. (2003) 'Religious identities and religious institutions,' in M. Dillon (ed.) *Handbook of the Sociology of Religion*, Cambridge, UK: Cambridge University Press, 207–24.

Andrejevic, M. (2007) *iSpy: Surveillance and Power in the Interactive Era*, Kansas: University Press of Kansas.

Aupers, S. and Houtman, D. (2010) (eds) *Religions of Modernity: Relocating the Sacred to the Self and the Digital*, Leiden: Brill.

Bauman, Z. (1996) 'From pilgrim to tourist – or a short history of identity,' in S. Hall and P. du Gray (eds) *Questions of Cultural Identity*, London: Sage, 18–36.

Baym, N. K. (2006) 'Interpersonal life online,' in L. Lievrouw & S. Livingstone (eds) *The Handbook of New Media*, London: Sage, 35–54.

Berger, P. (1999) 'The desecularization of the world: a global overview,' in P. Berger (ed.) *The Desecularization of the World: Resurgent Religion and World Politics*, Washington, DC: Ethics and Public Policy Center.

Berger, H. and Ezzy, D. (2009) 'Mass media and religious identity: a case study of young witches,' *Journal for the Scientific Study of Religion*, 48(3): 501–14.

boyd, d. (2007) 'Why youth (heart) social network sites,' in D. Buckingham (ed.) *Youth, Identity, and Digital Media*, Cambridge, MA: MIT Press, 119–42.

Brasher, B. (2001) *Give Me that Online Religion*, San Francisco: Jossey-Bass.

Bruns, A. (2008) *Blogs, Wikipedia, Second Life and Beyond: From Production to Produsage*, New York: Peter Lang.

Bunt, G. (2009) *iMuslims: Rewiring the House of Islam*, Chapel Hill, NC: University of North Carolina Press.

Burkhalter, B. (1999) 'Reading race on-line: discovering racial identity in usenet discussions,' in M. A. Smith and P. Kollock (eds) *Communities in Cyberspace*, London: Routledge, 60–75.

Butler, J. (1997) *Excitable Speech: A Politics of the Performative*, New York: Routledge.

Campbell, H. (2010) *When Religion Meets New Media*, London: Routledge.

Chandler, D. (1998) *Personal Home Pages and the Construction of Identities on the Web*. Online. Available: www.aber.ac.uk/media/Documents/short/webident.html (accessed November 26, 2002).

Cheong P. H., Halavais, A. and Kyounghee, K. (2008) 'The chronicles of me: understanding blogging as a religious practice,' *Journal of Media and Religion*, 7(3): 107–31.

Clark, L. S. (2003) *From Angels to Aliens: Teenagers, the Media and the Supernatural*, Oxford: Oxford University Press.

——(2005) 'The constant contact generation: exploring teen friendship networks online,' in M. Mazzarella (ed.) *Girl Wide Web: Girls, the Internet, and the Negotiation of Identity*, New York, NY: Peter Lang, 203–21.

Cowan, D. E. (2005) *Cyberhenge: Modern Pagans of the Internet*, New York and London, Routledge.

Dawson, L. L. (2000) 'Researching religion in cyberspace: issues and strategies,' in J. K. Hadden and D. Cowan (eds) *Religion on the Internet: Research Prospects and Promises*, Amsterdam, London and New York: JAI Press, 25–54.

Dawson, L. L. and Cowan, D. (eds) (2004) *Religion Online: Finding Faith on the Internet*, New York: Routledge.
DeNicola, L. (2006) 'The bundling of geospatial information with everyday experience,' in T. Monahan (ed.) *Surveillance and Security: Technological Politics and Power in Everyday Life*, New York: Routledge, 243–64.
Donath, J. S. (1999) 'Identity and deception in the virtual community,' in M. A. Smith and P. Kollock (eds) *Communities in Cyberspace*, London: Routledge, 29–59.
Durkheim, E. (1995) *The Elementary Forms of Religious Life*, New York, NY: Free Press.
Feltmate, D. (2010) ' "You wince in agony as the hot metal brands you": religious behavior in an online role-playing game,' *Journal of Contemporary Religion*, 25(3): 363–77
Giddens, A. (1991) *Modernity and Self-Identity: Self and Society in the Late Modern Age*, Stanford, CA: Stanford University Press.
Goffman, E. (1959) *The Presentation of Self in Everyday Life*, London: Penguin Books.
Hall, S. (1996) 'Introduction: who needs "identity"?' in S. Hall and P. du Gray (eds) *Questions of Cultural Identity*, London: Sage, 1–17.
Helland, C. (2004) "Popular religion and the internet: a match made in (cyber)heaven," in L. Dawson and D. Cowan (eds) *Religion Online: Finding Faith on the Internet*, New York: Routledge, 23–35.
——(2007) "Diaspora on the electronic frontier: developing virtual connections with sacred homelands," *Journal of Computer Mediated Communication*, 12(3). Online. Available: http://jcmc.indiana.edu/vol12/issue3 (accessed 10 June 2008).
Henderson, S. and Gilding, M. (2004) "I've never clicked this much with anyone in my life: trust and hyperpersonal communication in online friendships," *New Media & Society*, 6(4): 487–506.
Hewitt, J. P. (2000) *Self and Society: A Symbolic Interactionist Social Psychology*, 8th edition, Needham Heights, MA: Allyn & Bacon.
Højsgaard, M. and Warburg, M. (2005) 'Introduction: waves of research,' in M. Højsgaard and M. Warburg (eds) *Religion and Cyberspace*, London: Routledge, 1–11.
Hoover, S. M. (2006) *Religion in the Media Age*, New York: Routledge.
Hoover, S. M., Clark, L. S. and Rainie, L. (2004) *Faith Online*, report from Pew Internet and American Life Project. Online. Available: www.pewinternet.org (accessed November 6, 2006).
Jenkins, H. (2006) *Confronting the Challenges of Participatory Culture: Media Education for the 21st Century*. Online. Available: www.macfound.org (accessed March 29, 2011).
Kaare, H. B. and Lundby, K. (2008) 'Mediatized lives: autobiography and assumed authenticity in digital storytelling,' in K. Lundby (ed.) *Digital Storytelling, Mediatized Stories: Self-representations in New Media*, New York, NY: Peter Lang, 105–22.
Karapanagiotis, N. (2010) 'Vaishnava cyber-puja: problems of purity and novel ritual solutions,' *Online – Heidelberg Journal of Religions on the Internet*, 4(1). Online. Available: http://online.uni-hd.de (accessed May 12, 2011).
Kitchin, R. (1998) *Cyberspace: The World in Wires*, Chichester: Wiley.
Kollock, P. and Smith, M. A. (1999) 'Communities in cyberspace,' in M. A. Smith and P. Kollock (eds) *Communities in Cyberspace*, London: Routledge, 3–25.
Larsen, E. (2004) 'Cyberfaith: how Americans pursue religion online,' in L. Dawson and D. Cowan (eds) *Religion Online: Finding Faith on the Internet*, New York: Routledge, 17–20.
Lievrouw, L. A. and Livingstone, S. (eds) (2002) *The Handbook of New Media: Social Shaping and Consequences*, London: SAGE.
Linderoth, J., Lindström, B. and Alexandersson, M. (2004) 'Learning with computer games,' in J. Goldstein, D. Buckingham and G. Brougere (eds) *Toys, Games and Media*, London: Lawrence Earlbaum, 157–76.

Livingstone, S. (2002) *Young People and New Media: Childhood and the Changing Media Environment*, London: Sage.
Lövheim, M. (2004) 'Young people, religious identity, and the internet,' in L. Dawson and D. Cowan (eds) *Religion Online: Finding Faith on the Internet*, New York: Routledge, 59–74.
—— (2006) 'A space set apart? Young people exploring the sacred on the internet,' in J. Sumiala-Seppänen, K. Lundby and R. Salokangas (eds) *Implications of the Sacred in (Post) Modern Media*, Göteborg: Nordicom, 255–72.
—— (2007) 'Virtually boundless? Youth negotiating tradition in cyberspace,' in N. T. Ammerman (ed.) *Everyday Religion: Observing Modern Religious Lives*, Oxford: Oxford University Press, 83–100.
—— (2008) 'Rethinking cyberreligion? Teens, religion and the internet in Sweden,' *Nordicom Review*, 29(2): 203–15.
Lövheim, M. and Linderman, A. (2005) 'Constructing religious identity on the internet,' in M. Højsgaard and M. Warburg (eds) *Religion in Cyberspace*, London; Routledge, 121–37.
Lüders, M. (2007) *Being in Mediated Spaces: An Enquiry into Personal Media Practices*, Oslo: University of Oslo.
Lundby, K. (ed.) (2008) *Digital Storytelling, Mediatized Stories: Self-Representations in New Media*, New York: Peter Lang.
McKenna, K. Y. A. and Bargh, J. A. (2000) 'Plan 9 from cyberspace: the implications of the Internet for personality and social psychology,' *Personality and Social Psychology Review*, 4(1): 57–75.
Markham, A. (1998) *Life Online: Researching Real Experience in Virtual Space*, Walnut Creek, CA: AltaMira.
Miller, C. R. and Shepherd, D. (2004). 'Blogging as social action: a genre analysis of the weblog,' *Into the Blogosphere: Rhetoric, Community, and Culture of Weblogs*, 18. Online. Available: www.blog.lib.umn.edu/blogosphere/blogging_as_social_action_a_genre_analysis_of_the_ weblog.html (accessed September 19, 2009).
Miller, D. and Slater, D. (2000) *The Internet: An Ethnographic Approach*, Oxford: Berg.
O'Brien, J. (1999) 'Writing in the body: gender (re)production in online interaction,' in M. A. Smith and P. Kollock (eds) *Communities in Cyberspace*, London: Routledge, 76–104.
O'Leary, S. (2004) 'Cyberspace as sacred space: communicating religion on computer networks,' in L. Dawson and D. Cowan (eds) *Religion Online: Finding Faith on the Internet*, New York: Routledge, 37–58.
O'Leary, S. and Brasher, B. (1996) 'The unknown god of the internet: religious communication from the ancient agora to the virtual forum,' in C. Ess (ed.) *Philosophical Perspectives on Computer-Mediated Communication*, New York: State University of New York Press, 233–70.
Parks, M. R. and Roberts, L. D. (1998) ' "Making MOOsic": the development of personal relationships on line and a comparison to their offline counterparts,' *Journal of Social and Personal Relationships*, 15(4): 517–37.
Piela, A. (2011) 'Beyond the traditional-modern binary: faith and identity in muslim women's online matchmaking profiles,' *CyberOrient*, 5(1). Online. Available: www.cyberorient.net/article.do?articleId=6219 (accessed May 5, 2011).
Reid, E. (1999) 'Hierarchy and power: social control in cyberspace,' in M. A. Smith and P. Kollock (eds) *Communities in Cyberspace*, London: Routledge, 107–33.
Schmidt, G. (2006) 'The formation of transnational identities among young Muslims in Denmark,' in G. Larsson (ed.) *Religious Communities on the Internet*, Uppsala: Swedish Science Press, 150–63.
Senft, T. (2008) *CamGirls: Celebrity and Community in the Age of Social Networks*, New York: Peter Lang.

Slevin, J. (2000) *The Internet and Society*, Cambridge, UK: Polity Press.
Teusner, P. (2010) 'Imaging religious identity: intertextual play among postmodern Christian bloggers,' *Online – Heidelberg Journal of Religions on the Internet*, 4(1). Online. Available: http://online.uni-hd.de (accessed May 5, 2011).
Turkle, S. (1995) *Life on the Screen: Identity in the Age of the Internet*, New York: Touchstone.
Zaleski, J. (1997) *The Soul of Cyberspace: How New Technology is Changing our Spiritual Lives*, New York: HarperCollins.

4 Community

Heidi A. Campbell

The extent to which a group of people who meet and interact online can be considered a community has been a subject of great debate over the past three decades. The Internet's ability to facilitate and mediate social relations has shifted many people's notions of friendship, relationship, and community in an age of networked, digital technologies. This chapter deals with the question of how community is defined in relation to the online context and how the Internet alters many people's practice of community within a new media landscape. This requires several key questions to be addressed, including: How is community defined, enacted, and networked online? What challenges do new media pose to traditional religious communities? What is the connection between online and offline community?

In order to answer these questions, this chapter begins with an overview of the rise of groups online and how they began to be viewed as communities. Early online communities opened up new possibilities for social interaction, challenging traditional notions of community. Next, the study of online religious community is reviewed, outlining the different waves of research conducted into the concept of community online. This overview demonstrates how new forms of community have been described, analyzed, and interpreted to consider the offline impact of these online groups. Finally, exploring these examples and researching community online points to a distinctive understanding of how community is lived and viewed in contemporary society. The shift in the conception of community is, notably, linked to a networked understanding of community rather than notions of shared geography and familial ties. This illustrates that new forms of community, facilitated by networked interaction, indeed point to a revised understanding and practice of community in an age of new media.

The emergence of community online

Since its beginnings, Internet culture has cultivated strong collaborative and communal elements. The birth of email in the 1970s began to facilitate a social side to Internetworking, so much so that, by 1973, a study found that three-quarters of all traffic on ARPANET was email-related, and the volume of mail soon began to strain the system (Hafner and Lyon 1996). Not long after the creation of email, lists and discussion groups began to appear, encouraging group communication online. In 1975 ARPANET, the US government forerunner to the Internet, had created the first electronic discussion group in order to establish a space where users could work together to create networking protocol. Through these groups, communities of conversation quickly took root online (Hafner and Lyon 1996). These moderated message groups were initially established to oversee various aspects of network business and research. Yet soon unofficial groups, such as SF-Lovers – created by researchers to discuss science fiction – emerged, as people saw the possibilities of the network for facilitating social interactions (Rheingold 1993). In 1979, the newly established Usenet system initiated the concept of newsgroups, dedicated discussion forums to be used for systems and technical discussions. It was not long until non-systems groups emerged on this network. By the early 1980s, numerous special interest discussion groups could be found, including "net.religion," a forum dedicated to discussions on the religious, ethical, and moral implications of human actions (Ciolek 2004).

Using the network as a social rather than a research space, as it was initially intended, created new challenges and extensive traffic. By the mid-1980s, newsgroup traffic and controversial use of online conversational space led to the creation of systems categories such as "alt" for alternative, "comp" for computers and "rec" for hobby-related groups. It was at this point that debates between Jewish and Christian members of net.religion resulted in the creation of the first religion-specific community, "net.religion.jewish" (Helland 2007). The 1980s also saw the advent of various new computer forums, including personal computer networks. This allowed more users to gain access to Internetworking, forums such as bulletin board systems (BBSs), fantasy-based multi-user dimensions (MUDs), multi-user object oriented (MOOs), and Internet relay chat (IRC) rooms that allowed participants to "talk" to others through various types of software.

These online forums took on community identities as they generated loyal support from members. The collective nature of these groups was marked by systems of symbolism and textual significance devised by members to communicate common ideas and maintain order, such as shared rules of "netiquette" (Reid 1995). Through this standardization of behaviors and the emotional investment of members, computer-supported social networks began to be described as communities. By the late 1980s, popular press accounts of ARPANET and other online forums for social activity began to describe them as forms of "'virtual community' based on the Internet" (Ceruzzi 1999: 298). Throughout the 1990s, there was a growing fascination with these online communities, as more people migrated online and began to experiment with the social interactions offered by the network. Online communities represented technologically mediated gatherings of people around a specific topic or purpose, with some level of commitment to that topic or purpose, and each other.

Examples of online religious communities appeared in the 1980s. Lochhead's study of the emergence of Christian discussion groups found that online religious groups began to form "a sense of identity as a community that existed independently of whatever service they chose for their electronic communication"

(1997: 53). Groups such as Ecunet, an ecumenical Christian email listserve (www.ecunet.org), H-Judaic (www.h-net.org/~judaic), and BuddhaNet (www. buddhanet.net) utilized various platforms to create religious conversational communities online. In the mid-1990s, cyberchurches and cybertemples began to appear, as websites providing online worship experiences for individuals and groups. For example, the First Church of Cyberspace ran weekly services for over a decade via Internet relay chat, seeking to leverage the Internet in order to create a new form of faith community online. The Internet, Cyberchurch's founder Charles Henderson argued, possesses the same power as the Protestant Reformation for unleashing new ways "in which people practice faith, as well as communicate with each other and God" (1997). Religious communities began to form even in multi-user dimensions. An early study of online prayer meetings in multi-user virtual reality environments found "a prayer meeting in the virtual world may not provide the same type of religious experience as a conventional church service, but it certainly reproduces some of the essential features of the latter – albeit in a novel way" (Schroeder, Heather, and Lee 1998).

While the Internet continues to serve as a social space and gathering point for people who share common passions and connections, what constitutes a community online has been a heated topic of debate. Rheingold, an early adopter and proponent of the Internet, coined the term "virtual community" to refer to groups of persons who create, nurture, and invest in relationships maintained through computer connections, or

> Social aggregations that emerge from the Net when enough people carry on public discussions long enough, with sufficient human feeling, to form webs of personal relationships in cyberspace.
>
> (1993: 5)

This definition emphasizes that online communities are formed not simply where there is sustained conversation or a growing online membership, but where members are prepared to emotionally invest in a group. Community online in the 1990s was also defined as "social spaces in which people still meet face-to-face, but under new definitions of both 'meet' and 'face' … [v]irtual communities [are] passage points for collections of common beliefs and practices that unite people who were physically separate" (Stone 1991: 81). This understanding highlights the notion of a common place of both ideological and spatial connection. At its heart, community online is the understanding that, while the space of interaction may have changed, the basic act of social exchange has not. As computer networking became recognized as an increasingly important way for individuals to maintain social relations, this utilization of network technologies to maintain relationships began to influence conceptions of community. As Wellman, a sociologist of community, argued:

> When a computer network connects people it is a social network. Just as a computer network is a set of machines connected by a set of cables, a social

network is a set of people (or organizations or other social networks) connected by a set of socially meaningful relationships.

(1997: 179)

While individuals may exhibit differing levels of value for and attachment to an online group (Blanchard and Markus 2004), they often identify similar markers or behaviors that are valued as part of their experiences of online groups, including shared common boundaries and symbols (Kollock and Smith 1994), exchanged and received support (Boshier 1990), a perceived emotional connection with other members (Baym 1995), and a shared culture or identity (van Dijk 1998). Over the past two decades, many new forms of community have emerged online, from interactions in virtual worlds such as Second Life, to conversational communities created via blogs and Godcasting (religious podcasting) sites, to spiritual-social networking taking place on sites like Facebook. These new forms of gathering continue to evoke similar questions regarding how community is formed, validated, evaluated, and legitimated by users online. At the heart of these issues is the question of what it means to be in a relationship or community with others in a networked, information-based society. Such questions have fueled over two decades of research on the topic of community within Internet culture.

The study of religious community online

In the 1990s, scholars began to pay serious attention to the technologies and methods people were using to congregate online and the types of discussions and practices that became the focal points of these groups. Hojsgaard and Warburg (2005) described the development of the academic study of religion and the Internet in terms of three waves of research: the descriptive, the critical, and the theoretical. This progression demonstrates how research questions and methods have matured both within the study of religion online and as part of the wider development of Internet studies.

First wave: documenting and describing community formation online

Researchers of religion online initially approached the Internet with fascination, as they sought to describe the practices of life online and the blurring boundaries of online culture. Studies of religion online were similar to those within computer-mediated communications (CMC) research, as scholars attempted to describe in detail social practices and groups surfacing online. Beginning with Rheingold (1993), who presented the first key study of how an online discussion forum might be conceptualized as a "virtual community," researchers have explored how life online can be framed in terms of community. There was a sense of novelty in many early Internet studies, and sometimes researchers were caught up in the hype or in the utopian–dystopian discourses regarding the effect Internet was having on society. During the mid-1990s and beyond, numerous case studies were undertaken that sought to describe these emerging online communities, from studies of BBS-based fan communities (Baym 1995) to group interactions in textually or visually oriented multi-user fantasy environments (Reid 1995). In general, many early researchers of Internet culture focused on questions such as: What is happening online? How might these social aggregations be seen as communities? And what effect does life online have on individual and group identities? Similarly, within the study of religion, scholars attempted to pinpoint, conceptualize, and explain the rise of online religious community.

Most of these initial studies were highly descriptive and often used ethnographic approaches to offer an in-depth picture of a particular online community. For example, Howard (2000) showed how fundamentalist websites were facilitating online conversations that create a common voice based around a specific set of topics or shared religious convictions, thus creating a vernacular community. Fernback's (2002) study of a neopagan online community highlighted how the Internet allows groups to constitute and define themselves as a community through the creation of distinct conversation patterns and the observance of communal religious ritual practices. My early work explored how an online Charismatic-Pentecostal community could be described as a "congregation of the disembodied," as they transported traditional religious structures online while enabling participants to widen their perceptions of global Christian community through interactions with believers around the world (Campbell 2003).

Within these studies, tensions emerged for some regarding the very idea of referring to an online forum as a community. Studies of different expressions of Islam online (Bunt 2000; Lawrence 2002) demonstrated that online groups frequently sought to reinforce global religious structures by employing common metaphors found in Islam to connect online practice with the offline religious community, such as referring to Islamic practice online as the "virtual ummah." Herring's (2005) study of a Christian newsgroup found that, for the group, defining itself as a religious community meant it was important to employ theological framing to justify online practices and existence. Other scholars argued that the Internet provides a space especially suited to religious persons living in diaspora to reconnect with religious spaces and communities (Taylor 2003). Thus the Internet becomes a crucial centralized point for religious communities to reconnect and re-envision their religious lives. Overall, these first studies offered a descriptive analysis of specific religious online communities, either by providing a detailed analysis of a single community or by considering how online religious community was emerging in relation to a specific religious tradition. They helped identify the variety of expressions of religious community emerging online and reflect on how online practices could create an online version of an offline faith tradition.

Second wave: critical analysis of the effects of community life online

By the late 1990s, research on the question of community online had evolved from simply describing this phenomenon to become more definitional in its exploration. Studies moved toward critical forms of analysis, as hype over the transformative nature of the Internet began to subside and a more realistic perspective emerged about the positive and negative effects of the Internet on society. For instance, Jones in his *Cybersociety* collections shifted from the initial question of "How do we study computer-mediated community?" (1995: 11) to call for more critical analysis of what kind of "community" is an online community (1998). Emphasis was placed on how online community might be reshaping general definitions of community in an information age. This created a new wave of research that identified and compared different typologies or forms of online community. Researchers began to tease out the different roles and structures within online communities in order to analyze how these influenced the extent to which members became involved in that community. Commonalities between studies emerged, as researchers began to note that online community members often identified similar characteristics or valued traits as part of their lived experiences in these groups (Kollock and Smith 1994). This work also led to investigation of the direct connections between online and offline community patterns and behaviors. Research began to show what had previously been suspected, that online communities are unique in that they "are not tied to a particular place or time, but still serve common interest in social, cultural and mental reality ranging from general to special interests or activities" (van Dijk 1998: 40).

Those studying online religious community also moved towards asking more refined questions related to community members' practices, looking at not only at motivation for joining and investing in online communities (Berger and Ezzy 2004), but also at how online participation might affect offline religious participation. This meant investigating how online community members' traditional understandings of community were transformed through their online participation. A forerunner of this line of questioning was Anderson's (1999) study of the rise of new communities of interpreters within Islam. He identified three groupings – "creole" pioneers, activist interpreters, and "officializing" interpreters – and explained how the Internet facilitates new religious identities outside traditional structures. Thus, online community could be seen as a new source of authority, potentially challenging traditional religious structures. Kim's (2005) work on Buddhist discussion boards spotlighted the diverse functions of contemporary religious organizations – as interpretive, interactive, integrative, and instrumental communities – which draws attention to the fact that studying religion online can provide vital insights into the changing nature of contemporary religious communities and organizations at large. This was echoed by several studies that found online religious community is intrinsically connected to offline religious institutions and affiliation (Young 2004; Campbell 2005). It seems members of online religious communities consciously import traditional religious ritual into online contexts, even if these practices must be modified in some form in order for them to be online.

It is true that offline religious practitioners and organizations often fear that Internet-based community is in some way inauthentic, impoverished, deceptive, or holds the seductive potential power to lead people out of the pew and away from face-to-face community. Yet this research showed that, for most, online religious community is not a substitute, but rather a supplement to extend offline relationships and communication in unique and novel ways (Campbell 2004). Second-wave studies focused on "the question of community" by highlighting how characteristics of membership practice and motivations for online community involvement point to larger shifts in understanding of the concept of community as a whole. These studies provided important insights into the defining characteristics of online religious community, as well as highlighting the unique roles and forms of practice online that might lead to redefinition of people's conception of community.

Third wave: theoretical turn towards community's online–offline relationship in a networked society

In the past decade, studies of community online have moved toward a more theoretical and interpretive perspective. Internet researchers now employ broader theories of social capital, organizational identity, and interactivity in new media as tools to assess how the Internet both influences and reflects trends within the larger social sphere. CMC research on the question of community looks closely at what the conditions of online community reflect or illustrate about offline community, and how offline community patterns and discourse determine online use and beliefs. Studies have consistently found that Internet users conceptually and practically connect their online and offline social lives, rather than seeing them as separate or disconnected spheres (Wellman and Haythornwaite 2002; Wellman 2004). This has focused scholars' attention on how online–offline interaction and integration can point toward findings about life in an information-dominated culture. This exploration of the relationship between online and offline social involvement is echoed in studies of online religious community. Research has shown members often join and stay involved in an online community in order to meet specific relational needs. Yet this participation does not fully meet religious members' desire for face-to-face interaction and a shared, embodied worship experience (Campbell 2005). Therefore, online religious activities represent simply one part of an individual's overall religious involvement.

Research comparing online and offline participation has also laid the ground for developing theoretical frameworks for interpreting the conditions and functions of online religious communities. One emerging approach draws on the social shaping of technology approach and theories such as domestication (Silverstone, Hirsch, and Morley 1992) to investigate how religious and social values guide distinctive religious responses toward technology (Zimmerman-Umble 1992). For example, Barzilai-Nahon and Barzilai (2005) have shown that in fundamentalist communities female Internet users' views of the Internet were influenced by offline communal discourses initiated by religious leaders. Offline authorities' negative views of the Internet forced them to frame usage in terms of economic needs to justify using a technology that allowed them to transgress traditional communal social boundaries. Similarly, my work on the Jewish ultra-Orthodox negotiation of the cell phone to create the "kosher" cell phone demonstrates how religious users employ shared narratives and beliefs to frame and reconstruct new media technologies (Campbell 2007). Social-shaping approaches to technology provide a useful framework for studying how offline religious communities evaluate and negotiate their use of new forms of media technology (Campbell 2010). These studies provide interesting conclusions about how religious groups may culture a technology such as the Internet so that it can be incorporated into the community and provide opportunities for group or self-expression within these boundaries. It also shows that online and offline contexts are intimately interconnected. Studies of online religious community continue to broaden interpretive frameworks to explain the conditions and practices of religious community online in relation to larger social patterns and trends within networked society.

In summary, studies of online religious community have evolved from broad to more refined questions. Research began by describing new forms of online social interaction via studies of specific online religious communities. Helping document the new forms of religious expression online and how traditional religious community practices are adapted online gave rise to general questions about why religious users go online. Researchers then moved towards mapping typologies of online community and rituals. Current studies often focus on questions about the extent to which offline religious communities and structures can influence online expressions of community. Many investigate the interconnection between online religious communities and their offline counterparts. A key question within studies of online religious community is how power relations are constituted or challenged online and how offline religious community can elucidate the ritual aspect of online community life. These are questions explored in more depth in the case studies found in Chapters 12 and 13.

Understanding community in a networked society

Increasing attention is being paid to how participation in online groups influences members' conception of offline religious communities. Researchers have explored how involvement in online communities may inform members' understanding of what it means to be part of a faith community and may alter expectations of how community should be pursued offline. The result of this research has transformed discourse about the nature of religious community in a networked society, as online groups often function quite differently from traditional religious institutions. Rather than operating as tightly bounded social structures, they function as loose social networks with varying levels of religious affiliation and commitment. The concept of "networked community" has emerged as a way to describe this new conception and structural form of community, both in online and offline contexts.

Since the mid-1990s, researchers have recognized unique social patterns at work within online communities, which seem to point toward changes in traditional forms of community. Increasingly, individuals live within multiple social spheres and groups, creating a networked understanding of community in which individuals create webs of connection between different social contexts to result in a personalized network of relations. Similarly, social structures and interactions found within religious online groups require a new understanding of how contemporary religious organizations function. The network metaphor has become important to describe social relations online and offline. Studies of religious community online describe a blurring of boundaries within online social culture, and attempt to create boundaries within an unbounded space and translate social practices (Baym 1995). While seeking a framework to describe these online groups, researchers began to note how computer networks can function uniquely as social networks (Wellman 1988). Internetworking became a metaphor for new patterns of socialization emerging in Western society, mirroring general shifts from geographic, static affiliations based on needs or familial ties to loosely bound, dynamic networks of relations based on shared interests and preferences. Much attention has focused on the online–offline interaction between different groups and its implications. As researchers continue to emphasize, the Internet is "embedded" in everyday life; the study of online community further highlights social shifts and changing notions of the very nature of community occurring in contemporary society (Wellman and Haythornwaite 2002). In fact, it can be argued that approaching community as a network has become the dominant approach within studies of community online.

This is partially due to work which, based on social network analysis, has shown how computer-supported systems function as social networks. Social network analysis emerged in sociology during the late 1960s and early 1970s, and is based on the belief that communities are, in essence, social and not spatial structures. This approach to community sought to address trends toward the "privatization of community." Urban sociology studies tended to focus on neighborhoods and other small-scale communities, with large-scale social phenomena being overlooked (Wellman and Leighton 1979). Yet it became evident that modern urban dwellers associate with several groupings, rather than a single neighborhood group. These links between groups created networks of individuals whose social ties varied in strength and intensity. Some networks were relied on for general purposes, such as work or family networks, and others served specific assistance roles, such as emergency services or special interest clubs. In social network analysis, a set of nodes is identified and the ties between them mapped, to determine how the nodes are connected. The resulting map or network represents the social structure of different nodes (i.e. an individual or group) and their patterns of relationships (Wellman 1997). In this analysis, social relationships that transcend groups are identified and used to describe underlying patterns of social structure. Analysts study networks as "ego-centered" (personal) or whole networks (a given population) in their efforts to identify the range, centrality, and roles of networks and their members.

Computer networks support a variety of social networks, from tightly bound organizational information networks to loose networks of informal email exchanges. As computer networking has become an increasingly important way for individuals to maintain social relations, it cannot be overlooked that these actions may be redefining contemporary conceptions of community. While information technology extends and redefines work and social practices, Wellman argues that it does not change the nature of social relations, which are facilitated through the technology because ties online mirror individuals' real-life ties, and are intermittent and specialized, and vary in strength (Wellman 1988). A networked view of community offers a useful approach not only to examining patterns of online interaction, but also for describing the evolution of community relations within society as a whole. It sits well with an understanding of community based on flexible relationships. Today, the image of a community bound strictly to geographic, ethnic, or culturally fixed relationships does not always seem applicable, especially within Western urban society. When technology mediates and sustains relationships, geographical separation is no longer a factor in exclusion from a social network. Increased ease of travel and technology such as the telephone allow people to maintain social contact with those with whom they have limited face-to-face contact. Other technologies, such as television and computers, also break down barriers by providing access to information on a global scale. Conversely, it is not uncommon for individuals to be socially separate from those who live in close physical proximity. This was shown by Massey (1994), who found that people who live in the same street or geographical area may live in very different communities.

Approaching religious communities as social networks is not unique to studies of the Internet. Employing a social network approach in studies of contemporary religious community is becoming more common. For example, Ammerman's (1997) study of congregations clearly framed community as "functioning as a network" (p. 346) and asserted that "understanding of the social systems of modern life must start with the individual's network of relations," (p. 352) and thus congregations should be approached as part of the social network of a community. Social network analysis is also used in a number of studies of religious institutions and groups to assess levels of religious investment (Ellison and George 1994) or degrees of social capital (Smith 2003). It has also been asserted that the network metaphor provides a more accurate description of contemporary patterns of relationships and so proves very useful for sociological studies of religious community (Campbell 2004). Community as network provides an important new narrative and research tool for investigating emerging relations and interactions occurring within contemporary religious organizations and groups. So the concept of networked community offers a valuable lens for describing the function of community both online and offline. Rather than living in a single static religious community, the study of religious online community shows many people in contemporary society live among multiple religious networks that are emergent, varying in depth, and highly personalized.

The future of community in a new media age

Seeing media and technologically mediated environments as sources of community regeneration and innovation is not new. Since the development of radio in the 1920s and television in the 1940s, the relationship between media and community building has been an area of interest (Jankowski 2002). Studying community in an age of digital media provokes some of the same questions posed by these older forms of media. These include issues related to how social cohesion and collective identity are established and maintained. New media technologies draw attention to novel dimensions of these core issues.

Many of the concerns about online community have also been spotlighted in research and critiques of televangelism and the "electronic church." Criticism continues to be voiced over whether technologically mediated relationships can be defined as a legitimate form of community. The disembodied interactions facilitated by media may allow for social interactions, but whether or not such engagements can produce truthful or authentic relationships is still highly debated within religious contexts. Also, fear that participation in a media-created community causes people to plug in, log on, and drop out of offline community continues to cause much apprehension for religious leaders. Yet, just as predictions that television viewers would leave their local churches in favor of an electronic church were proved to be largely unfounded (Hoover 1990), so similar claims that Internet users will plug in and drop out of offline church have not yet been borne out. While online religious community has been shown to be different from traditional offline community, it cannot be fully separated from religion in the offline context. This means that concerns over how the concept of community is changing is not just an issue of how community is lived online, but also of how it is being perceived and lived out in the offline context.

With the rising popularity of social networking software, questions continue to emerge regarding new forms of technologically mediated community. Issues being explored include how the blogosphere reshapes our notions of community (Blood 2004) and how Twitter followers can cultivate a sense of community through creating interlinked personal networks (Gruzd, Wellman, and Takhteyev 2011). Research on online religious community also further considers how Web 2.0 technologies provide new possibilities for community creation online and challenge offline religious community. Recent work on online churches in virtual environments suggest an interdependent relationship between the digital and everyday life as online churches deliberately replicate familiar elements of everyday activity in their online behaviors (Hutchings 2008, 2010). Studies of religious blogging demonstrate that individuals may use their online activities to consciously resist traditional forms of community and instead opt to construct a fluid religious identity and network that allows them to experiment with new ways of religious interaction online (Teusner 2010). As network technologies increasingly facilitate our social, educational, and work-related interactions, and are tied to mobile devices that further shift our notions of place and interconnection, the changing nature of community will continue to be an important area of exploration. Our communities continue to function as diverse areas of networked social interactions; the Internet and new media worlds thus become valuable spheres for studying these new ways of being together.

As the image of the network and the notion of our living in a networked society (Castells 1996) have become more and more prevalent, the network metaphor has become an accepted way of explaining our social patterns and forms of gathering. Indeed Rainie and Wellman (2012) argue that the network is the social operating system of the twenty-first century, meaning our ways of working, socializing, and identity building are formed through networks of diverse associations rather than relying on tight social ties and bounded relations. This encourages people to live as "connected individual rather than embedded group members" (p. 19) or in terms of networked individualism. This tendency towards dynamic networked identity also arguably informs practices of public religion, as the influence of religious institutions is often replaced by one's personalized social network as the key influence in one's spiritual life. Thus scholars are increasingly highlighting how the logic of the network is replacing notions of place-based community, shaping how religious community is perceived as well as how it is understood to function in the twenty-first century.

Recommended reading

Blanchard, A. and Markus, M.L. (2004) "The experienced 'sense' of a virtual community: characteristics and processes," *ACM. SIGMIS Database*, 35(1): 64–79.

Blanchard and Markus provide a framework for identifying the key markers and unique traits of online community, as well as the different actors involved in the process of online community construction in various networked contexts.

Campbell, H. (2004) "Challenges created by online religious networks," *Journal of Media and Religion*, 3(2): 81–99.

This article highlights the key arguments religious practitioners often raise when critiquing the legitimacy of online community, and responds with research data to demonstrate that, while online community is unique, it is also connected to the offline context.

Campbell, H. (2005) *Exploring Religious Community Online: We Are One in the Network*, New York: Peter Lang.

This book offers the most comprehensive overview of the study of the concept of community online and the unique attributes of online religious community.

Dawson, L. (2004) "Religion and the quest for virtual community," in L. Dawson and D. Cowan (eds), *Religion Online: Finding Faith on the Internet*, 75–92, New York: Routledge.

Dawson provides a concise overview of research questions and approaches used in the study of religious community online.

Wellman, B. and Gulia, M. (1999) "Net surfers don't ride alone: virtual community as community," in Barry Wellman (ed.), *Networks in the Global Village*, 331–67, Boulder, CO: Westview Press.

This article explores sociology of community literature to demonstrate how social network analysis approaches to community help inform the study and analysis of online communities.

References

Ammerman, N.T. (1997) *Congregation and Community*, New Brunswick: Rutgers University Press.
Anderson, J. (1999) "The Internet and Islam's new interpreters," In D.F. Eickleman (ed.), *New Media in the Muslim World: The Emerging Public Sphere*, 41–55, Bloomington, IN: Indiana University Press.
Barzilai-Nahon, K. and Barzilai, G. (2005) "Cultured technology: internet and religious fundamentalism," *The Information Society*, 21(1). Online. Available: www.indiana.edu/~tisj/21/1/ab-barzilai.html (accessed October 12, 2005).
Baym, N. (1995) "The emergence of community in computer-mediated communication," in S. Jones (ed.), *Cybersociety*, 138–63, Thousand Oaks, CA: Sage.
Berger, H. and Ezzy, D. (2004) "The internet as virtual spiritual community: teen witches in the United States and Australia," in L. Dawson and D. Cowan (eds), *Religion Online: Finding Faith on the Internet*, 175–88, New York: Routledge.
Blanchard, A. and Markus, M.L. (2004) "The experienced 'sense' of a virtual community: characteristics and processes," *ACM. SIGMIS Database*, 35(1): 64–79.
Blood, R. (2004) "How blogging software reshapes the online community," *Communications of the ACM*, 47(12): 53–5.
Boshier, R. (1990) "Social-psychological factors in electronic networking," *International Journal of Lifelong Education*, 9(1): 59–75.
Bunt, G. (2000) *Virtually Islamic: Computer-Mediated Communication and Cyber Islamic Environments*, Lampeter: University of Wales Press.
Campbell, H. (2003) "A review of religious computer-mediated communication research," in S. Marriage and J. Mitchell (eds), *Mediating Religion: Conversations in Media, Culture and Religion*, 213–28, Edinburgh: T&T Clark/Continuum.
——(2004) "Challenges created by online religious networks," *Journal of Media and Religion*, 3(2): 81–99.
——(2005) *Exploring Religious Community Online: We Are One in the Network*, New York: Peter Lang.
——(2007) "What hath God wrought: considering how religious communities culture (or kosher) the cell phone," *Continuum: Journal of Media and Cultural Studies*, 21(2): 191–203.
——(2010) *When Religion Meets New Media*, London: Routledge.
Castells, M. (1996) *The Rise of the Networked Society*, New Jersey: Wiley Publishers.
Ceruzzi, P. (1999) *A History of Modern Computing*, Cambridge, MA: MIT Press.
Ciolek, T.M. (2004) "Online religion: the internet and religion," in H. Bidgoli (ed.), *The Internet Encyclopaedia*, vol. 2, 798–811, New York: John Wiley & Sons.
Ellison, C.G. and George, L.K. (1994) "Religious involvement, social ties, and social support in a southeastern community," *Journal for the Scientific Study of Religion*, 33(1): 46–61.
Fernback, J. (2002) "Internet ritual: a case of the construction of computer-mediated neopagan religious meaning," in S. Hoover and L.S. Clark (eds), *Practicing Religion in the Age of Media*, 254–75, New York: Columbia University Press.
Gruzd, A., Wellman, B., and Takhteyev, Y. (2011) "Imagining Twitter as an imagined community," *American Behavioral Scientist*, 55(10): 1294–318.
Hafner, K. and Lyon, M. (1996) *Where Wizards Stay Up Late: Origins of the Internet*, New York: Simon and Schuster.
Helland, C. (2007) "Diaspora on the electronic frontier: developing virtual connections with sacred homelands," *Journal of Computer Mediated Communication*, 12(3). Online. Available: http://jcmc.indiana.edu/vol12/issue3/ (accessed June 10, 2008).

Henderson, C. (1997) "The emerging faith communities of cyberspace," *Computer-Mediated Communication*, Online. Available: www.december.com/cmc/mag/1997/mar/hend.html (accessed March 15, 1998).

Herring, D. (2005) "Virtual as contextual: a net news theology," in L. Dawson and D. Cowan (eds), *Religion and Cyberspace*, 149–65, London: Routledge.

Hojsgaard, M. and Warburg, M. (2005) "Introduction: waves of research," in M. Hojsgaard and M. Warburg (eds), *Religion and Cyberspace*, 1–11, London: Routledge.

Hoover, S. (1990) "Ten myths about religious broadcasting," in R. Ableman and S. Hoover (eds.), *Religious Television: Controversies and Conclusions*, 23–39, New Jersey: Albex.

Howard, R.G. (2000) "Online ethnography of dispensationalist discourse: revealed versus negotiated truth," in J.K. Hadden and D.E. Cowan (eds), *Religion on the Internet: Research Prospects and Promises*, 225–46, New York: JAI Press.

Hutchings, T. (2008) "Creating church online: a case-study approach to religious experience," *Studies in World Christianity*, 13(3): 243–60.

——(2010) "Creating church online: an ethnographic study of five internet-based Christian communities," PhD thesis, Durham: Durham University.

Jankowski, N. (2002) "Creating community with media: history, theories and scientific investigations," in L.A. Lievrouw and S.M. Livingstone (eds), *Handbook of New Media: Social Shaping and Social Consequences of ICTs*, 55–74, Thousand Oaks, CA: Sage.

Jones, S. (ed.) (1995) *CyberSociety*, Thousand Oaks, CA: Sage.

——(ed.) (1998) *CyberSociety 2.0*, Thousand Oaks, CA: Sage.

Kim, M.C. (2005) "Online Buddhist community: an alternative organization in the information age," in M. Hojsgaard and M. Warburg (eds), *Religion and Cyberspace*, 138–48, London: Routledge.

Kollock, P. and Smith, M. (1994) "Managing the virtual commons: cooperation and conflict in computer communities," in S. Herring (ed.), *Computer-Mediated Communication: Linguistic, Social, and Cross-Cultural Perspectives*, Amsterdam: John Benjamins. Online. Available: www.sscnet.ucla.edu/soc/faculty/kollock/papers/vcommons.htm (accessed June 10, 2008).

Lawrence, B.F. (2002). "Allah on-line: the practice of global Islam in the information age," in S. Hoover and L.S. Clark (eds), *Practicing Religion in the Age of Media*, 237–53, New York: Columbia University Press.

Lochhead, D. (1997) *Shifting Realities: Information Technology and the Church*, Geneva: WCC Publications.

Massey, D. (1994) *Space, Place and Gender*, Minneapolis: University of Minnesota.

Rainie, L. and Wellman, B. (2012) *Networked: The New Social Operating System*, Cambridge, MA: MIT Press.

Reid, E. (1995) "Virtual worlds: culture and imagination," in S. Jones (ed.), *Cybersociety*, 164–83, Thousand Oaks, CA: Sage.

Rheingold, H. (1993) *The Virtual Community*, New York: HarperPerennial.

Schroeder, R., Heather, N., and Lee, R.M. (1998) "The sacred and the virtual: religion in multi-user virtual reality," *Journal of Computer Mediated Communication*, 4. Online. Available: www.ascusc.org/jcmc/vol4/issue2/schroeder.html#LANGUAGE (accessed May 10, 2010).

Silverstone, R., Hirsch, E., and Morley, D. (1992) "Information and communication technologies and the moral economy of the household," in R. Silverstone and E. Hirsch (eds), *Consuming Technologies: Media and Information in Domestic Spaces*, 15–29, London: Routledge.

Smith, C. (2003) "Theorizing religious effects among American adolescents," *Journal for the Scientific Study of Religion*, 32(1): 17–30.

Stone, A. (1991) "Will the real body please stand up? Boundary stories about virtual cultures," in M. Benedikt (ed.), *Cyberspace: First Steps*, 81–118, Cambridge, MA: MIT Press.

Taylor, J. (2003) "Cyber-Buddhism and the changing urban space in Thailand," *Space and Culture*, 6(3): 292–308.

Teusner, P. (2010) "Emerging church bloggers in Australia: prophets, priests and rulers in God's virtual world," PhD thesis, Melbourne: RMIT University.

van Dijk, J. (1998) *The Network Society*, Thousand Oaks, CA: Sage.

Wellman, B. (1988) "The community question re-evaluated," in Michael Peter Smith (ed.), *Power, Community and the City*, 81–107, New Brunswick: Transaction Books.

——(1997) "An electronic group is virtually a social network," in S. Kiesler (ed.), *Culture of the Internet*, 179–205, Mahwah, NJ: Lawrence Erlbaum.

——(2004) "Connecting community: on- and off-line," *Contexts*, 3(4): 22–8.

Wellman, B. and Haythornwaite, C. (2002) "The Internet in everyday life: an introduction," in B. Wellman and C. Haythornwaite (eds), *The Internet in Everyday Life*, 3–44, Oxford: Blackwell.

Wellman, B. and Leighton, B. (1979) "Networks, neighbourhoods and communities: approaches to the study of the community question," *Urban Affairs Quarterly*, 14(3): 363–90.

Young, G. (2004) "Reading and praying online: the continuity in religion online and online religion in internet Christianity, " in L. Dawson and D. Cowan (eds), *Religion Online: Finding Faith on the Internet*, 93–106, New York: Routledge.

Zimmerman-Umble, D. (1992) "The Amish and the telephone: resistance and reconstruction," in R. Silverstone and E. Hirsch (eds), *Consuming Technologies: Media and Information in Domestic Spaces*, 183–94, London: Routledge.

5 Authority

Pauline Hope Cheong

Before the contemporary advent of digital media, authority has historically been marked as having a contentious relationship with the development of newer communication technologies. Marvin (1988) illustrated, for instance, how the then-new medium of the electric bulb was accompanied by debates on the nature of authority and changing communication behaviors between the elites and masses. In the face of television, Meyrowitz (1985) argued that "authority is weakened when information systems are merged" (p. 63), that is, the authority of leaders diminishes when a medium allows different people to have open access and gain greater control over knowledge and social information. With web-based technologies there has been growing attention paid to authority and a set of interrelated issues of intensifying mediation, digital divides, participatory democracy, and grassroots activism.

While the topic of authority has been of longstanding interest to new media scholars and practitioners, the role of authority, including religious authority in faith communities, has received relatively less research attention and systematic analysis. This chapter discusses how religious authority has been framed in relation to the online context, and the ways, if any, in which the Internet facilitates changes in practices of religious authority. There are, of course, varied conceptions of authority. Thus it is instructive to probe a related set of questions, including: What is "religious authority"? How do scholars researching new media regard religious authority? And what general propositions about authority and communication technologies lie behind their published works?

Accordingly, this chapter provides a thematic analysis of recent studies examining implications of the Internet for religious authority. This critical overview observes that much of the literature on this issue operates on two rather different logics. The first is more rooted in the earlier emphasis on the Internet as a decentralized and free space. A dominant conceptualization is that forms of religious authority are altered by digital technologies, which are perceived to disrupt and displace traditional faith doctrines and domains, often embedded in forms of hierarchical communication. An alternative perspective is stimulated by the growing importance of situating religious authority among older media and faith infrastructures. The Internet may, to some extent, have facilitated changes in the personal and organizational structures by which religious leaders operate. But active and accommodative practices by some clergy, related to their engagement with digital media, may enable them to regain the legitimacy and trust necessary to operate in the religious sphere. This review demonstrates how emerging research highlights paradoxes in authority, as clergy negotiate tensions in their online representations as they attempt to harness the interactive, dialogic capabilities of mediated social networks. Thus emerging practices of religious authorities facilitated by networked interactions may prompt updating of our understanding of authority in increasingly mediated environments.

Considering religious authority and mediated communication

Given its rich and variable nature, "authority" is itself challenging to define and study. Although the words "clergy" and "priest" are commonly used, in the West, to connote religious authority, the variety of related titles is immense (e.g. "pastor," "vicar," "monk," "imam," "guru," "rabbi"). Studies focused on religious authority online have been few, compared to studies centered on religious community and identity. Despite interest in and acknowledgment of the concept, there is a lack of definitional clarity over authority online, and no comprehensive theory of religious authority (Campbell 2007). It is not the intention here to investigate the origins of "authority," but it is significant to point out that treatments of religious authority vis-à-vis communication and media studies have taken on varying forms.

For instance, religious authority can be descriptively categorized into different types, justified by varied forms of legitimation. As reflected in Weber's classic categorization (1947), authority is said to arise from sacred tradition, appointment to a superior office and perceived charisma of being instilled with divine or supernatural powers. Following this typology, and drawing on an exploratory study of Christianity, Judaism, and Islam (Campbell 2007), four layers of religious authority have been identified: hierarchy (roles or perceptions of recognized leaders), structure (community, patterns of practice, or official organizations), ideology (faith beliefs, ideas, or shared identity), and texts (recognized teachings or official religious books). It has also been observed that layers like hierarchy and structure are intertwined and "related," with priestly roles and perceptions derived and defined by their practices amid "structural power struggles" within Hindu temple management (Scheifinger 2010). In this light, recognition that religious authority is context-dependent complicates and enriches the varied forms of authority.

Authority can also be understood in more relational terms, as maintained in dynamic interactions between two realities that manifest and acknowledge the authority. Accordingly, authority is conceptualized as emergent:

> [the] effect of a posited, perceived or institutionally ascribed asymmetry between speaker and audience that permits certain speakers to command not just the attention but the confidence, respect, and trust of their

audience, or – an important proviso – to make audiences act *as if* this were so.

(Lincoln, 1994: 4)

In this sense, authority is performative and discursive, involving persuasive claims by leaders to elicit an audience's attention, respect, and trust. Religious authority thus can be approached as an order and quality of communication, which in an electronic age is media-derived and dynamically constructed (Cheong *et al.* 2011a).

Hence, religious authority can be vested or constructed, constituted from various perspectives referring to a range of thinking on divinely related control and influence, to exact obedience, judge, govern, and make consequential pronouncements. Its nature is multidimensional and dependent on legitimating systems associated with different cultural expressions. This interchange enables us to observe its wide-ranging and variable application in multimodal worlds. In this vein, a growing number of studies have examined or referenced religious authority in the online arena. The next section presents a critical overview of these studies.

Mapping religious authority and Internet research

Past reviews on the state of Internet studies have maintained that the field has progressed from a variety of disciplinary backgrounds into "three ages" or multiple stages that somewhat parallel the chronological and ontological development of digital media (Wellman 2011). This review has similarly found related and overlapping clusters of concepts mirroring the growth of the field. Relationships between religious authority and the Internet have primarily been characterized as relationships of dislocation or coexistence; this is mapped below under two general organizing logics: the logic of disjuncture and displacement, and the logic of continuity and complementarity. The former perspective refers to dominant approaches in which digital media are framed as corrosive and disruptive to traditional religious authority, stressing an erosion of the power of traditional institutions and leaders to define and determine the meaning of religious symbols. The latter refers to more recent thinking, which views digital media connections as supportive and complementary of religious authority, with evolving practices which are restructuring the legitimacy of their symbols and work contexts, amidst creative and countervailing (re)presentations. Beyond these two themes, the tensions in religious authority that are amplified by social media are discussed. This is followed by further observations about future research.

The logic of disjuncture and displacement

The dominant logic, inspired by initial studies of Internet research, is that religious authority is eroded by online religious activities. Here, the logic of "disjuncture" involves arguments which propose the relationship between religious authority and new media is characterized by upheaval and/or disconnectedness. "Displacement" refers to the acts of apparent change or movement, including supplanting power and furnishing an equivalent authority in place of another. The mainstream conception linking religious authority and the Internet is normative, taking hold in the shadow of utopian and dystopian thinking and research in the context of virtual communities. In tandem with the utopian rhetoric accompanying the pioneering stage of web-based developments, earlier research on religion online made extreme claims about religious authority in mainstream and new religious contexts. Early studies proposed that the Internet was a distinct and conducive "third space" for spiritual interaction, and that new flows of religious information and knowledge posed corrosive effects on the influence and jurisdiction of traditional religious authorities. The dominant logic associates offline religious authority with more static models of legitimation, seeing the Internet as promoting informational diversity and social fractures that are disruptive to the status quo. In alignment with this logic of discontinuity and displacement, new forms of web-based authorities have also been proposed.

One common view frames online religion as a viable and vibrant alternative, emphasizing its "revolutionary potential" for altering how religious faith is conceived and practiced. At the outset, virtual communities were often regarded as egalitarian, a cyber-oasis apart from the practices of traditional and organized religion. For instance, online religious interaction has been juxtaposed with offline realities, with the Internet said to be a "cybersangha" (religious community or monastic order) with no physical home (Prebish 2004) and to provide "alternative spiritual sanctuaries with few speech restrictions" (Kim 2005: 141). In a similar vein, reports on new religious movements and the virtual church focused on interpretative textual communities, which functioned without a central leader or institution (e.g. O'Leary 1996). This emphasis on the disjuncture between online and offline realms implied circumvention of existing face-to-face connections with religious authorities.

Another prevalent view is that the Internet challenges authority by expanding access to religious information in a way that can undermine the plausibility structure of a religious system. Many commentators have noted the ways in which religion online is growing and deepening in a variety of traditions, as sacred scriptures, expository and devotional materials have become available online. Search engines prompt the use of the Internet by many as an online library of textual, audio, and visual religious texts. This, in turn, opens up new spaces of persuasion arising from numerous sources of authority. Correspondingly, Soukup (2003) observed a shift from the church as "a locus of theology," as viewers assemble religious guides of their own volition, deferring to the authority of the webpage, which appears "completely self-contained" and "free of external certification and gatekeeping."

As the Internet allows access to information previously considered covert or only understood by elites who are certified and/or ordained, it is posited that religious authority may diminish, with non-professionals gaining greater control over access to religious knowledge. Numerous commentators highlight how many obscure, self-proclaimed religious guides have posted their teachings online, offering lay perspectives to expand their domain of religious discourse. In Islam for example, the ulama (trained Muslim scholars) have long held to the idea that it is not enough to recognize certain texts as authoritative (e.g. Sahih Bukhari, a hadith text from Sunni Islam), but it must also be recognized that the texts can only be properly understood by those who are "authorized" to interpret them (Zaman 2007: 28). Commentaries are one of the primary ways that ulama have traditionally disseminated their authoritative views to audiences, but lay Islamist thinkers have co-opted that platform. Anderson (1999) noted the rise of new communities of discourse that reflect "creolization," as commentators "cast religious talk in idioms of speech and thought previously or otherwise allocated to separate speech communities" (p. 56). Specifically, it was argued that "what emerges with the Internet is thus a sphere of intermediate people, new interpreters, drawn from these realms and linking them in a new social, public space of alternative voices and authorities" (p. 56).

A related facet of displacement logic points out how the status of authorities and ecclesiastical structure is undermined when followers gain more access to relevant knowledge, since "to preserve status, knowledge is often protected by encoding it in jargon, or by restricting access to it in other ways" (Meyrowitz 1985). In this light, the Internet is viewed as a danger to religious authority because it presents potentially oppositional information that negatively affects the credibility of religious institutions and leadership. The spread of unorthodox teachings calls attention to the possible weakening of the status of religious leaders as spiritual mentors. For example, Fukamizu (2007) argued that the authority of Japanese Buddhist priests has eroded with electronic forum use, as their followers develop "critical attitudes" and entertain doubts about traditional doctrines and their faith systems from their chat interactions. He also predicted that in "postmodern faith," "horizontal interaction among religious followers" will be more important than the "vertical, top down of traditional doctrines."

The Internet, by allowing schismatic leaders to emerge, also helps challenge more directly the ability of traditional authorities to define legitimate teachings and symbols. Turner (2007) stated that "global information technologies and their associated cultures undermine traditional forms of religious authority because they expand conventional modes of communication, open up new opportunities for debate and create alternative visions of the global community" (p. 120). He went so far as to propose that it is not difficult for a Muslim to quote some hadiths or issue a fatwa, as "in the modern global media, the ability to claim religious authority has been democratized in the sense that anybody can assume the role of an [imam]" (p. 120). With the rise of a multiplicity of online "experts," seekers and believers may now experience increased access and ability to initiate debates and even actively confront religious authorities with online information. The decline of a religious movement may ensue when leaders appear unwilling or inadequately equipped to deal with perpetrators of perceived deliberate misinformation and heresy online. For example, Introvigne (2005) observed religious leaders of a new Japanese religious movement were largely ineffectual in the face of online rumors, defamation or what was understood as "information terrorism"; it was stated that, "The leadership's reaction was from weak to non-existent." In part, as a result of the partially voluntary lack of legal and other reaction against attacks, "it was noted that this religious movement lost almost half of its membership in certain western countries" (pp. 112–13). Similarly, Cowan (2004) argued that the replication of religious propaganda in countermovement sites, such as anticult and countercult sites, confers "the semblance of authority" on those believed to be the originators of online materials, since these sites frequently refer to the operators of similar sites as "experts." Because most religious organizations may have limited energy for responding to misrepresentations online, the web "favors the countermovement" and helps further the cause of critics if propagation of (mis)information is their primary agenda (pp. 266–8).

Furthering the logic of displacement in which digital media is perceived to be corrosive and disruptive to traditional religious authority, online forum leaders and webmasters have been portrayed as new authority figures. For example, Herring (2005) noted that, notwithstanding criticisms and contested decisions, posters in an online Christian news group generally accepted the moderator as a "governing authority" and spiritual advisor. Campbell (2005) speculated that, within Christianity, there would be shifts in "congregational power structures," as formerly discounted "techies" find themselves in new leadership roles. The authority of Buddhist leaders is also displaced by non-monastic authorities like webmasters who are "conceived as the religious specialists or 'virtuosi' (in Weber's terms) for giving definitions and taking the place of monks as disseminators of knowledge" (Taylor 2003: 294). Busch (2011) examined an online Buddhist message forum and concluded that the founder and global moderators discursively and structurally shaped the web environment. This process is said to elevate the authority of the online moderators, as it "inherently allows those in control of the site the authority to set the boundaries of religious orthodoxy and identity and hence, who can take part in the community" (p. 58).

Moreover, it has been anticipated that the Internet helps create new mediators associated with new online services, altering the past hierarchical order of established religions. By allowing the conduct of "online ritual activities" functional solely in cyberspace, Helland (2007) argued that cyber-pilgrimages and long-distance ritual practices have enabled diaspora religious groups like the Hindus to develop connections among themselves and to India, although he maintained that the effects the presence of *puja* wizards and scholars on ritual service websites had on the activities normally conducted by the temple in the diaspora community were indeterminate. In a more recent analysis of *puja* ordering websites, Scheifinger (2010) argued that the *puja* service professionals were challenging the authority of the temple administration and priests in a "subtle" manner by "determining what should happen at temples and what is acceptable" (p. 647), restricting the participation of non-ethnic Indians, curtailing activities like animal sacrifices, and selling photographs of deities (where temple photography is not allowed). It was noted that the activities of *puja* service providers also undermined the financial position of priests by reducing their opportunities for receiving extra monies from devotees visiting the temple, leading to the conclusion that "those who have traditionally exercised authority are now being bypassed and that when it comes to the ordering of *pujas* online, it is the independent providers who are the ones exercising authority" (p. 652).

Collectively, these and other studies highlight how the logic of disjuncture and displacement that undergirds religious authority operates across a spectrum of religious beliefs and backgrounds. Religious interpretation, texts, ecclesiastical structures, and the importance of positions like webmasters and forum moderators (all framed as components of religious authority) are changed by online communication and the capabilities of the Internet to expand resource access, facilitate new ritual practices, and support new positions of power. As the Internet becomes more popular among the religiously oriented, it is perceived to be a largely though not universally positive resource for promoting social capital in online religious communication, which is seen by some offline religious leaders as disruptive or destructive.

The logic of continuity and complementarity

There are alternative perspectives challenging the conceptualization that the Internet leads to a decline or crisis of religious authority, mirroring the trajectory of Internet studies that has moved away from a focus on online phenomena and its disembodied customs. The logic of "continuity" involves arguments which propose or reason that the relationship between religious authority and new media is characterized instead by connectedness, succession, and negotiation. "Complementarity" refers to the acts of interrelation of socio-technical developments that co-constitute and augment authority. The past decade has witnessed a more integrated perspective that grounds the significance of the Internet in people's everyday lives, particularly the harmonization of online practices with local community-building activities. More recently, scholarship has gathered which is oriented toward investigating the synergetic relationships between online and offline faith beliefs and infrastructures. In this view, offline religious authority is reframed as shaping, sustaining, and being sustained by online practices.

So rather than be threatened by the Internet, some scholarship has recognized how religious organizations have addressed the presence of new online religious texts and controversial interpretations. For instance, the use of court orders against Internet opponents on the basis of copyright infringement and defamation (i.e. false malicious publication) illustrates forceful reactions undertaken by the leadership of the Church of Scientology to address disparaging and hostile online rhetoric (Introvigne 2005). Another case, of a Baha'i-oriented discussion group, is interesting to note in relation to its temporal sequence of events. Piff and Warburg (2005) proposed that, although the discussion group was initially allowed to function without the interference or supervision decentralized of Baha'i institutions, the eventual closure of the email list demonstrated how "American Baha'i authorities" could have "put pressure on individual posters to exercise restraint or self-censorship in expression of their views" (p. 98). As such, it was acknowledged that the chronicling of the rise and fall of this online group suggests that members do acknowledge and abide by the advice and instructions of their organizations. Therefore, "the much heralded bypass opportunity of the Internet may be more of an ideal construction than a reality in many cases" (p. 98).

Congruent with the logic of continuity and complementarity, Barzilai-Nahon and Barzilai (2005) highlighted how ultra-Orthodox Jewish elites in Israel controlled online information via censorship and supervision of websites that provided a platform for them to disseminate their teachings and provide counter-narratives to political criticisms. Internet usage, other than for professional and economic purposes, was banned, as prominent spiritual leaders issued proclamations that only allowed time for information technology training. It was argued that the process of "culturally shaping" the Internet led to the preservation of the hierarchical order of their fundamentalist community and social stratification of their membership. Campbell (2012) also noted how the Catholic Church has shaped the Internet in line with its formal hierarchy and clerical caste led by the Pope via the generation of automated email responses on the Pope's behalf and dismantlement of online interactive features like the ranking function and comment mode on the Vatican YouTube channel in order to preserve the Vatican's image and control of new media.

Similarly, albeit in a different context, Kluver and Cheong (2007), in addressing questions of religion and modernization, underscored the logic of complementarity between authority and Internet applications. Their study of religious leaders found that, instead of incongruence and criticism of new technology, cultural compatibilities were manifest in the development of new media and a variety of established faith traditions (Buddhist, Christian, Muslim, Taoist, and Hindu) in the highly wired context of Singapore. Religious leaders largely framed the Internet as a positive development for their community and embraced it as part of their religious missions and growth strategies. So as "not to subvert religious authority," several leaders also stressed the tool-like capabilities of the Internet to impute neutrality to the medium, "in order to reclaim net-based technologies for their religious practices" (pp. 1137–8)

Still other studies highlight how online religious discourse may not necessarily be inflammatory, critical, or damaging to established religious authorities. Cheong et al. (2008), in a multi-method study of Christian blogs, hyperlinks on blogrolls and interviews, found that several blogs were affiliated with local churches or congregations and many blogged about their engagement with local religious activities and referenced customary religious texts. Drawing on a content analysis, Campbell (2010) also concluded that Christian religious bloggers utilize their blogs to frame authority in ways that "may more often affirm" than assault sources of authority in terms of hierarchy, structure, roles, and text.

Furthermore, as an extension of the logic of complementarity, recent scholarship has proposed redefinitions of the constitutions and practices of religious authority to account for its perceived flourishing in increasingly integrated social media platforms (Cheong and Ess 2012). Horsfield (2012) observed that as digital media have increased "the potential for a diversity of voices," "the previously recognized criteria of religious authority such as formal qualifications or institutional positions are changing to more fluid characteristics applied by audiences, such as a person's charisma, accessibility and perceived cultural competence" (p. 255). Indeed, there appear to be changes in the modes of authority production, as some religious leaders have expanded their scope of influence, restructuring their communicative practices online, bridging and bonding forms of social capital to spur administrative and operational effectiveness (Cheong and Poon 2008).

An emerging corpus of studies highlights how religious leaders are weaving social media into their vocation. Lee (2009) illustrated how Won Buddhist priests have created personal blogs on Cyworld for self-cultivation, empowerment, and development of the relationship between leadership and laity. It was documented that some of the open diaries of monks and nuns were used to demystify the ideal life of a priest as pure and pious, and depict their accommodation and loyalty amid the dominant and gendered norms of their organization, or were used to "indirectly deliver" sermons to young Buddhists and potential believers. Fischer-Nielsen (2012) also stressed that Google, Facebook and YouTube have been integrated into the working lives of pastors. In an analysis of results from a survey completed by 1040 pastors of the Evangelical Lutheran Church in Denmark, he found that 95 percent of them are online daily and a significant proportion (94 percent of the pastors aged between 25 and 39 years) regarded the Internet as having positive influence on their work. Two-thirds of the respondents reported that the Internet had "caused more frequent contact with parishioners" and most endorsed "flesh and blood," "real church practice" in lieu of cyberchurch rituals and web-based services.

In this way, some commentators claim that the Internet, via social media platforms, is an avenue of renewal, rejuvenating the life (and legitimacy) of religious organizations. Lomborg and Ess (2012) noted how the presence of a Danish church on Facebook was praised in terms of its "progressive" "brand value." In another analysis, of Muslim-oriented podcasts, it was asserted that leaders may expand their authority through self-promotion and representation on multimedia platforms where podcasts are utilized with older media (Scholz et al. 2008). In particular, it was argued Muslim groups may disseminate doctrine and reinforce existing power structures by extending a group leader's presence via podcasting technologies:

> the authority necessary to legitimize this specific interpretation of Islamic belief and practice is generated by a set of acoustic and visual features signaling "Islamic" authenticity to the listener and by the bias of steady references to the high educational level (in terms of a traditional Islamic education) of the podcasts' key speakers.
>
> (p. 508)

Hence, to adapt pragmatically to an increasingly pluralistic spiritual sphere or "religious marketplace," leaders and laity are encouraged to enter into agreements characterized not merely by offline dogmatic pronouncements, but increasingly also by clergy's new competencies to connect interactively across a spectrum of media to persuasively reach congregational members (Cheong et al., 2011a). Clergy, it is proposed, are adjusting their social identity from that of commanders and sages to guides and mediators of knowledge in encounters both online and offline, an approach that Cheong et al. (2011a) have termed "strategic arbitration." Such strategic arbitration online facilitates the co-creation of information and expertise under conditions where laity cooperation is elicited by retaining discretionary power among the leadership to determine informational and interpersonal outcomes such that they do not destabilize the organization.

For example, findings from a study of Christian pastors showed how leaders monitored their online communication (for example by selectively curbing email response) and justified the validity of their authority (for example by drawing upon scripture and stressing their own interpretations via new "online ministries" and branding activities) in order to reinforce normative regulation (Cheong et al. 2011a). Another study, drawing on in-depth interviews, found Buddhist leaders also constructed their authority by promoting communication influence through offline–online mediation which in turn restores trust and increases congregational epistemic dependence upon them (Cheong et al. 2011b). The study illustrated how Buddhist leaders principally rechanneled online resources and messages back into priest and laity relationships by (a) stressing the benefits of Dharma classes and personalized real-life mentoring connections, which in some cases were framed as sacred relational ties or "karmic links," (b) promoting sensorial ritual practices (e.g. meditation and blessings) and festivals (e.g. Vesak or Buddha's birthday celebrations) enacted in the presence of monks and nuns within perceived temple sacred grounds, and (c) enacting multi-modal outreach across digital platforms. Findings also showed that Buddhist clergy were actively involved in heightening their web presence to meet demands for cognitive coherence in "low and high tech" representations so as to strengthen congregational affective interest and organizational loyalty.

In contemporary times, therefore, an added dimension of the logic of complementarity includes transmediation, a process whereby authority practices are appropriated and remediated across different communication platforms (Cheong 2011). In the context of new media's affordances for amplifying religious leaders' ability to reach faith seekers and believers, Lee and Sinitiere (2009) highlighted how media-savvy evangelical pastors or "holy mavericks" have attracted attention to their high-growth organizations in part by their vigorous adoption of corporate organizational branding in contemporary conditions of media convergence. Support for these religious authorities, who typically have a strong brand presence online, appears strong, because they are generally believed to be able to reconcile a duality of concern with the "other-worldliness" of spiritual life with the "this-worldliness" of new media marketing. In parallel, inscribed in recent expressively titled publications like *The Reason Your Church Must Twitter* (Coppedge 2009) is religiously tinted discourse that advocates for priests to adopt social media to advance their outreach and missions. There have been multiple ways in which churches have incorporated the use of Twitter and other micro-blogging practices into their daily institutional practices to create "ambient religious communication" and a sense of connected presence among members (Cheong 2010). For example, in some cases, the creation of "Twitter Sundays" encouraged members to tweet their reflections and questions throughout the service, but it is pertinent to note that tweets are typically reviewed by church staff and then posted as scrolling visual messages on a screen behind the preaching pastor.

In sum, a growing body of research points to the recurrent logic of continuity and complementarity of religious authority, situated in the contemporary zeitgeist surrounding Internet use as incrementally and routinely incorporated within individual, collective, and institutional norms, practices, and orderings. As the literature demonstrates, while religious leaders are recognized as being increasingly dependent on online resources, overall, they are increasingly portrayed as adaptive and as exercising significant control by, for instance, curtailing the negative impact of false and inflammatory interpretations and reclaiming their audience's respect and trust. Furthermore, religious leaders have also been portrayed as assuming expanded competencies as strategic arbitrators of online–offline religious information, to restore relational bonds and credibility important to the development of convergent multimedia and corporate promotional strategies.

The logic of dialectics and paradox and other future research directions

This chapter offers a critical conceptual framework for articulating the multiple links between new media and religious authority. It is clear from the above discussion that the Internet facilitates both the weakening and strengthening of religious authority, offering possibilities for conflict, yet also for understanding and accommodation. This insight into the dual logics prompts further examination of a dialectical perspective in mediated culture. A dialectical perspective on new media and culture recognizes the simultaneous presence of two interacting forces, seemingly opposite, interdependent, and complementary, akin to Eastern philosophies (such as yin and yang) on the completion of relative polarities (Cheong *et al.* 2012). Here, the logic of dialectics on religious authority would imply understanding the management of conflicting tensions, uneven gains, multiple opportunities, ambivalences, and challenges that new media users like religious leaders face within their online and offline experiences (Cheong and Ess 2012). As Schement and Stephenson (1996) noted, religion has to be understood in terms of "endemic tensions," localized and prevalent aspects of continuity and change, consumption and worship that constitute "unavoidable frictions" in the private and public spheres of religious practice within the information society. In effect, further research needs to investigate the ways religious leaders manage and resolve ambiguities in their ongoing negotiation of socio-technical tensions, for example their negotiations of privacy and connectivity, over- and underexposure in their experiences of new digital, mobile, and geolocational media applications.

To be sure, a small but growing number of studies have already observed the countervailing tendencies and double meanings of mediated religious authority. For instance, Barker (2005) suggested that the Internet can undermine "the strong vertical authority structure" and provide "an alternative source of information to be disseminated by the movement's leaders and enable this to be communicated through horizontal networks" (p. 80). Cheong *et al.* (2011b) recognized how competing online resources can also serve as a source of education, serving to enhance a priest's authority relating to and involving knowledge, since the latter is able to move beyond dictating to mediate between texts. In other words, "a paradox of epistemic authority is that it may be more effective when followers possess some level of knowledge that enables them to evaluate the legitimacy of clergy's knowledge" (p. 1163), for example in instances when congregational members converse with leaders by referring to established and new religious texts, allowing clergy to display their proficiency and sophistication by addressing their specific concerns. Lomborg and Ess (2012) stated that Facebook friendships may be relationally rewarding for leaders seeking to build closer relationships with their members, but that it is a "delicate balancing act" with "continuous tension" since the strategic presentation of the pastor as an ordinary person or "one of us" also possibly entails a risk of jeopardizing the professional respect so crucial for pastoral work and leadership within the community (p. 185).

Thus, these studies suggest the logic of dialectics and paradox, since leaders struggle with, negotiate, and build tensions related to processes of digital mediation in their work as they attempt to reconstruct religious authority. This interesting, complex, and somewhat counter-intuitive relationship warrants conceptual expansion and future-focused attention.

In a related manner, future research on religious authority should consider broadening the data repertoire to more accurately capture and archive over time developments in clergy communication. Methodologically, earlier studies have drawn their conclusions mostly from participant observation in virtual communities, while more recent studies have employed interviews, content analyses, and case studies. A few studies have used quantitative methods such as surveys and hyperlink analyses, prompting further consideration of new ways in which qualitative and quantitative data collection could be deployed to investigate religious authority in research studies. For example, webliometrics, which refers to a quantitative research method in information science used to analyze online patterns, could be used and triangulated with qualitative methods such as interviews and content analyses in order to understand more comprehensively the processes of corrosion, maintenance, and reconstruction of religious authority.

To conclude, in light of the scarce systematic attention paid to the topic of religious authority in digital contexts, this chapter has provided an initial mapping of the broad contours of research developments to illuminate key relationships undergirding authority in an increasingly mediated era. While coverage within a chapter is necessarily limited, it is hoped that this overview has identified significant themes, illustrated across a range of studies and religious traditions. A metatheoretical perspective on authority and communication technologies serves as a useful learning and discovery device for understanding emerging new media and their implications for religious authority.

Recommended reading

Lincoln, B. (1994) *Authority: Construction and Corrosion*, Chicago: University of Chicago Press.

In this book, Bruce Lincoln, professor of the history of religions, provides an engaging treatise on authority, its construction, maintenance, and corrosion. With regard to television, the new medium at the time of the book's publication, he conceptualizes the importance of observing how the exercise of authority implicates and is dependent on the use of electronic media.

Meyrowitz, J. (1985) *No Sense of Place: The Impact of Electronic Media on Social Behavior*, New York: Oxford University Press.

Inspired by what has recently emerged as media ecology research, Joshua Meyrowitz, professor of communication, argues that electronic media distort distinctions between social groups, including leaders and followers, as broadcast exposure helps humanize and demystify the powerful. Although the focus is on the saturation of television in society, his thought-provoking thesis (notwithstanding some criticisms of technological determinism) has implications for the projections of authority and control amid contemporary media convergences and accelerating spatial–temporal dynamics within digital media developments.

Cheong, P.H., Fischer-Nielsen, P., Gelfgren, S., and Ess, C. (eds) (2012) *Digital Religion, Social Media and Culture: Perspectives, Practices and Futures*, New York: Peter Lang.

This book offers a pioneering overview of the study of digital religion and social media practices. One component of the introductory chapter addresses the question of authority in light of prevailing digital and social media developments. Multiple chapters in this anthology, which brings together works by prominent researchers in related and interdisciplinary fields of study, highlight the contemporary implications of digital media for authority, identity, and community constructions in emerging religious networks and connections.

References

Anderson, J. (1999) "The Internet and Islam's new interpreters," in D. Eickelman (ed.), *New Media in the Muslim World: The Emerging Public Sphere*, 45–60, Bloomington: Indiana University Press.

Barker, E. (2005) "Crossing the boundary: new challenges to religious authority and control as a consequence of access to the Internet," in M. Hojsgaard and M. Warburg (eds), *Religion and Cyberspace*, 67–85, London: Routledge.

Barzilai-Nahon, K. and Barzilai, G. (2005) "Cultured technology: Internet and religious fundamentalism," *The Information Society*, 21(1): 25–40.

Busch, L. (2011) "To 'come to a correct understanding of Buddhism': a case study on spiritualising technology, religious authority, and the boundaries of orthodoxy and identity in a Buddhist Web forum," *New Media and Society*, 13(1): 58–74.

Campbell, H. (2005) "Spiritualizing the Internet: uncovering discourses and narratives of religious Internet use," *Online – Heidelberg Journal of Religions on the Internet*, 1(1). Online. Available: http://archiv.ub.uni-heidelberg.de/volltextserver/volltexte/2005/5824/pdf/Campbell4a.pdf (accessed May 10, 2007).

——(2007) "Who's got the power? Religious authority and the Internet," *Journal of Computer-Mediated Communication*, 12: 1043–62.

——(2010) "Religious authority and the blogosphere," *Journal of Computer-Mediated Communication*, 15(2): 251–76.

——(2012) "How religious communities negotiate new media religiously," in P.H. Cheong, P. Fischer-Nielsen, S. Gelfgren, and C. Ess. (eds), *Digital Religion, Social Media and Culture: Perspectives, Practices and Futures*, 81–96, New York: Peter Lang.

Cheong, P.H. (2010) "Faith tweets: ambient religious communication and microblogging rituals," *M/C Journal: A Journal of Media and Culture*. Online. Available: http://journal.media-culture.org.au/index.php/mcjournal/article/viewArticle/223 (accessed December 5, 2010).

——(2011) "Religious leaders, mediated authority and social change," *Journal of Applied Communication Research*, 39(4): 452–4.

Cheong, P.H. and Ess, C. (2012), "Religion 2.0? Relational and hybridizing pathways in religion, social media and culture," in P.H. Cheong, P. Fischer-Nielsen, S. Gelfgren, and C. Ess. (eds), *Digital Religion, Social Media and Culture: Perspectives, Practices and Futures*, 1–24, New York: Peter Lang.

Cheong, P.H. and Poon, J.P.H. (2008) "'WWW.Faith.Org': (Re)structuring communication and social capital building among religious organizations," *Information, Communication and Society*, 11(1): 89–110.

Cheong, P.H., Halavais, A., and Kwon, K. (2008) "The chronicles of me: understanding blogging as a religious practice," *Journal of Media and Religion*, 7(3): 107–31.

Cheong, P.H., Huang, S.H., and Poon, J.P.H. (2011a), "Religious communication and epistemic authority of leaders in wired faith organizations," *Journal of Communication*, 61(5): 938–58.

——(2011b), "Cultivating online and offline pathways to enlightenment: religious authority and strategic arbitration in wired Buddhist organizations," *Information, Communication & Society*, 14(8): 1160–80.

Cheong, P.H., Martin, J.N., and Macfadyen L. (2012), "Mediated intercultural communication matters: understanding new media, dialectics and social change," in P.H. Cheong, J.N. Martin, and L. Macfadyen (eds), *New Media and Intercultural Communication: Identity, Community and Politics*, 1–20, New York: Peter Lang.

Coppedge, A. (2009) *The Reason Your Church Must Twitter*. Available: www.twitterforchurches.com (accessed January 5, 2009).

Cowan, D. (2004) "Contested spaces: movement, countermovement, and e-space propaganda," in L. Dawson and D. Cowan (eds), *Religion Online: Finding Faith on the Internet*, 255–72, London: Routledge.

Fischer-Nielsen, P. (2012) "Pastors on the Internet: online responses to secularization," in P.H. Cheong, P. Fischer-Nielsen, S. Gelfgren, and C. Ess (eds), *Digital Religion, Social Media and Culture: Perspectives, Practices and Futures*, 115–30, New York: Peter Lang.

Fukamizu, K. (2007) "Internet use among religious followers: religious postmodernism in Japanese Buddhism," *Journal of Computer-Mediated Communication*, 12(3). Online. Available: http://jcmc.indiana.edu/vol12/issue3/fukamizu.html (accessed December 20, 2007).

Helland, C. (2007) "Diaspora on the electronic frontier: developing virtual connections with sacred homelands," *Journal of Computer-Mediated Communication*, 12(3). Online. Available: http://jcmc.indiana.edu/vol12/issue3/helland.html (accessed December 20, 2007).

Herring, D. (2005) "Virtual as contextual: a net news theology," in L. Dawson and D. Cowan (eds), *Religion and Cyberspace*, 149–65, London: Routledge.

Horsfield, P. (2012) "A moderate diversity of books? The challenge of new media to the practice of Christian theology," in P.H. Cheong, P. Fischer-Nielsen, S. Gelfgren, and C. Ess (eds), *Digital Religion, Social Media and Culture: Perspectives, Practices and Futures*, 243–58, New York: Peter Lang.

Introvigne, M. (2005) "A symbolic universe: information terrorism and new religions in cyberspace," in M. Hojsgaard and M. Warburg (eds), *Religion and Cyberspace*, 102–18, London: Routledge.

Kim, M.-C. (2005) "Online Buddhist community: an alternative religious organization in the information age," in K.T. Hojsgaard and M. Warburg (eds), *Religion in Cyberspace*, 138–48, New York: Routledge.

Kluver, R. and Cheong, P.H. (2007) "Technological modernization, the Internet, and religion in Singapore," *Journal of Computer-Mediated Communication*, 12(3): 1122–42.

Lee, J. (2009) "Cultivating the self in cyberspace: the use of personal blogs among Buddhist priests," *Journal of Media and Religion*, 8(2): 97–114.

Lee, S.L. and Sinitiere, P.L. (2009) *Holy Mavericks: Evangelical Innovators and the Spiritual Marketplace*, New York: New York University Press.

Lincoln, B. (1994) *Authority: Construction and Corrosion*, Chicago: University of Chicago Press.

Lomborg, S. and Ess, C. (2012) "'Keeping the line open and warm': an activist Danish church and its presence on Facebook," in P.H. Cheong, P. Fischer-Nielsen, S. Gelfgren, and C. Ess (eds), *Digital Religion, Social Media and Culture: Perspectives, Practices and Futures*, 169–90, New York: Peter Lang.

Marvin, C. (1988) *When Old Technologies Were New: Thinking About Communication in the Late Nineteenth Century*, New York: Oxford University Press.

Meyrowitz, J. (1985) *No Sense of Place: The Impact of Electronic Media on Social Behavior*, New York: Oxford University Press.

O'Leary, S. (1996) "Cyberspace as sacred space: communicating religion on computer networks," *Journal of the American Academy of Religion*, 64(4): 781–808.

Piff, D. and Warburg, M. (2005) "Seeking for truth: plausibility on a Baha'i email list," in M. Hojsgaard and M. Warburg (eds), *Religion and Cyberspace*, 86–101, London: Routledge.

Prebish, C. (2004) "The cybersangha: Buddhism on the Internet," in L.L. Dawson and D.E. Cowan (eds), *Religion Online: Finding Faith on the Internet*, 135–50, New York: Routledge.

Scheifinger, H. (2010) "Internet threats to Hindu authority: puja ordering websites and the Kalighat temple," *Asian Journal of Social Science*, 38(4): 636–56.

Schement, J.R. and Stephenson, H.C. (1996) "Religion and the information society," in D.A. Stout and J.M. Buddenbaum (eds), *Religion and Mass Media: Audiences and Adaptations*, 261–89, Thousand Oaks, CA: Sage.

Scholz, J., Selge, T., Stille, M., and Zimmerman, J. (2008) "Listening communities? Some remarks on the construction of religious authority in Islamic podcasts," *Die Welt des Islams*, 48(3/4): 457–509.

Soukup, P.A. (2003) "Challenges for evangelization in the digital age," Online. Available: www.iglesiaeinformatica.org/4–2Challenges%20for%20Evangelization%20in%20the%20Digital%20Age.pdf (accessed June 8, 2007).

Taylor, J.L. (2003) "Cyber-Buddhism and changing urban space in Thailand," *Space and Culture*, 6(3): 292–308.

Turner, B.S. (2007) "Religious authority and the new media," *Theory, Culture & Society*, 24(2), 117–34.

Weber, M., trans. Henderson, A. and Parsons, T. (1947) *Theory of Social and Economic Organization*, New York: Oxford University Press.

Wellman, B. (2011) 'Studying the Internet through the ages,' in M. Consalvo and C. Ess (eds), *The Blackwell Handbook of Internet Studies*, 17–23, Oxford: Blackwell.

Zaman, M.Q. (2007) *The Ulama in Contemporary Islam: Custodians of Change*, Princeton, NJ: Princeton University Press.

6 Authenticity

Kerstin Radde-Antweiler

The concept of authenticity is a much-debated notion in media studies and discourse. For example, performances of rituals or pilgrimages online are often doubted as being a mere simulation or a reproduction of something "real," rather than being authentic as such (Hill-Smith 2009). Researchers also raise questions in relation to the study of rituals within virtual worlds, such as Second Life or World of Warcraft, regarding whether online rituals are serious and authentic acts, or fakes or flawed simulations (Radde-Antweiler 2010). In Internet research in general there has been much debate about whether social actions within digital realms have the same quality as face-to-face interactions.

But why are online rituals not considered as real as offline rituals? Is there such a clear distinction between the real and the virtual? And is this an accurate or helpful analytical distinction? In order to investigate these questions, this chapter explores scholarly discussion around the concept of authenticity while focusing on the two main research themes. The first deals with the question of whether people's experiences, as well as their virtual bodies, can be considered authentic or real online. Connected with this, the second theme concerns the definition of the environment itself, considering whether cyberspace is a "real," authentic place, and the extent to which it can function as a sacred space. It becomes clear that both topics are based on the distinction and definition of the terms "online" and "offline," or "real" and "virtual."

Defining authenticity

According to the *Oxford Advanced Learner's Dictionary*, authenticity can be described as a "quality of being authentic" (Hornby 1989: 67). The adjective "authentic" itself can bear two meanings: it can be used to describe something as true or genuine, or something or someone as trustworthy or reliable. The *Cambridge Dictionary* (n.d.) stresses the first meaning when it connects it with "the quality of being real or true." Persons are judged as authentic if they present themselves as they truly are, in other words if they are not pretending to be someone else or playing another role. Originally the term "authenticity" was derived from the Greek *auto* and *entes*, and meant, "to fulfill something in oneself" (Kalisch 2000: 32).

In contrast to "authentic" the term "virtual" is often used to describe a lack of reality, for example due to the fact that materiality is missing. This is a crucial point to be explored in more detail later in this chapter.

In religious and anthropological studies, the concept of authenticity has served as an important way of exploring and interrogating the essence and uniqueness of religious and cultural traditions. Based on Hobsbawm's distinction between invented traditions from modern times and so-called genuine traditions (Hobsbawm 1983: 8, 13), the view of foreign, especially non-Christian traditions was romanticized. A prominent example is the framing of "African religion," which was in most anthropologists' reports presented as "still possessing an authenticity that the civilized, modern Westerner has lost" (de Witte 2004: 136). As this notion that cultural and religious systems are not fixed but socially constructed became accepted within these areas of study, it also became clear that the concepts of religion and culture were dynamic or fluid, rather than fixed. This meant that they were portrayed as changing across time and place. In this context, the concept of authenticity was greatly criticized, as authenticity was seen as "a cultural construct of the modern Western world" (Handler 1986: 2). The fluid nature of religion and culture meant one could not give a substantial definition of authenticity, or define what it actually is. As a result, scholars often approached the term "authenticity" as having a certain meaning of trueness as well as trustworthiness for religious actors. So religious studies deals with ascriptions and processes of negotiation engaged in by religious actors, which can be defined by the terms "religion" or "religious." These concepts are thereby variant and fluid and can be determined only discursively – in their relationship to the concept of culture, for example. Previously, religion was seen from a scholarly perspective as a system of definable, consistent and uniform symbols and theology. When considering a single actor's perspective, it becomes clear that there is a wide variance in religious ideas dominating religious discourse. Also, constructions of what religious experiences and "real" religion are cannot be regarded as static entities. Religion, can thus be defined as a fluid system of symbols with variant meanings ascribed to it by individual religious actors. "Authenticity" has in this context two meanings. First, it serves as a category which allows these actors to judge whether certain objects, for example particular beliefs and performances, are part of a given religious system. Second, actors are judged to be "authentic" if they are the agents of these beliefs or performances (see for example de Witte 2004).

The study of authenticity online

Giving an overview of research studies on authenticity online is quite problematic. Despite the fact that the concept of authenticity plays an important role in nearly all analysis of religious activities online, authenticity as such is not explicitly brought up as a central topic, but is presupposed in most studies. This presumption can be seen in the three different waves or stages of Internet research outlined by Højsgaard and Warburg (2005). The first wave, in the mid-1990s, can generally be characterized as filled with dystopian fears on the one hand and utopian fascination on the other. Due to the fact that online activities were new, a description of these phenomena was necessary. In the second wave, a more reflective and critical analysis of the field was conducted by prominent researchers like Dawson (2005) and Lövheim (2004). During the third wave, the majority of Internet research was defined by theoretical approaches that focused on the connectivity between offline and online religiosity (Wellman 2004). In all three stages, the topic of authenticity emerged through two major research themes: first, in researchers' evaluation of people's experiences and presentation of their bodies online; and second, in the classification and analysis of the environment or online space itself. Both topics are of course interconnected, based on the offline–online relationship; in other words, they highlight the distinction between what is referred to as the "virtual" and the "real" in relation to the Internet.

People's authentic experiences and bodies in cyberspace

Users experience their role, body and actions in cyberspace in quite different ways. In early Internet research, cyberspace was presented in a utopian frame, connecting Gibson's *Neuromancer* and the idea of a "cyber-heaven" where people in front of the screen could fly in an "illusory datascape that radically differs from the reality of physical existence" (van Doorn 2011: 532). This contrasted with much of the research, which showed that actions and experiences online were seen as highly connected with contexts, as well as with the body, offline (Campbell 2004; Jenkins 2006). With growing technical opportunities in virtual environments, observing the role of the body became increasingly important, due to the fact that the visual nature of virtual worlds meant it was not merely writing or text but bodily performances, such as walking or running via avatars, that constituted users' experiences online. However, many researchers still presupposed a strict separation between the online body and offline activities. For example, Hayles stated:

> As long as the human subject is envisioned as an autonomous self with unambiguous boundaries, the human–computer interface can only be parsed as a division between the solidity of real life on one side and the illusion of virtual reality on the other, thus obscuring the far-reaching changes initiated by the development of virtual technologies.
>
> (1999: 290)

Dawson stresses the ambiguity of religiosity online as different and at the same time similar to offline experiences, which are identified by him as the "real" experiences (Dawson 2005). Yet most recent research agrees that social actions online do have an effect on how users experience their bodies, gender and sexuality. For example, van Doorn stresses that:

[t]hese "virtual" experiences extend beyond their conventional associations with the embodied spaces that are created and inhabited by the physical body and move into the textual space of IRC, where they produce digital "bodies of text". These bodies cannot be understood as mimetic textual copies of the "real thing", but rather work to transfer embodied articulations of gender and sexuality "from one plane of meaning and appearance to another".

(2011: 535)

A prominent example highlighting the effects and implications of social action online in offline contexts is a well-publicized discussion of a rape in Second Life. In 2007, two Belgian newspapers, *De Morgen* and *Het Laatste Nieuws*, reported details of a virtual rape that happened to a Belgian female resident in the virtual world, leading to local, offline police investigations. Several blogs picked the story up and broadcast it. Regardless of the recently solved question of whether the whole story was a newspaper hoax, the event raised interesting issues related to discussions of authenticity on several blogs, for example virtuallyblind.com (www.virtuallyblind.com/2007/04/24/open-roundtable-allegations-of-virtual-rape-bring-belgian-police-to-second-life), destructoid.com (www.destructoid.com/second-life-now-with-more-rape--28711.phtml) and vtoreality.com (www.vtoreality.com/2007/how-exactly-does-virtual-rape-even-occur-in-second-life/909/). Most of the blog posts dealt with the question of whether this rape could be compared with an offline rape, or if the abuse of an avatar and the "mere" online body could have any effect on the offline body at all:

> Can this rape be considered as a "real" rape even if it did not affect the "real" offline body?
> The main question that arose again and again in discussions was not whether the virtual rape of an avatar in an online environment was possible, but how much the user-victim might be traumatized by the event.
> (Heidbrink, Miczek, and Radde-Antweiler 2011: 183)

So what is "virtual rape"? Is it control of an avatar against a user's will, a textual or graphical depiction of a forced sexual act, or something else completely? Can virtual rape occur without even the appearance (in a graphical world) or description (in a text-based world) of physical contact, or is that "just" harassment – essentially the equivalent of an obscene phone call? How should crimes perpetrated only in a virtual space be punished? Is it just harassment (of the user), no matter what the crime (against the avatar)?

The question of authenticity was raised here by the fact that users who experience such offenses and violations often show the same after-effects as victims of offline rapes (Kirwan 2009). Most of the arguments against the efficacy or realness of such actions were based on an assumed distinction or separation between the online and offline fields. Social actions within online environments were not considered to be equal to offline actions. Similarly, religious performances online, such as rituals, are often heavily doubted, especially by religious institutions. For example, anthropologist Felicia Hughes-Freeland in 2006 stressed that

> There is a strong evidence for the claim that ritual cannot be subsumed or reproduced through media representations. Although symbolic communication brings ritual and media into the same analytical frame, ritual has an instrumentality that most media representations do not have. Ritual is really real, not symbolic.
>
> (pp. 613f.)

However, the discussion of how the online body can be defined – in contrast to or as an enhancement of the offline body – is not a new one. In the 1990s the role of the body was discussed in relation to learning in virtual school environments (Bruckmann and Resnick 1995; Reid 1995). Nevertheless, due to the fact that the Internet was at this time a primarily textual medium, the body itself was also seen as a mere textual construction:

> In cyberspace, people are seen as "disembodied", detached or freed from the constraints of the physical. Online bodies are constructed through words. People present their bodies by the words they select.
>
> (Campbell 2004: 217)

This is in contrast to newer 3D environments that present the user with new possibilities and allow them to have a body in cyberspace, in the form of a graphical representation. Users can now not only type and converse in virtual environments such as Second Life, they can walk, fly, speak, and carry out other bodily actions online with the help of an avatar. These developments also change the possibilities for the religious use of the Internet. For example, religious activities like church services online are no longer limited to writing texts or chatting, but can also integrate gestures such as meditation poses or folding the avatar's hands for prayer. Thus users now have the ability to immerse themselves bodily in the environment via their avatar and emulate religious actions.

Even if the connection between online and offline bodies is recognized and seen as a point of agreement, the question remains how the relationship between them can be defined. For example, Hutchings (2010) draws a line between online and physical arenas by stating that users need specific tactical methods to deal with these different spaces. So by using traditional settings in religious online performances, such as creating a virtual church that mirrors elements of standard offline churches, the user is provided with a feeling of familiarity that gives them security and allows them through the mediated symbolism to "participate in their perceived 'authenticity'" (Hutchings 2010: 82). Research on wedding rituals in Second Life has also shown that a kind of familiarity in religious performances seems to be necessary:

> The presented examples made clear that virtual wedding ceremonies are in general very traditional in their style and procedures. Besides the fact that a

ritual has to be recognized as a ritual by the participants, as Gladigow stresses, for instance, the question arises whether rituals in Virtual Worlds in which change and instability are the norm and common in daily life rituals should pursue a certain continuity.

(Radde-Antweiler 2010: 350f.)

Taylor (1996) speaks of this distinction in terms of two bodies which become noticeable in online activities: a "corporeal" and a "digital" body, which are created and used online to help create the user's identity (p. 439). Radde-Antweiler (2008) also points to this idea when she speaks of the users' status and desire to be "free of real-life body conditions" as well as the possibility of performing religious actions "with his 'embodied body'" (p. 174).

But the role of the online body and how it can be understood is also a methodological research question. Grieve discusses the need to carefully consider methods in studying online bodies, especially within the context of Virtual Worlds and how virtual ethnography can be done (Grieve 2010). James Clifford raises reservations also voiced by classical anthropology when he asks, "What if someone studied the culture of computer hackers ... and in the process never 'interfaced' in the flesh?" (1997: 61). The problem of verifiability and reliability in research is also discussed by Taylor, who critically asks whether issues raised by virtual research are general methodological problems – offline as well as online – for example the verification of a subjective experience of an interviewee or the problematic assumption of the "true, authentic other to get past persona" (Taylor 1996: 443). In general, with the increase in Internet use and emergence of virtual environments, the role of the online body became seen as more important. In research the question remains how the relationship between the offline and the online body can be defined, and whether online bodily experiences can be judged to be as authentic as offline experiences. It is important to note that, based on the examples of virtual rape and virtual rituals, many Internet users attribute a high degree of authenticity to their online experiences.

The concept of an authentic sacred place online

The question of authenticity has been further complicated by the fact that with the implementation and rising popularity of virtual 3D environments entire religious rituals and acts, such as weddings and worship services, can be performed online. This leads to discussions of the authenticity of these activities and spaces, generating questions like "Can one 'just sit' online?" (Grieve 2010: 37) Or, is virtual space "an authentic ritual space?" (Heidbrink, Miczek, and Radde-Antweiler 2011: 182). Such concerns indicate that the concept of body, as discussed above, as well as the concept of space itself, are judged differently by different people. The evaluation of the authenticity of the online space is often based on definitions of what constitutes the "virtual" and "real" for different people in these contexts. Wertheim, in her book *The Pearly Gates of*

Cyberspace, argues that cyberspace was constructed as an alternative space, a "heavenly realm," and therefore as something completely different from reality, namely physical space (1999: 41). Many people, such as those discussed in relation to the example of online rape, share the assumption that the virtual space is not a "real" space. Therefore virtual worlds like online communities or games are seen as spaces that do not meet the criteria and conditions to be seen as constituting tangible reality.

In this perspective, virtual worlds are seen as mere simulations, as stressed by Baudrillard (1994) in his theory of simulation. According to him, it has become impossible to distinguish between the original and a copy, reality and fiction, model and image, due to the fact that the images of reality are nowadays portrayed primarily through mass media, and have become more important and powerful than the reality itself. Thus the world presented by the media is a simulated, illusory world, what Baudrillard defines as the "simulacrum," which captures the real world in the form of a hyper-reality. The meaning of "simulacrum" can thereby be pejorative, in the sense of deceptive appearances, but it can also be interpreted positively, as part of a concept of productive imagination. In this sense virtual worlds and those spaces in which online religion and religious actions take place, as well as the online body itself, can be seen as mere simulations.

With the emergence of the blogosphere and virtual worlds the question arises as to whether such places or spaces can be judged as authentic. Authenticity is here seen as something real, in contrast to "virtual," which does not have the same influence on the online user or actor. This concept presupposes a clear distinction between offline and online worlds:

> We found that the chief reason for the reluctance of others to see cyberspace as a valid site of ethnographic research is because the virtual is assumed to be fake, and thus one is considered to not really be there.
>
> (Grieve 2010: 39)

Most debates and concerns are connected with the discussion of the relationship between "online" and "offline," which is often identified in terms of the "virtual" versus the "real." In the 1990s, research into the Internet moved from considering online activities as primarily communication exchanges, to seeing them more in terms of building virtual communities (Rheingold 1993; Turkle 1995; Reid 1995). This analysis put more attention on the motivations of and benefits to users who participated in such online communities. In 1999, Ågren pointed out that the building of social capital depends on trust. His approach was based on the theory of social capital originated by the sociologist James Coleman, which said that social capital in its four different forms (information potential, norms, authority relation and obligations/expectations) meant that trust was only truly available online in relationships among people (Coleman 1988). In the context of virtual communities this trust has to be developed under particular circumstances. As Ågren suggests, users face problematic circumstances which make building trust in cyberspace unique, in that the user is confronted with unknown people, whom he has never met in the physical world and who may not be human at all, but rather mere software or simulations.

Nevertheless, the dichotomy between these two different realms – the virtual world versus the physical, the "real" world – is an important one. Stone emphasized in her definition of virtual community that the Internet is a space where "physically separated" people could meet (1991: 85). In her research on the influences of modern technology on gender identity she argued that the gain of social capital online has no significant effects on the offline identity (Stone 1995). O'Leary also pointed in the same direction when he stressed that religious performances, like rituals, are only artificial constructions "with no material stakes or consequences" (O'Leary 1996: 804). Similarly, according to Turkle virtual worlds serve as mere playgrounds, due to the fact that they are more simulations of real life than real life itself, and are based on a "distinctly real-life bias" (1995: 324).

However, other researchers have criticized this binary division between fantasy and reality. Prominent examples include Gunn and Brummett, who are against the "perceived opposition between authenticity and commercialization or globalization" (2004: 707). In analogous discussions in cultural studies they stressed the constructivist mode of such categories. Handler argued that clear concepts like authenticity present a "cultural construct of the western world" mostly for the purposes of political or romanticizing legitimation (Handler 1986: 2). Other early researchers, such as Deleuze, saw cyberspace as an integral part of reality (Deleuze 1988) and replaced the binary "virtual" and "real" with "virtual" versus "actual." He pointed out that virtuality can be considered as complete and real, and "must be defined as strictly a part of the real object" (Deleuze 2004: 260).

Theoretical advancements were made by Jakobsson regarding the real–virtual relationship when he distinguished between virtual actions and the virtual space in which they take place. Based on Goffman's theory of the presentation of self in everyday life, he argued directly against Turkle's concept of virtuality as a mere simulation. For Jakobsson, social actions within virtual environments have real effects on the offline body and mind. Religious performances and experiences online generate effects that are not limited to the online arena. However, if these effects can be considered real, the space does not automatically have the same status. Things in cyberspace – for example, a beer – consist of different elements or characteristics from their physical counterpart; only the "symbolic significance is left intact" (Jakobsson 1999, 2001). Nevertheless, in his later works Jakobsson dismisses the dichotomy "real life" and "virtual life" as being "poorly suited for denoting the difference between the physical world and the virtual world" (Jakobsson 2006: 64). Other researchers have also demanded a dismissal of this understanding. Researchers on virtual worlds like Second Life or World of Warcraft make clear that qualifications such as "virtual," "real" or "authentic" depend totally on users' understanding: "What happens in virtual worlds often is just as real, just as meaningful to participants" (Taylor 2006: 1). For many users their offline and online lives are seen as contexts that are merged and interwoven (Consalvo and Ess 2011), and they are not seen as contradictory (Baym 2010). As Boellstorff stresses:

> What makes these virtual worlds real is that relationships, romance, economic transactions, and community take place with them – in short, that they are places of human culture. It is this social reality that links virtual and actual.
> (2008: 245)

Interestingly, most of the classical approaches that still stress the distinction between "virtual" and "real" seem to be based on Benjamin's thesis that everything is mediatized – or in other words, entangled inseparably with the medium, lacking the quality of the original – and thus loses its authenticity:

> The authenticity of a thing is the essence of all that is transmissible from its beginning, ranging from its substantive duration to its testimony to the history which it has experienced.
> (Benjamin 1968: 223)

Through the reproduction process within the medium, the object becomes separated from the original tradition, a process defined as "the liquidation of tradition." However, if we take this seriously we have to ask, critically, what kind of objects, as well as actions, are not mediatized? Another crucial argument against the sharp distinction between "virtual" and "real" is the assumption that there is no longer any non-mediatized area. In recent years, research discussion has focused on the question of mediatization by interrogating how mediation is actually carried out.

It can be argued that our present everyday experience is media saturated. This increasing "mediation of everything" is interrelated with our understanding of religion, as our experience of religion in Europe and North America is something that is deeply mediatized, not only by so-called "digital media," but also by traditional "mass media." In contrast to mediation processes, the concept mediatization tries to focus on is the "transformations of society and everyday life that are shaped by the modern media" (Lundby 2009: 4). According to Krotz (2001), "mediatization" is a concept used to describe a meta-process in which modern institutions and whole societies are shaped. Meyer and Moors point in the same direction when they stress that religious processes are always mediated:

> Religion, we argue, cannot be analyzed outside the forms and practices of mediation that define it … the point is to explore how the transition from one mode of mediation to another, implying the adoption of new mass media technologies, reconfigures a particular practice of religious mediation.
> (2006: 7)

In contrast to Hjarvard's theory of media logic (Hjarvard 2008a), Krotz's concept of mediatization is not restricted to recent phenomena and does not signify only something that is modern or postmodern. He identifies five processes in which mediatization takes place: the change of media environments, the rise of different media genres, changing functions of classical media, in contrast to growing new functions of digital media, and "changing communication forms and relations between the people on the micro level, a changing organization of social life and changing nets of sense and meaning making on the macro level" (Krotz 2008: 24). Given the possibility of the media acting as a distributor and producer of information about religious issues, it could itself become a religious or cultural environment (Hjarvard 2008b). In contrast, Lundby's approach focuses on the perspective of religious actors and reflects religion "through the forms and processes of *mediation* in practices that are considered 'religious' by people" (Lundby 2011).

The question arises how a dichotomy between the online and offline bodies can hold up, if presently everything is highly mediatized? This is especially evident with the invention of new technologies, such as augmented reality or mobile Internet technologies. For example, gaming via Kinect on the Xbox 360 allows the user to move within the game only by making body movements, instead of using conventional controllers. In this case the online and offline body are completely intertwined; one mirrors the other so they cannot be seen as separate.

Another problematic issue concerning authenticity online can be seen in the aspect of truthfulness or credibility. Due to the fact that anyone has the ability to access and publish almost anything they choose on the Internet, users must learn to deal with a huge amount of data. Users must identify or create their own specific criteria in order to develop selection processes, and differentiate between useful and false information. In the classical publication process, a strict hierarchy of experts dominates the flow of communication and monitors what information is published. If, for example, someone wants to learn about a certain religious tradition they can read a book that – in most cases – is written by an expert in the area, since most publishing houses have strict criteria for publishing. If the same person uses an Internet search engine they will find a wide variety of articles from many different sources and kinds of people – experts as well as laymen. Compared to classical publications, the online user may not find it as easy to identify whether the article is written by an expert or a laymen, or whether it was meant to be taken seriously at all. The use of nicknames and anonymity exacerbate this, meaning that the reader cannot easily find out who the author is, nor what their background is.

With the emergence of the so-called Web 2.0, the situation has become even more problematic. In the time of ARPANET, the majority of religious communication and information was provided via e-mail and bulletin board systems, for example on Usenet (Ciolek 2004). Therefore single contributions to particular discussions, for example in forums, could easily be connected to specific authors. The use of hyperlinks and online networking, however, means that more than one person may now be involved in the production of content. Decentralized knowledge production becomes common, as the consumer becomes at the same time a producer. An example of such processes is apparent in the blogosphere, where texts are often produced and shared by many users, and are at the same time connected to other texts via hyperlinks:

> New media is emancipatory ... in that it frees both text from the producer and people from the audience. Emancipatory media is decentralized, where each receiver is a potential transmitter, where the masses are mobilized, where production is collective and control is fueled by self-organization.
> (Teusner 2010: 116)

But not only have the characteristics of religious information changed, blogs serve as a platform for identity building as well. For example, bloggers who blog about their religious experiences and discuss them with other bloggers often do so in order to construct a distinctive religious profile, so as to be seen as an emerging church blogger (Teusner 2010). Lövheim (2004) also stressed in her studies on online interactions between young people that social trust serves as a necessary element in people's interaction and identity construction, especially on the Internet. The user builds up this trust in their social relationships both online and offline. Many people assume that trust building can become problematic online, due to the fact that communication on the Internet lacks face-to-face contact, where the user could use visual cues, physical appearance and gestures to support their evaluation of the person they are speaking to.

To sum up, regarding the Internet as a space as it relates to the concept of authenticity involves certain difficulties. As we have seen with the relationship between online and offline bodies, the dichotomy of "virtual" versus "real" plays an important role in judging online space as authentic or as mere simulation. Current researchers have frequently criticized this binary division. Another problematic issue concerning authenticity and the Internet relates to discussions of credibility. Online users are confronted with a huge amount of data that they must classify and evaluate. This is complicated by the fact that such assessments must be made without face-to-face contact, meaning that the Internet requires different criteria for judging whether other users are trustworthy.

Conclusion

When considering discussions of religion online, it seems that authenticity serves as a figure of speech, especially when it comes to researching religion on the Internet. Previously, religion or religions were approached, for example in the study of theology, from a scholarly perspective, and seen as a system of definable, consistent and uniform symbols. Considering the single actor perspective, it becomes clear that there is in fact a large variance in the religious ideas current in religious discourse. Also, what constitutes a religious experience can no longer be regarded as a static entity; nor can what is considered a "real" religion be seen as a fixed system. In fact, debates over questions of what makes religious practice or experience authentic are no longer reserved for higher theological discourse, they are also part of common public discourse, and increasingly arise in contemporary mass media. It is obvious that, in contrast to traditional settings, in a mediatized world the authority for defining what is real or "authentic" is no longer only in the hands of religious experts. For example, religious experiences and performances can happen in a virtual environment independent of religious institutions. Therefore the answer to the question "What is real?" depends on the actors' perspectives, and mostly on their criteria for "reality" and "virtuality." It also depends on whether their concepts of the real and the virtual are dichotomous, interdependent or analogous. It is no surprise that most of the critical voices on the question of authenticity come from offline communities, especially authorities in religious institutions. Dawson mentioned the worry of losing authority when he spoke of "a crisis of authority" connected with "a crisis of authenticity" (2000: 43f.). As has been argued in this chapter, and as Pace (2004) stressed, authenticity and trustworthiness present a special challenge for religion online, due to the fact that the relationship between online and offline settings, as well as online and offline bodies, are still seen as open questions:

> As in real-world religions, believers must trust or "have faith in" their leaders; the development of trust in virtual space may not occur as easily as it does in the real world, especially if there is no connection to real-world information.
> (Robinson-Neal 2008: 232)

Therefore future research on authenticity must concentrate on the strategies and legitimating processes employed by religious users and must analyze how authority and credibility is constructed in a mediatized world. Nevertheless, one has to ask if authenticity as an analytical category is still helpful. Like the dichotomy "virtual" versus "real," the concept of authenticity can be seen as coming from an "emic" perspective. The distinction between "etic" and "emic," originated by the linguist Kenneth Pike, is used to differentiate between statements made from an inside perspective ("etic") and from an outside perspective ("emic"; Pike 1967). Research in the field of religious studies makes clear that it is critical to use terms from an emic perspective as analytical categories, since they always imply judgment, as is perfectly demonstrated in the case of authenticity. De Witte suggests further research could focus on the "work of construction itself and the dilemmas and struggles involved in it" (de Witte 2004: 136). Interesting questions are then raised: Why do some religious actors judge certain performances or traditions as authentic, and why do others not? How do they legitimatize these judgments? Are there differences between individual religious actors and the official institutions regarding argumentation and what is classified as authentic or as fake? And which forms of argumentation are convincing, and for whom?

Recommended reading

Campbell, H. (2003) "Congregation of the Disembodied," in M. Wolf (ed.), *Virtual Morality*, 179–99, London: Peter Lang.

This chapter deals with the interplay between technology, religion and the communication of religious meaning. The study makes clear that, despite the fact that the Internet raises issues of disembodiment, online communities are able to realize authentic religious identity and meaning.

Heidbrink, S., Miczek, N. and Radde-Antweiler, K. (2011) "Contested Rituals in Virtual Worlds," in R. Grimes, U. Hüsken, U. Simon and E. Venbrux (eds), *Ritual, Media and Conflict*, 165–88, Oxford: Oxford University Press.

This chapter discusses the negotiation of online rituals in virtual worlds, such as Second Life and other MMOGs (massively multiplayer online games). It becomes obvious that the different framing of these different environments by users can create conflicts. The interpretations of such environments – ranging from games to online communities – are based on the different notions of "virtuality" and "reality" and the relationship between them.

Grieve, G. (2010) "Virtually Embodying the Field: Silent Online Buddhist Meditation, Immersion, and the Cardean Ethnographic Method," *Online – Heidelberg Journal of Religions on the Internet*, 4(1): 35–62. Online. Available: http://archiv.ub.uni-heidelberg.de/volltextserver/volltexte/2010/11296/pdf/03.pdf (accessed 20 June 2011).

This article theorizes and discusses the relationship between the virtual and actual as part of an ethnographic research method.

Jakobsson, M. (2006) "Virtual Worlds and Social Interaction Design," PhD thesis, Umeå: Umeå University. Online. Available: http://umu.diva-portal.org/smash/record.jsf?pid=diva2:144420 (accessed 25 July 2011).

This dissertation presents a study of social interaction in virtual worlds and their design. Jakobsson's investigation of the qualities of social interaction in virtual worlds results in the thesis that virtual worlds can be seen as being as authentic or real as the physical world. People interacting within these worlds are seen to evoke real and true emotions. One cannot, therefore, identify fixed boundaries between the virtual and physical arenas.

Taylor, T.L. (1996) "Life in Virtual Worlds: Plural Existence, Multimodalities, and Other Online Research Challenges," *American Behavioral Scientist*, 43(3): 435–49.

This article presents methodological considerations for research in virtual environments. The topics of authenticity and creditability are critically discussed as necessary categories in offline and online interviews.

References

Ågren, P.O. (1999) "Virtual Community Life: A Disappearance to Third Places for Social Capital," in K. Braa and E. Monteiro (eds), *Proceedings of IRIS 20 "Social Informatics"*, 683–69, Oslo: University of Oslo.

Baudrillard, J. (1994) *Simulacra and Simulation*, Michigan: University of Michigan Press.

Baym, N. (2010) *Personal Connections in the Digital Age*, Cambridge: John Wiley & Sons.

Benjamin, W. (1968) "The Work of Art in the Age of Mechanical Reproduction," in W. Benjamin, trans. H. Zohn, *Illuminations*, 217–51, New York: Schocken.

Boellstorff, T. (2008) *Coming of Age in Second Life: An Anthropologist Explores the Virtually Human*, Princeton, NJ: Princeton University Press.

Bruckmann, A. and Resnick, M. (1995) "The MediaMOO Project: Constructionism and Professional Community," *Convergence*, 1(1). Online. Available: http://www.cc.gatech.edu/~asb/convergence.html (accessed 21 October 2004).

Cambridge Dictionary (n.d.) "Authenticity." Online. Available: dictionary.cambridge.org/dictionary/british/authenticity?q=authenticity (accessed 1 November 2004).
Campbell, H. (2004) "The Internet as Social-Spiritual Space," in J. MacKay (ed.), *Netting Citizens: Exploring Citizenship in the Internet Age*, 208–31, Edinburgh: St Andrew's Press.
Ciolek, T.M. (2004) "Online Religion: The Internet and Religion," in H. Bidgoli (ed.), *The Internet Encyclopaedia*, 2, 798–811, New York: John Wiley & Sons.
Clifford, J. (1997) *Routes: Travel and Translation in the Late Twentieth Century*. Cambridge: Harvard University Press.
Coleman, J.S. (1988) "Social Capital in Creation of Human Capital," *American Journal of Sociology*, 94: 95–120.
Consalvo, M. and Ess, C. (2011) *The Handbook of Internet Studies*, Chichester: John Wiley & Sons.
Dawson, L.L. (2000) "Researching Religion in Cyberspace: Issues and Strategies," in J.K. Hadden and D.E. Cowan (eds), *Religion on the Internet: Research Prospects and Promises*, 25–54, New York: Elsevier Science.
——(2005) "The Mediation of Religious Experience in Cyberspace," in M.T. Højsgaard and M. Warburg (eds), *Religion and Cyberspace*, 15–37, New York: Routledge.
Deleuze G. (1988) *Bergsonism*, New York: Zone Books.
——trans. P. Patton (2004) *Difference and Repetition*, London: Continuum.
Doorn, N. van (2011) "Digital Spaces, Material Traces: How Matter Comes to Matter in Online Performances of Gender, Sexuality and Embodiment," *Media, Culture & Society*, 33: 531–47.
Gibson, W. (1984) *Neuromancer*, New York: Ace.
Grieve, G. (2010) "Virtually Embodying the Field: Silent Online Buddhist Meditation, Immersion, and the Cardean Ethnographic Method," *Online – Heidelberg Journal of Religions on the Internet*, 4(1): 35–62. Online. Available: http://archiv.ub.uni-heidelberg.de/volltextserver/volltexte/2010/11296/pdf/03.pdf (accessed 20 June 2011).
Gunn, J. and Brummett, B. (2004) "Popular Communication After Globalization," *Journal of Communication*, 54: 705–21.
Handler, R. (1986) "Authenticity," *Anthropology Today*, 2(1): 2–4.
Hayles, K. (1999) *How We Became Posthuman: Virtual Bodies in Cybernetics, Literature, and Informatics*, Chicago: University of Chicago Press.
Heidbrink, S., Miczek, N. and Radde-Antweiler, K. (2011) "Contested Rituals in Virtual Worlds," in R. Grimes, U. Hüsken, U. Simon and E. Venbrux (eds), *Ritual, Media, and Conflict*, 165–88, Oxford: Oxford University Press.
Hill-Smith, C. (2009) "Cyberpilgrimage: A Study of Authenticity, Presence and Meaning in Online Pilgrimage Experiences," *Journal of Religion and Popular Culture*, 21(2). Online. Available: http://www.usask.ca/relst/jrpc/art21%282%29-Cyberpilgrimage.html (accessed 20 June 2011).
Hjarvard, S. (2008a) "The Mediatization of Society: A Theory of the Media as Agents of Social and Cultural Change," *Nordicom Review*, 29(2): 105–34.
——(2008b) "The Mediatization of Religion: A Theory of the Media as Agents of Religious Change," *Northern Lights*, 6(1): 9–26.
Hobsbawm, E. (1983) "Introduction: Inventing Tradition," in E. Hobsbawm and T. Ranger (eds), *The Invention of Tradition*, 1–14, Cambridge: Cambridge University Press.
Højsgaard, M. and Warburg, M. (2005) "Introduction: Waves of Research," in M. Højsgaard and M. Warburg (eds), *Religion and Cyberspace*, 1–11, London: Routledge.
Hornby, A.S. (1989) *Oxford Advanced Learner's Dictionary*, Oxford: Oxford University Press.
Hughes-Freeland, F. (2006) "Media," in J. Kreinath, J. Snoek, and M. Stausberg (eds), *Theorizing Rituals: Issues, Topics, Approaches, Concepts*, 595–614, Leiden: Brill.

Hutchings, T. (2010) "The Politics of Familiarity: Visual, Liturgical and Organisational Conformity in the Online Church," in S. Heidbrink and N. Miczek (eds), *Online – Heidelberg Journal of Religions on the Internet*, 4(1): 63–86. Online. Available: www.ub.uni-heidelberg.de/archiv/11298 (accessed 21 July 2011).

Jakobsson, M. (1999) "Why Bill was Killed: Understanding Social Interaction in Virtual Worlds," in A. Nijholt, O. Donk and B. van Dijk (eds), *Interactions in Virtual Worlds: Proceedings of the Fifteenth Twente Workshop on Language Technology*, Enschede: Twente University.

——(2001) "Rest in Peace, Bill the Bot: Death and Life in Virtual Worlds," in R. Schroeder (ed.), *The Social Life of Avatars*, 63–76, Springer, London.

——(2006) "Virtual Worlds and Social Interaction Design," PhD thesis, Umeå: Umeå University. Online. Available: http://umu.diva-portal.org/smash/record.jsf?pid=diva2:144420 (accessed 25 July 2011)

Jenkins, H. (2006) *Fans, Bloggers, and Gamers: Exploring Participatory Culture*, New York: New York University Press.

Kalisch, E. (2000) "Aspekte einer Begriffs-und Problemgeschichte von Authentizität und Darstellung," in E. Fischer-Lichte and I. Pflug (eds), *Inszenierung von Authentizität*, 31–44, Tübingen: A. Francke-Verlag.

Kirwan, G. (2009) *Presence and the Victims of Crime in Virtual Worlds*. Online. Available: www.temple.edu/ispr/prev_conferences/proceedings/2009/Kirwan.pdf (accessed 1 November 2011).

Krotz, F. (2001) *Die Mediatisierung des kommunikativen Handelns. Der Wandel von Alltag und sozialen Beziehungen, Kultur und Gesellschaft durch die Medien*, Opladen: Westdeutscher Verlag.

——(2008) "Media Connectivity: Concepts, Conditions, and Consequences," in A. Hepp, F. Krotz, S. Moores and C. Winter (eds), *Connectivity, Networks and Flows: Conceptualizing Contemporary Communications*, 13–31, Cresskill, NJ: Hampton Press.

Lövheim, M. (2004) "Young People, Religious Identity, and the Internet," in L.L. Dawson and D.E. Cowan (eds), *Religion Online: Finding Faith on the Internet*, 59–73, New York: Routledge.

Lundby, K. (2009) *Mediatization: Concept, Changes, Consequences*, New York: Peter Lang.

——(2011) "Patterns of Belonging in Online/Offline Interfaces of Religion," *Information, Communication and Society*, 14(8): 1219–35.

Meyer, B. and Moors, A. (2006) *Religion, Media, and the Public Sphere*, Bloomington: Indiana University Press.

O'Leary, S.D. (1996) "Cyberspace as Sacred Space: Communicating Religion on Computer Networks," *Journal of the American Academy of Religion*, 64(4): 781–808.

Pace, S. (2004) "Miracles or Love? How Religious Leaders Communicate Trustworthiness through the Web," *Journal of Religion and Popular Culture*, 7. Online. Available: www.usask.ca/relst/jrpc/art7-miraclesorlove.html (accessed 23 June 2011).

Pike, K.L. (1967) *Language in Relation to a Unified Theory of the Structure of Human Behavior*, 2nd (ed.), The Hague: Mouton.

Radde-Antweiler, K. (2008) "Virtual Religion: A Religious and Ritual Topography of Second Life," *Online – Heidelberg Journal of Religions on the Internet*, 3: 174–211. Online. Available: www.ub.uni-heidelberg.de/archiv/8294 (accessed 5 June 2012).

——(2010) "'Wedding Design' Online: Transfer and Transformation of Ritual Elements in the Context of Wedding Rituals," in C. Brosius and U. Hüsken (eds), *Ritual Matters: Dynamic Dimensions in Practice*, 328–53, New Delhi: Routledge.

Reid, E. (1995) "Virtual Worlds: Culture and Imagination," in S. Jones (ed.), *Cybersociety*, 164–83, Thousand Oaks, CA: Sage.

Rheingold, H. (1993) *The Virtual Community*, New York: HarperPerennial.
Robinson-Neal, A. (2008) "Enhancing the Spiritual Relationship: The Impact of Virtual Worship on the Real World Church Experience," *Online – Heidelberg Journal of Religions on the Internet*, 3(1): 228–45. Online. Available: www.ub.uni-heidelberg.de/archiv/8294 (accessed 5 June 2012).
Stone, A.R. (1991) "Will the Real Body Please Stand Up? Boundary Stories About Virtual Cultures," in M. Benedikt (ed.), *Cyberspace: First Steps*, 81–118, Cambridge, MA: MIT Press.
——(1995) *The War of Desire and Technology at the Close of the Mechanical Age*, Cambridge, MA: MIT Press.
Taylor, T.L. (1996) "Life in Virtual Worlds: Plural Existence, Multimodalities, and Other Online Research Challenges," *American Behavioral Scientist*, 43(3): 435–49.
——(2006) *Play Between Worlds: Exploring Online Game Culture*, Cambridge, MA: MIT Press.
Teusner, P.E. (2010) "Imaging Religious Identity: Intertextual Play among Postmodern Christian Bloggers," *Online – Heidelberg Journal of Religions on the Internet*, 4(1): 111–30. Online. Available: www.ub.uni-heidelberg.de/archiv/11300 (accessed 21 July 2011).
Turkle, S. (1995) *Life on the Screen: Identity in the Age of the Internet*, New York: Simon & Schuster.
Wellman, B. (2004) "Connecting Community: On- and Off-line," *Contexts*, 3(4): 22–28.
Wertheim, M. (1999) *The Pearly Gates of Cyberspace*, London: Virago.
Witte, M. de (2004) "Afrikania's Dilemma: Reframing African Authenticity in a Christian Public Sphere," *Etnofoor*, 17(1/2): 133–55.

7 Religion

Gregory Price Grieve

Often when you log onto a video game you are assigned a quest, challenge, or puzzle that you must solve. Religious studies has been given a similar quest, because, as Lorne Dawson and Douglas Cowan write, "[t]he Internet is changing the face of religion worldwide" (2004: 1). Yet, while digital media have become one of the most important ways in which people practice their faith, because of religious studies' preoccupation with scripture and the printed word, the discipline has left communication studies and sociology to do the heavy interpretive lifting (Grieve 2006: 12–16). Fortunately, these fields have made much headway into the subject of digital religion, which, as Heidi Campbell writes, was just a few years ago "an underdeveloped area of inquiry" (2005: 309). Still, while communications and sociology have made progress, they have been hampered because they have not clearly articulated of what digital religion consists (Jansen *et al.* 2010). In other words, scholars of digital religion still need to investigate exactly what counts as digital religion, and why people practice it.

For example, is the Vatican's website (www.vatican.va) religion? Is the official Scientology website (www.scientology.org) religious? Is the Pastafarian "Church of the Flying Spaghetti Monster" website (www.venganza.org) religious? Is the National Association for Stock Car Auto Racing website (www.nascar.com) religious? My point is neither to argue that some of these examples are religious and others are not, nor is it to provide a definition by example, i.e., that the Christian Jesus is more religious than the Scientologist Xenu, the alleged ruler of a 75 million-year-old Galactic confederacy. Instead, this chapter aims to employ such concrete examples as a means to investigate what constitutes "digital religion" as a subject of academic inquiry.

To investigate an academic understanding of how religion should be understood when it goes online, or in other words "digital religion," this chapter engages in two key concepts, those of religion and the digital. First, the category of religion is interrogated. This becomes complex, as "religion" as a concept is only a few hundred years old, contains no essential or absolute quality and holds many different interpretations. Thus we focus on an understanding of religion forged in the Enlightenment, also known as the Age of Reason, beginning in early 1700s in Europe, in which religion is understood in terms of non-scientific metanarratives, or overarching stories that answer such comprehensive questions as: Where do I come from? Why am I here? And, what happens after I die? From this perspective we highlight three essential features of religion: (1) myth or non-scientific stories that are told about the world, (2) rituals or actions that are seen to have a mythic significance, and (3) faith, which describes those beliefs which are not immediately susceptible to rigorous proof.

Second, we extend the definition of religion into digital media, where it can be understood through three features: as aspects of the new media themselves, as a particular technological ideology, and as a workaround for the conditions of a liquid modern life. Digital media differ from analog media because they are electronic and can thus be handled by computers as a series of numeric data, which creates a new type of medium that is interactive, hypertextually linked, and dispersed. A "technological ideology" is a coherent system of practices and beliefs that reflects the way in which a technology is linked to economics, politics, and culture. Digital media is tied to an ideology that, for better or worse, understands this technology as a revolutionary force that will bulldoze existing social institutions, communities, and practices. Lastly, it is argued that digital religion operates as a workaround, or an innovative temporary solution, to our experience of religiosity in contemporary life. Digital religion emerges within what Zygmunt Bauman (2005) calls "liquid modernity," a period of global capitalism where life is constantly changing, highly mediated, hurried, and uncertain. As a workaround, digital religion is a means of overcoming the problems of a "liquid modern life," but because it is an impromptu and temporary response, it also implies that a permanent solution is not ready at hand.

Looking at these categories together, religion and the digital, allows us to understand the concept of "digital religion" or how religion is lived out and experienced online. This leads to discussion of how scholars have imagined and discussed digital religion through the lens of new media's technological ideology over the last 15 years and through three dominant waves of scholarly investigation.

Investigating the category of religion

Often "religion" is assumed to be as old as humanity, and the category is seen to be applicable universally as being present in every human culture that has ever existed anywhere on Earth. In such a case, there would be no problem in placing the Vatican's website in the same category as Paleolithic cave images as expressions of religiosity. Yet "religion" is not inevitable, nor did it develop – from cave paintings to digital media – in a uniform and orderly linear fashion. In fact, religion's current meaning is only a few hundred years old, and can be traced back to the European Enlightenment. Also known as the Age of Reason, and centered in eighteenth-century Europe, the Enlightenment was an intellectual, scientific, and cultural movement that advocated reason as the primary source of legitimacy and authority and stressed freedom and rational thought over dogma, tradition, and blind faith.

Maintaining that the category of religion was born in the Enlightenment is not to argue that people did not believe or worship gods or God before that time, or that the word "religion" cannot be found before 1700. It is rather to argue that it was not until the Enlightenment that the many different ways that people interacted with deities were subsumed under one category, and that this category – "religion" – was seen as the opposite of Enlightenment thought. The non-Enlightenment beliefs and practices by which people interacted with deities are examples of "metanarratives," those grand stories that give a comprehensive explanation of existence (Lyotard 1979). Metanarratives are stories that people tell about themselves and their place in history to make their world significant and meaningful. They are the grand stories that are told in order to legitimize various versions of "the truth." For instance, the webpage "God's Plan of Happiness" on The Church of Jesus Christ of Latter-Day Saints' site (www.mormon.org) answers a series of questions, including: "Where did I come from?" "Why am I here?" "What is God's Plan for us?" and "What happens when I die?" In summary, "religion" as a term has come to signify non-scientific stories that explain the world, and also that describe people's place in it.

Religion's family resemblances to myth, ritual, and faith

Metanarratives are stories that tell fundamental truths. The modern understanding of the term "religion" was born in the Enlightenment to categorize metanarratives that the Enlightenment defined as different from its own because they were not based on scientific laws. Scientific laws are universal and invariable facts about the physical universe, such as Archimedes's principle that any floating object displaces its own weight of fluid. By defining religion as what is not based on scientific laws, Enlightenment thought is able to categorize together a vast number of differing metanarratives that have nothing to do with each other except that they are perceived as unscientific. For instance, Paleolithic cave paintings, the Vatican's website, and Hubbard's book *Scientology: A New Slant on Life* (2007), can all be seen as religious. However, because these non-scientific metanarratives cannot be reduced to one common feature (such as belief in God, prayer, or scripture), it is often difficult to articulate why a particular phenomenon is religious. Instead of one essential feature, the category of religion is defined by a series of overlapping similarities. This list of family resemblances would seem endless, except that some qualities are more prototypical, or central, than others. Just as a group of family members are recognized because they display certain central traits (say red hair, hazel eyes, and freckles) (Rosch 1975), the category of religion is recognized through the family resemblance of myth, ritual, and faith.

Myth is a key characteristic of religion and marks its first family resemblance. In the popular imagination "myth" often denotes widely shared beliefs that are simply false, and is also used to gloss those apparently fictional metanarrative stories that non-Enlightenment groups tell about themselves and their world. While these ideas of myth as representative of other people's stories and as falsehood stem from dramatically different historical contexts (ancient Greece and European colonialism), they both fit comfortably into the Enlightenment's use of the word "religion" to denote non-scientific metanarratives. Both uses of the term "myth" are readily apparent in digital media. For instance, there are many sites such as "scientology myths 2.0," which asks "what is fact and what is myth?" (www.scientologymyths.info). Yet, because the word "myth" has the sense of being false, few, if any, groups define their own sacred narratives as coming under this category. There are many places, however, where "myth" is used to denote other people's metanarratives, such as the Native American myths listed on the Living Myths website (www.livingmyths.com).

The second family resemblance is ritual, which defines those practices that deliberately work to contrast themselves with the ordinary by creating a mythic significance. If you could imagine a Martian coming down and watching a scientist working in her lab, and a Catholic priest working in his cathedral, how these performances differ would not at first be readily apparent. Both humans would be executing a sequence of special disciplined actions performed for specific occasions, in a specially demarcated location. From an Enlightenment perspective, an experiment is an action that is regulated by the scientific method, which gathers observable, measurable evidence that can be subjected to logical reasoning. Rather than instrumental, from the perspective of the Enlightenment ritual is seen as mythic, in that its actions have a "metapragmatic" significance beyond themselves. As Catherine Bell writes in her classic work, *Ritual Theory, Ritual Practice*, ritual "always suggests the ultimate coherence of a cosmos in which one takes a particular place ... that places one securely in a field of action and in alignment with the ultimate goals of all action" (Bell 1992: 141).

Religion's third family resemblance is faith. From an Enlightenment perspective, scientific evidence refers to observable facts based on empirical and measurable methodologies that are employed to counter or support a hypothesis. Religious faith, on the other hand, is assumed to refer to what a person "believes," and is not immediately susceptible to rigorous proof. In fact, to interpret a religion people often want to know the tradition's beliefs, as represented by such things as Hindu online practice and cave paintings. It might be surprising, then, to learn that before the seventeenth century religion did not center on "belief." In Roman and Early Christian usage, "religion" referred primarily to "cult," the careful performance of ceremonial obligations. The importance of practice can still be seen in many non-Protestant traditions, such as Judaism and Hinduism, which tend to be concerned with orthopraxis, "right-doing," rather than orthodoxy, "right-thinking." In Northern Europe, in a transition begun by Reformation figures such as Huldrych Zwingli (1484–1531) and John Calvin (1509–64), the ritual was cleansed from the category of "religion," and the term came to refer primarily to pious faith. For instance, Samuel Johnson, in the *Dictionary of the English Language* (1755), defines religion as "Virtue, as founded upon reverence of God" (quoted in Smith 1998: 271). From this overview we synthesize that religion can be understood as based on the Enlightenment concept that categorizes religion in terms of metanarratives that possess features or attributes of myth, ritual, and faith.

Investigating "digital" religion

As stated above, religion defines stories and practices that are used by individuals and groups to mark out the meaning they attach to their world and life practice, and can be identified through a set of common features. These characteristics also provide a basis for discussing what constitutes digital religion. In order to understand digital religion, however, we must consider how new media shapes religious practice, so we can investigate how the digital differs from how religion engages in or is expressed through other types of media. In other words, we need to be able to articulate how and why phenomena such as the Scientology website differs from the printed book *Scientology: A New Slant on Life* (Hubbard 2007). Digital religion is marked by three features: a specific form of media, a particular technological ideology, and as possessing a "work-around" or strategy for managing the conditions of what can be understood as living a "liquid" form of modern life.

First, one could argue that what makes digital religion different from other forms of religion is the fact that it is wrapped in a particular form of media. Digital, or new, media are composed of such things as digital audio, digital video, and computer games, as well as online media such as websites, e-mail, social sites, and multiplayer games. Digital media, as opposed to analog media such as newspapers, film, and vinyl discs, can be glossed as those electronic media that are handled by computers as a series of numeric data. Digital religion differs in three main aspects from "analog religion": interactivity, hypertextuality, and its method of dispersal. "Interactivity" defines the technical ability of users to intervene, respond, and see the effects of their intervention in real time. For instance, at the Rudra Centre's website one can conduct online *puja*, or Hindu ceremonial worship. Here one can use a cursor to go through the steps of conducting worship, such as *arti*, in which light from wicks soaked in ghee (purified butter) is offered to the images of deities (www.rudraksha-ratna.com/shivapuja.htm). Hypertextual navigation allows users to make reading choices by engaging with "links" that transfer them directly to another location in a digital text document, or to another webpage. For example, one can navigate through the "Hypertext Bible" using "hot links" that not only link the user to different locations in the text, but also to different versions and translations of the Bible (www.public-domain-content.com/books/bible). Lastly, "dispersal" describes how digital media are both decentralized and also spread throughout the fabric of everyday life. For instance, if one needs to be reminded about the correct time for *adhan* (Islamic prayer) and in which direction to face there is a downloadable iPhone application for that, iPray 1.1 (www.iphoneislam.com). These three traits differ from analog media, and hence analog religion, which is typically static in its production and engagement, as well as linear in its format, which demands sequential engagement. Thus digital religion offers higher degrees of flexibility of engagement.

Second, digital religion cannot be located by merely tying it to a particular medium. Instead, it must also be identified as part of a "technological ideology" that reflects the ways in which technology is linked to economics, politics, and culture. A technological ideology represents the beliefs and logic system which support a given technology. For instance, the dominant American ideology sees digital media as a positive and revolutionary technological development through which all the world's problems can be creatively and innovatively solved. As Esther Dyson argues in "Cyberspace and the American Dream: A Magna Carta for the Knowledge Age," digital media will lead to the "creation of a new civilization, founded in the eternal truths of the American Idea" (1994). Digital religion is tied to a similar technological ideology of new media, in that it is seen as more than a new way of communicating, but as a new vision for society: its practices are often posed as revolutionary, and tied to the triumph of human creativity and freedom over dogma and blind tradition. As Brenda Brasher writes in *Give Me That Online Religion*, "[m]uch as the printing press sparked a radical transformation of society and culture in the sixteenth century, the computer and CMC [computer-mediated communication] are electronically bulldozing the symbolic terrain of religions around the world" (2001: 27–8).

Lastly, but tied to the first two features, digital religious practices often operate as "workarounds" for or ways to cope with the conditions of living in a world full of ambiguity and change, representing a "liquid modern life." Life in our global networked world is constantly changing, highly mediated, hurried, and uncertain. The sociologist Zygmunt Bauman characterizes this predicament as "liquid modernity," an era stemming from the late global capital market economic system that began in the early 1970s, and has linked it to the rise of new digital media (2005). Bauman argues that in liquid modernity we have moved from a solid, hardware-focused modernity toward a light and liquid software-focused one, which has brought profound changes to the human condition. Because of its under-defined, fluid state, in a liquid modern life one must run just to stay in place. Social forms do not have time to solidify, so individuals have to plan and hastily organize their lives by splicing together an unending series of short-term projects that do not add up to concepts like "career" and "progress."

Often digital practices stem from and are the product of the stresses produced by liquid modernity, which has dissolved traditional religious communities and institutions so that individuals have to actively explore and create novel, elastic, temporary, and flexible forms. In a liquid modern life one must be constantly ready to change tactics and abandon commitments without regret, so as to pursue all opportunities when they arise. Yet, such digital religious practices are rarely if ever permanent solutions. Instead they are understood better as "workarounds," a term taken from computer programming that indicates a temporary creative solution to a problem. Workarounds typically imply that a genuine solution to the problem is still needed, and tend to be brittle, breaking under further pressure or due to unforeseen change. For example, meditation groups that practice virtually in the online world of Second Life can be seen as workarounds for a liquid modern life (Grieve and Heston 2011). On one hand virtual worlds create a new opportunity for religious practice. By clicking their mouse, practitioners can opt out of the day's stress through meditation, and also have the ability to meditate together in real time online. Yet, the anxieties which necessitate the meditation, and also the fact that there are few traditional face-to-face opportunities or locations to meditate, are produced by a liquid modern life, and stem from the conditions of late capitalism in which traditional religious communities, institutions, and practices have dissolved under pressure from a market-driven economy.

The characteristics of digital technology in many ways imprint and inform the character of digital religion. Yet digital religion cannot be characterized as simply traditional religion packaged in a new media form. Instead, digital religion is unique because it addresses the anxieties produced in a liquid modern world by using new media's technological aspects to weave together religious metanarratives and the ideology surrounding the digital.

Studies of digital religion

During the last fifteen years there have already been three waves of scholarship addressing digital religion. The goal here is not a comprehensive literary review which describes all the work (see Cho 2011). Instead, key articles and books are highlighted to map out the "technological ideology" which has informed the three periods and how the different aspects of the media have been discussed, as well as to understand how these relate to religion as it is practiced within a state of liquid modernity.

Beginning in the mid-1990s the initial wave of scholarship on digital religion was caught in an ideology of awe. When digital media first caught the imagination of both scholars and journalists, the first charismatic wave looked on in horror or stood in reverence of digital religion's transformative possibilities. These earlier studies centered on the question of whether the Internet is a liberating utopia that will lead toward a "global village" and humanity's salvation or a dark dystopia that isolates individuals from society and will ultimately lead to the desert of the real. Occurring at the start of the "dot.com bubble," these often exploratory studies were generated by the launch of the Internet and based on text-dominated media such as chat rooms, listserves, bulletin boards, and text-based MUDs (multi-user dungeons). These first studies tended to be highly speculative, drawing heavily on researchers' own experience, and were triggered by the surprise of finding religion on the Internet. In a sense, the first wave of scholarship was caught up in the revolutionary qualities seen in digital media (Grieve 1995). The major goal of the first wave was "to establish," as Stephen O'Leary writes, "the credibility of the thesis that our conceptions of spirituality and of community are undergoing profound and permanent transformation in the era of computer-mediated-communication" (O'Leary 1996: 782).

The sources from the first wave can be divided into popular literature and key academic articles. The three most influential book-length popular works include: Brenda Brasher's *Give Me That Online Religion*, which sees the Internet as a source of a new transcendence equal in importance to that of the printing press during the Reformation (Brasher 2001); Margaret Wertheim's *The Pearly Gates of Cyberspace*, which argues that the Internet is a repository for spiritual yearning (Wertheim 1999); and Jeff Zaleski's *The Soul of Cyberspace*, which explores online ritual and asks what role the net plays in humanity's spiritual renaissance (Zaleski 1995). The pivotal academic article is Stephen O'Leary's seminal piece, "Cyberspace as Sacred Space: Communicating Religion on Computer Networks," which argues for a "transformation of religious beliefs and practices" (O'Leary 1996: 783). While O'Leary paints a utopian picture of the Internet as a transformative and liberating space, Jay Kinney's "Net Worth? Religion, Cyberspace and the Future" sees digital media as dystopic and maintains that it will atrophy users' inner spiritual life (Kinney 1995).

Brought on by the commercialization of the World Wide Web, by 2002 digital media had become a routine part of American life. The second wave of scholarship reflects this routinization of digital ideology among the general public, the stage that comes after innovative beginnings and is often a reaction against the disorderly freedom of individual creativity. By the turn of the century, hundreds of millions of people were using digital media everyday, and 25 percent of American users had searched the web for explicitly religious purposes. By 2002, it was clear that online religion was here to stay. Rather than treating digital media with awe or horror the field turned to systematic analysis of the construction of online identity and community. The second wave differed from the first, moreover, because there was a sense that, while cyberspace was really not that unusual, its consequences for religion were not yet known. As such, the driving question was no longer whether there can be religious communities and identities online, but what types of communities and identities exist in this new social space. Following in the wake of the cultural turn of research on religion and media more generally (Hoover and Clark 2002), the second wave of scholarship included longitudinal studies (Campbell 2005), the nature and quality of people's experience (Dawson 2005), on- and offline connections (Højsgaard 2005), and practice (Young 2004), as well as how technology was actually being utilized (Barker 2005).

Again, reacting to the first wave, the studies of the routinizing phase called into question the supposed dichotomy posed between online and offline practice. For example, Gary Bunt questioned whether new religious practice really provides new, hypertextual articulations or whether it simply mirrors offline religion (Bunt 2004). That is, does the web merely convey information about religion, providing supplements to actual-world practice, or does it make available experiential immersion that can be considered unique? Christopher Helland refines this position by making a distinction between "online religion" (websites in which users can act with unrestricted freedom and a high level of interactivity) and "religion online" (which provides only religious information and is not interactive) (Helland 2000; see Maxwell 2002; Karaflogka 2002). A final focus asks if there is a "strange kind of fit" between specific religions, religious practice, and digital media (Maxwell 2002). For instance, Douglas E. Cowan distinguishes between "open sources," which encourage innovation, and "closed sources," which are not open to modifications (Cowan 2005).

Between 2000 and 2005, a number of edited volumes and monographs were published on the study of religion and digital media. On the cusp of the second wave is Jeffrey Hadden and Douglas Cowan's *Religion on the Internet: Research Prospects and Promises* (Hadden and Cowan 2000). Hadden and Cowan's work is the first systematic study, yet many of its research questions and perspectives map earlier conceptions of digital media. A second early work is Elena Larsen's *CyberFaith: How Americans Pursue Religion Online*. This report by the Pew Internet & American Life Project established an empirical baseline for many of the studies that followed. A summary of this report (Larsen 2004) was published in the second wave's first entirely academic work, Lorne Dawson and Douglas Cowan's *Religion Online: Finding Faith on the Internet* (Dawson and Cowan 2004). Dawson and Cowan's volume brings together emerging voices in the field, as well as republishing "classics" such as O'Leary's early work on "Cyberspace as Sacred Space" and Charles Prebish's work on cybersanghas. The final volume is Morten Højsgaard and Margit Warburg's *Religion and Cyberspace*, which emerged from the 2001 international conference on "Religion and Computer-Mediated Communication"(Højsgaard and Warburg 2005). Approaching the key questions of the second wave, *Religion and Cyberspace* explores religious authority, religion and the construction of online identity and community, and the connections between on- and offline environments.

Also, between 2003 and 2005, four important monographs that reflect the routinization of the digital were published. First, Gary Bunt's *Islam in the Digital Age: E-Jihad, Online Fatwas and Cyber Islamic Environments* documents the use of the Internet in the Arab world, specifically the emergence of *e-jihad*, and the influence and authority of online *fatwas* (Bunt 2003). Second, Heidi Campbell's *Exploring Religious Community Online: We Are One in the Network* results from her seven years of research on how Christians have adopted digital media (Campbell 2005). Besides documenting these Christian groups, she offers a theory of how digital media generate narrative-formed identities and communities. A third work is Douglas Cowan's *Cyberhenge: Modern Pagans on the Internet*, which counters the vigorous promotion of his earlier work and provides a deeply pessimistic view of the possibilities of the Internet for online practice (Cowan 2005). The final monograph in this phase which I wish to mention is Paolo Apolito's *The Internet and the Madonna: Religious Visionary Experience on the Web*, which analyzes visions of the Virgin Mary on the Internet (2005). Apolito focuses on how many users perceive the web as a place of transcendence and mystery, but ends by echoing what many of the second-wave scholars found – that new media are really not that new and often simply imitate the actual world.

Mirroring the Internet itself, a new phase of the ideology of the digital has begun. In 2005, Højsgaard and Warburg wrote, "the third wave of research on religion and cyberspace may be just around the corner" (Højsgaard and Warburg 2005: 9). In predicting the third wave in 2005, O'Leary argued that the future of the Internet would be "catholic," by which he meant that not just text, but iconography, image, music, and sound, if not taste and smell as well, would be part of the online experience (O'Leary 2005). The third wave differs from earlier studies because of the appearance of Web 2.0, which includes interactive applications such as YouTube, Facebook, and Second Life.

In the third wave of research on digital religion, scholars have continued to explore questions of identity and community, but also more closely examine issues of authority, co-production, and convergence. Initiating the start of a new, more theoretical turn, is Campbell and Lövheim's edited journal special issue on "Religion and the Internet: Considering the Online-Offline Connection" (2011), and an edited volume by Cheong, Fischer-Nielsen, Gelfgren, and Ess, titled *Digital Religion, Social Media and Culture: Perspectives, Practices and Futures* (2012). The first published monograph is Bunt's *iMuslims: Rewiring the House of Islam*, which analyzes social networking sites to show how they have become influences outside the traditional spheres of Islamic authority. Bunt also explores how the Internet has influenced forms of Islamic activism and radicalization, including *jihad*-oriented campaigns by networks such as al-Qaeda (Bunt 2009). Campbell's *When Religion Meets New Media* focuses on how different religious communities are engaging with digital religion. Rather than simply embracing or rejecting new communication technologies, different groups negotiate a complex set of differing strategies depending on their religious-social histories (Campbell 2010). Current work such as this seeks to consider how factors in online and offline religion become integrated, so that digital religion becomes a way to explore how religion is being transformed and expressed in multiple contexts in digital culture.

Conclusion: the reward for investigating digital practice

This chapter has investigated what constitutes "digital religion." It has demonstrated that digital religion is not simply a repackaging of traditional religious beliefs in a new media wrapping. Instead, digital religion is unique because it uses the technological aspects of new media to weave together non-scientific metanarratives with the technological ideology surrounding the digital as a way to address the anxieties produced in a liquid modern world. The chapter has demonstrated that there is not one essential quality that defines digital religion's metanarratives. Instead, "religion" can be recognized through the family of resemblances of myth, ritual, and faith. "Myth" refers to non-scientific metanarratives; "rituals" are actions that are seen to have a mythic significance; and "faith" describes those beliefs that are not immediately susceptible to rigorous proof.

The chapter has also described the last 15 years of scholarship on digital religion. It has traced how in the mid-1990s digital religion was caught up in a charismatic ideology of awe in which both scholars and journalists looked on in horror or stood in reverence at digital religion's transformative possibilities. A second wave of scholarship began in the early 2000s and reflected the routinization of digital media that followed the Internet's commercialization. By the late 2000s scholarship began to express features of a third wave of theoretical reflection, especially in relation to studies of interactive and social media applications such as YouTube, Facebook, and Second Life. This work continues to be expanded to consider religious engagement in multiple new media spheres, because, as O'Leary has stated, when looking for the future of digital media and religion "it may be more useful to examine the world of computer games than religious websites" (O'Leary 2005: 43).

After one finishes a quest, one is usually given a reward. The repayment for investigating digital religion is not a litmus test to definitively answer the question of what is religious and what is not. Rather, what the chapter has delivered is both a map on which to locate current and past digital religious practices, and a glimpse of what digital religion may look like in the near future.

The first reward is that, by investigating the category of religion, scholars are able to see through new media's technological ideology, and thus better describe, explain, and analyze how people have practiced and are currently practicing digital religion. For instance, looking at the digital through a theory of myth as other people's metanarratives problematizes a "transmission view" of media, and allows one to articulate how individuals not only communicate, but dwell together in the shared communal space on the Internet, specifically in discussion forums, e-mail listserves, and virtual worlds. A theory of rituals as practices that have a significance beyond themselves demonstrates how, as the Internet has become more and more ingrained in everyday life, scholars find a more intimate and less dichotomous connection between on- and offline. Finally, an understanding of faith as those metanarratives excluded from the Enlightenment problematizes the technological ideology of "newness" that surrounds new media – for while there are obvious differences in digital practice, online religion is not a dichotomous break with earlier offline beliefs, behaviors, and institutions. Rather than simply embracing or rejecting new communication technologies, users engage with digital religion in a variety of ways, the specific combination of possible methods varying according to their religious-social history.

The second reward is that investigating new media enables scholars to understand how not only digital religion but religion in general may evolve in the near future into a "smart mobile interactive cloud." As always there is danger in making predictions; the changes mentioned here describe more of an evolution from current forms and do not take into account unexpected innovation. Still, we can wager that there will be four major features of digital practice in the new future. First, the Web will be smarter, knowing not just what users say, but what they mean. We will see more semantic content, and the applications that support it. One could imagine applications that predigest digital content for different religious groups, such as Hasidic sects, screening followers from information that counters their beliefs. Second, new media will be mobile and we will see an increase in augmented reality (AR) in which digital media are laid over physical, real-world environments. For instance, there could be an application that gives pilgrims to the Buddhist holy site of Bodhgaya a ritual map provided by a mobile device lay-over of the actual location. Third, the web will continue to grow more interactive. In the near future, websites such as www.vatican.va will be infinitely more interactive, incorporating wikis, video, audio, and in many cases their own social networks. Lastly, more and more applications will be outsourced to the cloud, with users accessing information stored on the web remotely from netbooks, tablet computers, smart phones, or other devices. One can imagine electronic rosaries that count and upload the number of times a user prays to a social networked site.

What combination of these features of new media will win out we cannot tell. It is safe to predict, however, that digital media in whatever form it takes will play an increasingly significant role in the future of religious practice. Because of its flexibility and relatively low expense, digital religion will continue to be key to allowing people to actively explore and create novel, temporary, and flexible forms of practice. Moreover, if we have not already reached the tipping point, the Web will soon be at the center of information and content distribution, having absorbed newspapers, printed books, movies, and even television. Because the discipline of religious studies often assumes that "religion" can be reduced to printed scripture, new and popular religious practices that are based in these new media tend to be marginalized. By understanding the future of the digital, however, we can glimpse the near future of religious practice more generally, especially as it is a response to and product of a liquid modern life.

Recommended reading

Campbell, H. (2010) *When Religion Meets New Media*, New York: Routledge.

A bellwether text in the emerging third wave of research on digital religion. Campbell focuses on how different religious communities are engaging with new media. She demonstrates that, rather than simply embracing or rejecting new communication technologies, different groups negotiate a complex set of differing strategies depending on their religious-social histories.

Eliade, M. (1969) *The Quest: History and Meaning in Religion*, Chicago: University of Chicago Press.

Written late in his career, the preface to this book clearly and concisely summarizes Eliade's thought (pp. i–v). What is most useful is the first chapter, "A New Humanism," in which he describes the intellectual task of religious studies (pp. 1–11). For Eliade's notion of the sacred see *The Sacred and the Profane: The Nature of Religion* (1957); for his method of comparison see *Patterns in Comparative Religion* (1949); for his concept of history see *Cosmos and History: The Myth of the Eternal Return* (1954).

Helland, C. (2000) "Online Religion/Religion Online and Virtual Communities," in J. Hadden and D. Cowan (eds) *Religion on the Internet: Research Prospects and Promises*, 205–23, London: JAI Press/Elsevier Science.

The key article of the routinizing second wave of research on digital religion, Helland (2000) makes a distinction between "online religion" (websites in which users can act with unrestricted freedom and a high level of interactivity) and "religion online" (which provides only religious information and not interaction). While later coming under much scrutiny, Helland's article is still a foundational text on which many other scholars have built their own projects.

O'Leary, S. (1996) "Cyberspace as Sacred Space: Communicating Religion on Computer Networks," *Journal of the American Academy of Religion* 64(4): 781–808.

The first widely read academic article written about digital media from the angle of religious studies, fifteen years after it was written, it has stood the test of time. O'Leary seeks to prove the credibility of religion online, and indicate how it is changing how we see religion. He draws on Walter Ong, a theorist of media and religion, to argue that online religion will bring about a transformation of religious beliefs and practices.

Smith, J. Z. (1982) *Imagining Religion: From Babylon to Jonestown*, Chicago: University of Chicago Press.

In Smith's seminal work, he argues that religion is solely the creation of the scholar's imagination and posits three conditions for its use: (1) a mastery of both primary and secondary materials; (2) an example that is used to display an important theory or fundamental question; and (3) a method for explicitly relating the theory to the example.

References

Apolito, P. (2005) *The Internet and the Madonna: Religious Visionary Experience on the Web*, Chicago: The University of Chicago Press.
Barker, E. (2005) "Crossing the Boundary: New Challenges to Religious Authority and Control as a Consequence of Access to the Internet," in M. Højsgaard and M. Warburg (eds) *Religion and Cyberspace*, 67–85, London: Routledge.
Bauman, Z. (2005) *Liquid Modernity*, New York: Polity.
Bell, C. (1992) *Ritual Theory, Ritual Practice*, New York: Oxford University Press.
Brasher, B. (2001) *Give Me That Online Religion*, San Francisco: Jossey-Bass.
Bunt, G. (2003) *Islam in the Digital Age: E-Jihad, Online Fatwas and Cyber Islamic Environments*, London: Pluto Press.
——(2004) "'Rip, Burn, Pray': Islamic Expression Online," in L. Dawson and D. Cowan (eds) *Religion Online: Finding Faith on the Internet*, 112–22, New York: Routledge.
——(2009) *iMuslims: Rewiring the House of Islam*, London: C. Hurst & Co.
Campbell, H. (2005) *Exploring Religious Community Online: We Are One in the Network*, New York: Peter Lang.
——(2010) *When Religion Meets New Media*, New York: Routledge.
Campbell, H. and Lövheim, M. (eds) (2011) "Special Issue: Religion and the Internet: Considering the Online-Offline Connection," *Information, Communication & Society* 14(8).
Cheong, P., Fischer-Nielsen, P., Gelfgren, S., and Ess, C. (eds) (2012) *Digital Religion, Social Media and Culture: Perspectives, Practices and Futures*, Peter Lang, New York.
Cho, K. (2011) "New Media and Religion: Observations on Research," *Communication Research Trends*. Online. Available: http://findarticles.com/p/articles/mi_7081/is_1_30/ai_n57221190 (accessed January 11, 2011).
Cowan, D. (2005) *Cyberhenge: Modern Pagans on the Internet*, New York: Routledge.
Dawson, L. (2005) "The Mediation of Religious Experience in Cyberspace," in M. Højsgaard and M. Warburg (eds) *Religion and Cyberspace*, 15–37, London: Routledge.

Dawson, L. and Cowan, D. (eds) (2004) *Religion Online: Finding Faith on the Internet*, New York: Routledge.

Dyson, E. (1994) "Cyberspace and the American Dream: A Magna Carta for the Knowledge Age," Online. Available: www.alamut.com/subj/ideologies/manifestos/magnaCarta.html (accessed June 10, 2011).

Grieve, G. (1995) "Imagining a Virtual Religious Community: Neo-Pagans on the Internet," *Chicago Anthropology Exchange* 7(2): 98–132.

——(2006) *Retheorizing Religion in Nepal*, New York: Palgrave-Macmillan.

——(2010) "Virtually Embodying the Field: Silent Online Buddhist Meditation, Immersion, and the Cardean Ethnographic Method," *Online – Heidelberg Journal of Religions on the Internet* 4(1). Online Available: http://archiv.ub.uni-heidelberg.de/volltextserver/frontdoor.php?source_opus=11296 (accessed November 10, 2011).

Grieve, G. and Heston, K. (2011) "Finding Liquid Salvation: Using the Cardean Ethnographic Method to Document Second Life Residents and Religious Cloud Communities," in N. Zagalo, L. Morgado, and A. Boa-Ventura (eds) *Virtual Worlds, Second Life, and Metaverse Platforms: New Communication and Identity Paradigms*, 288–305, Hershey, PA: IGI Global.

Hadden, J. and Cowan, D. (eds) (2000) *Religion on the Internet: Research Prospects and Promises*, London: JAI Press/Elsevier Science.

Helland, C. (2000) "Online Religion/Religion Online and Virtual Communities," in J. Hadden and D. Cowan (eds) *Religion on the Internet: Research Prospects and Promises*, 205–23, London: JAI Press/Elsevier Science.

Højsgaard, M. (2005) "Cyber-Religion: On the Cutting Edge Between the Virtual and the Real," in M. Højsgaard and M. Warburg (eds) *Religion and Cyberspace*, 50–64, London: Routledge.

Højsgaard, M. and Warburg, M. (2005) *Religion and Cyberspace*, London: Routledge.

Hoover, S. and Clark, L. (2002) *Practicing Religion in the Age of Media: Explorations in Media, Religion and Culture*, Thousand Oaks, CA: Sage.

Hubbard, L. R. (2007) *Scientology: A New Slant on Life*, Commerce City, CA: Bridge Publications.

Jansen, B., Tapia, A. and Spink, A. (2010) "Searching for Salvation: An Analysis of US Religious Searching on the World Wide Web," *Religion* 40(1): 39–52.

Karaflogka, A. (2002) "Religious Discourse and Cyberspace," *Religion* 32(4): 279–91.

Kinney, J. (1995) "Net worth? Religion, Cyberspace and the Future," *Futures* 27(7): 763–76.

Larsen, E. (2004) "CyberFaith: How Americans Pursue Religion Online," in L. Dawson and D. Cowan (eds) *Religion Online: Finding Faith on the Internet*, 16–19, New York: Routledge.

Lyotard, J. F. (1979) *The Postmodern Condition: A Report on Knowledge*, Minneapolis: University of Minnesota Press.

Maxwell, P. (2002) "Virtual Religion in Context," *Religion* 32(4): 343–54.

O'Leary, S. (1996) "Cyberspace as Sacred Space: Communicating Religion on Computer Networks," *Journal of the American Academy of Religion* 64(4): 781–808.

——(2005) "Utopian and Dystopian Possibilities of Networked Religion in the New Millennium," in M. Højsgaard and M. Warburg (eds) *Religion and Cyberspace*, London: Routledge, pp. 38–49.

Rosch, E. (1975) "Cognitive Representations of Semantic Categories," *Journal of Experimental Psychology: General*, 104(3): 192–233.

Smith, J. Z. (1998) "Religion, Religions, Religious," in M. C. Taylor (ed.) *Critical Terms for Religious Studies*, 269–84, Chicago: The University of Chicago Press.

Wertheim, M. (1999) *The Pearly Gates of Cyberspace: A History of Space from Dante to the Internet*, New York: W. W. Norton & Co.

Young, G. (2004) "Reading and Praying Online: The Continuity of Religion Online and Online Religion in Internet Christianity," in L. Dawson and D. Cowan (eds) *Religion Online: Finding Faith on the Internet*, 86–97, New York: Routledge.

Zaleski, J. (1995) *The Soul of Cyberspace*, San Francisco: Harper.

Part II
Thematic case studies

8 Hindu worship online and offline

Heinz Scheifinger

At the heart of any consideration of religious ritual practice online is the extent to which a ritual in its online manifestation has undergone an alteration from the corresponding ritual carried out in its traditional context. Such an assessment is necessary in order to approach important sociological questions regarding whether and in what ways the Internet is affecting both religious practices and religious experiences. In addition, it is necessary to investigate issues concerning the validity or efficacy of rituals that are undertaken via the Internet. If a ritual appears to be transformed online but it is still deemed to be acceptable, then it suggests that the ritual itself has not changed significantly and that there are unlikely to be fundamental changes in the religious experience that it gives rise to.

In light of this, I adopt a comparative approach in the following discussion of Hindu worship online – an especially important topic since, as Christopher Helland notes, "many members of the Hindu tradition have embraced the Internet ... as a valuable (and viable) tool for doing their religion" (Helland 2010: 148). In my investigation, I will focus upon the *puja* ritual. *Puja* means worship and it involves making a number of offerings to a deity. These rites are variable but each sequence of procedures constitutes a ritual which is commonly referred to as *a puja*. Therefore, in my discussion, *puja* will refer to Hindu worship in general, while "a *puja*" or "the *puja*" will refer specifically to a ritual that consists of a number of acts. Details regarding such rituals will be introduced shortly.

Prior to this, a brief note regarding the nature of ritual is required. As Stephen Jacobs (2007) points out, defining ritual is extremely problematic, and consequently there is no agreement upon what constitutes ritual activity. However, Ronald Grimes's observation that "All ritual ... is addressed to human participants and uses a technique which attempts to re-structure and integrate the minds and emotions of the actors" (Grimes 1990: 196 in O'Leary 2004: 56) is a useful benchmark that can be used in order to differentiate between ritual and non-ritual activity, albeit with an important caveat in the case of Hinduism. Unlike in other religious traditions, in Hindu worship the presence of others is unimportant (see Gupta 2002: 37) and so there is no attempt to integrate the minds of the various individuals who are participating in the ritual.

There can be little doubt, however, that the performance of a *puja* is an attempt to restructure the mind and emotions of its practitioner and few, if any, would argue that a *puja* is not a ritual. Therefore, in my discussion, and in line with other authorities (e.g. Eck 1985), a traditional *puja* carried out in the offline context will simply be accepted as being a ritual. Furthermore, for the purposes of comparison with an online *puja*, I will assume that a *puja* conducted in a physical environment is successful in bringing about the restructuring of the minds and emotions of devotees and that this restructuring constitutes a religious experience.

Case study: *puja* offline and online

Although it encompasses a diverse array of beliefs and practices, Hinduism has a number of "prototypical" features (Eichinger Ferro-Luzzi 1997: 301) – one of which is *puja*. A *puja* is a ritual performed regularly by millions of Hindus in which an image or *murti* believed to be the embodied form of a god or goddess is worshipped. During a traditional *puja*, which can be undertaken in temples and at shrines (including those within the home), a devotee is able to interact with the deity by way of the *murti*. Simple or elaborate offerings are made (sometimes mediated by *pujaris* or priests), which can include flowers and food. Consequently, depending upon the scale of the ritual, a worshipper's senses are stimulated to different degrees.

In a complex *puja*, the clashing of cymbals, the beating of drums, and the blowing of conch shells can all be heard. Edible *prasad* or consecrated food satisfies the sense of taste, while incense stimulates a devotee's sense of smell. Incense is likely to be used even in a simple form of the ritual, but the key feature that links the most elaborate temple ritual and the most basic one undertaken at a wayside shrine or in the home is that of *darshan*. A prototypical feature of Hinduism in its own right, *darshan* is an integral part of *puja*. It involves a devotee gazing into the eyes of the *murti* and, at the same time, being seen by the deity. As Gwilym Beckerlegge puts it: "an exchange takes place through the eyes, and devotees may feel that they have been granted a vision of the deity or have experienced the divine, favored glance" (Beckerlegge 2001: 62).

The facility to perform a *puja* via the Internet has been available for more than a decade. Various websites, whether associated with or unconnected to Hindu temples, offer an image of a deity, and typically, while devotees gaze at this image (often from the comfort of their own homes), they can use a mouse or other navigation device in order to set in motion animated versions of some of the processes that are carried out in a traditional *puja*. Thus, for example, clicking upon the relevant icon will result in the appearance of flowers, which settle in front of the deity's image. In addition, the website may offer religious music or sacred chanting to accompany the image of the deity on the screen. An individual who conducts the ritual in this way is performing an online *puja*, a term not to be confused with the ordering of a *puja* online, which results in worship being carried out on a devotee's behalf at a physical temple.

An example of an opportunity to conduct an online *puja* can be found on the official website of the Vishwanath temple in Varanasi, an important Indian pilgrimage city roughly halfway between Delhi and Kolkata. Vishwanath is a name used to refer to the god Shiva in Varanasi, and this temple is the preeminent one to Shiva in this city, which is especially associated with the worship of this pan-Indian deity. It is also one of the most important Hindu temples in India. The image made available for online *puja* on the Vishwanath temple's website (see www.shrikashivishwanath.org/en/online/epooja.aspx) is that of the *lingam*, the symbol of Shiva, which is housed in the temple's inner sanctum and which is the focus of conventional offline devotional activity for Vishwanath. Although the *lingam* is a non-anthropomorphic symbol of the deity, which means that it does not feature human-like eyes, it can still facilitate the process of *darshan*. Indeed, according to the Temple Trust, *darshan* of the *lingam* "confers liberation from the bondages of *maya* [illusion] and the inexorable entanglements of the world. A simple glimpse of the [*lingam*] is a soul-cleansing experience that transforms life and puts it on the path of knowledge and *bhakti* [devotion]" (Shri Kashi Vishwanath Mandir n.d.).

A Hindu devotee, or even a curious non-Hindu – unlike in the case of worship directed toward the physical *lingam* situated within the temple, which is usually off limits to non-Hindus – can freely perform an online *puja* to Vishwanath. While gazing upon the image of the *lingam*, an individual can begin the online *puja* by clicking on the first button visible on the screen above this symbol of the god, which sets off the chanting of *Om Namah Shivaya* – a *mantra*, or sacred phrase, in praise of Shiva. Clicking on further buttons gives rise to a number of animated actions such as the pouring of milk over the *lingam* and the sprinkling of leaves associated with the worship of Shiva upon this deity's symbol. In each case, hands appear on the screen which carry out these processes. The appearance on the screen of smoking incense, which sways from side to side in front of the *lingam*, completes the practical processes that constitute the online *puja* to Vishwanath.

Discussion

While during a *puja* to Vishwanath in the physical temple's inner sanctum corresponding acts of worship to those that are simulated online will also occur, there is clearly a vast difference between the online *puja* and one carried out within the temple. For example, the former constitutes a solitary exercise with little sense stimulation, while bustle, noise and smells will accompany the latter. Some of the stark differences between online worship and Hindu worship performed in a traditional setting are mentioned by Brenda Brasher, who at the outset of *Give Me That Online Religion* (2004; first published in 2001) briefly compares *puja* undertaken at a physical temple with that carried out via the Internet. She points to the fact that in the latter case, there is no journey to or waiting time at the physical site, that there is no interaction with fellow devotees, and that online *puja* can be carried out at one's own convenience (Brasher 2004: 4–5). She further highlights that, online, full stimulation of the human sensorium no longer occurs. For example, the odor of flowers and fruits is absent. Because of this, she concludes that undertaking online *puja* is a "profoundly different religious experience" (Brasher 2004: 4) to performing *puja* in the traditional offline context.

In coming to her conclusion, Brasher compares only the outward features of *puja* carried out at a temple with those of online *puja*. She is certainly correct to highlight the fact that the absence in online *puja* of many of the sensual aspects that are a part of traditional *puja* constitutes a major difference. However, she does not consider in detail fundamental aspects of *puja* that may lead to the conclusion that the difference between online worship and that carried out in the traditional manner is not as significant as she makes out. Furthermore, there are issues regarding the Hindu notion of purity that also need to be taken into account in a consideration of online *puja*.

The need for a more sophisticated analysis of online Hindu worship than that provided by Brasher has been alluded to by Joanne Waghorne (2004). In her book *Diaspora of the Gods*, Waghorne investigates issues surrounding the construction of Hindu temples in India and elsewhere by middle-class Hindus. Online *pujas* are not therefore her concern. However, in the final paragraph of the book, Waghorne unexpectedly mentions that she is "left wondering what kind of sacrality will accrue to the temples in cyberspace with their virtual *pujas*" (Waghorne 2004: 241). Recently, this issue has been explored by Nicole Karapanagiotis (2010), while in my own work I have attempted to provide detailed analyses of online Hindu worship that take into account the nature of *puja* and its central element of *darshan* (see Scheifinger 2008, 2010a). In the light of these developments, it is now possible to assess more fully the possible implications of *puja* conducted by way of the Internet.

The sacrality of the environment

Regardless of whether a *puja* is carried out in a temple or directed to a deity housed in a shrine in the home, the environment is necessarily kept clean and marked off as being pure and sacred. Therefore, questions regarding the ways in which the online *puja* environment differs from the essential sacred environment where the conventional form of the ritual is carried out are important. If sacrality cannot be achieved in the new venue, then the efficacy or capacity to produce the desired effect of the ritual in giving rise to a religious experience is threatened. In her study, which takes into account the views of devotees of the Hindu god Vishnu, Karapanagiotis (2010) explains that devotees assert that there is no reason why the deity cannot inhabit cyberspace, but that some are concerned with issues regarding purity. For example, the computer itself which facilitates online *puja* is associated with secular activities such as work, while the webpage which contains the image of the deity may also feature non-religious images such as advertisements.

Karapanagiotis refers only to devotees' reservations concerning non-religious images sharing the screen with an image of Vishnu and inappropriate material stored within the computer, but I suspect that at least some of her informants were actually voicing concerns regarding material considered impure (pornography is mentioned as being especially problematic) which is present in the shared environment of cyberspace (see Karapanagiotis 2010: 183–85). Otherwise, simply accessing a webpage that offers the opportunity to undertake an online *puja* that does not feature non-religious images – as in the case of the online *puja* to Vishwanath described above – would overcome any threats to impurity accruing from Vishnu's presence in cyberspace. However, Karapanagiotis herself states that many devotees "believe that both cyberspace and the computer are problematic places for housing Vishnu" (2010: 180). Regardless, what is clear is that devotees have genuine concerns regarding the sacrality of the new environment in which *Vishnu* is housed. This also poses a danger to the mental purity required of devotees in order to conduct an efficacious *puja*. In contrast, the sacred environment associated with physical shrines and traditional temples specifically encourages such a state of mind.

Although some devotees express reservations regarding the purity of the online *puja* environment, there are a number of ways in which "Vishnu's cyber-altar can be spatially purified and his worship online made more easily generative of mental purity" (Karapanagiotis 2010: 189). Strategies employed by Karapanagiotis's informants in order to purify the cyber-altar include making sure that the computer and the immediate area around it is clean, playing devotional music, closing computer windows extraneous to the *puja*, restarting the computer prior to the commencement of the ritual, keeping the computer away from items associated with work, and placing the computer on an altar (Karapanagiotis 2010: 190–91). In addition, there is the popular idea, present in devotional literature and in oral traditions, that any problems concerning purity associated with the worship of Vishnu can be overcome if the devotee approaches this activity with a pure heart (Karapanagiotis 2010: 192–93).

Since there is a prevalent belief within Hinduism that Hindu gods and goddesses cannot themselves be affected by perceived impurity, and that instead it is the environment in which they dwell that becomes adversely affected if a person considered to be impure approaches the *murti* (Hamilton 1998: 72), any fears that devotees may have regarding the state of purity of the environment of cyberspace in general are also assuaged. In addition, the notion that gods and goddesses cannot be affected by impurity means that the location of an image of a deity in cyberspace can actually have a positive impact, in the view of some Hindus, when it comes to issues surrounding the notion of purity. For example, there is the belief that because they do not enter a shared physical space, those individuals who undertake an online *puja* without first undergoing the necessary purification rites do not have a negative impact on the sacred environment, which can subsequently affect the ability of other devotees to foster a pure attitude conducive to worship (see Scheifinger 2009: 284; 2010b: 336–38).

Core characteristics of **puja**

In addition to the concept of purity not being fatal to the efficacy of an online *puja*, it is important to note that while this form of the ceremony is indeed very different from one carried out in a traditional setting, the central aspect of the ritual remains. Because the replication of deities within Hinduism is unproblematic (see Pocock 1973: 89–92), as is the mediation of sacred images via the screen (see Herman 2010: 158; Scheifinger 2010b: 333), the practice of *darshan* – the key feature of *puja* – can be successfully mediated via the Internet. While the other senses may not be stimulated in the way that they are when conducting a *puja* in the offline setting, the importance of the sense of sight remains in an online *puja*. In both cases, a devotee is able to see and be seen by the deity. Therefore, in this crucial respect, the *puja* is not altered radically in its online form.

Because the processes that are carried out in a traditional *puja* are symbolic, the fact that in the corresponding online ritual physical props are not used means that further fundamental aspects of *puja* are not abandoned online (see Scheifinger 2008: 246). Indeed, in Hinduism, the acceptance of the idea that a *puja* ritual is symbolic is made explicit through the existence of a type of *puja* in which "the physical form [of the deity] is carefully mentally reconstructed, with such rituals as libations and flower offerings being exactly performed in the virtual reality inside the head" (Smith 2003: 144). Any abbreviation associated with the practicing of an online *puja* is also unproblematic. It does not interfere with the ritual's efficacy because "ritual abbreviation and simplification are ubiquitous procedures that are allowed by the [Hindu sacred] texts themselves" (Fuller 1992: 246).

Conclusion

I have shown that threats to the sacrality of the online *puja* environment can be overcome, that the ability to partake in the core practice of *darshan* remains in online worship, and that a *puja* is symbolic, which means that the omission of certain aspects of a *puja* in its online form is unproblematic. This suggests that an online *puja* is a valid and efficacious form of a ritual that is central to Hinduism, which in turn provides an explanation as to why many Hindus are using the Internet in order to conduct worship. It also indicates that performing an online *puja* does not constitute a fundamentally different experience from the carrying out of worship in a traditional setting. Of course, there are noteworthy differences between a *puja* carried out at a temple and one undertaken online, but the important point is that crucial aspects remain. Furthermore, if a comparison is made between an online *puja* and a basic one carried out at a shrine, then the contrast is less marked, while the differences between an online *puja* and a *puja* performed in the mind are minimal. In short, Hindu *puja* rituals that are performed online are not fundamentally different from traditional forms of the ritual and hence possess efficacy.

Discussion questions

- To what extent can computer space be considered sacred space, and acceptable for conducting religious rituals?
- In your opinion, can a deity inhabit or be connected with online? How might this perception impact the devotee's practice of the ritual?
- Do you think the ability to practice religion online has the potential to radically affect various religious traditions? If so, in what ways?

References

Beckerlegge, G. (2001) "Hindu Sacred Images for the Mass Market," in G. Beckerlegge (ed.) *From Sacred Text to Internet*, 57–116, Milton Keynes: The Open University.

Brasher, B. (2004) *Give Me That Online Religion*, New Brunswick, New Jersey: Rutgers University Press.

Eck, D.L. (1985) *Darśan – Seeing the Divine Image in India*, Chambersburg: Anima Books.

Eichinger Ferro-Luzzi, G. (1997) "The Polythetic-Prototype Approach to Hinduism," in G.D. Sontheimer and H. Kulke (eds) *Hinduism Reconsidered*, 294–304, New Delhi: Manohar.

Fuller, C.J. (1992) *The Camphor Flame – Popular Hinduism and Society in India*, Princeton: Princeton University Press.

Grimes, R. (1990) *Ritual Criticism: Case Studies in Its Practice, Essays on Its Theory*, Columbia, South Carolina: University of South Carolina Press.

Gupta, S.S. (2002) *Puri – Lord Jagannatha's Dhaam*, New Delhi: Rupa & Co.

Hamilton, M. (1998) *Sociology and the World's Religions*, Basingstoke: MacMillan Press.

Helland, C. (2010) "(Virtually) Been There, (Virtually) Done That: Examining the Online Religious Practices of the Hindu Tradition – Introduction," *Online – Heidelberg Journal of Religions on the Internet*, 4(1): 148–50.

Herman, P.K. (2010) "Seeing the Divine Through Windows – Online Darshan and Virtual Religious Experience," *Online – Heidelberg Journal of Religions on the Internet*, 4(1): 151–78.

Jacobs, S. (2007) "Virtually Sacred: The Performance of Asynchronous Cyber-Rituals in Online Spaces," *Journal of Computer-Mediated Communication*, 12(3).

Karapanagiotis, N. (2010) "Vaishnava Cyber-*Puja* – Problems of Purity and Novel Ritual Solutions," *Online – Heidelberg Journal of Religions on the Internet*, 4(1): 179–95.

O'Leary, S. (2004) "Cyberspace as Sacred Space: Communicating Religion on Computer Networks," in L.L. Dawson and D.E. Cowan (eds) *Religion Online – Finding Faith on the Internet*, 37–58, New York/London: Routledge.

Pocock, D.F. (1973) *Mind, Body and Wealth – A Study of Belief and Practice in an Indian Village*, Oxford: Basil Blackwell.

Scheifinger, H. (2008) "Hinduism and Cyberspace," *Religion*, 38(3): 233–49.

——(2009) "The Jagannath Temple and Online *Darshan*," *Journal of Contemporary Religion*, 24(3): 277–90.

——(2010a) "Hindu Embodiment and the Internet," *Online – Heidelberg Journal of Religions on the Internet*, 4(1): 196–219.

——(2010b) "*Om*-line Hinduism: World Wide Gods on the Web," *Australian Religion Studies Review*, 23(3): 325–45.

Shri Kashi Vishwanath Mandir (n.d.) "Introduction." Online. Available: www.shrikashivishwanath.org/en/myth/history.aspx (accessed April 8, 2011).

Smith, D. (2003) *Hinduism and Modernity*, Oxford: Blackwell.

Waghorne, J.P. (2004) *Diaspora of the Gods – Modern Hindu Temples in an Urban Middle-Class World*, New York: Oxford University Press.

Website

Shri Kashi Vishwanath, www.shrikashivishwanath.org/en/online/epooja.aspx (accessed April 8, 2011).

9 Virtual Buddhism
Buddhist ritual in Second Life

Louise Connelly

Online ritual raises a number of questions for scholars of religion, such as: How are rituals from specific religious traditions structured online? What are the difficulties and limitations of online rituals? Can online ritual provide the same outcomes as offline ritual, specifically in relation to the obtainment of liberation and enlightenment or nirvana? Studying Buddhist ritual online enables a greater understanding of how technology is being used by religious practitioners to negotiate between the offline and online world. It also illustrates how various Buddhist groups and individuals practice Buddhism today in relation to the Internet.

This case study focuses on Buddhist ritual in Second Life, which is an online virtual world launched in June 2003 and created by Linden Lab, a company based in San Francisco. In Second Life, there are "avatars" (online personas), known as "residents" (hereafter referred to as "participants," in the context of ritual), who can engage with certain Buddhist rituals such as spinning a prayer wheel, chanting, prostration and meditation. Second Life enables individuals to purchase land and create an online world where they interact with others and engage in various activities. It cannot be considered a massively multiplayer online role-playing game (MMORPG), as it does not have an end goal or reward structure. Instead, it functions as a society with residents and an online currency known as the Linden Dollar (L$).

There are many aspects of Buddhist ritual online, but for the purpose of this case study the focus is on the exploration of the silent meditation ritual found at the Buddha Center in Second Life (in-world address 137, 130, 21). A number of other themes, such as authority, community and identity, can also be examined, and so ritual should be considered within the wider context of these dimensions; however, since such themes are explored elsewhere in this book this case study will focus solely on the theme of ritual.

The practice of Buddhist meditation online raises a number of considerations for the examination of both religion online and the position of religion in society (Casey 2006: 73–74). Kim (2005), Ostrowski (2006), Connelly (2010) and Grieve (2010) have contributed significantly to the analysis of Buddhism online and these earlier discussions focus primarily on why users engage with Buddhism online, including the development of an online Buddhist community and identity (Kim 2005; Ostrowski 2006). More recent examinations of Buddhism in Second Life provide an analysis of Zen Buddhism and virtual embodiment (Grieve 2010), as well as the importance of aesthetics in relation to religious practice and how religious practice is negotiated online and offline (Connelly 2010).

The key question that arises is: why would someone engage in virtual ritual? Some have suggested that this may be due to a lack of Buddhist centers or teachers available to the participants offline (Ostrowski 2006: 100), or the need to be part of a community or create and maintain an identity (Grieve 2010). The communal aspect of being involved in the Buddha Center is illustrated by many residents who display the group name above their avatar name, indicating that they have chosen to join this particular online Buddhist group.

It is in Second Life that the interaction with others and participation in online ritual provides meaningful experiences – an opportunity to engage with, learn about and participate in Buddhist rituals – whereas offline, these opportunities may not be available (Ostrowski 2006: 100). Therefore the Buddha Center in Second Life provides an easily accessible environment where anyone can engage with Buddhism.

The online environment presents a number of unique challenges in relation to communication and the provision of a complete sensory experience. The online world is a highly visual and auditory mode of communication, dependent on the use of both voice and text (public chat, private instant messaging, and note cards). This has an impact on the type of Buddhist rituals that can be practiced, since it privileges those that rely on the auditory, such as chanting (voice), and the visual, which includes silent meditation (voice and text). However, since technology does not enable smell, touch or taste, visual representations are often used to imply or invoke these senses, such as the visual representation of the incense in the main temple at the Buddha Center. This example illustrates continuity between offline and online temples as well as the implication of an authentic replicated experience.

This case study examines online Buddhist silent meditation, which can vary within different schools of Buddhism. For example, within Zen Buddhism, it can be referred to as "zazen". At the Buddha Center they use the generic term of "silent meditation," as they believe this will appeal to a wider audience, including yogis and non-Buddhists; whereas at other Buddhist temples in Second Life, where there is only Zen practice – such as at the Kannonji Zen Retreat (in-world address 214, 79, 22) – "zazen" will typically be used. The following discourse provides a description of the environment and the silent meditation ritual, as well as considering the possible outcomes and implications of online meditation.

Case study: meditating online in Second Life

For many Buddhist groups and individuals, ritual is an important component of religious practice and it may incorporate physical artifacts such as incense, a singing bowl, scripture and a Buddha statue. The ritual may be individualistic or communal and in the communal setting will be overseen by a facilitator who may or may not be an ordained Buddhist monk or priest. At the Buddha Center, there is a variety of different Buddhist traditions and facilitators, including "two Theravada monks, a Tibetan Lama, two Chan monks, a Zen monk and three Zen Dharma teachers/Zen priests" (extracted from a discussion with Delani Gabardini, co-founder of the Buddha Center, on March 27, 2011).

The Buddha Center is not affiliated with a specific school of Buddhism, and as one of the co-founders and facilitators, Delani Gabardini, maintains, the Buddha Center focuses on a "universal Buddhism". Furthermore, as co-founder Zino March states, there is "not 'one' Buddhism," and many different schools of Buddhism (Tibetan, Theravada, and Zen) and associated rituals and practices can be found at the Buddha Center.

Between 2009 and 2010, 14 interviews were conducted with the main facilitators and participants in order to determine why they practiced and taught Buddhism within Second Life. The interviews were undertaken in both voice and text and were usually one-to-one, except on two occasions when the interview was conducted within a group setting. The interviews focused on two questions: why did the facilitators and participants practice or engage with Buddhism in Second Life?; and how are virtual artifacts used in relation to Buddhist ritual in Second Life? In addition to the interviews, direct observation and participation in a number of Buddhist rituals, including silent meditation, provided a greater understanding of Buddhist ritual online.

To understand the ethos of the Buddha Center, it is important to provide a brief historical background. The Buddha Center is a non-profit organization founded by Zino March and Delani Gabardini in September 2008. It was originally a small temple; although by 2010 it had significantly expanded. It now hosts a number of buildings and facilities, and in September 2010 had more than 2,500 participants. The Buddha Center is arguably one of the largest Buddhist groups in Second Life, although there are other groups, such as the Zen Buddhist retreat Kannonji (http://kannonjiretreat.com, in-world address 214, 79, 22) and the Pure Land Buddhist Practice Group (in-world address 211, 223, 29).

In order to illustrate how ritual manifests in Second Life, this case study focuses on Buddhist silent meditation practice (often referred to as "zazen"), which is facilitated by Delani, Tashi Aura, and others. Facilitators often work at several temples and present the rituals differently. Although the generic term, "silent meditation" is used at the Buddha Center, for Eihei Dogen (1200–53), a Japanese Soto Zen master, "zazen"– or silent seated meditation – is a communal ritual and a means of realization and enlightenment that is gained in the here and now (Leighton 2007: 177), since it is "a ritual enactment and expression of awakened awareness" (p. 167). For those who engage with the silent meditation ritual at the Buddha Center, it could be said that it is a communal activity and a ritual to obtain awareness and realization, although it is not necessarily defined as zazen.

The following discussion will consider three areas: how virtual artifacts are used, the characteristics and structure of online silent meditation, and how this specific ritual is negotiated in the offline environment.

Buddhist meditation

Before entering the temple, there is the opportunity for the participant to donate to the Buddha Center. This is a feature found in many locations in Second Life because the landowners rent the land from Linden Lab and so must raise funds to maintain it. Significantly, the design of the donation pots resembles that of traditional donation pots found at many offline temples. It could be argued that these can be associated with the practice known as giving, or *dana*. Although this is not the primary focus of this discussion, it is pertinent to note that *dana* is a meritorious action (*karma*) found in many South Asian cultures, and that this artifact therefore directly contributes to the imitation of offline customs, practices and rituals (for a detailed discussion of *dana* see Heim 2004).

On entering the temple, the participant can click on the "prostration" icon and prostrate three times, which denotes devotion to the "three refuges" of the *Dhamma* (truth), the Buddha and the *sangha* (community). This action is carried out by many of the participants and is a feature found in other Buddhist temples throughout Second Life. The virtual ritual of prostration demonstrates a level of respect and authenticity not dissimilar to that shown by participants visiting a temple offline. However, as with real-life practice, prostration is not compulsory and is carried out by those who feel comfortable with it, especially as there are both Buddhists and non-Buddhists who participate in the practices and activities found at the Buddha Center.

Inside the temple, a maximum of 22 participants can sit crossed-legged (in the lotus position) on the meditation cushions that are positioned in a semi-circle around the pool and face the large gold Buddha statue. On either side of the Buddha statue, there are pots containing virtual incense and plants, and a singing bowl is placed beside the facilitator's cushion. Other artifacts, such as a gong and scriptures, are often introduced, depending on the practice. There is also sound within the temple, which includes the noise of the water in the pool and the tinkling of the wind chimes that hang above the entrance, all of which contribute to the ambience.

As there is a noticeable absence of three of the five senses online, the visual and auditory aspects are heavily relied upon for the facilitation of and engagement in religious practice and ritual. Therefore it is significant that the creators of the Buddha Center have given considerable attention to the aesthetics of the artifacts and the temple, in order to compensate for these absent senses. The co-founder and primary creator, Zino March, states that many of the designs are intentionally taken from real life (from a discussion with Zino on August 10, 2010). Consequently the visual artifacts provide an element of authenticity, as "Religious seeing is set within a series of ritual rules that *frame* the experience for the viewer providing boundaries for *what* is seen and *how* objects are seen"

(Plate 2002: 162; italics in original). This is also highlighted by Morgan, who argues that "Seeing is part of the embodied experience of feeling, and therefore is properly understood as a fundamental part of many religious practices" (2009: 133). In this way, virtual artifacts can be seen to contribute to the ritual of online silent meditation. The description below of silent meditation sessions within the main temple at the Buddha Center further illustrates this point.

During July and August 2010, a number of silent meditation sessions facilitated by Delani were observed. The sessions took place at different times of the day and a number of avatars participated, some dressed in monastic robes, others in a variety of ensembles. From discussions with different participants, it became apparent that they were from different countries and affiliated with different schools of Buddhism, or in some cases were not practicing Buddhists but found Buddhism in Second Life to be a convenient and accessible introduction to Buddhism. Others stated that they participated because they liked being part of a community not affiliated with one particular school of Buddhism.

The meditation led by Delani, who is an ordained Zen Buddhist priest offline, is presented in voice as well as text. Delani, like many of the facilitators, commences the session by stating "please use whichever form of meditation you are comfortable with," so that those from different Buddhist affiliations and non-Buddhists can engage with the practice in a manner with which they are comfortable. In one session, she follows this statement by reading a poem titled "beautiful things before meditation." In some sessions, note cards are issued to the participants. The note cards are text-based virtual objects that might contain scriptures, sutras, quotes or Zen koans, and the participant can read them during the meditation session or save them within their inventory. To begin the session, Delani chimes the singing bowl three times to signify the start of the meditation, and there is one chime at the end of the session. Delani explains that it is the responsibility of the facilitator to keep track of time, and so the chime is used not only at the Buddha Center but also in other Buddhist temples in Second Life (as well as in real life); this also provides continuity between the different online temples (from a discussion with Delani on March 27, 2011).

During the session participants will often have the word "away" floating above their heads to signify that the avatar has been inactive for some time, and thus they are likely to be meditating offline; this is confirmed by many of the participants and facilitators. After the single chime, participants will thank Delani and will often say "namaste" or use paralanguage such as hands in prayer – "_/_" – known as *gassho*, to indicate respect and thanks (Kozinets 2010: 23). Thanking the facilitator is common in both real-life and Second-Life ritual and practice. Then the participants will wait for Delani to leave the temple, and some will prostrate again before exiting. On occasion, a few participants may continue to meditate and are left sitting in the lotus position on the meditation cushion.

From discussions with many participants and with the facilitators, it has become apparent that the online meditation practice is not confined to Second Life, since participants are practicing meditation in real life while their avatars virtually meditate in Second Life. Therefore, for some, the meditation online is mediated offline, but the virtual practice enables them to belong and to engage with a community and to be taught or guided by a facilitator, which may not be possible in their offline world (Ostrowski 2006).

Findings: online Buddhist meditation

Buddhist ritual in Second Life provides an opportunity for the offline global community to easily engage with different schools of Buddhism and different types of Buddhist ritual. At the Buddha Center, the co-founders and facilitators provide an environment that replicates the offline Buddhist environment, albeit in a more eclectic form. The artifacts, buildings, and environment provide a level of authenticity and enable Buddhists and non-Buddhists to participate in a variety of non-religious as well as religious practice and ritual. Delani states that she is "seeing more and more intermingling of the traditions (even by the monks) in SL" than she has seen "in real life" (from a discussion on March 27, 2011). Although this is true of this particular Buddhist temple online, this may not represent the situation in other Buddhist temples, and so further examination of Buddhist ritual online is needed in order to fully comprehend the nuances of online Buddhist ritual.

The purpose of online ritual considered

Ritual has a number of purposes in Buddhism, but is perhaps most importantly considered as an aid for greater understanding and to gain awareness and spiritual awakening, resulting ultimately in liberation from the cycle of rebirth (*samsara*). It is possible that this is also true of online Buddhist ritual, as it is also used as a means for gaining awareness. Furthermore, the virtual artifacts are created and used in ritual in a similar manner to that found offline. For example, the singing bowl is used in the silent meditation session or, for some, the artifacts are used to gain merit directly, through, for example, placing a donation (*dana*) in the virtual donation pot or spinning the virtual prayer wheels that are found in many locations at the Buddha Center. Although the senses of touch, smell, or taste are absent online, it is through sight, sound, and "imitation touch" that merit "can be obtained from a virtual object as long as it is done with the same intention" (extracted from a discussion with Zino on 10 August 2010; Connelly 2010: 18). It could be said, therefore, that virtual artifacts have a soteriological purpose, which means they are intrinsic to obtaining liberation from suffering and ultimately gaining enlightenment.

Not only are the artifacts important, but so too is the visual design of the environment in which the Buddhist ritual takes place, as "visual practices help fabricate the worlds in which people live and therefore present a promising way of deepening our understanding of how religion works" (Morgan 2000: 51). The design of virtual objects and the environment replicate the offline world in a way that enables not only a level of authenticity, but also a means through which one can participate in Buddhist ritual. The Buddhist ritual online can be said to be analogous with the ritual offline, as both provide an opportunity to gain merit through action which in return directly contributes to the ultimate goal of Buddhism: liberation from the continual cycle of birth and rebirth (*samsara*) and the obtainment of enlightenment or nirvana.

Conclusion: understanding Buddhist ritual in Second Life

Three areas have been discussed in this case study: first, the structure of meditation ritual online at the Buddha Center; second, the limitations of technology in relation to the senses and online ritual; and third, the possible reasons for practicing online Buddhist ritual. Significantly, it is also evident that online ritual, for some, is not purely contained within Second Life, and so there is a negotiation between online and offline meditation practice, with online meditation initiating and framing simultaneous offline practice (Connelly 2010: 28).

The Buddha Center provides an environment in which participants can be selectively engaged with Buddhist ritual in order to gain a greater understanding of Buddhism. The acceptance and utilization of virtual artifacts which are intrinsic to offline ritual, such as the donation box, incense, and meditation cushions, can be seen as significant to online ritual. For some, the online artifacts, temples, and rituals are being accepted as equally authentic as those found offline. Although the examination of Buddhist ritual online is still in its infancy, existing studies indicate a growing trend of people engaging with Buddhism online. Moreover, the development of new technologies and modes of communication should be considered in relation to the characteristics of ritual and the impact this may have on religion generally – both online and offline (Casey 2006: 73, 84). The potential for developing a new, eclectic style of Buddhism online could have ramifications for Buddhist doctrine and practice both online and offline.

Discussion questions

- What are the similarities and differences between online and offline ritual?
- Can online ritual be considered authentic when it does not constitute a complete sensory experience?
- What limitations exist and what challenges can arise from practicing Buddhist ritual online?

References

Casey, C. (2006) "Virtual Ritual, Real Faith: The Revirtualization of Religious Ritual in Cyberspace," *Heidelberg Journal of Religions on the Internet* 2(1). Available: www.online.uni-hd.de (accessed March 5, 2011).

Connelly, L. (2010) "Virtual Buddhism: An Analysis of Aesthetics in Relation to Religious Practice within Second Life," *Heidelberg Journal of Religions on the Internet* 4(1). Available: www.online.uni-hd.de (accessed February 10, 2011).

Grieve, G. (2010) "Virtually Embodying the Field: Silent Online Meditation, Immersion, and the Cardean Ethnographic Method," *Heidelberg Journal of Religions on the Internet* 4(1). Available: www.online.uni-hd.de (accessed March 5, 2011).

Heim, M. (2004) *Theories of the Gift in South Asia: Hindu, Buddhist, and Jain Reflections on Dana*, New York: Routledge.

Kim, M. (2005) "Online Buddhist Community: An Alternative Religious Organization in the Information Age," in M. Højsgaard and M. Warburg (eds), *Religion and Cyberspace*, 138–48, Oxon: Routledge.

Kozinets, R.V. (2010) *Netnography: Doing Ethnographic Research Online*, London: SAGE.

Leighton, T.D. (2007) "Zazen as an Enactment Ritual," in S. Heine and D.S. Wright (eds) *Zen Ritual: Studies of Zen Buddhist Theory in Practice*, 167–84, New York: Oxford University Press.

Morgan, D. (2000) 'Visual Religion', *Religion* 30: 41–53.

——(2009) "The Look of Sympathy: Religion, Visual Culture, and the Social Life of Feeling," *Material Religion* 5(2): 132–55.

Ostrowski, A. (2006) "Buddha Browsing: American Buddhism and the Internet," *Contemporary Buddhism* 7(1): 91–103.

Plate, S.B. (2002) *Religion, Art, and Visual Culture: A Cross-Cultural Reader*, New York: Palgrave Macmillan.

10 Playing Muslim hero
Construction of identity in video games[1]

Vit Sisler

Video games are popular mainstream media and constitute an important social activity for a substantial part of Muslim youth (Sisler 2008; Tawil-Souri 2007). Unlike other audiovisual media, video games immerse consumers, offering action and engagement, rather than inaction and passive reception. At the same time, they provide youngsters with a convenient source of cultural symbols, myths, and rituals, helping them to form their own identities. The question of identity construction is thus central to video games, since they enable a risk-free and socially acceptable way of engaging in a virtual role play (Murphy 2004).

This case study analyzes three contemporary Muslim games and explores the ways in which the hero's identity, meaning the virtual representation of the player's self, is constructed and communicated to the players. The case study is based on content analysis of these games and on interviews with their producers. The key research question of this study is how identity can be construed on the level of game play – that is, through the interactive transactions between the player and the game, as enabled by the game's rule system. In addressing this, the study compares the different concepts of identity in three Muslim games while simultaneously analyzing how these concepts are (or are not) embedded in the game play. On a more general level, this study aims to lay down a theoretical and methodological framework for analyzing video games from the perspective of cultural studies, and Islamic studies in particular.

Unlike film or other audiovisual media, video games are interactive, which implies that any content analysis has to cover three intertwined levels: audiovisual signifiers, narrative structure, and game play. On all these levels, culturally, socially, or even religiously relevant messages can be communicated to the players.

The interactive element of game-playing is of crucial importance for the gaming experience, yet it poses substantial theoretical and methodological difficulties for analysis. It is not possible to describe using classical audiovisual methods, for example segmentation into sequences and shot-by-shot analysis. Instead, the system of rules shaping the choices players can make during the game has to be studied. In this respect, Bogost (2007) argues that games open a new domain of persuasion. He calls this new form *procedural rhetoric*: the art of persuasion through rule-based representations and interactions rather than spoken words, images or moving pictures.

The following examples will analyze all of the above-mentioned levels: audiovisual, narrative, and game play, and explore how the different concepts of identity are constructed on these levels. We have employed a shot-by-shot analysis (Vanoye and Goliot-Lété 2001) for the review of cinematic sequences and a Petri net (Natkin and Vega 2003) for the analysis of game play. Hence, this case study also explores the procedural rhetoric of the games studied and discusses how identity is presented via their rule systems.

Example 1: *Abu Isa's Quest for Knowledge*

Abu Isa's Quest for Knowledge is an edutainment game published by the UK-based company Abu Isa Games in 2006. According to its mission statement, the company focuses on "developing and providing educational and fun based games enabling Muslims and non-Muslims to learn and grow their knowledge about Islamic Culture, Civilization and Science" (Abu Isa Games 2006). The game puts the player in the role of a student of Islam, whose task is to fight evil wizards and recover ancient manuscripts of Islamic knowledge, including the Quran. The introductory story presents the narrative in a simple textual form:

> Asalaamu Alaikum, Peace be upon you, O student of knowledge. You have chosen to embark upon Abu Isa's Quest for Knowledge. Sadly, 1 ancient manuscript of the Quran and 8 other books of knowledge covering Ahadith and Fiqh have been stolen by a group of evil wizards. Their plan is to hide these books from mankind unless someone meets their challenge and proves himself worthy of possessing the manuscripts through his knowledge. You have been tasked by the scholars to venture forth and recover these manuscripts. You must answer the questions which are posed to you to prove your worth, while eliminating as many wizards as you find in your path. Remember, only your knowledge of the Deen will get you through. Begin in the name of Allah.

The game itself utilizes a 3D boardgame pattern, blending simple game play with testing Islamic knowledge. For the analysis of game play of *Abu Isa's*, we use a Petri net, a modeling language for the description of distributed systems, including games. A Petri net is essentially a graph (Figure 10.1) in which the nodes represent transitions (i.e. events that may occur, signified by bars) and places (i.e. conditions, signified by circles). The directed arcs describe what places are pre- and/or post-conditions for which transitions (signified by arrows). In other words, a Petri net is a graphic representation of the actions players can take in the game and their possible outcomes.

In the game play of *Abu Isa's Quest for Knowledge* (Figure 10.1), the player fights evil wizards (Q1) and searches for hidden books of knowledge (Q2). For every successful move on the board, he/she needs to answer a basic question about the tenets of Islam (c_1–c_6) such as "What is salat?" or "How many items

138 *Vit Sisler*

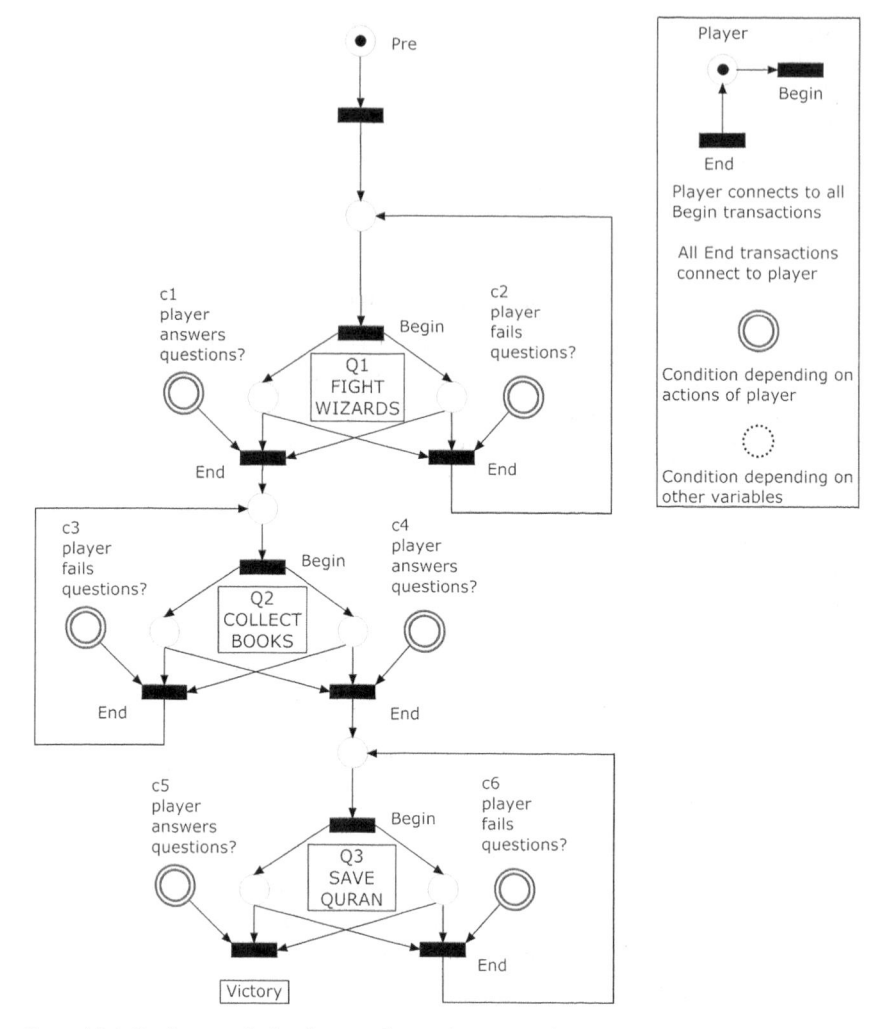

Figure 10.1 Petri net analysis of game play in the game *Abu Isa's Quest for Knowledge*

in the Islamic belief system are called 'pillars' of belief?" When the player collects the required number of books of knowledge, he or she can finally recover the manuscript of the Quran (Q3) and win the game.

Although the Islamic message is central to the game, the game play is not related to it and consists of typical procedural forms of the edutainment genre. The gaming and the educational parts constitute two separate elements. Correspondingly, the hero lacks an elaborated background and gender and is presented simply as a Muslim student on a quest to save the Quran; an adventure into which the player can project him- or herself. Yet nowhere in the game does he or she face a challenge or ethical problem through which the teaching of Islam could guide him or her. The Islamic knowledge in the game is reduced to answering trivia-style questions. Recovering Islamic books is then reduced to objectives and/or bonuses.

Example 2: *Under Siege*

A significantly different approach to identity construction can be found in the game *Under Siege*, published by the Syrian company, Afkar Media, in 2005. Unlike *Abu Isa's Quest for Knowledge*, *Under Siege* introduces real events into the virtual world. Its opening mission, "The Massacre," begins with a mass killing at the Mosque of Abraham in Hebron, where in 1994 a radical Jewish fundamentalist, Baruch Goldstein, shot 29 Muslims during Friday prayers. The background story is presented to the player in an emotional cinematic sequence:

Table 10.1 Transcript of the introductory cinematic sequence for "The Massacre" mission in the game *Under Siege*

Video	Audio
"The city of Hebron. Morning prayer – winter 1994."	
The camera slowly flies through the city of Hebron, toward the Mosque of Abraham, at dawn.	Sounds of city at dawn. Birds singing and dogs barking. A prayer can be heard in the distance.
The mosque fills the screen. The camera slowly moves toward the entrance. We can see Goldstein moving toward the entrance.	Prayer (in Arabic): "In the name of God, Most Gracious, Most Merciful." Footsteps.
Prayer hall of the mosque. People are sitting and listening to the imam.	"O my Lord! I do seek refuge with Thee …"
Detail on Goldstein's grim face. He is loading his machine gun.	Magazine clicks.
The camera moves through the mosque. People are standing with their heads bowed down. Detail on the imam's face.	Imam: "Allahu Akbar!" People (in response): "Allahu Akbar!"
In slow motion, Goldstein enters the mosque firing his machine gun.	Goldstein crying. Machine gun firing.
Goldstein lowers his hand, holding the empty machine gun. Cartridge cases are slowly falling to the ground. Fade out.	Empty cartridge cases clinking on the ground. Dramatic music.

Immediately after the dramatic introduction, the player takes control of Ahmad. As the game play begins (Figure 10.2), he has to survive the first minutes of Goldstein's shooting by hiding between pillars in the mosque (Q1), then carefully move close to Goldstein (Q2) and finally disarm him (Q3) while he is loading his machine gun (c2). If the player is hit by Goldstein's

140 *Vit Sisler*

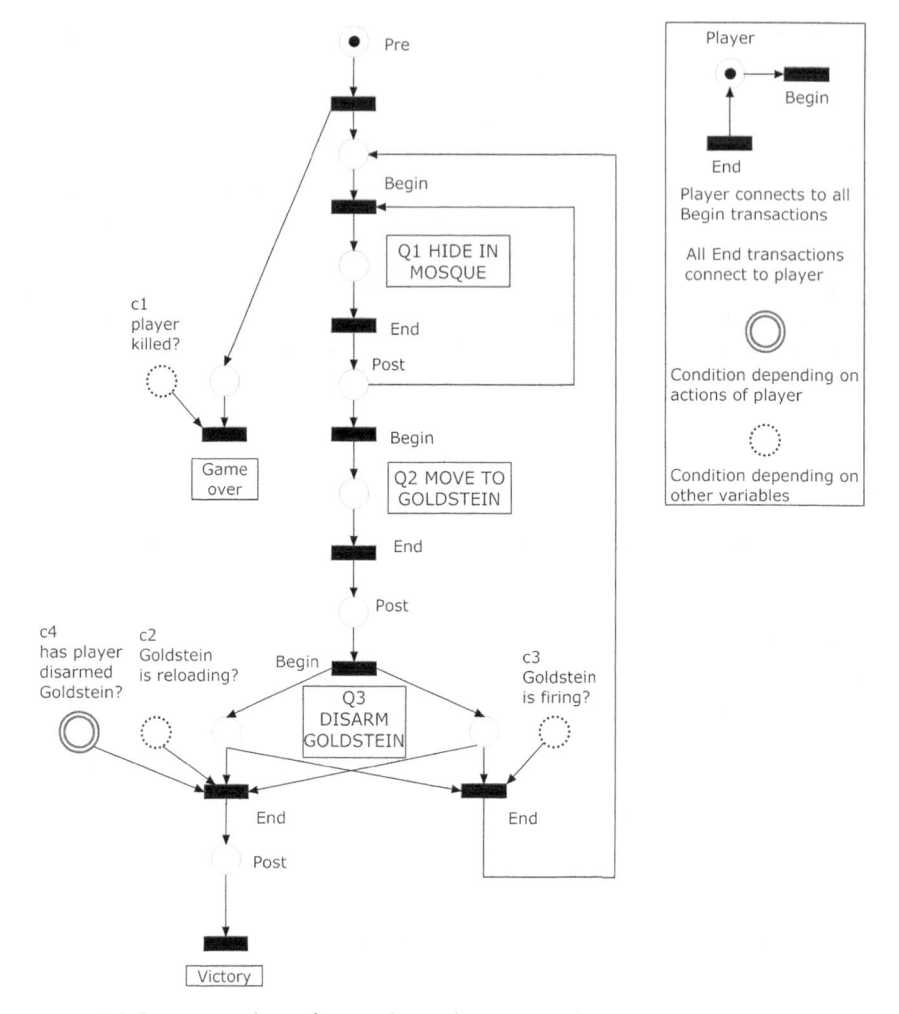

Figure 10.2 Petri net analysis of game play in the game *Under Siege*

indiscriminate shooting (c1) or misses the right moment to disarm him (c3), he dies. The scene is depicted in a very emotional way, previously unknown in video games, as the mosque is full of wounded and dying people, crying and shouting.

The game play designed by Afkar Media departs significantly from the canon of the first-person shooter genre. Ahmad has no real option for fighting back, except a rather desperate attempt at disarming Goldstein, and he at first figures in the game in the position of victim. Later on, in the missions that follow, he tries to escape from the mosque, which is besieged by the Israeli army, and is caught up in an armed struggle with the Israelis. This finally leads him to join the resistance movement and embark on a risky mission revolving around saving his friend from Israeli jail and interrogation. In the game, the player therefore witnesses a radical change in Ahmad's identity, which he or she can actively re-enact. Yet the player has no real ability to affect this change in identity, since it is firmly set in the game play.

Rollings and Adams (2003) describe a concept titled the "mono-myth," in which the hero exists in an ordinary world, where he or she receives a call to adventure. At first the hero refuses the call, but is finally forced by circumstances to embark on one. Strikingly, the narrative of *Under Siege* matches this concept. In the beginning, Ahmad is described as a normal, fearful person, who has reconciled himself to life as a second-rate citizen and shuns violence. Yet later in the game he is exposed to an attack and thus forced to defend himself, which explains the further violence and development of combat game play. Newgren argues that the concept of the "mono-myth" reflects an internal narrative that strikes a chord with most people and "helps players identify with the hero, entering into the game narrative and immersing them in the game" (2010: 138).

It is important to note that the Muslim identity of the hero is not central to the game play of *Under Siege*. Although Ahmad is clearly a Muslim and the whole mission takes place in a mosque, there are other perhaps more salient identities in play: Palestinian, Arab, ordinary citizen, victim of a terrorist attack, and so on. In comparison to *Abu Isa's Quest for Knowledge*, in which the identification of the players with Islam was crucial to the developers, *Under Siege* aims to construct a more multifaceted identity, that of the ordinary citizen confronted with unavoidable violence. As Radwan Kasmiya, the manager of Afkar Media, told me: "It is not our aim to strengthen national identity among Arabs or religious identity among Muslims and to define ourselves in this way vis-à-vis the others. To strengthen identity in such a way leads only to increasing tensions among people. ... It was our aim to show what happens in Palestine behind politics, to show people's stories and problems."

Example 3: *Quraish*

The last game in our study is *Quraish*, a real-time strategy game also created by the Syrian Company, Afkar Media, in 2005. *Quraish* deals with pre-Islamic Bedouin wars and the early Islamic conquests. Throughout the game, many concepts of pre-Islamic Arab culture and early Islamic history are communicated to the player.

For this study we have chosen to focus on the game's sixth level, "The Choice," which puts the player face to face with a moral decision unusual in the realm of digital entertainment. The introductory cinematic sequence to this level is inspired by Muhammad Ibn Isḥāq's description of the Battle of the Trench (*Ghazwat al-khandaq*), taken from the traditional Muslim biography of the prophet Muhammad, *Sīrat rasūl Allāh* (Life of Allah's Messenger):

142   Vit Sisler

Table 10.2 Transcript of the introductory cinematic sequence for the level "The Choice" in the game *Quraish*

Video	Audio
"Arabia 627 A.C."	
The camera flies through the desert ...	Narrator (in Arabic): "It has been five years since I fled from Mecca to carry out my beliefs."
... and a narrow canyon, toward the oasis of Medina.	"Fear struck my heart when Arabs and Jews gathered their forces and decided to eliminate this new religion from the Earth."
People are digging a trench under the burning sun.	"The Prophet eases our hearts and orders us to dig a trench around our city and prepare for victory if only we keep our oath to God."
Two Muslims are struggling with a huge rock, unsuccessfully trying to break it with their shovels.	"Under the burning sun, our strength was vaporized when a huge rock blocked our trench and refused to bend to our heartfelt strokes."
They give up their futile attempts and turn to the camera.	"Desperately, we asked Muhammad for help."
A hammer fills the screen, rises into the sky, and strikes the rock.	"The Prophet raised the hammer and struck the rock while shouting ..."
Muslim army charges Roman legion. The rock cracks.	"Allahu Akbar!" "I have been promised the keys of Syria!"
Muslims in a siege machine are swinging a ram. Catapults are firing on the walls of a fortification.	"Allahu Akbar!"
The rock cracks even more.	"I have been promised the keys of Persia!"
Flags are falling down from a fortress in a besieged city. Muslim warriors cheer.	"Allahu Akbar! I have been promised the keys of Yemen!"
A lonely rider moves off into the setting sun.	"Ten years have passed since that day and I witnessed with my own eyes how God fulfilled His Messenger's promises when we fulfill our oath. But what about our future generations?"
Logo and text appear on the screen (in Arabic): "*Quraish*. Do you have what it takes to make history?"	"Will they keep their oath? God always keeps His ..."

In the sixth level of game play (Figure 10.3), the player represents a leader of the pagan Shayban tribe, which is allied with the Quraish tribe during the time of their struggle with Muhammad's Muslim forces in Medina. The player's first quest (Q1) is to build an army and then (Q2) join the tribes besieging Medina in the famous Battle of the Trench. In this historical battle (627 AD), the outnumbered Muslims under Muhammad's command successfully defended the city of Medina, partly because of the trench they dug around it. The game's main narrative follows the historical events, so that, after an unsuccessful

Playing Muslim hero 143

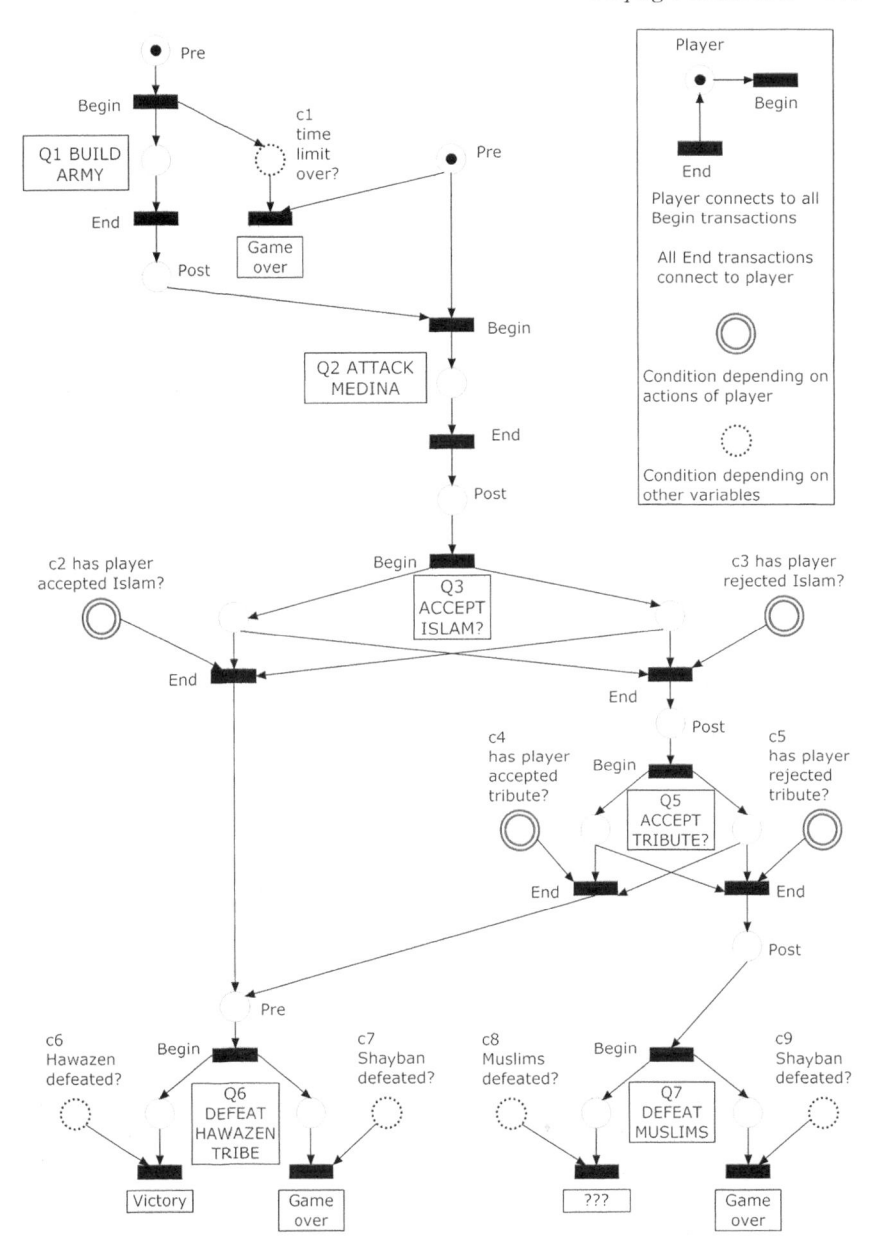

Figure 10.3 Petri net analysis of game play in the game *Quraish*

charge, the leaders of the Quraish tribe decide to withdraw from battle. The player with his Shayban tribe is then offered Islam (Q3). If he accepts, the Shayban tribe joins the Muslims in order to defeat the rest of the attacking Hawazen tribe (their former allies) (Q6). If he refuses, he is given another option: to keep his religion and pay a tribute (*al-jizya*) to the Muslims (Q5). If he accepts, the game continues as already described (Q6). If he refuses both Islam and the tribute, his quest (Q7) is then to defeat the Muslim forces in Medina.

The game play analysis of this level demonstrates how Afkar Media transcended the simplistic pattern of edutainment. Instead of limiting the educational and persuasive aspect of the game to simple exposure to Islamic content, they have constructed a virtual environment that allows the player to explore numerous strategies for action and decision, enabling him, finally, to experiment with the very identity of his virtual self. Although the authors' preference is clearly communicated through the game play (defeating the Muslims [Q7] borders on the impossible), they have introduced the concepts of free choice and performative construction of identity into the realm of Muslim games. The fact that the player can win the game while either accepting Islam or keeping the hero's original (pagan) identity reflects the rather ambitious mission of Radwan Kasmiya, who perceives video games as cutting-edge technology for cultural dialogue, conveying different points of view and enabling the exchange of ideas.

Discussion

These examples suggest that the issue of religious and cultural identity is central to many Muslim games. Until recently, games of US, European, or Japanese origin have almost exclusively dominated the markets in the Muslim world. These games raised serious concerns and have regularly been criticized for inciting violent behavior, displaying sexuality and misrepresenting Islam (Mernissi 2006; Sisler 2008). There has therefore been a desire to present Muslim youth with alternative games that would reflect their culture and religion in a more appropriate way. By doing so, the Muslim games offer different, oftentimes conflicting concepts of Muslim identity (Table 10.3).

Abu Isa's Quest for Knowledge offers a singular, simply outlined identity of a Muslim student, into which the player can easily project him- or herself. The

Table 10.3 Different identity concepts constructed by the three Muslim games analyzed

Hero and game	Narrative	Audiovisual signifiers	Game play
Student in *Abu Isa's Quest for Knowledge*	Muslim	—	—
Ahmad in *Under Siege*	Palestinian victim Arab (implicitly Muslim)	male Arab (implicitly Muslim)	resistance fighter
Hani in *Quraish*	Bedouin Arab pagan	Bedouin Arab male	Muslim (optional) pagan (optional)

hero has no background, gender, or distinctive visual representation. Moreover, his or her identity plays no role in relation to game play. In *Under Siege*, Ahmad has the multi-layered identity of a Palestinian Arab, with a well-developed background story capitalizing on real world events. The narrative and audiovisual signifiers suggest that he is a Muslim, although his religious identity is not emphasized in the game. Evolution of his identity from that of victim to resistance fighter is central to the game play, but the player has no opportunity to change this. Finally, the virtual chieftain, Hani, in *Quraish* is a Bedouin Arab whose identity is clearly manifested at all three levels of the game. Moreover, his religious identity is central to the game play, since the player can accept or reject Islam and thus directly participate in the construction of Hani's identity.

Gee (2007) suggests that the play of identities created through video games can cause users to actively reflect on the construction of their own identities. Yet, as Shaw (2010: 39) argues, we cannot assume that the act of playing a game in which the character is Muslim and created by Muslims will cause an ontological shift or change in the nature of the gaming experience for a Muslim gamer. Without further empirical research on which identifiers are important to players, we cannot predict a deterministic relationship between identification as a member of a group and identification with a game character. In other words, playing as a character does not necessarily imply identifying with that character (Shaw 2010: 196). Nevertheless, unlike film or other audiovisual media, video games such as *Quraish* can convey significant concepts of identity at the level of game play, translating them into a new digital domain – the domain of procedural rhetoric.

Conclusion

This case study offers an instructive lesson on procedural rhetoric and ethical choices in Muslim games. Whereas *Abu Isa's Quest for Knowledge* presents, to paraphrase Bogost (2007: 287), ethical positions through logic that enforce player behavior according to a particular moral register, *Quraish* presents ethical doubt through logic that disrupts movement along one moral register, with orthogonal or intersecting movement along another. In other words, where Muslim edutainment fails to utilize the full potential of the medium while "taking direction from textbooks and spelling out ideas in a literal fashion" (Newgren 2010: 144), *Quraish* capitalizes on the strength of the medium and allows the gamer to experience ethical dilemmas and draw their own conclusions, possibly resulting in a change in the hero's religious identity.

From a broader perspective, the growing interest of game developers in the Muslim world in the issue of identity (Sisler 2008; Tawil-Souri 2007; Campbell 2010) indicates the role the video game industry could play as the cutting-edge conveyors of contemporary Islam, as well as the increasingly important economic relevance of video games in the emerging Muslim consumption culture. The latter appropriates global brands and products and refashions them along the lines of Islamic principles.

Discussion questions

- Does religious and cultural representation in video games matter, or is it "just a game"?
- How is the hero's identity, as constructed by the game developers, significant for the player? To what extent might video games shape or inform a player's religious identity?
- Can video games be used as a medium for facilitating cultural and religious dialogue?

Note

1 This study was supported by research grant number DF11P01OVV030, financed by the Ministry of Culture, Czech Republic and carried out at the Charles University Faculty of Arts in Prague, 2010.

References

Abu Isa Games (2006) "About Us." Online. Available: www.abuisagames.com/aboutus.html (accessed April 16, 2011).
Bogost, I. (2007) *Persuasive Games: The Expressive Power of Videogames*, Cambridge: MIT Press.
Campbell, H. (2010) "Islamogaming: Digital Dignity Via Alternative Storytellers," in C. Detweiler (ed.) *Halos and Avatars: Playing Video Games with God*, 63–74, Louisville: Westminster John Knox Press.
Gee, J. P. (2007) *What Video Games Have to Teach Us about Learning and Literacy*, New York: Palgrave Macmillan.
Mernissi, F. (2006) "Digital Scheherazades in the Arab World," *Current History: A Journal of Contemporary World Affairs*, 106(689): 121–6.
Murphy, S. C. (2004) "Live in Your World, Play in Ours: The Spaces of Video Game Identity," *Journal of Visual Culture*, 3(2): 223–38.
Natkin, S. and Vega, L. (2003) "Petri Net Modelling for the Analysis of the Ordering of Actions in Computer Games," in Q. H. Mehdi, N. E. Gough, and S. Natkin (eds) *4th International Conference on Intelligent Games and Simulation (GAME-ON 2003), 19–21 November 2003, London, UK*, London: Eurosis.
Newgren, K. (2010) "Bioshock to the System: Smart Choices in Video Games," in C. Detweiler (ed.) *Halos and Avatars: Playing Video Games with God*, 135–48, Louisville: Westminster John Knox Press.
Rollings, A. and Adams, E. (2003) *Andrew Rollings and Ernest Adams on Game Design*, Indianapolis, IN: New Riders.
Shaw, A. (2010) *Identity, Identification, and Media Representation in Video Game Play: An Audience Reception Study*, unpublished PhD thesis, University of Pennsylvania.
Sisler, V. (2008) "Digital Arabs: Representation in Video Games," *European Journal of Cultural Studies*, 2(11): 203–20.
Tawil-Souri, H. (2007) "The Political Battlefield of Pro-Arab Video Games on Palestinian Screens," *Comparative Studies of South Asia, Africa and the Middle East*, 27(3): 536–51.
Vanoye, F. and Goliot-Lété, A. (2001) *Précis d'analyse filmique*, Paris: Nathan.

11 Digital storytelling and collective religious identity in a moderate to progressive youth group

Lynn Schofield Clark and Jill Dierberg

Storytelling has long been an important aspect of memory and identity. People tell stories about their past as a way of underscoring concerns about their present and future, as Ochs and Capps have argued in their influential research on narratives (Ochs and Capps 1996). We choose to tell certain stories as a means of communicating our concerns to particular audiences, and when our stories are received positively, we feel affirmed in our sense that we, and our stories, hold value. As Lövheim has noted in her chapter on identity in this volume, digital media offer new means of constructing religious identities, both as such media mediate self-representation and as they offer enhanced means of social interaction. As individuals use digital tools to produce and share religious narratives, they perform a certain form of self that is enacted in relation to others. Digital media therefore contribute to trends in the personalization of religion, as individuals can reflect on their own narratives and can also participate in collective reflection on what it means to assume a religious identity in a particular context.

As Nancy Ammerman has noted, our religious identity narratives occur at the intersection of two kinds of stories: autobiographical stories about ourselves as individuals, and stories of religious traditions, sacred actors, shared experiences, and religious institutions that help to shape the meaning we attach to our autobiographical stories (Ammerman 2003). Whereas much of the literature on religious identity and spiritual narratives has focused on how individuals tell these kinds of religious identity stories, the case study presented here explores the collective aspects of religious identity storytelling, in which a group of young people who were members of a moderate-to-progressive faith community were given an opportunity to create a narrative of identity using digital storytelling.

Case study: digital storytelling

Digital storytelling has arisen as a movement that teaches ordinary people both narrative development and digital authoring technologies, enabling them to tell meaningful stories that are of significance to them (Lambert 2009; Davis and Weinshenker 2012). Perhaps now more than at any previous moment in history, people can use digital authoring technologies to bring longstanding interests in storytelling into a confluence with multimedia production techniques (Gauntlett

2011; Jenkins 2006; Lessig 2008). What sets apart a digital storytelling experience from the production of a news package, a promotional video, or a do-it-yourself production is that digital storytelling engages participants more directly in a process that focuses on the construction of the story to be told. Group members who participate in a digital storytelling project are therefore encouraged to see the story that emerges as "their" story rather than a story or a commentary put together by experts. Group members who wish to engage in a digital storytelling process often seek the help of a facilitator, whose work can range from providing instruction on certain aspects of the process to overseeing both story development and the final production's technical aspects.

Because of its accessibility and ease of use, digital storytelling has come to be of interest to religious groups, particularly among communities that wish to counter misinformation or stereotypes that might lead others to make false assumptions about who they are or what they stand for. The process of constructing an identity narrative using digital storytelling allows participants to recognize their agency and claim their right to tell their own story (Hess 2010). In their study of digital storytelling among Norwegian youth, Kaare and Lundby (2008) found that the digital storytelling process also enabled young people to consider what it meant to create what they saw as an "authentic" narrative of individual religious identity within their particular context. The case study reviewed here similarly found that the young people involved in digital storytelling needed encouragement as they sought to connect their individual biographical narratives with those of their religious traditions. It differed from the Norwegian study in that, rather than creating individual narratives, participants were encouraged to work together to construct a collective religious identity narrative.

Methodology

The research project titled "Digital Storytelling and Religious Formation" followed after a six-month interview-based research project that explored the cultures of religious youth groups (Dierberg *et al.* 2009). Clark wanted to further develop the research relationship with a local Jewish and a local Lutheran (ELCA) congregation, to consider how they might benefit more directly from our interaction with them; as researchers we wondered how we might not only *write about* but *work with* these groups. This turn to a redefinition of roles between researcher and researched is consistent with calls for greater reflexivity in ethnographic projects which seek to work with communities "to capture and build upon community and social movements," as Fine and Weiss have written (1998: 277–78; see also Fine 1994; Dimitriadis 2001). Gary Knutson, the youth leader at Christ Lutheran Church where Dierberg had been the primary contact, expressed willingness to extend this relationship, but stipulated that Dierberg needed to attend weekly meetings as a volunteer so as to build trust within the group. She did this for two months. Then, she began engaging the young people in the digital storytelling process. As part of that process, she led discussions concerning what members of the group felt were most important to them, as a group. This chapter is based on field notes from the experience of creating the digital story over a six-month period and subsequent interviews with the five young people and the youth leader who had been most centrally involved in its production.

Discussion

The narrative of collective religious identity

Members of the group decided that their group's collective life could be captured in relation to three stories: (1) the story of how they were unique and how they differed from other Christian communities, as captured in the catchphrase "We're different"; (2) the story of how they felt they engaged in community service as a means not only of changing their communities, but also of changing themselves; and (3) the story of how they took these experiences of transformation and made them a key part of how they accepted others into their youth group community regardless of who they were, what they believed or what they struggled with personally. This latter idea was captured in the phrase of their youth group leader, who related this accepting ethos to living out a relationship with God through living out relationships with one another: "incarnational relationships are it" (personal interview with Gary Knutson, April 6, 2009).

Once the group had identified three central stories that they believed characterized who they were, Dierberg encouraged them to think about how they would express those stories visually through photos and film footage. Young people gathered photos from key moments in their experience with the group, and in consultation with the group members Dierberg and other members of the research team developed a set of questions for on-camera interviews with members of the group. Members of the team then scripted and edited a final version of the story.

The resulting digital story opened with a photo and video montage of young people interacting with one another and with the community. Then the young people discussed their youth group as a "safe space" in which young people could be themselves, could raise questions about beliefs and behaviors, and could find acceptance among their peers. In a second section, group members discussed the ways in which their experiences of service had transformed their understandings of people whose life experiences differed from their own. The third section included statements about and images of mutual support and shared experiences. The 15-minute video also included photo and video montages of the young people engaged in conversation with one another and in service projects involving people outside their group (Christ Lutheran Church, video, June 2, 2010).

"I wish I would have been in the film"

Immediately after it was completed, group participants who hadn't been in the film expressed some regrets about their absence, which was a sign that the resulting video expressed a group narrative of which they wished to be a part. These regrets came from students who had been invited but had declined to participate in the video's production. One youth, Kelsey, explained this common regret, and noted, "If we did the process again, I think we would want to include more youth group members" (personal interview with Kelsey, October 20, 2010). Another youth, Hailey, shared similar sentiments: "I feel that more kids would want to voice their opinions, even if they seemed like they wouldn't" (personal interview with Hailey, October 20, 2010). Perhaps these regrets voiced after the fact emerged because it had been difficult for participants to envision ahead of time what the final video would look like or how it would represent the group as a whole. As a result of this experience, we followed a different procedure with group members at Temple Emmanuel, a second congregation with which we developed the digital storytelling process. In that congregation, youth group members were invited to view an incomplete version of their group's video that highlighted only two young people on screen. After that screening, ten other young people volunteered to participate in the interviews so as to have their experiences represented in the final digital storytelling product. The Christ Lutheran Church video might similarly have looked different had there been an opportunity for its further development.

Shared communal identity

Overall, members of the group and the youth director reacted positively to the finished digital storytelling product. They recognized themselves in the completed video, as Kelsey stated: "I do think the video accurately portrays the youth group. It represented the strong relationships we share and the love that we have for each other" (personal interview with Kelsey, October 20, 2010). Another young person, Kyle, even suggested that some of the youth have become more aware of what the youth group is all about after the process. "I think this video accurately portrays this youth group in a way that not even some of the kids realized until they saw it," he said (personal interview with Kyle, October 19, 2010).

When asked if the video allowed them to better understand who the group is in relation to the community, the answers were surprising. It seemed the video allowed the group, as a whole, to take ownership of who they believed themselves to be in the context of the local church as well as in the wider Christian community. In the context of the local church body, for example, Kyle reflected, "I believe it made us feel as though we really are part of the church as a whole, not just a separate entity that helps the church out occasionally" (personal interview with Kyle, October 19, 2010). Hailey suggested: "I think that the adults in the congregation should see [the video]. They need to have their eyes opened about how truly smart and genuine we are about these topics" (personal interview with Hailey, October 19, 2010). Overall, it seemed that the video allowed the youth an outlet through which to voice their sense of identity to, and in relation to, the larger church body. When speaking of this relationship to the wider church, Hailey noted that she believed that the video helped her and other group members to articulate how they were different from other more conservative Christian groups while affirming that their group held value that was apart from, rather than inferior to, those other groups.

The youth director in particular had an especially positive response to the video. He felt the video resonated with most of the youth, and he was eager to share the video with parents, with potential new group members, and with the wider church body. In fact, he screened the video at a district-wide meeting of his church's denomination. When asked how the video was received, he said enthusiastically, "everyone wants one of these for their church youth group!" (e-mail correspondence with Gary Knutson, November 2, 2010).

Interpretation and analysis: fluid identities and anchoring narratives

As Jerome Bruner (1990) has pointed out, as humans we seek to organize our experiences into narrative form so that we can make sense of our lives. We reflect on the narratives we construct as we consider who we are and who we want to be, and this process of reflection in turn influences how we will pursue our own ends. Such reflection can actually encourage us to change our behaviors and our actions, resulting in personal transformations (Davis 2005; Ochs and Capps 1996). Moreover, as the process of participating in and creating a digital storytelling project can result in stories that are in a certain sense "fixed," they allow both the creator and the audience to reflect upon the story and to consider how well it does or does not represent both who they are and who they aspire to be (Davis and Weinshenker 2012). In this sense, digital stories provide *anchoring narratives*: narratives of identity that help people to reflect upon a story that held resonance and meaning for them at a particular time and in a particular context. As people view a digital story over time, they can continue to reflect on the extent to which they see continuity or change between that anchoring narrative and the narratives that they use in subsequent settings. Digital storytelling, therefore, provides a means by which individuals or groups are afforded opportunities not only to tell but to listen to their own stories. Such listening to the narratives of the self is a key aspect of identity development, as Holland and her colleagues (1998) have noted:

> People tell others who they are, but even more importantly, they tell themselves and they try to act as though they are who they say they are. These self-understandings, especially those with strong emotional resonance for the teller, are what we refer to as identities.
>
> (p. 3)

Yet as Davis and Weinshenker (2012) note, with reference to the question of whether or not digital stories are an enactment of identity, "Without the ongoing support of a community, the self-realizations [digital stories] report and the personal transformations they testify to are likely to fade from consciousness without translation into action" (p. 22). Digital storytelling may, therefore, provide groups with anchoring narratives that contain significant aspirations, but they only become catalysts for movement toward those aspirations with the support of a community. In the case of collectively produced digital stories such as the one explored here, the communal nature of the process and its interpretations in various screenings has demonstrated the importance not only of expressing those aspirations, but of revisiting those group narratives among communities that are willing to share the work of enacting them. Digital storytelling can therefore serve as a catalyst for both individual and collective purposeful action.

Although it was not the original intent of this project, the participants' comments about wanting to screen the video for parents and other members of the congregation revealed a felt need to be seen by those constituents as members of the wider church community, albeit on their own terms. In this sense, it affirmed Frank Rogers' (2010) Narrative Pedagogies project and the idea that "the narratives of our lives intermingle with the narratives that ground our faith and [participating in storytelling can] inspire people to journey toward hope as empowered agents of healing in our world" (n. pag.). Stories, therefore, can play a key role in helping young people to be integrated into the life of the faith community.

Participating in a digital storytelling project also engaged young people in the important process of *articulation*, giving them an opportunity to practice talking about and expressing what it means to them to embrace a religious identity. Such work is important, for "articulacy fosters reality," as Smith and Denton (2005) have written in their argument for greater opportunities to practice such talk. In this case, such articulation occurred *relationally* rather than individually. Taking on a digital storytelling process required the young participants to work together, to think through commitments, and even to do research on the history of their community and tradition in order to consider how it relates to their own lives. Digital storytelling – because it provides effective prompts for discussion and an engaging and vivid process for rendering that discussion into tangible public form – served as an opportunity for this kind of relational development of identity.

Conclusion

This case study illustrates that digital storytelling can serve as a resource for both the expression of and continued commitment to a collectively held identity. Over a period of six months, young people in Christ Lutheran Church made decisions about which stories to tell about their group, they collected photos and music that they believed would bring those stories to life, and they viewed the digital storytelling product both immediately after its production and in subsequent settings. Through this process, the participants in this digital storytelling project authored their collective identity and took ownership of the aspirational elements it entailed.

The final product itself served as a catalyst that galvanized the group, helping them to identify their desire to be viewed by parents and congregation members as part of a larger church body, and providing further encouragement for them to participate in meaningful service activities and to continue to provide a safe space for those who might become part of their group.

Digital storytelling is not always an enactment of collective identity. If young people feel coerced to tell a story that they don't believe in, or if they feel left out of a key telling of the collective narrative, digital storytelling can serve to expose tensions rather than enhancing inclusion. In this particular case study, however, the digital storytelling process enabled young people to write themselves, and their community, into being in a way that was fresh and meaningful for them. In doing so, the process became a means by which they could employ the tools of digital media for the creation of an enhanced and collective narrative of religious identity.

Discussion questions

- Do you think that communicating your religious commitments in a video format is easier or more difficult than communicating through a written or oral form? Why do you think this?
- Over the past two decades, in an increasingly diverse and plural world, the concept of religious identity has shifted. How might a collaborative process of narrative construction in digital storytelling assist young people in developing a sense of identity in this religiously plural context?
- What does digital storytelling tell us about how people understand how religious identity is constituted in a participatory digital culture?

References

Ammerman, N.T. (2003). "Religious identities and religious institutions," in M. Dillon (ed.), *Handbook of the Sociology of Religion*, 207–24. Cambridge: Cambridge University Press.

Bruner, J. (1990). *Acts of Meaning*. Cambridge, MA: Harvard University Press.

Christ Lutheran Church (June 2, 2010). Video. Available: www.storyingfaith.org/sharing (accessed June 4, 2012).

Davis, A. (2005). "Co-authoring identity: Digital storytelling in an urban middle school." *Technology, Humanities, Education and Narrative (THEN Journal)* 1: 1–12.

Davis, A. and Weinshenker, D. (2012). "Digital storytelling and authoring identity," in C.C. Ching and B. Foley (eds), *Constructing the Self in a Digital World*. Cambridge: Cambridge University Press.

Dierberg, J., Bamford, A., Clark, L.S., and Monserrate, R. (2009, October). "'We're not just here to hang out': Exploring collective identity in moderate and progressive youth groups." Presented at Society for the Scientific Study of Religion, Denver, CO.

Dimitriadis, G. (2001). "Coming clean at the hyphen: Ethics and dialogue at a local community center." *Qualitative Inquiry* 7(5): 578–97.

Fine, M. (1994). "Working the hyphens: Reinventing self and other in qualitative research," in N.K. Denzin and Y.S. Lincoln (eds), *Handbook of Qualitative Research*, 70–82. Thousand Oaks, CA: Sage.

Fine, M. and Weiss, L. (1998). *The Unknown City: Lives of Poor and Working Class Young Adults*. Boston: Beacon Press.

Gauntlett, D. (2011). *Making is Connecting*. London: Polity.

Hess, M. (2010, November). "In the flow: Learning religion and religiously learning." Presidential address to the Religious Education Association, Denver, CO.

Holland, D., Lachicotte, W. Jr., Skinner, D., and Cain, C. (1998). *Identity and Agency in Cultural Worlds*. Cambridge: Harvard University Press.

Jenkins, H. (2006). *Convergence Culture: Where Old and New Media Collide*. New York: New York University Press.

Kaare, B.H. and Lundby, K. (2008). "Mediatized lives: Autobiography and assumed authenticity in digital storytelling." In K. Lundby (ed.), *Digital Storytelling, Mediatized Stories: Self-representations in New Media*, 105–22. New York: Peter Lang.

Lambert, J. (2009). *Digital Storytelling: Capturing Lives, Creating Community*, 3rd edition. Berkeley, CA: Digital Diner Press.

Lessig, L. (2008). *Remix: Making Art and Commerce Thrive in the Hybrid Economy*. New York: Penguin.

Ochs, E. and Capps, L. (1996). "Narrating the self." *Annual Review of Anthropology* 25: 19–43.

Rogers, F. (2010). "Introduction: God in the graffiti," *Narrative Pedagogies*, unpublished manuscript.

Smith, C. and Denton, M. (2005). *Soul Searching: The Religious and Spiritual Lives of American Teenagers*. New York: Oxford University Press.

12 Charting frontiers of online religious communities

The case of Chabad Jews

Oren Golan[1]

Since its inception, the question of community on the Internet has puzzled scholars. Researchers have inquired whether the Internet can produce a viable and meaningful community (Rheingold 2000; Green 1999; Beninger 1987), and whether it can indeed facilitate the growth and social integration of its members. Within the religious world, a tension around Internet use has been growing in the past few years. Religious leaders appreciate the pervasiveness and strong potential of the Internet for fostering outreach, proselytizing the faith, strengthening connections among congregation members, and promoting fundamental worldviews. However, the loose commitment of web surfers and their tendency to "shop around," that is, to enter and exit websites of completely different orientations, poses a threat to religious communities' ability to uphold their social frontiers – a tension that has led many religious leaders to object to Internet practices.

In this study, the following question is explored: how do religious communities use the Internet to invite new members and expand their influence while catering to their own communities and consolidating existing membership? To examine this question in detail, we focus on the case of the Chabad, a Jewish ultra-Orthodox group that has been a pioneer on the Web, having an online presence as early as the 1980s.

Chabad's case is unique, as it is an ultra-Orthodox group that maintains the tension of keeping up an enclave lifestyle while promoting outreach. A religious enclave is a cultural system that ensures insiders will conform to the collective's worldview and lifestyle. Chabad members live within an enclave society, yet at the same time their philosophy advocates outreach to Jews of all denominational affiliations, and to some extent even beyond the Jewish world, for the purpose of what they perceive as "bettering the world" and advancing the imminent arrival of the messiah. This has been most apparent in their continuous efforts to send emissaries around the world, create centers of worship and teaching, publish books and generally promote Chabad's philosophy and practices.

The Chabad movement and outreach

Chabad is a subgroup within ultra-Orthodox Judaism, and more specifically of the wider Hassidic movement. The movement emerged in the eighteenth century as a charismatic religious faction that swept through Poland and the Russian Empire. Alongside its growth, it distinguished itself by a creed that emphasized popular mysticism, reforming the use of Jewish liturgy, and modifying ritual and the Jewish Eastern European dress code (Stadler 2009; Baumel 2006; Fishkoff 2003; Friedman 1991). The Hassidim are divided into several dynastic groups known as "courts," each headed by its own rabbi and following their respective customs. These groups differ in their conception of social boundaries and interaction with non-community members, and may fluctuate from an extreme seclusion and separation from outsiders, as in the case of the Satmars, to an outreach to Jews and gentiles around the world, as in the case of Chabad. Unlike other ultra-Orthodox Jews, who prefer to turn inward and fortify their boundaries, the Chabad movement turns outward as well, assuming responsibility for the Jewish collective and striving to teach its ways to a broader community.

It has been contended that members of the Chabad community readily use tools of modern technology, including the media, for the dissemination of its teachings (Shandler 2009). Although not the largest Hassidic court, Chabad surpasses others in its impact on the outside world, Jewish or non-Jewish. In fact, both in Israel and in the US, Chabad members periodically engage in campaigns of religious influence in locations from street centers to army bases and beyond (Ravitzky 1994: 304). Chabad's institutional aspects are highly developed and are governed from its center (Friedman 1994). In the past, leaflets, newsletters, books, and other means were utilized as part of campaign endeavors, and a fervent zeal for religious activism marked the approach. Most apparent perhaps is the work of the emissaries (*Shlichim*), who develop contacts with local Jewish establishments on university campuses and in town centers around the world. Since the death of their leader, the highly venerated Rabbi Schneerson, the Chabad community has ruptured, with some seeking to affirm the rabbi's continuance and even looking for his Messianic return (see Bilu 2009; Kravel-Tovi 2009). However, this study highlights the communal institution-building that sprang up prior to Schneerson's demise and has continued to develop in its aftermath. In the Schneerson era, Chabad's emissaries created a strong mechanism for expanding Chabad's influence and for integrating the community in respect of its common mission, while fortifying Chabad's center in Brooklyn as its main hub. After the rupture in Chabad's charismatic movement following the death of Rabbi Schneerson, these emissaries gained further importance by becoming a central form of social action for the movement, committing the community to its organization while reinforcing their common values of outreach. These tendencies have re-emerged in the age of the Internet and new media, when the tools for mass dissemination of information have been rationalized and significantly expanded. Accordingly, it would be of interest to learn how these modern tools of communication demarcate the Chabad "territory" and facilitate interaction among Chabad members and the wider audiences it aims to influence.

Methodology

This study consists of in-depth interviews and observations of Chabad websites. In-depth interviews were conducted with 25 webmasters (website leaders, public relations personnel, web designers, content managers) for three websites (http://chabad.org, www.crownheights.info and http://col.org.il) between 2009 and 2012, in Israel and the US. The core set of interviews were conducted face to face in the webmasters' office environments. During 2009–10, frequent visits were made to Jewish website offices in Brooklyn, New York, which enabled observations of websites' workings and insights into other community members and websites, including that of Chabad.org and crownheights.info. To select websites for observation, as well as to assess Jewish responses towards Chabad's virtual activities, informal discussions and interviews were conducted with avid surfers and webmasters that use Chabad's websites from within and beyond the community. Accordingly, conversations were held with Yeshiva students, Rabbinical students, webmasters of other websites, and avid web surfers.

This research included observation and analysis of the websites, with particular attention given to services offered, the creed expressed in respect of the websites' online practices, use of language and visual culture. Sites were selected according to two main criteria: traffic and subject recommendations. Traffic and activity were strong determinants in the cases of Chabad.org and col.org.il, while crownheights.info was recommended by key informants. Observational investigation is unobtrusive and grounded in the natural setting of Chabad members' digital activities, and facilitates in-depth insight into the symbols and metaphors of the rich multimedia world of Internet culture (including sounds, colors, and style of language). To address the ways that communities employ the Internet to spread their influence while catering for and fostering integration within their own communities, the three websites are explored in terms of their outward and inward community reach.

Outward community reach: Chabad.org

Chabad uses multiple strategies to spread its worldview. Accordingly, the Internet is used as a tool by Chabad for highlighting its practices (e.g. international emissaries, and community and religious celebrations) and particular identity markers as an ultra-Orthodox community (most apparent in their URL, chabad.org, the name "Chabad online," and their frequent display of pictures of the late Rabbi Schneerson and his famed house). Chabad's online presence and work can be traced back to the 1980s, when the Internet was not yet mainstream and garnered attention only from smaller groups of computer enthusiasts, students, and followers of academia (Danet 2001). Chabad emerged online through spaces such as electronic bulletin boards (BBS) like Keshernet, where Chabad community members, most notably the late Rabbi Kazan, started their religious online activism (Zaleski 1997), that is to say, their intentional action to bring about religious awareness and change. According to my interviewees, as early as 1988 the first "Ask the Rabbi" emerged over these bulletin boards and, a few years later, the entire *Tanya*, the basic text of Chabad philosophy, which contains daily lessons, was made available online along with other Jewish texts and teachings (at the "Chabad in Cyberspace" online discussion network). By the end of 1993, with the blessing of the highly revered leader of Chabad, Rabbi Schneerson, Chabad.org had been established. From a few grassroots initiatives of Rabbi Kazan and others, Chabad.org emerged as a legitimized and center-based institution, rooted in the heart of Chabad's Brooklyn home. From its beginnings, its goals were directed outward, as Kazan discussed in an interview:

> Our setup was never for our own group. On the contrary, this was set up strictly to deal with the outside world. I don't know if your average Chabad person is going to want his kid running around on the net. It's like putting him in the middle of a newspaper store with all the magazines there ... .
> My perspective here is of getting out to the world. Getting a message of Judaism to the Jew who doesn't know much, to the Gentile who is interested in finding out what Judaism has to offer.
>
> (Zaleski 1997: 14)

At the time, Kazan did not foresee the fervent fascination that ultra-Orthodox communities would have for the Internet (see Campbell and Golan 2011); however, he articulates the website's goal of outreach, which has continued to the present. In an interview with a leading figure at Chabad.org, the perception of the Internet was explained to me: "a lot of people shun it. The technology is here for a purpose, for something positive – Chabad try to use everything we can in a positive way" (February 2010). This corresponds to Chabad's philosophical guideline of broadening the scope of religious involvement (Ravitsky 1994) and different view of the Internet as being a tool for advancing godliness into the world, in contrast to other ultra-Orthodox viewpoints, from which the Internet is a source of livelihood at best, and of evil inclinations and sin at worst (Campbell and Golan 2011; Horowitz 2001). Chabad's point of view, which gained support from its leaders, drove it to invest in this enterprise with great passion and devote considerable resources to it.

Since its inception, the website has undergone significant growth. In early 2010, the website leaders boasted 350,000 subscribers, and, according to compete.com, Chabad.org's traffic in September of 2010 reached 502,824 unique users. More than 50 percent of its users are regulars, and it tops the list of Jewish education sites, with an average surfer time of 4.7 minutes (*Jewish Internet Metric Study 2009*). This places Chabad.org as currently the leading Jewish website in the world in terms of its popularity and exposure. It has also been acclaimed by the Smithsonian as well as leading American press agencies for its historically early delivery of religious education over the net (Fishkoff 2003: 282–3).

Nowadays Chabad.org has significantly expanded its tools and services, providing additional texts and content including news (often pertaining to Jewish issues in the US and Israel), blogs, daily study options for the *Chumash-Torah*, the *Tanya* and other well-known texts, as well as new interpretations of the *Parasha* (the week's reading of the Torah), blogs, a live feed of "Jewish TV," animated instructional accounts, and other forms of free instructional and information services, and links to the site's counterparts in several other languages, all of which utilize up-to-date forms of Internet media.

Although the site's title and URL is "Chabad.org," which creates an expectation of engagement with the world of Chabad, it is more challenging than one might expect to find distinguishing marks of the movement. For example, a leading article on the *Parasha* discusses the question "How does Judaism view wealth?" This is hardly a Chabad-oriented question. This is also true of other parts of this webpage, except for the search platform for Chabad at its center. This is not to say that the website does not modify its content in a way that conforms to the Chabad perspective. For example, interviewing "Hanna," a rabbinical student of the reform movement in Brooklyn, she described her preparation for discussing a *Parasha* every week. In her efforts to keep the discussion current and relevant, rather than just scholarly, Hanna told me that she consults various websites. In her search, she finds that "I keep getting useful materials from Chabad.org, but I am cautious. Some ideas I don't agree with, such as their approach to God's relationship to people" (personal interview, March 2, 2010). Hannah's reflection mirrored responses from other webmasters and Jewish instructors I interviewed. They are appreciative of the fact that Chabad.org (alongside other popular websites they mentioned, such as aish.com, the non-Orthodox myjewishlearning.com or even Wikipedia) is a powerful player that provides information and rich ideas that are extremely useful to them. However, the image of Chabad, as well as the perspective it represents, makes them wary of its content and to an extent distrustful.

In spite of their misgivings, people from various denominations, including (albeit to a lesser extent) the ultra-Orthodox communities, noted Chabad.org's rich repositories of information, its visibility and influential role.

When asking webmasters in Chabad.org about the uses community members made of the website, webpages dedicated to daily study (of the *Tanya*, for example) and repositories of Jewish texts held on the website were noted. In this sense, the community of Chabad believers are viewed as a compartmentalized sector who may enjoy the services offered by the website, but who are certainly not the site's key audience. It should be noted that Chabad.org does offer localized services to emissaries, for a price, allowing emissaries to create their own website to cater to their local communal needs, while making use of the contents and social legitimacy that the website bestows. However, the bulk of the website is geared towards a broader audience with blurred identities in regard to their affiliation with Chabad or even with Judaism. This stands in contrast to other Chabad websites, as will be explained.

Inward community reach: Chabad online and crownheights.info

Beyond Chabad's outreach concerns, several of its websites are devoted to community members and are directed inward, rather than outward. In this sense, an alternative approach to communal boundaries can be seen on two other websites: col.org.il – referred to here as "COL," an acronym for "Chabad online" – and crownheights.info. On these websites, there is a focus on communal concerns as well as Chabad's network of active participants (e.g. global emissaries, Rabbis). Let me clarify by examining the specific case studies.

Much like Chabad.org, COL and crownheight.info emerged much later in the maturation period of the Internet (in the 2000s) and were founded by teenaged entrepreneurs. COL, a Hebrew website based in Israel, mostly in Jerusalem and the town of Kfar Chabad, was initiated by Menachem Cohen, who worked as a journalist for local Chabad newspapers from the age of 15.

Crownheights.info, meanwhile, was founded by a 17-year-old entrepreneur (referred to here by the pseudonym "Daniel") with the hope of earning a livelihood, and is based in the heart of a Chabad-dominated part of Brooklyn. It claims 28,000 unique visitors per day and is focused on local news, Israeli news and – most importantly – Chabad community news. The office functions as a newsroom. While I was visiting the website office, a phone call informed Daniel, the web manager, of a bus accident, and he dashed off to the scene of the event to ask people questions and snap photos with his camera. The whole episode was short; however, it provided a live example of the function of the website – supplying (mostly) photographs of current events. Daniel takes pride in the responsiveness of the website: "if there's a siren outside or helicopter, you would go online and find out what happened," he said (personal interview, June 2, 2010). He spoke of the importance of his work in informing the public of possible hazards, even if they are occasionally offensive to their way of life. For example, he reported an atrocious kidnap-rape that occurred in an adjacent street. In spite of the fact that "Jews were not involved," he said that the public should know what is happening around their homes. Daniel defines the mission of the website as informing and protecting the community. Furthermore he seeks to cater to the many emissaries and their contacts abroad. In this aspect, crownheights.info operates in the same vein as COL.

According to a COL webmaster, connections among the emissaries are very important online. Browsing through COL's webpages, a recurring theme is that of emissaries' pictures posted from around the world. "Chabad is like a family," he says:

> Not everyone knows each other, but they care; when you do something you get responses from everyone. Rabbi "Jacob" is an emissary in Bangkok. He was raised in Jerusalem of a big family. When he publishes a piece, all of his friends and family respond, on talkbacks; responses in English, Yiddish and Hebrew. People who are on the website do not expect to read an update from the prime minister or from the ultra-Orthodox. Nothing but from the courts of the Chabad community. We have flash bulletins of congratulations for newborn babies, reminders on upcoming weddings, *Brith* [rite of circumcisión] celebrations, and the like. In cases of disaster, like the story of the daughter of a Chabad emissary who died in a fire after playing with matches, we got 300 post responses. Unlike talkbacks, where

people hide, here people state their full names. The success of the website can be seen if every emissary will use it as his homepage."

(personal interview, August 9, 2009)

According to this webmaster, the website operates as a community (or an "imagined community," in Anderson's terms; 1991) where people who are of the community or are loosely connected to its key figures (e.g. emissaries, rabbis) can all participate in the communal events and happenings. This facilitates and simulates a sense of familial relations and transfers them to the cybernetic realm on the safe, trustworthy, and familiar plane that is COL.

Conclusion

This chapter has focused on the ways that religious communities utilize the Internet to foster their inner solidarity and promote religious and communal growth beyond regional and symbolic boundaries. In the case of Chabad, we have seen how the movement has grown institutionally and been strengthened through its web presence. This growth is increasingly significant, given the challenges the movement has faced in recent years.

The early legitimation of the Internet by Chabad illustrates the movement's positive view of engaging with the tools of modernity to interact with the non-Hassidic world, and paved the way for the work of future webmasters and social networking (e.g. Facebook, Twitter). The Internet has become an acceptable space where Chabad websites (intentionally or unintentionally) complement each other's work, in a "division of labor" between those dedicated to the outreach vision of Chabad and those devoted to internal community use. For the Chabad, as for other religious communities, the Internet provides visibility to outsiders as well as internally. In many ways, these websites serve as the "face of the community" and a way to cross its boundaries; while in other ways it is a social landscape in which to work and play through user participation.

This study has highlighted the viewpoint of webmasters and of content on Chabad websites; however, future research is called for into communal concerns about media effects on users. Hence research is needed on user participation and involvement in the Internet. More specifically, one could ask how Chabad users adopt the new medium and how they integrate it into their formal communal activities (e.g. schooling, synagogue, the workplace, and dealings with the state and various institutions) as opposed to informal activities (e.g. dance, music, recreation, and leisure). Also, additional research might question the Internet's influence on communal religious practices: for example whether it provides mobilizing spaces of worship, and its effect in unifying or changing liturgy.

Discussion questions

- How can the Internet challenge a religious community's solidarity, values, or boundaries?

- What aspects of the Internet are adapted by the Chabad community, and what strategies are used to confront the challenges they perceive as being posed by the Internet?
- Who are the agents of change and power in the community? How does their perception and use of the Internet differ? Why?

Note

1 I take this opportunity to thank the Fulbright program and Judy Stavsky, the Deputy Director of the US-Israel Educational Foundation, for their generous support of this study. Furthermore, I thank the Center for Religion and Media at NYU and its directors Angela Zito and Faye Ginsburg for warmly encouraging and facilitating this project. Further gratitude is due to the volume's editor, Heidi Campbell, for her illuminating comments and support, as well as Batia Siebzehner for her important insights on an early draft of the chapter.

References

Anderson, B. (1991) *Imagined Communities: Reflections on the Origin and Spread of Nationalism*, London: Verso.

Baumel, S. D. (2006). *Sacred Speakers: Language and Culture among the Haredim in Israel*, New York: Berghahn.

Beninger, J. R. (1987) "Personalization of Mass Media and the Growth of Pseudo-Community," *Communication Research*, 14: 352–71.

Bilu, Y. (2009) " 'With Us More Than Ever': Making the Late Lubavitcher Rabbi Present in Messianic Chabad." In K. Caplan and N. Stadler (eds), *Leadership and Authority in Israeli Haredi Society*, 186–224, Tel Aviv: Hakibutz Hameuchad (in Hebrew).

Campbell, H. and Golan, O. (2011) "Creating Digital Enclaves: Negotiation of the Internet Among Bounded Religious Communities," *Media, Culture & Society*, 33(5): 709–24.

Danet, B. (2001) *Cyberpl@y*, London: Berg.

Fishkoff, S. (2003) *The Rebbe's Army: Inside the World of Chabad-Lubavitch*, New York: Schocken Books.

Friedman, M. (1994) "Habad as Messianic Fundementalism." In M. E. Marty and R. S. Appleby (eds), *Accounting for Fundamentalisms: The Dynamic Character of Movements*, 328–73, Chicago: University of Chicago Press.

——(1991) *Haredi Society Sources, Trends and Processes*. Jerusalem: Machon Yerushalim Leheker Yisrael (in Hebrew).

Green, L. (1999) "The End of the Virtual Community," *M/C Journal: A Journal of Media and Culture*, 2(8). Online. Available at: http://journal.media-culture.org.au/9912/virtual.php (accessed November 19, 2010).

Horowitz, N. (2001) "The Ultra-Orthodox and the Internet," *Kivumim Hadashim*, 3: 7–30 (in Hebrew).

Jewish Internet Metric Study (2009). Available at: www.scribd.com/doc/19774969/1-Jewish-Internet-Metric-Study

Kravel-Tovi, M. (2009) "To See the Invisible Messiah: Messianic Socialization in the Wake of a Failed Prophecy in Chabad," *Religion* 39(3): 248–60.

Ravitzky, A. (1994) "The Contemporary Lubavitch Hasidic Movement: Between Conservatism and Messianism." In M. E. Marty and R. S. Appleby (eds), *Accounting for*

Fundamentalisms: The Dynamic Character of Movements, 303–27, Chicago: University of Chicago Press.

Rheingold, H. (2000) *The Virtual Community: Homesteading on the Electronic Frontier*, revised edition, Cambridge, MA: MIT Press. See also: www.rheingold.com/vc/book

Shandler, J. (2009) *Jews, God and Videotape: Religion and Media in America*, New York: New York University Press.

Stadler, N. (2009) *Yeshiva Fundamentalism: Piety, Gender and Resistance in the Ultra-Orthodox World*, New York: New York University Press.

Zaleski, J. (1997) *The Soul of Cyberspace*, New York: HarperCollins.

13 Considering religious community through online churches

Tim Hutchings

The emergence of religious communities online facilitates shifts in patterns of commitment and belonging with significant implications for offline activity. This chapter focuses on "community" and pursues three questions concerning discourse, practice, and context: How is the term "community" defined, attributed and contested? What networks, boundaries and norms emerge in spaces defined as "communities"? Finally, how do online communities challenge or support more traditional religious formations?

These questions are particularly relevant where online activity replicates, and thus potentially replaces, characteristics of local religious community. In Christian "online churches," key practices – worship, preaching, prayer, support proselytism – are translated into digital formats and pursued through online media. These churches could compete with their local counterparts, extend their influence, or reflect shifting understandings of what "belonging" to a community entails. Online churches are of great interest to scholars exploring the meaning of community, and have already prompted much discussion in Christian circles about the merits of digital communication (Estes 2009).

Academic attention to online churches has so far focused on virtual worlds and online ritual. The first published study (Schroeder, Heather, and Lee 1998) examined the language of a small charismatic group in a graphical world, framed in terms of a house-group prayer meeting. Subsequent research focused on virtual worlds, specifically Church of Fools (Ostrowski 2006; Jenkins 2008; Kluver and Chen 2008) and Second Life (Robinson-Neal 2008; Miczek 2008), and consistently found that ritual patterns replicate offline forms with limited innovation. Reliance on the familiar also extends to visual design and organizational structure (Hutchings 2010b), serving social, psychological, and theological functions. If visitors are already attuned to a particular religious tradition, then reproducing symbols online signals expectations of behavior, reduces creative demands, and frames the space as an "authentic" Christian church.

Attention to rituals and virtual worlds is justified, but addresses only part of the spectrum of online church activity. Churches have emerged in almost every digital medium, including e-mail lists, chatrooms, websites, forums, video, and social network sites; and text- or broadcast-based groups can dwarf virtual world congregations in size, funding, and persistence. The relative importance of practices also varies, reflecting diverse Christian understandings of "church." The essence of "church" may be found in worship, but also in preaching, participation in wider ecclesial structures, or supportive community, and participants may take little interest in the rituals that researchers have explored.

Research into religious media, from radio and television (Hoover 1988) to the Internet (Campbell 2005), has consistently reported that audiences use mediated resources to augment local activity. According to the Pew "Cyberfaith" survey, for example, "Religion Surfers" see the Internet as "a useful supplemental tool that enhances their already-deep commitment to their beliefs and their churches, synagogues, or mosques" (Larsen 2001, Executive Summary). This general conclusion also applies to the specific case of online churches (Hutchings 2010a). Most participants continue to attend a local church, and those who do not have almost always done so in the past. Online community operates within and responds to larger social contexts, and we must look to these contexts to fully understand the balance of styles, symbols, and practices that emerge online.

Media, theology, and religious activity operate here in a complex, mutually influential relationship. This chapter demonstrates the diverse social formations arising from this interplay by selecting two contrasting online churches, one non-denominational, the other operated by an American Evangelical megachurch. These churches use different media, pursue different goals and have developed different cultures. Each generates different discourses, practices, and offline consequences, deriving in part from rival understandings of what it means to be a "community."

Case study: "St Pixels" and "Church Online"

Methodology

These case studies are based on ethnographic research conducted from 2006 to 2009. Ethnographic methodology involves long-term participant observation of a field site, aiming to understand what practices, structures, and concepts actually mean to participants themselves. This approach is well-suited to the topic of "community," drawing attention to ways in which that term is defined, used and performed, and has been successfully applied to online research for more than a decade (Hine 2000; Boellstorff 2008).

St Pixels (www.stpixels.com) and Church Online (http://live.lifechurch.tv) both operate a central website and Facebook page, but participants also use Facebook groups and profiles, e-mail, instant messaging, telephone, and offline gatherings to develop networks of communication outside these officially supervised spaces. There is no single, bounded field site here: the researcher must construct the object of study by tracing out relationships between different regions of activity. Each region may pose different research opportunities and offer different kinds of information, forcing constant reflection on the most appropriate methods to apply (Marcus 1995: 100).

My own research combines multiple approaches, responding to the different possibilities and limitations of each space and medium. I became a regular visitor to both churches, participating in conversations and worship events and seeking to make connections, gain trust, and develop my own understanding of each community. As a participant, I was able to discuss my experiences and perceptions with others – one of the most important advantages of ethnographic study over purely observation-based research. I also conducted 25 semi-structured, recorded interviews with each group, reflecting a range of views and roles. Most were conducted by telephone, but I also organized face-to-face interviews at offline meets, used in-world text chat with Second Life users, and agreed to interview more cautious participants by e-mail or instant messenger. Each medium favored different kinds of conversation, varying in duration and detail, but useful information emerged from every format. Other methods applied only to one of the case studies: I spent time at Church Online's Second Life campus, analyzed video at the Church Online website, conducted content analysis of month-long samples of St Pixels' forums and blogs, and analyzed any survey data or demographic statistics published by each church.

Variations in medium, practice, community expectations and perceptions of privacy generate unique ethical considerations and opportunities for collaboration. I discussed my research methods with St Pixels members through an on-site blog, but no equivalent platform was available at Church Online. Many St Pixels participants considered their (publicly accessible) church to be a private space, and we agreed that I should only quote material with the author's written consent. At Church Online, the audience for each broadcast is large and ever-changing, and chatroom contributions show no indications that participants are speaking to a private circle of friends. I therefore treated Church Online chatroom postings as public statements that I could quote without author permission, and sought informed consent only when organizing formal interviews. All interviewees apart from paid staff members are referred to in this chapter by pseudonyms.

Case study 1: St Pixels

My first case, St Pixels, is an independent, non-denominational Christian community, founded as "Church of Fools" in 2004 (Jenkins 2008). St Pixels operates a website where registered members can construct a profile, send private messages, write a blog, post to discussion forums, play word games, join a private group for "peer-to-peer discipleship" and access a chatroom for conversation and prayers. Members can also post images and design a cartoon "avatar" for their profile.

St Pixel's core values emphasize respect, honesty, and companionship within a broad Christian framework:

> We aim to create sacred space on the Internet where we can seek God together, enjoy each other's company and reflect God's love for the world. Those of any belief or none are welcome to take part in our activities,

providing they accept the Christian focus of our community and respect other participants.

(acorn 2008)

Forum discussions reflect this diversity, and liberal, Evangelical and Catholic positions are common. Participation is often prompted by offline frustrations. One member visited the forums in search of "the intellectual activity that I craved" after years of childcare, releasing "thoughts that hadn't been expressed for years" (Sandy, telephone interview, May 3, 2008). Another interviewee found escape online from the restrictions of his conservative Protestant local church, and used anonymous online debates to help think through his shift to a more liberal private theology (Daniel, personal interview, February 27, 2008).

Blogs play a more important role in building ties, providing space to "share what is happening in our lives" (Anon., n.d.). According to a forum poster, "Blogs give members the opportunity to share parts of their lives, their joys, sorrows, worries, mountain top experiences or depth of the valley times ... to share in the lives of others as people do off line." Another described blogging as "one of the biggest builders of community we have." Chat is more immediate, but "emotion can be expressed better here." Interviewees agreed: blogging "helps you build up relationships," (Carol, personal interview, February 20, 2008) by "opening a mind" to the reader (April, personal interview, February 14, 2008).

Chat is another key location of community-building conversation. One interviewee explained by instant messaging that "i almost live at st p it seems – there till 4:30 am this morning :-)" (Harriet, personal interview, February 22, 2008). The chatroom is custom-designed to facilitate worship, held up to five times daily during my research. Services follow a liturgical pattern, with prayers, responses and a brief homily, and worship leaders, usually without formal training, can post images and play audio files.

The community is also active beyond the primary website. Many join Facebook to play games. Members participate in exchanges of gifts, books and postcards, organized through the website, and have auctioned artworks for charity. Over 20 offline meets were held in 2008, and the most important, an annual gathering at a member's UK retreat center, developed great cultural significance. Rooms were renamed after sections of the website, online names were used, avatars were worn as badges, and partners and children were decorated with honorary user names. The offline gathering also impacted the online community. Attendees posted updates and photos throughout, telephones and laptops were passed around for conversations with distant friends, and photographs and sounds were recorded for use in chatroom worship throughout the year.

Case study 2: Church Online

Church Online is part of LifeChurch.tv, a "multisite" Evangelical megachurch based in Oklahoma. LifeChurch.tv operates more than a dozen "campuses" in six states and has been named the second largest church in the US (*Outreach*

Magazine, 2009). Each campus uses giant screens to show Pastor Craig Groeschel's sermons, but also has its own local pastor, worship band, and home groups. Churches worldwide can register as "Network" or "Open" partners, receiving free video resources to help structure their activity according to the LifeChurch system.

Church Online was launched in 2006 as an Internet-based campus. Visitors to "Experiences" – services – watch broadcasts, interact through a supervised chatroom, pray with volunteers in one-to-one chat, view a world map marking visitor locations, take electronic notes on the sermon or post pre-scripted invitations to social network sites. No asynchronous interaction is supported – there are no profiles, blogs, or forums – and the chatroom closes shortly after each service.

Chatroom contributions are dominated by enthusiastic responses to video worship and preaching. Sustained conversation was rare during my research, and indeed discouraged. The following chatroom exchange took place in August 2009, scattered over unconnected intervening posts, when a self-described atheist mentioned the Dead Sea Scrolls. Here A is the Church's Online pastor, B the atheist, C a volunteer, and D a visitor.

A: B this is not the place to write me at [e-mail address]. I love the conversation
B: Brandon, why isn't this the place?
B: I mean, that's the purpose of having a chat, right?
C: B – e-mail [e-mail address] and he would love to talk to you about your questions.
A: This chat is built around this video message to the left. It is to help us engage further with the content there
D: B, it's really to keep on track with the teaching going on
D: But B, if you want to keep in touch, I invite you to follow me on Twitter
D: I'm @[Twitter account] I'd like to keep in touch

It is interesting to note D's eagerness to promote himself as a Twitter evangelist, using LifeChurch.tv as a platform for his own ministry.

LifeChurch.tv's declared mission is "to lead people to become fully devoted followers of Christ" (LifeChurch.tv 2011). Church Online is a prominent tool in the LifeChurch arsenal, promoted offline and online through posters, flyers, and electronic invitations. Google Ads target users searching for pornography, and MySpace and Facebook campaigns are regularly announced. Experiences end with a call to conversion, inviting viewers to click a button to announce their decision. New believers can request a "What's Next Kit," containing a Bible and sermon CDs.

More sustained communication takes place in "LifeGroups," meeting through chatrooms, Facebook, Second Life, e-mail lists, and webcam conferences. Church Online also encourages offline "Watch Parties," in which families and friends watch the broadcast together. According to the LifeGroup Pastor, the LifeGroup is "where you're going to develop community, it's where you're going to receive encouragement, it's where you get some accountability ... you can't be known in a crowd" (Davis, personal interview, November 11, 2008). Some participants shared these expectations. One described her LifeGroup as "family," a place where God worked "healing" for her (Pamela, telephone interview, March 10, 2008). For most, however, this high commitment offers little appeal. Groups are rare, and several leaders spoke to me of disappointment. According to one Second Life leader, it was hard "seeing so many people come and go ... I just haven't seen the stability in our group that I would like, and which I think would be easier to maintain in an RL group" (Florence, personal interview, September 22, 2008).

Findings and analysis

St Pixels and Church Online represent different kinds of online "community." St Pixels is highly relational and encourages social interaction alongside prayer and debate. Church Online is much larger, more controlled, and attention is focused on the video stream of officially sanctioned content. Relationships do emerge, particularly in LifeGroups, but few see this as a priority.

Despite these differences, participants in both churches speak warmly of "community." An Austrian woman explained to me that she enjoyed "the community of people [at LifeChurch] who are my age – I'm 30" (Christina, e-mail interview, September 28, 2008). Community existed at Church Online because "people are ACTUALLY THERE. It's this virtual place where they meet, but the way they participate online is real: they sing, listen, take notes, talk to each other, etc. With their minds, people are at the same place at the same time." When I asked about relationships, she replied:

> No, I haven't started to make friends there, and it isn't important to me. It's a process that takes time, and one that is usually based on sharing a certain life situation, helping each other, similar interests, etc. ... doing life together, I guess.

Community here is separate from "sharing life," the phrase used so often to describe the core purpose and highest value of St Pixels.

If the "community" of St Pixels emerges through electronic sharing, the "community" of Church Online is better understood as a movement. Visitors are connected to one another through their shared attention to and support for the work of LifeChurch.tv, and demonstrate that connection by expressing their appreciation. Leaders seek to promote a more active, relational understanding of "community" through videos and sermons, encouraging viewers to join LifeGroups, volunteer as chatroom coordinators, post to the Facebook page and invite their friends to Church Online, but this attempt to redefine "community" through performance and discourse has limited impact on actual viewer behavior.

The movement community of Church Online and the relational community of St Pixels relate in different ways to local churches worldwide. St Pixels builds community with those who come to its website, but Church Online promotes itself vigorously by distributing resources to global networks of church partners and undertaking online evangelism projects. LifeChurch.tv is both friend and rival to local churches, offering material free of charge while demonstrating a level of rhetorical and media talent that local preachers will struggle to match. In each case, I encountered a minority who had chosen to attend no local church, either through ill health or previous negative experiences, but only in Church Online did I meet individuals who simply thought the quality of online ministry was better.

Conclusion

This chapter began with three questions, regarding the definition, structure and offline impact of online community. As we have seen, St Pixels and Church Online suggest different answers. St Pixels understands "community" as the practice of "sharing life," and has developed a network of blogs, forums, chatroom events, and offline meets. Church Online has created a "community" that emphasizes shared ideas over relationships, a discipleship movement based on broadcasts and advertising. Each church primarily attracts offline churchgoers, but offers them different possibilities: St Pixels has created space for debate and friendship, while Church Online offers world-class preaching and the chance to share in an evangelism movement that claims to be highly successful.

At the level of official discourse, these differences are somewhat less apparent. The pastors of Church Online emphasize the importance of relationships, tell stories of successful Watch Parties and encourage viewers to join a LifeGroup or comment on the church Facebook page. Discipleship, they explain, demands that believers become active, involved, and accountable. Audience response is mixed, and the frequency and tone of these requests – framed as an option the viewer really should explore – suggest leadership concern that the majority are too comfortable in their passive anonymity.

As suggested in the introduction, each church develops through the interplay of theology, practice, and media. The combination of video feed and chatroom encourages a particular kind of focus in Church Online, well suited to a preaching-oriented ecclesiology, while the custom-designed St Pixels chatroom demonstrates an attempt to enhance the fit between theology and setting by creating new digital tools. Leaders, participants, supporters, and critics are all involved in an ongoing exchange of ideas and actions, seeking to shape the emergence of the forms of "community" they deem theologically and socially desirable. Practice, discourse and offline significance will continue to be shaped through these many factors, in ways that are not yet fixed or predictable.

Discussion questions

- Does the word "community" mean something different online and offline? How does a group's understanding of "community" change when that group becomes active online?

- Who decides what "community" means? How do they persuade others to accept their definition, and what do they gain from doing so?
- In what ways do online communities challenge or support local religious commitments or involvement?

References

acorn (2008) "Our core values." Online: www.stpixels.com/article?article=54bdb29d-03f0–4a18-ab65–2dc59c7ff102 (accessed January 31, 2011).

Anon. (n.d.) "Explore St Pixels blogs." Online. Available: www.stpixels.com/intro-users (accessed January 31, 2011).

April (February 14, 2008) Personal Interview in Manchester, UK.

Boellstorff, T. (2008) *Coming of Age in Second Life: An Anthropologist Explores the Virtually Human*. Woodstock: Princeton University Press.

Campbell, H. (2005) *Exploring Religious Community Online: We Are One in the Network*. New York: Peter Lang.

Carol (February 20, 2008) Personal Interview by telephone.

Christina (September 28, 2008) Personal interview by e-mail.

Daniel (February 27, 2008) Personal Interview by telephone.

Davis, R. (November 11, 2008) Personal Interview in Oklahoma, US.

Estes, D. (2009) *SimChurch: Being the Church in the Virtual World*. Grand Rapids: Zondervan.

Florence (September 22, 2008) Personal Interview via Second Life text.

Harriet (February 22, 2008) Personal Interview via MSN.

Hine, C. (2000) *Virtual Ethnography*. London: Sage Publications.

Hoover, S. (1988) *Mass Media Religion: The Social Sources of the Electronic Church*. London: Sage Publications.

Hutchings, T. (2010a) *Creating Church Online: An Ethnographic Study of Five Internet-Based Christian Communities*. Unpublished PhD thesis, Durham University.

——(2010b) "The politics of familiarity: visual, liturgical and organizational conformity in the online church." *Online – Heidelberg Journal of Religions on the Internet* 4(1): 63–86. Online. Available: http://archiv.ub.uni-heidelberg.de/volltextserver/volltexte/2010/11298/pdf/04.pdf (accessed January 31, 2011).

Jenkins, S. (2008) "Rituals and pixels: experiments in an online church." *Online – Heidelberg Journal of Religions on the Internet* 3(1): 95–115. Online. Available: http://archiv.ub.uni-heidelberg.de/volltextserver/volltexte/2008/8291/pdf/jenkins.pdf (accessed January 31, 2011).

Kluver, R. and Chen, Y. (2008) "The Church of Fools: virtual ritual and material faith." *Online – Heidelberg Journal of Religions on the Internet* 3(1): 116–43. Online. Available: http://archiv.ub.uni-heidelberg.de/volltextserver/volltexte/2008/8292/pdf/Kluver.pdf (accessed January 31, 2011).

Larsen, E. (2001) "Cyberfaith: how Americans pursue religion online." *Pew Internet and American Life Project*, December 21. Online. Available: www.pewInternet.org/Reports/2001/Cyber Faith-How-Americans-Pursue-Religion-Online.aspx (accessed January 31, 2011).

LifeChurch.tv (2011) "Welcome to LifeChurch.tv." Online. Available: http://www.lifechurch.tv/who-we-are (accessed January 31, 2011).

Marcus, G. (1995) "Ethnography in/of the world system: the emergence of multi-sited ethnography." *Annual Review of Anthropology* 24: 95–117.

Miczek, N. (2008) "Online rituals in virtual worlds: Christian online services between dynamics and stability." *Online – Heidelberg Journal of Religions on the Internet* 3(1): 144–73.

Online. Available: http://archiv.ub.uni-heidelberg.de/volltextserver/volltexte/2008/8293/pdf/nadja.pdf (accessed January 31, 2011).

Ostrowski, A. (2006) "Cyber communion: finding God in the little box." *Journal of Religion and Society* 8. Online. Available: http://moses.creighton.edu/JRS/2006/2006–10.html (accessed January 31, 2011).

Outreach Magazine (2009) "2009 Outreach 100 tracks top U.S. churches." October 2. Online. Available: www.outreachmagazine.com/resources/outreach100/2009-outreach100/3158-2009-Outreach-100-Tracks-Top-Churches.html (accessed 31 January 2011).

Pamela (March 10, 2008) Telephone Interview.

Robinson-Neal, A. (2008) "Enhancing the spiritual relationship: the impact of virtual worship on the real world church experience." *Online – Heidelberg Journal of Religions on the Internet* 3(1): 228–45. Online. Available: http://archiv.ub.uni-heidelberg.de/volltextserver/volltexte/2008/8293/pdf/nadja.pdf (accessed January 31, 2011).

Sandy (May 3, 2008) Telephone Interview.

Schroeder, R., Heather, N. and Lee, R. (1998) "The sacred and the virtual: religion in multi-user virtual reality." *Journal of Computer-Mediated Communication* 4(2). Online. Available: http://jcmc.indiana.edu/vol4/issue2/schroeder.html (accessed January 31, 2011).

14 The kosher cell phone in ultra-Orthodox society

A technological ghetto within the global village?

Tsuriel Rashi

As modernity and secularization swept from west to east across Europe in the nineteenth century, some Jewish religious leaders (especially in Eastern Europe) spoke out fiercely against the changes in an attempt to forestall an inevitable wave of assimilation. Members of the Orthodox community who were opposed to such social and religious changes came to be known as "Haredim," literally "fearers" (of heaven) (Heilman and Friedman 1991). This opposition included a fear or concern about media.

In recent years, a number of studies have been conducted on the way the Jewish ultra-Orthodox (Haredi) community generally views modernization and digitalization (Zarfati and Blais 2002; Friedman 2006) and particularly how it relates to the Internet (Livio and Weinblatt 2007; Horowitz 2000; Rovanna 2007). The unique social structure of ultra-Orthodox society has also received attention (Friedman 1991; Grylak 2002; Caplan 2007), as has the ultra-Orthodox media and its status within that society (Caplan 2001; Friedman, I 2005; Rashi 2011). This case study seeks to explore these complex issues through surveys of the factors behind a three-year ultra-Orthodox campaign (from late 2004 to the beginning of 2007) against third-generation (3G) cell phones. Ultra-Orthodox community media played an important role in this public struggle, which forced Israeli cell phone companies to produce and market a "kosher" phone that would not have Internet or SMS capability and would block access to "indecent" phone numbers such as erotic and gambling services. The case of the kosher phone demonstrates that, by exploiting the print media, the religious leadership managed to partially block 3G cell phones and to reaffirm and enhance their status within the community.

Methodology

This study explores ultra-Orthodox Israelis' concerns about and resistance to the introduction of 3G phones into their community, which were deemed harmful to moral and social aspects of their society. This is done by investigating the role mass communication (newspapers and posters) played in framing the public struggle against these cell phones and the impact of this victory for the wider ultra-Orthodox community. In order to analyze the struggle, issues of two ultra-Orthodox daily newspapers in Israel, *Hamodia* and *Yated Ne'eman*, from December 2004 to February 2007 were examined, including news reports, editorials and op-ed articles, letters to the editor, official announcements, and advertisements. A qualitative content analysis of this material was performed in order to examine the positioning and degree of prominence of the various items. The study took into account the nature of the discourse, the language, and the dominant themes and argumentation employed, to frame the events surrounding the rise of the kosher phone. To complete the picture, *pashkvilim* (wall posters commonly displayed in ultra-Orthodox communities) that related to the kosher phone were examined for the same period. *Pashkvilim* serve as an important form of communication for the ultra-Orthodox, providing information on upcoming events, promoting issues affecting the community, and serving as advertisements related to community issues.

Case study in context: the beginning of the campaign and its driving force

The kosher cell phone campaign started when a member of one of the ultra-Orthodox sects working with a group of youth at risk discovered young people were using 3G phones to surf the Internet and enter chat rooms, forums, and other sites perceived as immodest. Various attempts made by community leaders to get the cell phone companies to block built-in surfing on the Internet and to avoid selling the 3G cell phones in ultra-Orthodox areas were unsuccessful, until in the summer of 2004 a group of rabbis from different ultra-Orthodox sects established the Rabbi's Committee for Communications Issues to deal with the "problem" of the 3G phones. One of the committee's first steps was to ban advertising by all Israeli cell phone companies (including Cellcom, Orange, Pelephone, and Mirs) in any ultra-Orthodox newspapers until they agreed to three conditions:

1 They were to provide and market a cell phone without Internet access.
2 There was to be external identification of those models to clearly identify a "kosher" phone.
3 They were to formalize an association with the committee of rabbis by signing a contract.

(Grobies 2005)

Five months later, in December 2004, the heads of the ultra-Orthodox educational systems held an urgent meeting at which "war" was formally declared against the cell phone companies and the 3G phones until the demands of the committee were met; plans were also made to hold a major conference. The ultra-Orthodox newspaper *Hamodia* published editorials informing the public about the resolutions made at the meeting: the use of cell phones by yeshiva students and girls studying at ultra-Orthodox seminaries would be absolutely forbidden (December 19, 2004, editorial; September 29, 2005, editorial).

Adults were requested in an editorial in the newspaper *Yated Ne'eman* to restrict their use of 3G phones and not to enter into financial obligations with cell phone companies (December 6, 2004, editorial).

The ultra-Orthodox press mobilized to solidify the status and power of the rabbis by publishing information about the upcoming conference, including pictures of the preparations for the conference itself. In January 2005 it published warnings and examples cited by the rabbis about the physical and emotional damage reportedly caused by cell phones, along with notices banning their use and front-page decrees calling for such a ban, such as the one in *Hamodia* under the heading "According to the Torah and Halakhah" (May 16, 2005, editorial) The conference was held in March 2005 and six months later the Mirs cell phone company signed a contract with the committee. Pelephone and Cellcom signed up at the end of August 2005 and Orange followed suit in April 2006. Notwithstanding a plethora of important issues on the national and international agenda, the successful campaign to market the kosher cell phone generated interest in major international media (Friedman, I 2005; MacKinnon 2005; Holmes 2006; Sarmad 2006) and the struggle against 3G phones received extensive and prominent coverage.

The rhetorical framing of the campaign

The analysis presented in the next few sections examines specific concepts and language used by ultra-Orthodox newspapers in their coverage of the emergence of the kosher phone. These papers tried to frame the campaign in terms of an all-out war against 3G phones. Several rhetorical strategies are explored in relation to how the public were encouraged to see this as (a) a community-wide mobilization and struggle against the phone, (b) a call for ostracism of those who evaded the "war," and (c) a way to build or affirm obedience to community leadership.

"Our cities are on fire": language of an historic all-out war

Throughout the entire campaign, the press used warlike language. Although this rhetoric is common in the ultra-Orthodox press when dealing with issues it chooses to oppose, it reached new heights in the struggle against the 3G phone. Against the backdrop of the preparations for the March 2005 conference on the matter, the press defined the struggle as "war, a struggle for our Jewish lives to which we have no alternative" (Tennenbaum 2004). It seems that as early as the beginning of the campaign ultra-Orthodox press wanted readers to understand that the "war" had reached its climax: a headline in *Hamodia* announced that "our cities are on fire" (December 15, 2004). One of the *pashkvilim* that appeared in Jerusalem and B'nei B'rak announced that "the battle is at its peak" and another warned against the dangers of the 3G phones, concluding that "we must defend ourselves against the enemy's network." "Warlike" headlines continued to appear in various articles, editorials, and letters to the editor. Three months after the "declaration of war," one of the *Yated Ne'eman* reporters called for a "blitz" (Ze'evi 2005). The 3G phone was described in militaristic terms, for example as a "mine" (Gilbo'a 2006) and a "biological bomb" (Sofer 2005).

After the four contracts negotiated between cell phone companies and the rabbis' committee were signed, and the cell phone companies agreed not to sell 3G phones in the ultra-Orthodox community, the ultra-Orthodox press reported that they had "surrendered" and hailed this "war of survival" as part of the struggle against secularity and another heroic historical struggle in the annals of the Jewish people. The first conference, which had brought the religious leadership together to announce the opening of the campaign, was referred to as "historic" and the process itself was called "an astounding social revolution" (Cohen 2005).

"Those who join the enemy – out": ostracism of anyone not taking part in the "war"

Describing this as a "war of survival" of historic proportions mandated the mobilization of the entire ultra-Orthodox population. Individuals and businesses that did not join in the effort were condemned. For example, when some newspapers continued carrying cell phone company advertisements past the stated ban, contravening the dictates of the rabbis, the Rabbis' Committee for Communication Issues published a protest condemning them (*Hamodia*, June 10, 2005, p. b; *Yated Ne'eman* June 10, 2005, p. 2).

At the same time, the gap between the reality of the response to the rabbis' call and the picture presented to ultra-Orthodox readers was significant. There were approximately 350,000 potential cell phone subscribers within the ultra-Orthodox community. At the beginning of 2007, a total of 135,000 individuals owned cell phones. The phone companies did not provide accurate information, but the estimate was that the distribution of subscribers at the peak of the struggle in 2007 was as follows: 80,000 Orange subscribers had 3G phones and 20,000 had kosher cell phones; 60,000 Pelephone subscribers had 3G phones and 30,000 had kosher cell phones; and 85,000 Cellcom subscribers had 3G phones and 46,000 had kosher cell phones (Ettinger 2007).

Even though many people did not follow the rabbis' orders to buy only kosher cell phones, those who disobeyed were referred to as the "the very last that have not transferred to a kosher phone, the fringe element of the camp" (Bar-Yosef 2006) and as "the rebellious fringe element," in direct contrast to the majority, who obediently changed phones (Levor 2007). Similarly, *pashkvilim* in Jerusalem announced that "indeed all of them have returned," saying that:

> thousands of people have signed and promised not to give their children cellular phones, to make every effort to ensure that their own phones are blocked to every undesirable line or program, and to help the community in the efforts to build a clean and kosher system.

At one point, Ariel Attias, the ultra-Orthodox Minister of Communication for the Israeli government, was vilified by community reports for stating in an interview that only 30,000 of the ultra-Orthodox community's reported 200,000 cell phones were kosher, which suggested that many members of the ultra-Orthodox community did not obey their rabbis. However, according to one ultra-Orthodox reporter, cell phone company data revealed that 90,000 kosher phones were sold (Hanoch 2006). Nevertheless, based on reports in ultra-Orthodox newspapers, community members were made to feel that if they changed their phones they were making the right decision, backed by the highest spiritual authority, and that those who did not do so belonged to the minority, victims of their own base desires, and should be seen as outcasts.

"Nothing can stop us from accomplishing our goals": obedience to the ban affirms community leadership

For the purpose of making the kosher phone successful and the consumer ban on the cell phone companies effective, it was stated that absolute obedience to the rabbis was necessary, as echoed in an editorial in *Hamodia*: "There is no half-hearted obedience, no conditional obedience and no considerations of convenience, comfort etc" (March 20, 2005). This call for complete obedience was presented as a halakhic obligation (March 11, 2005) and portrayed as an accepted tradition (Hanoch 2006). For instance, when Mirs agreed to abide by the rabbis' conditions, a front-page news item in the ultra-Orthodox press told people to only use the Mirs kosher phone (March 11, 2005). *Pashkvilim* showed models of the approved cell phones with a headline that read, "observe and do whatever you are taught," a verse from Deuteronomy 17:10 demanding obedience to the Sanhedrin.

Some publicists went further and made a connection between the warning against 3G phones and the words of the prophet Amos (3:6): "Shall a shofar be sounded in the city and the people not be afraid?!" (Gerlitz 2004). The demand for obedience was even used to underscore the reliability of one Cellcom distributor in an ultra-Orthodox neighborhood in Jerusalem, who advertised the reopening of his shop on the front page of *Hamodia* and *Yated Ne'eman* after Cellcom signed up with the committee of rabbis on media matters. His ad noted, "We have been closed for six months by order of our Torah sages, but now you are invited to sanctify the Holy Name by buying one of these Cellcom cell phones in our store" (August 31, 2005).

During the struggle and its aftermath, obedience to the rabbis, which was credited for eventual victory over the threat of the 3G phone, was presented as a fundamental, legitimate halakhic obligation that was essential for the future of the community. After Cellcom and Pelephone signed the contract, an editorial in *Hamodia* attributed the success to the people of the community, who had obeyed their rabbis (August 13, 2005).

Outcomes of the ban for the wider ultra-Orthodox community

The victory of the ultra-Orthodox leadership over the cell phone companies in Israel created waves in other Jewish communities around the world and engendered discussion about the future of relations between ultra-Orthodox society and the business world. Ultra-Orthodox American rabbis signed a contract with the American cell phone company Sprint to market kosher phones (Baum 2006). The initiative failed for financial reasons, but the American ultra-Orthodox leadership's desire to emulate the Israeli model is still very strong (Nathan 2007). The 3G campaign clearly demonstrated that the battle against the cell phone companies was not so much about consumer power, but more about control and societal discipline. It became very clear that it is such discipline, coupled with community mobilization, that leads to effective consumer power in the marketplace.

Consumer power and the discipline that this initiative created were expressed not only in the actions of the public, but also in the conduct of the newspapers' editorial boards. According to Tzippi Rotlevi, marketing manager of *Yated Ne'eman*, the ban on the cell phone companies began when their advertising was at its peak, causing the newspaper a loss of millions of dollars in revenue (Rotem 2007). Readers and rabbis alike lauded the ultra-Orthodox press for joining in the struggle by refusing advertising from the cell phone companies as the rabbis had decreed, and for developing a media response to the public ban on 3G phones. This praise was published in the form of editorials (December 17, 2004), articles (Kahan 2006), and letters to the editor (April 19, 2005). Furthermore, after the first three companies began to market kosher phones, *Hamodia* advertised on its front page that, beginning on October 1, 2005, it would not publish unauthorized or "non-kosher" phone numbers (September 27, 2005), describing this step as "a most basic, necessary, self-explanatory obligation" (October 2, 2005).

Discussion: influence and lessons of the kosher phone campaign

The ultra-Orthodox battle against the private use of 3G phones was only partially successful: tens of thousands did indeed buy the kosher phones, but many in the ultra-Orthodox community did not. Moreover, some of the tens of thousands who did subscribe to kosher cell phones held on to their 3G models. On the other hand, publicly the victory was more complete. After the campaign, displaying a non-kosher cell phone in public caused the user considerably more discomfort. That the victory was only a partial one was clear not only from the numbers, but also from words and actions. So much talk about the importance of obedience to the rabbis indicates that this value was not fully implemented in spite of the unequivocal ultra-Orthodox educational-ethical line on this issue. Indeed, the fact that sanctions regarding the acceptance into ultra-Orthodox educational institutions of children whose parents owned non-kosher cell phones was published more than two years after the opening of the campaign, when victory cries were already being heard, speaks louder than a hundred witnesses.

However, notwithstanding the fact that it was only a partial victory, the kosher cell phone campaign still serves as a case study through which we can look at religious authoritarianism in a society that cuts itself off from the outside world and views any intrusion, particularly that of advanced technology, as a potential threat that must be countered. The nature of ultra-Orthodox conduct and the degree of success in the campaign might well provide a theoretical infrastructure for examining similar cases in closed groups of other religions. A number of different methods were used by community leaders to create a system that preserves the authority of the existing leadership. First, educators were approached and told to enforce the cell phone ban in the part of the community under their authority – the students at various educational institutions. At the same time, the ultra-Orthodox press emphasized the ban, at the same time as identifying potential dangers of cell phones.

The ultra-Orthodox news media played an important role in relating, albeit in a biased fashion, different aspects of the situation: it presented the battle over the cell phone as a historic struggle, linked to a chain of struggles faced by the ultra-Orthodox in society due to their values and way of life. Press accounts presented the community as dichotomized between those who obey their spiritual leaders, who will be rewarded spiritually and gain joy from their children, and those who disobey the leadership, bringing tragedy upon themselves and the society in which they live. The media presented the obedient as the majority and the disobedient as an ostracized minority. Threats and sanctions accompanied the rhetoric published in the newspapers, which throughout the whole period continued to call for an uncompromising consumer ban, on the one hand, and unfailing loyalty to the firms that met the religious leadership's demands, on the other. Israel's ultra-Orthodox community managed to derail technological inroads it deemed harmful to its society when such curtailment was so clearly running against the tide of the current trends in worldwide culture. This was achieved largely through the support of its print media (newspapers and *pashkvilim*), which assisted the leadership in its efforts to persuade people to resist the temptation of 3G phones.

Technological progress in the form of the cellular revolution was interpreted by the rabbis as causing a war of survival that threatened the identity of their community and its established centers of authority. We can learn from this case study that, even though it seemed that the centers of power would collapse under the temptations offered by modernity that followed the advent of new media, religious authorities, through the daily newspapers and *pashkvilim*, were able to retain their power. This shows that anyone who believes that hierarchical religious societies can easily be pulled down by technology in the hands of the younger generation may well be mistaken.

Discussion questions

- Do you think other religious societies could reproduce such a campaign, which here kept power in the hands of traditional religious authorities (i.e. the rabbis) in the ultra-Orthodox Jewish community?
- Which factors within new media culture might challenge the control or influence of established leaders within a given religious community?

References

Bar-Yosef, N. (2006) "A Year Since the Kosher Cellular Revolution," *Yated Ne'eman*, February 7, p. 11. [In Hebrew.]

Baum, K. (2006) "After Orange Surrendered, the Kosher Cellular Hit New York." www.scoop.co.il/article.html?id=2060 (accessed May 25, 2006). [In Hebrew.]

Caplan, K. (2001) "The Media in Haredi Society in Israel," *Kesher*, 30: 18–30. [In Hebrew.]

——(2007) *Internal Popular Discourse in Israeli Haredi Society*, Zalman Shazar Center, Jerusalem. [In Hebrew.]

Cohen, A. (2005) "The Sages Helped," *Yated Ne'eman Yated – This Week supplement*, December 23, p. 28–30. [In Hebrew.]

Ettinger, Y. (2007) "Rabbi Elyashiv: Ultra-Orthodox Schools Will Not Accept Students Whose Parents Do Not Have a Kosher Cellular," *Ha'aretz*, February 4, p. 11a. [In Hebrew.]

Friedman, I. (2005) "Meeting Modernity," *The Jerusalem Report*, June 13, p. 12.

Friedman, M. (1991) *The Haredi Ultra-Orthodox Society: Sources Trends and Processes*, The Jerusalem Institute for Israel Studies, Jerusalem. [In Hebrew.]

——(2005) *The Pashqevil (Pasquinade) and Public Wall Poster/Bulletin Board Announcements in Haredi (Ultra-Orthodox) Society: The Exhibition Catalog in the Eretz-Israel Museum (June–July 2005)*, The Eretz-Israel Museum and Yad Ben-Zvi, Tel-Aviv-Jerusalem. [In Hebrew.]

——(2006) "Dreading Technology and Progress: The Penetration of Digitalization to the Religious Sector," *Z'man Digitali*, 11: 28–33. [In Hebrew.]

Gerlitz, M. (2004) "Can a Man Take Fire in His Bosom?" *Hamodia*, December 23, p. c. [In Hebrew.]

Gilbo'a, A. (2006) "A Dangerous Mine at Home," *Hamodi'a*, June 13, p. 3. [In Hebrew].

Grobies, A. (2005) "The Cellular Struggle and Its Aspects," *Hamodia*, March 18, p. g. [In Hebrew.]

Grylak, M. (2002) *The Haredim: Who Are We Really?* Keter, Jerusalem. [In Hebrew.]

Hanoch, A. (2006) "The Joy of Obedience," *Hamodia*, June 30, p. c. [In Hebrew.]

Heilman, S.C. and Friedman, M. (1991) *The Haredim in Israel: Who Are They and What Do They Want?* New York: [s.n.].

Holmes, K.E. (2006) "A Call from above: Religion Finds a Way to Keep Up With Technology," *The Philadelphia Inquirer*, October 14, p. B4.

Horowitz, N. (2000) "The Ultra-Orthodox and the Internet," *Kivunim Chadashim*, 3: 7–30. [In Hebrew.]

Kahan, B. (2006) "Partner-Orange to Supply Cellular Phones Approved by The Council of Rabbis for Media Matters," *Yated Ne'eman*, April 11, p. 2. [In Hebrew.]

Levor, A. (2007) "Everybody Has Reached the Same Conclusion," *Hamodia-madorim*, January 15, pp. 16–17. [In Hebrew.]

Livio, O. and Weinblatt, K. T. (2007) "Discursive Legitimating of a Controversial Technology: Ultra-Orthodox Jewish Women in Israel and the Internet," *The Communication Review*, 10(1): 29–56.

MacKinnon, I. (2005) "Kosher Phone Taps into New Market for Mobiles," *The Times*, March 3. www.timesonline.co.uk/tol/news/world/middle_east/article417509.ece (accessed April 20, 2007).

Nathan, D. (2007) "Orthodox Jewish Group Sues Sprint over 'Kosher Phone' Deal," http://news.findlaw.com/andrews/bt/tel/20061215/20061215_yeshiva.html (accessed January 3, 2007).

Rashi, T. (2011) "Divergent Attitudes within Orthodox Jewry toward Mass Communication," *The Review of Communication*, 11(1): 20–38.

Rotem, T. (2007) "More Than Anything I Wanted to Succeed," *Ha'aretz – This Week*, April 8, p. 20. [In Hebrew.]

Rovanna, G. (2007) "The Penetration of the Internet into the Religious and Ultra-Orthodox Society (Fears, Problems and Solutions)," *Tzohar*, 27: 55–68. [In Hebrew.]

Sarmad, A. (2006) "New Cell Phone Services Put God on the Line," *Wall Street Journal*, March 27. http://online.wsj.com/public/article/SB114342358113508709-V7XmysEhOqxO_fUfy3FqdrPzNgI_20070327.html (accessed March 27, 2007).

Sofer, B.S. (2005) "Happy Is He Who Is Always Fearful," *Hamodia*, May 6, p. d. [In Hebrew.]

Tennenbaum, Y.M. (2004) "The Cellular 'Persecutor,'" *Hamodia*, December 3, p. c. [In Hebrew.]

Zarfati, O. and Blais, D. (2002) "Between 'Cultural Enclave' and 'Virtual Enclave': Haredi Society and the Digital Media," *Kesher*, 32: 47–55. [In Hebrew.]

Ze'evi, N. (2005) "Indeed, We Are the Market Powers," *Yated Ne'eman*, March 13, p. 5. [In Hebrew.]

15 Formation of a religious Technorati
Negotiations of authority among Australian emerging church blogs

Paul Emerson Teusner

The extent to which traditional and institutional patterns of authority are reflected, reinforced and/or challenged in online settings of social interaction is a question of interest among many who study religion online. Web 2.0 applications, such as blogs, carry with them the promise of creating democratizing space, where anyone with access to online media production may have an equal voice on the Web. However, some users' voices in the blogosphere are considered more authoritative than others, especially since search engines like Google and Technorati have come to measure the perceived performance of authority online. This raises important issues of how the blogosphere shapes religious discourse and authority.

Web logs, commonly known as blogs, have emerged in the last decade to become an important vehicle for self-publishing and expression online. Blogging was introduced in 1999 as a platform on which personal web pages could easily be updated, without having to edit the entire page. Users would enter text that would appear as "posts," arranged in reverse chronological order, so that the web page would resemble an online journal, made publicly available on the Net. Over time, new features were added to the blogging platform, which facilitated the conversational element of this medium. "Comments" features enable readers of blog pages to respond to posts with their own opinions, starting a conversation between blog authors ("bloggers") and their audiences via entire threads of interactions recorded online. "Permalinks" allow posts and their ensuing comments to have their own URL, thereby enabling bloggers to refer back to a previous article via these links. "Tagging" allows bloggers to assign one or more keywords to a blog post that can later be sorted by topic for readers. These features also allowed search engines to identify and collect the permalinks and tags of multiple bloggers' posts so they could be easily sorted and accessed by readers.

Technorati is a search engine that collects information from blog pages and arranges them according to tags, making blog posts accessible to a wider audience. The Technorati search engine also allows posts to be ranked by popularity, or "authority," as determined by the number of permalinks published on other blogs within a given time period (Blood 2004; Bortree 2005; Kumar *et al.* 2004). These features became important tools in helping facilitate online conversation as well as analyzing the influence of blogging conversation in society. It also means the name "Technorati" is often synonymous with the idea of one having influence and authority online, especially in the blogosphere.

These new additions to the technology have enabled blogs to evolve from simple web publishing tools to global social networking platforms. Blogs become sites for interaction between multiple users, where issues of public interest can be explored and discussed across a multitude of sites, offering a wide range of opinions and perspectives. Thus, in the last decade the blogosphere has rapidly emerged as an important alternative source of information, challenging the power of institutional mass media and their prominent voices of authority (Beer and Burrows 2007; Efimova and de Moor 2005).

Blogging raises important issues related to religious authority online. Recent research has shown that the Internet provides an alternative space for the construction of religious identity, free from the constraints of institutional authority and with the potential to create and explore new symbolic practices (Lövheim and Linderman 2005). Blogging also promises a democratization of voices and the freedom to express personal views on public religious issues, and the capacity to create global networks to share information and resources, find support and care, and build trusting relationships (Cheong *et al.* 2008; Murley 2005).

For those who feel excluded or silenced in their local faith communities, the blogosphere provides a public voice and a space to be heard. Of key importance here is how the blogosphere offers emerging church bloggers the potential to create alternative voices of authority on issues of theology, leadership and polity in religious institutions. Blogging presents an opportunity to explore and develop religious identity in an open and public forum that allows one to question cultural, symbolic, economic, and theological practices of modern church life in ways not often possible within traditional religious institutions.

This case study explores the challenges these online conversational spaces can pose to traditional understandings of religious authority, through the lens of Christian bloggers who associate themselves with the emerging church. The central question being explored is: What attracts people to use blogging to create a voice on issues of religion, and on what conditions are some religious bloggers considered more authoritative than others? This case study addresses this question by examining the posts and comments of twenty Australian religious bloggers involved in the emerging church movement over two three-month periods, and by analyzing the network of links between blogs in the same sample.

Case study: emerging church bloggers in Australia

This case study looks at 20 bloggers from a variety of Protestant and Evangelical faith traditions in Australia. Through their online activities, they are networked with a global group of bloggers who associate themselves with what is sometimes called the "emerging church" or "missional" movement. Functioning more like a conversation than a movement, those in this study who connect with the emerging church seek to instigate change within their denominations, rather than the establishment of a new church. Those associated with the emerging church tend to show disillusionment with both the structures and rituals of mainstream Protestantism, and the perceived consumerist attitudes of modern Evangelicalism, or "mega-churches." The movement tends to favor close, intimate communities, the proper use of new media technologies and the engagement of lay leadership. The bloggers in this study use phrases like "in exile" from their denomination, "looking for something different," or even "churchless" to describe their sense of affiliation with the tradition of their upbringing and they use blogging to confess their needs and seek like minds.

The emerging church movement is attractive to those who have a strong disaffection with current church structures that divide clergy from the rest of the church, including, at times, its academic theological institutions. People in the emerging church seek new ways to talk about theology, which promotes the involvement of those who do not have access to formal theological education, incorporates new everyday language and symbols, and affirms the contribution of minority groups, especially women and young people. They find that discursive practices have developed that determine bloggers' place within the movement and that patterns of authority have even emerged. Ironically, those who use blogging to explore their place in the Christian church offline discover that they must also negotiate authority within the online community. Thus, these bloggers represent an interesting group to study when considering how authority is presented and perceived online.

In order to determine this sample of Australian emerging church bloggers, a keyword search was conducted via Technorati in April 2006 to identify bloggers associated with the tags "emerging church," "emergent church" and "postmodern church." Over 150 blogs were identified in the search, ordered according to their "authority" (i.e. ranked according to the number of links found on the Internet that point to their sites, according to Technorati's search engine). Within this sample, attention is given to the 20 blogs written by Australians. The majority of bloggers were men; two blogs were authored by women, and another was authored by a male-female couple. Over half ($n = 11$) of these bloggers were working professionally in a religious setting (i.e. were ministers or other forms of clergy, held positions in church administration offices, or coordinated church-based projects). For this sample, all blog entries posted between the periods July 1 to October 31, 2006 and February 1 to May 31, 2007 were collected, plus up to 28 days' comments after each post. In addition, during these sample periods, hyperlinked references to other bloggers in the sample were counted.

Blog posts and perception of authority

Within the time periods stated above, approximately 80 posts were read that contained bloggers' opinions about the emerging church blogosphere and thus provided insight into what attracts people to religious blogging and how authority is established or perceived online. In these posts, bloggers discussed the benefits of blogging about religion, what makes someone an authoritative blogger, and the effectiveness of Technorati's authority rankings as a measure of good blogging practice.

Data collected from blog posts and conversations show these religious bloggers have much to say about the perceived benefits of blogging, such as providing a space to discuss religion and finding people who will listen. For many writers, blogging provides an opportunity for sharing stories and developing relationships outside the confines of an institutional church. For those involved in the emerging church, which seeks to discuss the reform of traditional forms of church, the blogosphere is seen as valued space and an extension of the movement's ethos. Making connections and developing relationships online is viewed positively by bloggers, as a source of support for people who may otherwise be isolated.

Yet these writers acknowledge that the blogosphere has negative potential. Some lament the narcissistic attitude with which people approach online social media technologies. They criticize bloggers for whom counting visitors, rather than connecting with people, is a primary goal. Bloggers in the sample would rather develop deep connections with a few people who read and comment on their work than know they have a vast but passive global audience. This highlights that, for these bloggers, online authority is connected to the quality of one's online contributions rather than the volume of one's posts or social network. For example:

> It truly is the deep engagements that count. I prefer one good face to face conversation to a dozen blog hits. That's the influence I live for, to spend time sharing with others in the spiritual journey. And I get far more gratification out of interacting with people in comments and private emails than watching my tracker.
>
> (Matt, blog post, July 21, 2006)

Blogging is considered by some in the sample as an important component of professional ministry. Connecting with people on the Internet is seen as an extension of their offline work and carries with it similar ethical expectations for these clergy. Certain blogging conventions are identified as important for online professional conduct, including responding to comments with respect and citing references and hyperlinks. These practices are equated with the behavioral expectation of proper Christian practice, thus online practice is informed by offline expectations.

> Citing your sources models your approach to research, to breadth of reading and filtering information. Linkage models discernment. Finally, a failure to link well breaks the blogosphere … . These kinds of ethical considerations also apply to comments. In part, this is why I think it is helpful for pastors (and theological educators) to blog – it puts us in contact with difference; with a world of opinion and ideas. Responding to comments helps one deal with other points of view …
>
> (Fernando, blog post, February 22, 2007)

The blogosphere also contributes to a distinctive perception of authority amongst bloggers in the emerging church movement. Technorati's authority ranking system is often criticized by bloggers as a false indication of influence, in that it establishes the authority of a blogger based simply on the links to their posts:

> [D]oes it really matter what electronic statistics are found at Technorati? The list of links and the corresponding ranks given there are, as far as I can make sense of them, rather ephemeral. ... I prefer to ask the question about the quality of the content of particular posts and of blogs: do they deserve the permanency that the printed-pixelated word achieves? ... A highly ranked blog on technorati is not automatically coterminous with profundity of thought.
>
> (Philjohnson, blog post, March 28, 2007)

For these bloggers, Technorati rankings are a poor measure of what they believe is real authority. Instead, Technorati rankings are seen to exclude people from participation in the emerging church conversation by reducing authority online to a numerical value, which to these bloggers highlights that the blogosphere is not the egalitarian environment it promises to be.

In these posts and comments, it can be seen that bloggers approach the Internet as a space for the sharing of stories, experiences and opinions about religion beyond the confines of church. However, bloggers recognize the Internet is not a classless space. Some are wary of users' campaigns for popularity and influence within the blogosphere. Technorati's idea of authority is considered highly suspect by most bloggers. Indeed, authority does not link to "good" blogging, from which true authority should be derived. For these bloggers, good blogging means that posts are original, well-referenced, personal, reasoned and sensitive. Bloggers should write with the aim of developing strong, honest and open relationships with their readers, and this requires them to blog regularly and often.

Links between blogs and authority rankings

When one blogger reads the post of another and believes the work is worth letting other people know about it, they may make a hyperlink to it on their own blog. These hyperlinked references promote relationships between bloggers, but, more than that, they are considered an exchange of authority from the link's author to its destination. Technorati counts such links as a measure of authority, and examining such links indicates which bloggers are more frequently read and thus are seen as more authoritative.

In the first study period, the 20 blogs studied contained 103 hyperlinks to other blogs in the sample, and of these 103 links, 61 pointed to just six blogs. Thus, a few blogs in the sample are considered more authoritative than the rest. Of these six blogs, all but one is authored by offline religious professionals, namely pastors and workers in diocesan offices, and only two by women (with one being authored by a male-female team). In the second study period, 68 hyperlinks were made on the 20 blogs, with 38 pointing to only four sites. These most-referenced blogs were again authored by religious professionals, and none were authored by women.

This simple study of connections made between the bloggers through hyperlinks demonstrates that a blogger's sex and profession are indicators of their authority, as determined by links to their blog. This means that, in the sample, those bloggers who are professionals in a religious setting (like clergy) are more likely to have greater authority than those who are not. It also means that men are more likely to have higher authority rankings than women.

Findings about authority in emerging church blogs

Bloggers in this study are not reluctant to discredit authority rankings, as determined by Technorati, on the basis that certain people are left out of the conversation. Why, then, are males and professionals in religious settings more likely to receive links from other bloggers in the sample? A clue to answering this question lies in bloggers' assertions about what makes for good blogging: writing that is original, well-referenced and reasoned. Bloggers also believe that good blogging is based on being well-read, exposing oneself to a range of information both in the blogosphere and elsewhere.

Online, many bloggers endeavor to remove themselves from the institutional structures that create borders and distinctions. These bloggers do share, however, a certain level of formal education and have access to resources that allow them to engage in academic theological discourse, with their opinions often being drawn from the same range of published works. Bloggers are keenly aware that academic discourse excludes voices from the emerging church conversation and that those bloggers who can engage in it are given greater authority than others. They try to bring other forms of information, such as other websites, music and art, and the sites of lesser-known bloggers, to the attention of readers. Yet, since it is easier to produce words than other media in a blog, the blogosphere tends to favor writing. Bloggers who are considered good writers are often given more attention, and those that can offer well-versed criticisms of other writings attract comments and links. Therefore, bloggers who approach topics of public conversation – such as theology, church structure and authority – are more likely to receive attention and be referenced in other sources than those who write mainly on personal and private discourses – such as individual faith practices – or use alternative media texts (e.g. videos, photos). In addition, bloggers in the sample that write often and advocate certain standards of practice are more likely to receive the attention of other bloggers in the sample, be linked to from their sites, and generate a Technorati ranking.

Women in particular are less likely to be among the high-ranked blogs. While the emerging church appears supportive of women standing alongside men in leadership roles, the blogosphere appears to favor the works of men in terms of links and comments. This could be because women in the sample tend to blog more infrequently than men; this also correlates with the fact that there are fewer women in full-time professions in the church. Furthermore, previous research has shown that women by and large tend to blog less about public issues and more about private practice (more about reading books or watching movies, for example, and less about the issues presented in such works) (Harp and Tremayne 2006; Herring *et al.* 2004).

Conclusion: lessons on authority from the blogosphere

To summarize, when dealing with religious authority, bloggers find themselves in a contradictory space. Some people turn to the blogosphere because they feel disaffected by authority structures that exclude lay people, especially women, from participating in normal religious discourse. These bloggers utilize this public space to articulate their convictions through the promotion of good blogging practice, based on the quality of writing and adherence to blogging standards. Yet they learn that the blogosphere has its own structures of authority designated by the Technorati machine, where authority rankings are given to those who write more often and regularly than others and to those who tend to write about public issues. The result is that the emerging church blogosphere emulates the authority structure of the offline religious world; those with high levels of authority offline (i.e. males and religious professionals) are often those who have the perceived authority online.

The blogosphere attracts those who, like emerging church bloggers, want to challenge institutional structures that exclude certain people from having a voice in public religion. Yet, this study contributes to a growing awareness that in reality, Web 2.0 is not a level playing field. There are systems like Technorati that calculate and decide whose online presence is more authoritative than others. Indeed, Technorati's ability to tag and rank blogs means those with high Technorati rankings are often portrayed as those having elite voices online. Furthermore, there are online practices and forms of speech that attract the attention of some and exclude others. These are more accessible to those who have access to formal education and time to write and read regularly. So it is a paradox within online religion that groups like emerging church bloggers challenge institutional structures and patterns of authority, yet they must also confront and adapt to these same patterns and structures online.

Discussion questions

- What constitutes a religious authority for a given community? Why are they given this privilege and responsibility?
- What qualifies one as an authority figure offline, as opposed to online?
- Are there alternative spaces (outside traditional structures) that facilitate religious dialogue and debate for those who do not hold positions of authority? In what ways does the Internet create such spaces for women, young people and others?

References

Beer, D. and Burrows, R. (2007) "Sociology and, of and in Web 2.0: Some initial considerations." *Sociological Research Online.* Online. Available: www.socresonline.org.uk/12/5/17.html (accessed 30 September 2007).

Blood, R. (2004) "How blogging software reshapes the online community." *Communications of the ACM,* 47(12): 53–5.

Bortree, D. S. (2005) "Presentation of self on the web: An ethnographic study of teenage girls' weblogs." *Education, Communication & Information,* 5(1): 25–39.

Cheong, P. H., Halavais, A. and Kwon, K. (2008) "The chronicles of me: Understanding blogging as a religious practice." *Journal of Media and Religion,* 7(3): 107–31.

Efimova, L. and de Moor, A. (2005) "Beyond personal web publishing: An exploratory study of conversational blogging practices." In *HICSS '05: Proceedings of the 38th Annual Hawaii International Conference on System Sciences,* Los Alamitos, IEEE Press. Online. Available: https://doc.telin.nl/dsweb/Get/Document-44480/ (accessed 28 May 2007).

Fernando (22 February 2007) "Ethics and Blogging." Blog post found at *Fernando's Desk.*

Harp, D. and Tremayne, M. (2006) "The gendered blogosphere: Examining inequality using network and Feminist Theory." *Journalism & Mass Communication Quarterly,* 83(2): 247–64.

Herring, S. C., Kouper, I., Scheidt, L. and Wright, E. L. (2004) "Women and children last: The discursive construction of weblogs," in L. J. Gurak, S. Antonijevic, L. Johnson, C. Ratliff and J. Reyman (eds) *Into the Blogosphere: Rhetoric, Community, and Culture of Weblogs.* Online. Available: http://blog.lib.umn.edu/blogosphere/women_and_children.html (accessed 11 June 2007).

Kumar, R., Novak, J., Raghavan, P. and Tomkins, A. (2004) "Structure and evolution of blogspace." *Communications of the ACM,* 47(12): 39.

Lövheim, M. and Linderman, A. (2005) "Constructing religious identity on the Internet." In M. T. Højsgaard and M. Warburg (eds) *Religion and Cyberspace,* 121–37, London, Routledge.

Matt (21 July 2006) Comment on "50 Most Influential Blogs" found at *Eclectic Itchings.*

Murley, B. (2005) "The mediahood of all receivers: New media, new 'church' and new challenges." Paper presented at Civitas Conference, Cornerstone University, Michigan.

Philjohnson (28 March 2007) "Emerging/Missional Bloggers." Blog post found at *Circle of Pneuma.*

16 Alt-Muslim

Muslims and modernity's discontents

Nabil Echchaibi

The actions of Muslims have often been inscribed in a cultural and political discourse that casts them in subordinate terms as traditional, introverted, and fatalist. Reinstituting faith in a culture that sees itself mostly at the receiving end of a powerful imported secular culture, no matter how liberating it might be, is unequivocally considered regressive and anti-modern by those who see no emancipation in the dogmas of the religious. Indeed, Islam's visibility in Western public space is threatening, as tensions flare up around mosques, minarets, veiling, and food taboos. The pattern in this debate is a rising visceral fear, largely exploited by populist politicians, of an anachronistic religion whose adherents not only disturb the architectural harmony of public space, but also interrupt the "natural" harmony and "linear" evolution of Western Judeo-Christian civilization. The placards and posters used during such highly publicized controversies as the minaret ban in Switzerland, the "Ground Zero Mosque" polemic in New York, and the Niqab ban in France all belabor this facile association between the symbols of Islam and a threat to national security and cultural unity.[1]

But such a simplistic view largely banalizes our understanding of the complexity of contemporary Muslim discourses and practices as they relate to modernity and their negotiation of cultural difference. In fact, a number of Muslims have turned to modern media technologies like satellite television and the Internet not necessarily to reinvent religious tradition and stir up pious passions but to seek original ways to render religious discourse more deliberative and dialectically engage a Western modernity they seek both to embrace and reform. Today, Islamic television is a far cry from the staid sheikh delivering his sermon on a state-owned channel. Men and women host talk shows, reality programs, and music variety shows where formerly taboo issues like politics, sexuality, relationships, and women's rights are openly debated. A growing number of teleIslamists effectively weave Quranic narratives into elaborate programs of social change and civic engagement. And traditional institutions of religious authority like Al-Azhar University in Egypt and other state-sanctioned constituencies are also adopting aggressive media strategies to counteract what they see as an emerging culture of semantic disarray over what Islam means today. On the Internet, videobloggers and otherwise marginal actors are capitalizing on much cheaper means of media production to join this massive fray of new cultural producers in Islam.

This case study explores the nature and significance of this dynamic cultural production in Islam through an analysis of a Muslim website based in the United

States in order to reflect on how authentic Islam is perceived and performed online. Alt-Muslim.com is described as a space for introspective comments on the Muslim world and a forum for progressive Muslims. With contributing editors and writers from the US, Canada, Australia, and the UK, Alt-Muslim bills itself as being at the forefront of an emerging independent Muslim media in the West. Its articles, opinions, media reviews, podcasts, and video commentaries seek to project an alternative view of Muslims as intellectuals, politicians, and artists. Specifically, this chapter will examine the dialogic and deliberative aspects of Alt-Muslim in its attempt to foster a more authentic religious experience for its users and in its claim to fashion a modern Muslim identity.

Muslim media and the religious order

The study of Muslims in the media has been primarily concerned with issues of representation and the shaping of public perceptions of Islam, but a number of scholars have recently turned their attention to Muslims as agents of media production on a variety of platforms, such as web blogging, social media, and film (Bunt 2009; Eickelman and Anderson 2003; Siapera 2009; Aydin and Hammer 2010). Studies of media representation, though of critical significance, tend to overemphasize the image of Muslims trapped in a structured system of signification that is impossible to overturn. While the power structure out of which public perceptions of Muslims emerge is indeed relentless, it is not necessarily static, and Muslims have become increasingly cognizant of the critical importance of media production as an effective mechanism to fight against their marginalization and otherization in public discourse. A focus on Muslim media production also privileges a view of Muslims as agents of what French sociologist Alain Touraine (1977) calls "historicity" or "the symbolic capacity of social actors to construct a system of knowledge and the technical tools that allow them to intervene in their own functioning, act upon themselves, and thereby produce society" (Buechler 2000: 6).

Of course, as social actors, Muslims exist in a larger power social structure and their actions may not necessarily seek to subvert that power configuration. The Internet, however, has afforded Muslims new and at times rival spaces to reinforce, cultivate, and act on a variety of ideological views, positions, and projects. Much like the print and audio-cassette technologies that came before it, Muslims are using the Web either to remediate or, in some cases, challenge the hegemonic interpretations of established religious authorities in ways that are more public and effective. As Eickelman and Anderson describe, new media technologies help create a new Muslim public sphere in which religious discourse is disembedded from its social and political structure:

> Situated outside formal state control, this distinctly Muslim public sphere exists at the intersections of religious, political, and social life. Facilitated by the proliferation of media in the modern world, the Muslim public can challenge or limit state and conventional religious authorities and contribute

to the creation of civil society. With access to contemporary forms of communication ... Muslims ... have more rapid and flexible ways of building and sustaining contact with constituencies than was available in earlier decades ... . This combination of new media and new contributors to religious and political debates fosters an awareness on the part of all actors of the diverse ways in which Islam and Islamic values can be created and feeds into new senses of a public space that is discursive, performative and participative, and not confined to formal institutions recognized by state authorities.

(2003: 2)

Nor is this new discursive and performative practice in Islam tied to a specific location or a particular set of traditions. In fact, the kind of Islam these new producers of religious meaning such as Alt-Muslim seek to project is a mobile Islam that adapts to and clashes with different cultural settings and spatial arrangements. Muslims in this new media culture are called on to develop a different relationship with their faith, to objectify it beyond tradition, and revise it in light of the exigencies of modern life. Specifically, this new face of public Islam appropriates slick media aesthetics (more visual and non-linear) and communication modes (more interactive) to draw inspiration and nurture a different religious experience.

Another important dimension of this form of agency lies in Muslims' embracing their religiosity as a defining marker of their cultural identity and their eagerness to renegotiate the place of Islam in the secularist narratives of modernity. Turkish sociologist Nilüfer Göle calls this category of new Muslims "second-wave" or "cultural" Islamists – as distinct from political Islamists – composed of "new social groups such as Muslim intellectuals, cultural elites, entrepreneurs, and middle classes that more greatly define the public face of Islam, thinking and acting in reformist terms" (2006: 173). This kind of activist Islam provides its adherents with not only a language and platform to defy conventional and static interpretations of Islam, but also an empowering source of cultural distinction with which they can negotiate the terms of their entry to modernity. Göle sees in this movement a "banalization" of Muslim identity, in the sense that Muslim actors do not seek refuge from the material expressions and values of modernity but quite the opposite, as "they blend into modern urban spaces, use global communication networks, engage in public debates, follow consumption patterns, learn market rules, enter into secular time, get acquainted with values of individuation, professionalism, and consumerism, and reflect critically upon their practices" (2006: 174).

Case study: Alt-Muslim – performing authentic Islamic identity

Context

Shahed Amanullah, the founder of Alt-Muslim, fits perfectly the profile of what Jon Anderson (2003) calls the "new interpreters of Islam," a new generation of

Muslims who seek to distance themselves from conventional nodes of religious authority by fashioning an alternative discourse that rivals official uses of the symbolic language of Islam. Amanullah has become an influential Muslim American over the years, earning him a spot in the Georgetown University list of the "500 most influential Muslims in the world"[2] in 2009 and 2010, alongside some prominent Muslim religious leaders such as Sheikh Al-Qaradawi and Egypt's Grand Mufti, Ali Gomaa. As a Muslim American journalist based in Washington, DC, Amanullah believed Muslims in post-9/11 America could not afford to antagonize mainstream media at a critical historical juncture, when their American-ness was being fiercely questioned. A few days after 9/11, he launched his blogging site, Alt-Muslim, both as an introspective voice to help Muslims critically address various faith and cultural issues and as a window to introduce non-Muslims to a new generation of well-trained Muslim commentators who do not fear or despise the media.

With associate editors in San Francisco, Toronto, and London and an international readership,[3] the site has quickly evolved into a highly visible reading stop for reflections on topical news, reviews of books, films and music by Muslim writers and artists, and self-criticism by Muslim commentators. Recent postings from contributors in the United States, Europe, the Middle East, and Australia have included commentaries on sexual harassment in Egypt, Muslim youth radicalization in the United States, the chaotic proliferation of halal consumer products, the faith of Christians in the Arab world, the twinning of mosques and synagogues to promote dialogue, faith, and civic duty, reviews of books on the Quran and climate change, the place of Islam in European pluralism, the new Muslim Brotherhood in the West, as well as reviews of films and profiles of Muslim newsmakers including artists, politicians, and athletes.

Methodology

It is this face of Islam, which seeks to intervene in, not retreat from modern secular public life, which awaits more scholarly attention. It is important to study these emerging Muslim media cultures as significant loci for the construction of contemporary Muslim subjectivities beyond the deterministic binaries of traditional religious and modern secular identities. I have chosen to focus on Alt-Muslim primarily because it is intensely engaged in shaping this activist Muslim subjectivity and because its mediating role reveals how Muslims discursively engage modernity as a source of both contention and identification. I also ask how the site's founders and contributors imagine an alternative religious experience that is socially, politically, and spiritually committed. Over the course of one year, I conducted multiple interviews with the founder of the site and analyzed dozens of posts, articles, and reviews from the blog and other companion sites. I have also attended various presentations by the founders on the history and objectives of Alt-Muslim and followed the coverage of the site in both mainstream media and Muslim media in the United States and the UK.

Analysis

The diversity of topics and opinions on Alt-Muslim is also reflected in the way its editors describe the site's mission as being to forge a welcoming space for Muslims with different ideological orientations and religious sensibilities. Amanullah equates the significance of creating this open space with the critical importance of bringing Muslims with disparate views together to listen to one another:

> We're trying to create that safe space that allows for all these diverse opinions and for all to respect them so that liberal Muslims, secular Muslims, conservative Muslims can feel like they are part of the same discourse. Also, before Alt-Muslim came around, you had a lot of mini-communities that were like, "well I'm saying what Islam is and we believe this" and somewhere else on the web someone says, "no no, we believe this," and they didn't really interact. Even today, there are very few places where Muslims with a wide variety of backgrounds can feel comfortable being in the same discussion space.
> (Amanullah, telephone interview, March 2, 2011)

Here Amanullah articulates an elaborate mission of Alt-Muslim to expand the discussion of Islam beyond its monologic tendencies and include nontraditional interlocutors who are often excluded. The public discussion of Islam in many Muslim countries, and to a lesser extent in the West, had traditionally followed a rigid and heavily centralized power structure in which religious bureaucrats close to officials dictated what constituted the religious and sought to control public expressions of virtue. The mission of Alt-Muslim is to free this discussion from the hierarchy of previous power structures and democratize participation. It is difficult to verify, however, whether the site has been successful in mediating a diverse conversation, as most articles generate only a handful of short comments, but the topics and analysis featured do reflect a variety of interests and opinions. They also reflect and promote a competing social imaginary where Muslim individuals – the writers, in this case – are encouraged to think for themselves through the stories they choose to foreground, instead of following a well-defined structure of religious givens and dogmas. The site then functions as a space for the production and negotiation of what Göle, following Charles Taylor, calls a "horizontal social imaginary" in which Muslim individuals create an alternative and supposedly hierarchy-free "frame of collective reference for self-definition" for other Muslims (2006: 180).

That frame of reference has expanded over the years, as six other sites have been added to Alt-Muslim in what has become a wide network of Islamic-themed websites grouped under a company called Halalfire Media. One of these sites, Salatomatic, allows users to review mosques in the United States and abroad in a crowd-sourcing fashion, based on their governance, their tolerance of women, and even their architecture. Amanullah, says the site, does not tell people these are the mosques Halalfire thinks you should go to or stop frequenting, but Muslims themselves feel empowered to recommend these mosques to others and rate the quality of an imam and his khutbah (sermons) in a democratic way. The site has accumulated reviews on 400 mosques in the United States alone, and, based on that, Amanullah says he can draw some interesting conclusions.

> Based on this data, between five to ten percent of mosques in the U.S. do not allow women to sit on their board. Five percent of mosques in the U.S. do not have accommodations for women at all. We also have statistics on how many imams deliver their khutbas in English, which is important for American Muslims. A significant portion of the reviews on the site are by women complaining about their treatment in mosques. You see, this is not about challenging authority. It's about transparency. It may be a new source of authority, but it's not my authority. It is the authority of the people.
> (Amanullah, telephone interview, March 2, 2011)

Amanullah's discreet use of words to describe the mission of Salatomatic indicates a subtle but determined effort to pressure other Muslims to become more accountable and accept public, including non-Muslim, criticism of their practices and actions. A big mosque in the Washington, DC area, for example, had both positive reviews (great architecture, ideal position, clean bathrooms) and some bad reviews (khutba mostly in Arabic, not women-friendly, disorganized management). Another Sunni mosque in the San Francisco area received poor ratings and many complaints from users who are frustrated by the poor management skills of its leadership. A reviewer had this comment about the mosque:

> It is not the mosque you should be disappointed by it is the people who run it, I think what this mosque needs is more ladies to help run it (they have a say now too!!!) and the younger generation to start taking over, I've spoken to a lot of the youngins [sic] and they are up for the challenge! we need all that and on top of that we need to hear out the life members!!!! this dilemma will not and I repeat WILL NOT be solved by police officers being called every chance they get. ... sooner or later the police will even get tired of this if they aren't already!!!! haven't they ever heard of the boy that cried wolf? if they don't like this post ... TOUGH ... this problem shouldn't have arrised [sic] in the first place!
> (Mosque Review 2008)

Salatomatic, Amanullah says, has not been created to target "bad" mosques or praise "good mosques," but to serve as a forum for people to help improve the quality of the prayer experience. The site is perceived as having an organic power to change the status quo of mosque management, and particularly the treatment of women, from the ground up with no direct interference from the founder of the site. Amanullah downplays his role in this process by attributing all agency to the users of the site, as their own arbiters in this relationship with mosques.

Visitors to Halalfire can also read commentaries on Alt-Muslimah, a collective blog on gender in Islam, read reviews on Zabiha, a guide to local halal restaurants and products, and shop for Muslim apparel, toys, books, music, and more on halalapalooza. Amanullah is again reluctant to think of himself as a pioneer interpreter or a leader, but he is clearly using all these Halalfire sites to project a model of how religiosity should penetrate modern life practices, such as consumption of market goods and services. The point for this generation of Muslims is not to render the religious, the source of their stigmatization in secular modernity, discreet in order to then participate in public life. Quite the contrary: they seek to magnify their religious differences through bodily politics and market intervention to domesticate modern public space. The music or toys that visitors to halalapalooza can buy, for instance, are symbolically contrasted with the blaring sexuality and materialism of their non-Muslim counterparts and accredited for their modesty and spiritual value. A review of the music of a Malaysian veiled woman who sings in a distinctly Western style and in English is described on Alt-Muslim as a crafted "singer-songwriter who manages to dispel scores of stereotypes about Muslim women – their independence, their creativity, and their ability to fashion a comfortable hybrid of cultures at peace with their religiosity." Here, the reviewer celebrates how this singer maintains her religious distinction even as she ventures into what Göle (1996) calls the forbidden spaces of modernity, in this case the world of showbiz and the Western music industry. The site therefore functions as an ethical compass for Muslim consumers as they navigate modern life and its materialist articulations. It also acts on both fronts: on Muslim tradition and on the secularist assumptions of Western modernity. Far from seeing themselves as religious subjects still waiting to be modernized through a process of secularization, the Muslims the site targets arguably seek a personally reworked version of their religion to shape their individual identity and inform their public behavior.

Conclusion

What is quite revealing about the work of Alt-Muslim, and all the other Halalfire sites, is what it defines as religiously authentic, and how it does this. A pop artist's music or a simple act of consumerism, even if not seemingly religious, can be as spiritual as a religious moment experienced in more traditional and less mediated settings, as in the mosque, for instance. Acting on a firm religious belief that Islam permeates all aspects of daily life, Alt-Muslim helps not only determine but also legitimate which of these spaces requires a Muslim's religious intervention. Authenticity in this case is framed not as a return to a "pure" form of Islam that lives in a body of doctrines, but rather as an active investment of faith to transform both the self and society. The founders of Alt-Muslim subscribe to a culture of mediated religion that sees market commodities not as signs of moral corruption but a site ripe for moral intervention.

The guidance the site offers therefore serves to reinforce the legitimacy of its religious discourse, and the authenticity of its practices and vision for a more disciplined Islamic public life.

Discussion questions

- How do sites like Alt-Muslim cultivate and sustain an authentic religious experience for their visitors?
- Do alternative digital media produce reformist, nontraditional, or unorthodox religious discourses and practices? How transgressive is this form of digital Islam?
- How does the projection of Islamic difference or distinction in online forums challenge the hegemonic narrative of Western modernity? What can this Muslim visibility and intervention reveal about the project of modernity and its ideological assumptions?

Notes

1 One popular poster used in the Swiss campaign to ban minarets separated minarets from mosques and showed them as missiles attacking the Swiss flag. A placard during the Park 51 demonstrations in New York City repeated such clichés as "All I needed to know about Islam, I learned on 9/11" and "Islam builds mosques on the land of its conquests." In France, the ban on the Niqab was turned into a threat to national identity and women's freedom despite the fact that only a negligible number of Muslim women don the full-face veil.
2 Georgetown University's Waleed bin Talal Center for Muslim-Christian Understanding, in collaboration with the Jordan-based Royal Islamic Strategic Studies Centre, started compiling an annual list of the 500 most influential Muslims globally in 2009. The list divided Muslims into four broad ideological categories: fundamentalists, traditionalists, modernists, and secularists.
3 According to its founder, Alt-Muslim has an audience of two million unique readers per year. Their parent company, Halalfire Media, which includes six other sites, has a total of 12 million viewers per year.

References

Amanullah, S. (March 2, 2011) telephone interview.
Anderson, J. (2003) "The Internet and Islam's new interpreters," in D. Eickelman and J. Anderson (eds) *New Media in the Muslim World: The Emerging Public Sphere*, 41–55, Bloomington: Indiana University Press.
Aydin, C. and Hammer, J. (2010) "Muslims in the media," *iContemporary Islam*, 4(1): 1–9.
Buechler, S. (2000) *Social Movements in Advanced Capitalism*, Oxford: Oxford University Press.
Bunt, G. R. (2009) *iMuslims: Rewiring the House of Islam*, London: Hurst & Co.
Eickelman, D. and Anderson, J. (eds) (2003) *New Media in the Muslim World: The Emerging Public Sphere*, Bloomington: Indiana University Press.
Göle, N. (1996) *The Forbidden Modern: Civilization and Veiling*, Ann Arbor: University of Michigan Press.
——(2006) "Islamic visibilities and the public sphere," in N. Göle and L. Amman (eds) *Islam in Public, Islam in Public*, 163–89, Istanbul: Bilgi University Press.

"Mosque Review." (June 5, 2008) Online. Available: www.salatomatic.com/d/South-San-Francisco+3467+Fiji-Jamatul-Islam-of-America (accessed August 10, 2010).

Siapera, E. (2009) "Theorizing the Muslim blogosphere: blogs, rationality, publicness, and individuality," in A. Russell and N. Echchaibi (eds) *International Blogging: Identity, Politics, and Networked Publics*, 29–46, New York: Peter Lang.

Touraine, A. (1977) *The Self-Production of Society*, Chicago: University of Chicago Press.

17 You are what you install

Religious authenticity and identity in mobile apps

Rachel Wagner

We are immersed today in what Wade Clark Roof calls "a time of paradigm shifts," a disruption between experiential and "institutionalized" forms of religion (2001: 171, 173). Contemporary "spiritual searching," according to Roof, "is largely a private matter involving loosely based social networks and small groups" (p. 177). Today's religiously minded person is a "bricoleur," one involved in building with whatever is at hand from a variety of sources, who "cobble[s] together a religious world from available images, symbols, moral codes, and doctrines," all the while "exercising considerable agency in defining and shaping what is considered to be religiously meaningful" (p. 75). In this case study, we look at mobile device applications (or apps) in order to consider how our prolific use of religious apps defines how we see ourselves even as it also reveals new challenges to traditional religion and authority. As our use of religious apps places control of religious interpretation and ritual performance increasingly in the hands of individuals, it also suggests a fluidity, hybridity, bricolage, and flow that gesture against traditional notions of fixed religious authority. The questions raised about authenticity by our use of religious apps also gesture toward a renewed sense of ownership and awareness of who we are and what we choose to believe, and thus presage a new kind of individualized, personalized authenticity of religious experience.

Description of case study

In this study six different types of smartphone app have been identified which present significant challenges to our thinking about how religious authenticity and presentation of the self is reflected through the mobile devices we use. These categories were derived through an analysis of apps found in the iTunes store as of September 2010 which contained explicit references to existing religions or religious texts; from this range, the most common types of religiously oriented apps are presented.

Prayer apps These apps enable users to pray by typing and sending prayers through mobile devices. Prayers may be sent to a human recipient in a temple, church or even to the Western Wall in Jerusalem, or directly to God.

The "Pray" app, for example, promises *only* spiritual delivery: you type in your prayer to God, tap "send prayer," and a box pops up: "Your prayer has been sent" ("Pray," Frog Army 2008). Apps like these raise questions about who or what we encounter when we use them, whether it is other users, God or perhaps just the program itself. As Turkle notes, we are "drawn to do whatever it takes" to maintain a view of interactive robots and chat-bots as "sentient and caring" (2011: 85). Such impulses seem also to apply to our use of prayer apps. Since digital media, like social media, are used for a host of social encounters, if we send our fears and desires through the digital ether, we may assume an authentic encounter with God (or other believers) has taken place when all we have done is engage in a solo media performance.

Ritual apps These apps offer guidance in the performance of recognized religious practices. Some, like various digital rosaries or virtual menorahs, offer visual props that replicate items one might use in real life. Others offer guidance on how to perform recognized rituals such as the proper blessing of food. Recently, Catholics debated the efficacy and authenticity of "Confession: A Roman Catholic App" (Little I Apps 2011), an app approved by an American Catholic Bishop but cautioned against by the Vatican. While the app leads users through officially condoned ritual procedures, Vatican spokesperson Federico Lombardi cautioned "the sacrament of penitence requires the personal dialogue between the penitent and the confessor and the absolution by the confessor" (Gilgoff and Messia 2011). This reveals a potential challenge apps pose to religious authenticity: if the app provides a recognizable script for rituals, what need is there for interaction with living church officials, and how would one know if the app had been used properly?

Sacred text apps These apps are digitized versions of sacred texts, offering varying degrees of interactivity. The "Al Bukhari" app puts the words of one of the greatest collectors of Muhammad's sayings and deeds into the hands of any smartphone user who buys it ("Al Bukhari," Soft & Wireless 2009). "Bible Shaker" allows users to enter a category such as "anger" or "finances," then shake the iPhone much like a Magic 8 Ball ("Bible Shaker," Brandon Woest 2011). Programmers have pre-selected verses to be associated with specific categories of inquiry, thereby shaping the theological possibilities of the replies. Apps like these encourage users to see sacred texts themselves as selectable "apps" or mini-programs that users have freedom to run, "play" with and in a sense control.

Religious social media apps Churches interested in developing their own apps for use by members have a number of fixed options. First, they can use open source software. ChurchKreatives (www.churchkreatives.com), for example, has created open source code for use by churches without the funds or ability to design their own individualized app. The resources programmed into the code include messaging, sermon streaming (video or audio), a news tab, a generic media tab and links to pre-existing social media such as Facebook and Twitter, as well as basic contact information for the bricks and mortar church. However, churches using open source code must have people on hand who know how to implement it and who can address any problems that arise over time. If they prefer, churches can create their own apps in-house. But, as Tim Turner of *The Church App Blog* explains, churches will meet predictable and formidable difficulties, including the need to hire a full-time programmer for making the app work with difficult Apple provisioning, for standardizing the app across multiple platforms like Android and Windows phones, and for keeping up with evolving standards for implementation in an ever-changing digital environment (Turner 2010). Thus many churches import content into pre-coded app vehicles that are supported by third-party businesses. These apps typically offer limited options like streaming video, messaging and providing information about worship times. More creative uses, such as dynamic prayer trees or GPS-enabled software for location of church members in one's vicinity, remain beyond the reach of most churches. Paying attention to what is possible via such pre-packaged apps is important, since as Heidi Campbell observes "there is evidence Internet use may transform the ways people conceive of religious community and local church," particularly in "a new conception of religious community as social network" (2005: 192). If churches utilize pre-designed apps with limited modes of community-building, will the church shape itself to match what the technology allows? If authenticity lies in self-determination of what constitutes meaningful worship and healthy community, then such considerations are quite important, since secular businesses may in some respects be shaping what is possible for church development. Again, control of religious practice may move from recognized religious authorities to individual users and designers, creating new "scripts" and experiences that raise questions about religious authenticity.

Self-expression apps These apps are a means of personal digital self-expression. Some apps, like digital wallpapers and backgrounds, include favorite Bible verses or religious images and are enjoyed primarily by the owner of the device. Other apps, such as ring tones or audible recitations of sacred text or songs, can be used as public expressions of faith by users. Mobile device owners may also buy religiously themed decorated cases for their devices that function as a visual statement of faith.

Focusing/meditation apps Focusing apps are less controversial than ritual apps, since the focusing they invite is not dependent on religious authority in real life. Examples include various digital Zen Garden apps, apps for gongs that ring at pre-specified intervals for help with meditation, and the intriguing "Guru Meditation" app that requires its users to hold the mobile device in their hands, with thumbs planted and unmoving on the device's screen, thus enacting the focus that resists using the phone for other purposes ("Guru Meditation," Ian Bogost 2008–9). Nevertheless, the ease with which such apps can be used outside of any religious context or community can indicate some potential issues relating to authenticity and authoritative practice.

Religious apps raise a number of questions about the authenticity of digitized religious practices, due to issues such as the inability to clearly identify a recipient of an app's prayer or to officially sanction its performance; the unsupervised performance of rituals via apps; the individualized interpretation of sacred texts using app-based tools; industrially rather than institutionally shaped forms of religious social media apps; the out-of-context use of sacred texts and symbols for personal expression via apps; and user-determined use of focusing applications on apps. All of the apps say something about the user who chooses them, as they demonstrate a fluid, streaming religious self, and all place control in the hands of individual users. They may receive an authentic "script" from recognized religious authorities, but are still provided, to varying degrees, with the power to interact in self-determined, unsanctioned ways. Such individualized experiences challenge received assumptions about religious authority in traditional contexts, and ultimately redefine authenticity, with the individual user increasingly in control of belief and practice.

Interpretation and analysis

The use of such apps may point to a process of renegotiation of what religious authenticity entails, as authority shifts from institution to individual and as people turn to their mobile devices for competing religious "scripts." Users may no longer feel obligated to interact with religious officials or even to interact directly with other people at all. As Victoria Vesna points out, we are experiencing a "transition from projecting ourselves as bodies to collapsing into a space of information and geometrical patterns" (2004: 258). More and more often we encounter others as projectable pixels and craft images of ourselves in transient data-based "blurbs." Every identity crafted online is "a temporary formation," subject to change based on any current whim (Hillis 2009: 95). Authenticity, then, is also a construct: users must decide for themselves what constitutes authentic religious practice, as their belief that another person hears their prayers or shares digital ritual experiences may be merely an illusion reinforced by a computer program.

This suggests the use of digital media can, at times, reinforce existing social and religious structures. Although believers in various traditions may engage with sacred texts or rituals in unorthodox ways via apps, the same digital devices that invite greater freedom may also be used to limit or even monitor belief. As Campbell (2010: 33) notes, "while cyberspace pushes the boundaries of religious life and discourse, it also provides a tool that can be adapted to traditional forms of monitoring and social control," especially in contexts in which a majority religion also has political power. Religious groups may also choose not to use smartphones at all, as a way of preventing the fluidity inherent in these devices from affecting believers. Campbell describes the phenomenon of the "kosher cell phone," which is modified to prevent Internet usage, text messaging and video (2010: 163). For those who utilize smartphones in unmonitored contexts, however, attempts at control are stymied by the market itself, which offers a neverending stream of new and unsanctioned religious applications, many encouraging experimentation and exploration of new religious ideas.

Mia Lövheim and Alf Linderman also point out that the Internet "greatly increases the possibility for an individual seeker to find information about established as well as alternative religious organizations" (2005: 126). Apps become a conduit for this information, when one installs ritual or sacred text apps for unfamiliar religious traditions. Diana Eck of Harvard University's Pluralism Project acknowledges the accessibility of such information, arguing that in contemporary "urban and global contexts" we encounter "new textures of religious diversity with increasing frequency" (2003: 168). She asserts that "our sharply heightened awareness of religious diversity" requires that everyone, not just the most educated or privileged in society, develop the ability to understand what these encounters mean (p. 42). Therefore authenticity of religious experience is no longer just in the hands of recognized religious authorities or received fixed rituals, it is in our hands – and also in the mobile devices we hold *in* our hands.

The "symbolic toolbox" available to today's religiously minded people allows, as Wade Clark Roof says, for forms of "religious reframing" that may enable "breaking through encrusted tradition and opening up new possibilities for an encounter with religious and metaphysical truths" (2001: 170). Stewart Hoover similarly observes that "media objects" can function as "symbolic resources" in the formation of personal identity (2006: 40). Today's seekers, he says, "seem to be always on a quest for enlightenment and will simply get it where they can, in popular culture or not, according to the logic of their own quest for self" (p. 77). What better visual metaphor for this selection of media items as identity markers than our mobile devices, where we can see such choices in action? On our smartphones, religious apps are installed alongside secular ones, and games and rituals coexist. Our mobile devices show what we care about, and offer us a primary portal into as many different digital realms as we wish, from social networks, to Internet websites and game-play, and even to explicitly religious church or ritual apps, sacred texts and other apps offering guidelines on how to practice our tradition (or traditions) of choice. Thus, the flow of religious apps mimics the flow of religious options generated every day, as users decide what to pay attention to and how to practice what they believe.

Although challenges to existing religious authority are obvious, the fluidity evident in digital downloads need not lead only to fragmentation. Ken Hillis (2009) notes what he calls a "cosmopolitan Web dynamic" which is simultaneously "a culture of networks" and "a culture of individualism." He suggests that even in this dichotomy there are "everyday manifestations of a desire for a worldwide *oikos* or *ecumene*," or the hope for a unified world, as he sees expressed within notions of Christian evangelism (p. 2). Similarly, in *Alone Together*, Turkle critiques technology's ability to alienate even as it binds. Turkle nonetheless acknowledges the *desire* that drives those seeking connection, quipping that "we will settle for the inanimate, if that's what it takes" (2011: 281). So our digital questing may in fact be about seeking a sense of wholeness and belonging. As Campbell (2005) notes, online church communities can provide a "sense of belonging" and of "being valued" even if one never meets the other members in person. In some cases, online religious communities may even be able to generate dialogue that is "at a more profound level than offline parishes" (pp. 179, 183). Religious social media apps can serve as portals into such communities, as well as signify a desire for such grounding. So to install a church's social media app may express a wish to be involved with the real people behind it. Drawing on Turkle's early work on identity, Campbell notes that "attaching oneself to an online community provides definition and boundaries for the self within the vast online world" (p. 189).

Choosing and utilizing social media apps connected to a specific community show we can function as entities-in-motion that also seek to ground themselves in singularly defined religious communities. This means that app use and selection can become a move toward authenticity, an act of deliberate performance. Thus the use of social media challenges claims that digital activities lack religious authenticity, and in fact it may nurture true relationships, if in novel forms. These relationships with information and communities can be rich and powerful, even if they depend upon the perception of personalized pixels as "a trace of the referent," a sign indicating the presence of a real person beyond the screen (Hillis 2009: 13).

Therefore it is claimed that the performance of app selection can *itself* be read as ownership of the religious quest. This argument is particularly striking if we view the mobile device as a sort of bodily proxy. Ritual theorist Theodore Jennings (1996) argues that the body is the site of noetic experimentation; that is, a place for what we could also call a knowing-in-motion. Ritual is "the means by which its participants discover who they are in the world and 'how it is' with the world" (p. 326). A smartphone privately reflects its user's concerns, preferences and activities. Individuals digitally install apps that represent what matters most in their search for authenticity in religious experience. The smartphone can be viewed as reflective of a person's ritual engagement with the worldviews inherent in the apps used, so the digital body becomes an extension of the physical or spiritual self.

The fluid experimentation involved in deciding which apps we will use and how we will find ourselves within the sequences they introduce is a quest that engenders, if we are conscious of it, increasing self-knowledge. Similarly, for Jennings, ritual entails the discovery of "the right action or sequence of actions" as a mode of discovering how one fits into the cosmic order reflected in the ritual itself (1996: 327). Roy Rappaport seems to agree on this point when he observes that ritual can "transmit information concerning [the performer's] own current physical, psychic, or sometimes social states to themselves and to other people" (1996: 429). App selection and maintenance, then, are kinds of ritual performance. We learn about ourselves by looking at the apps that we choose and observing how we use them. This, it seems, is also a form of authenticity-in-motion.

Conclusion

Our ongoing selection of apps challenges existing modes of religious authority, calling into question traditional means of determining religious authenticity.

At the same time, our use of religious apps privileges a "seeker" mentality and encourages individualized forms of religious experience. This, in turn, reinforces a pluralist mode of encounter with religion offline, signifying an order of fluidity, a structure of streaming identity, and deliberate performance of authenticity. Apps are optional. They are things that we choose, display, utilize and potentially discard. Therefore our selection and use of particular apps reveals our concern about what constitutes authentic religious performance and to what degree this depends upon traditional authority and contexts.

Fluidity alone does not deny authenticity of religious experience if it is matched with conscious awareness of the choices one is making. Drawing on Robert Jay Lifton's work, Turkle points out that the "unitary view of self correspond[s] to a traditional culture with stable symbols, institutions, and relationships," a situation confounded today by the options for streaming self-identity, especially in the religious sphere. Lifton and Turkle agree that the "protean self" is capable of "fluid transformations" while still being "grounded in coherence and a moral outlook," able to be "multiple but integrated." In short, says Turkle, "you can have a sense of self without being [just] one self" (1995: 258). This fluidity is reflected in the metaphorical proxy of our mobile devices. Our smart phones have multiple apps, but can still reflect a coherent sense of self; indeed, one that can handle more than one mode of religious encounter.

Turkle observes, "a more fluid sense of self allows a greater capacity for acknowledging diversity" (1995: 261). Perhaps then, simply by the very selection and collection of diverse apps that come and go based on our current identity status, we imitate and reinforce an attitude of openness to multiple religious paths. Or as Turkle puts it: "What most characterizes the model of a flexible self is that the lines of communication between its various aspects are open. The open communication encourages an attitude of respect for the many within us and the many within others" (1995: 261). What emerges is a natural, if digitally mediated, pluralism that is reflected in the very functionality of our mobile devices, which model for us the ability to live in a state of determined flux. Even as traditional modes of religious authority are in crisis, the individual religious self is alive and seeking. Authenticity, then, comes in self-awareness of the flow.

Discussion questions

- If you own a mobile device, take a look at the apps on it and ask yourself why you selected those particular apps, and what, if anything, they say about you.
- How might the selection of apps for one's mobile device be seen as an act of identity formation? Can apps be used to help one construct an authentic or holistic religious identity?
- To what extent are apps engineered to shape our behavior? Could owning or using apps itself be seen as an expression of authentic religiosity or an attempt to cultivate religious behavior?

References

Campbell, H. (2005) *Exploring Religious Community Online: We Are One in the Network*, New York: Peter Lang.

——(2010) *When Religion Meets New Media*, Oxon: Routledge.

Eck, D. (2003) *Encountering God: A Spiritual Journey from Bozeman to Benares*, Boston: Beacon Press.

Gilgoff, D. and Messia, H. (2011) "Vatican Warns about iPhone Confession App," *CNN News*, February 10. Online. Available: http://articles.cnn.com/2011-02-10/world/vatican.confession.app_1_new-app-confession-iphone?_s=PM:WORLD (accessed May 21, 2011).

Hillis, K. (2009) *Online a Lot of the Time: Ritual, Fetish, Sign*, Durham, NC: Duke University Press.

Hoover, S. (2006) *Religion in the Media Age*, Oxon: Routledge.

Jennings, T.W. (1996) "On Ritual Knowledge," in *Readings in Ritual Studies*, R. Grimes (ed.), 324–34, Upper Saddle River, NJ: Prentice Hall.

Lövheim, M. and Linderman, A.G. (2005) "Constructing Religious Identity on the Internet," in *Religion and Cyberspace*, M.T. Højsgaard and M. Warburg (eds), 121–37, Oxon: Routledge.

Rappaport, R. (1996) "The Obvious Aspects of Ritual," in *Readings in Ritual Studies*, R. Grimes (ed.), 427–40, Upper Saddle River, NJ: Prentice Hall.

Roof, W.C. (2001) *Spiritual Marketplace: Baby Boomers and the Remaking of American Religion*, Princeton, NJ: Princeton University Press.

Turkle, S. (1995) *Life on the Screen: Identity in the Age of the Internet*, New York: Simon & Schuster.

——(2011) *Alone Together*, New York: Basic Books.

Turner, T. (2010) *The Church App Blog*. Online. Available: http://thechurchapp.org/blog/2010/04/points-to-consider-re-mobile-technology-for-churches/ (accessed May 21, 2011).

Vesna, V. (2004) "Community of People with No Time: Collaboration Shifts," in *First Person: New Media as Story, Performance, and Game*, N. Wardrip-Fruin and P. Harrigan (eds), 249–61, Cambridge, MA: MIT Press.

Apps

"Al Bukhari" (iPhone app) 2009, Soft & Wireless FZCO. Online. Available: www.apple.com/itunes

"Bible Shaker" (iPhone app) 2011, Brandon Woest. Online. Available: www.apple.com/itunes

"Confession: A Roman Catholic App" (iPhone app) 2011, Little I Apps. Online. Available: www.apple.com/itunes

"Guru Meditation" (iPhone app) 2008–9, Ian Bogost. Online. Available: www.apple.com/itunes

"Pray" (iPhone app) 2008, Frog Army. Online. Available: www.apple.com/itunes

18 Japanese new religions online
Hikari no Wa and "net religion"

Erica Baffelli

New religious movements and the Internet

Earlier studies of the Internet and religion pointed out that the Internet might provide a useful medium for marginal and small religious organizations, especially for groups less related to older religious traditions or for groups emphasizing a direct contact with the "divine." Some researchers indicated that the possibilities offered by the Internet for accessing religious information, and sharing religious beliefs and systems might even "help facilitate the development of new religions" (Hozak and Stanina, n.d.) because people can patch together a religious system of their own based on beliefs and ideas they gather from others on the Internet. People who have never met in person may unite and form their own religion based on conversations in discussion groups. Zaleski (1997) argued that religious groups and teachings "that tend toward anarchy and that lack a complex hierarchy" (p. 111) might be favored by the Internet. Other scholars discussed the fact that the Internet "might well pose serious problems for religions that have historically stressed the role of a strong central authority, like the Roman Catholic Church or Scientology" (Dawson and Hennebry 1999: 34). In their work, Dawson and Hennebry discuss the impact of the Internet on new religious movements and point out the possibility of increasing competition between new religions "to secure a marked edge" on the Internet (1999: 35). They also discuss the fear over the possibility of "spiritual predators" on the Internet (1999: 19), especially following the tragic mass suicide of 39 members of Heaven's Gate at Rancho Santa Fe, California on March 26, 1997. After the tragic event, the media reported that Heaven's Gate not only had a sophisticated website and ran a web design company, but also that it used the Internet for online proselytism.

The survey in Dawson and Hennebry's 1999 paper, one of the earliest surveys conducted on new religious movements on the Internet, included two Japanese new religions, Sōka Gakkai and Kōfuku no Kagaku (pp. 22–3). The term "new religious movements" (often abbreviated to NRMs) is an umbrella term used especially in the sociology of religion for movements or organizations also described as, for example, "alternative religions," "non-conventional religions," "contemporary sects," "new religious groups," or "new religious sects." new religious movements are sometimes labeled with the derogatory term "cult." Defining new religious movements involves determining how to distinguish new from traditional religious movements and new groups from sectarian organizations: scholars often disagree on the criteria used to define how and in what ways NRMs are "new" (Melton 2004; Barker 2004; Robbins 2005). For scholars in the sociology of religion, "new" is always a relative term. Indeed, some "new" religions are now more than one hundred years old (for example Tenrikyō, or a number of other new religious movements founded in Japan in the late nineteenth century).

In Japan, the concept of "new religions" was first used following the end of World War II to denote the numerous groups whose historical development traces back to the mid-nineteenth century (Astley 2006: 93). These groups have been defined, according to the period of their development and the classification criteria adopted, as "new religions" (*shinshūkyō*), "new-new religions" (*shin-shinshūkyō*) and "new spiritual movements and culture" (*shinreisei undō*). Many classifications have been proposed in order to distinguish the most recently formed groups from the so-called "institutionalized religions" (*kisei shūkyō*) or "traditional religions" (*dentō shūkyō*), namely the various schools of Buddhism and shrine Shintō. The definition of *shinshūkyō* (*shūkyō* is the standard term for religion and *shin* means new) is rendered problematic by the fluidity and complexity of the various groups, their phases of development and their affiliation. Summing up, characteristics attributed to Japanese new religions include:

- the role of leader: the group is often centered around a charismatic leader;
- syncretism and eclecticism: groups can draw on different religious traditions and change their affiliation over time; and
- dynamism: they are dynamic and can change quite radically in a short time.

In addition, many new Japanese religious groups have been known for their intensive (and sometimes aggressive) use of the media and for their enthusiastic, at times even pioneering, approach to technology (Baffelli 2010b: 255) in order to present the image of an up-to-date religion (Reader 1991: 218–19). However, many Japanese new religions were latecomers to the Internet and their use of it is normally restricted to information-based websites aimed at enhancing their public profile (Dawson and Hennebry 1999: 26). Indeed, the online content often replicates material available in other of the group's publications and viewers are encouraged to visit the group's center in person. The reasons for this cautious approach may be explained as the effect that the sarin gas attack – perpetrated by members of the group Aum Shinrikyō in the Tokyo subway in 1995 – had on how new religions are portrayed and perceived in Japan (Baffelli 2010a: 119; Baffelli *et al.* 2010). After the attack, which left 12 people dead and thousands injured, aggressive criticism was leveled at all new religious movements and their leaders, and in many cases the use of the Internet by new religious movements in Japan still strongly reflects these criticisms. In particular, new religions saw the Internet as an environment too difficult to control effectively, and one in which the group and the leader – who is usually an extremely important figure within the group – will be unprotected from external attacks.

This case study introduces a distinct case of a Japanese new religion that, because of exceptional circumstances in its history and development, has decided to use the Internet as its main means of proselytism and interaction between the leader and members, especially new members. Nowadays Japan is one of the countries with the highest rates of Internet penetration (Ministry of Internal Affairs and Communications 2008; Baffelli 2010a: 121) and almost all new religions have an official website. However, their use of official websites is still largely limited to the provision of information (Kawabata and Tamura 2007). Many organizations have been slower in embracing new forms of online interactions. Indeed, blogs, forums and social networking services are largely delivered by enthusiastic members, and not part of a prepared group communication strategy, with groups still focusing mainly on printed media, especially books and magazines. Here a specific case of one Japanese new religious movement's innovative use of the Internet is explored in order to consider how new media offer important opportunities for public presentation in a society where most other avenues are unavailable to them.

Exploring Hikari no Wa on the Internet

Aum Shinrikyō (literally, Aum Supreme Truth), the group responsible for the sarin gas attack in the Tokyo subway, among other crimes, was one of the most active groups on the Internet in Japan. The group was founded in 1984 by Asahara Shōkō, who started a small yoga center that eventually developed into a bigger millennialist organization, which included various forms of Buddhist teachings and involved members living together in a community (Reader 2000).

In 1991, Aum launched its own private network (Watanabe 2005) and set up a discussion room on Fujitsu Nifty Serve, which at the time was one of the largest networks in the country (Watanabe 2005: 47). About 300 registered users – half of whom were members – communicated on this "Aum Shinrikyō Net," via a bulletin board system, chat, and e-mail (Watanabe 2005). Aum also had a relatively flashy website for its time, which included a lot of information, an appealing design and audio and video downloads.

Aum Shinrikyō changed its name into Aleph in 2000 (Aleph is the first letter of the Hebrew alphabet and symbolizes a new beginning) and announced changes in its doctrine. In particular, the group declared that they wanted to retain practices of yoga and meditation but would discontinue teachings considered "dangerous," and " start from ground zero" with the organization's structure (Jōyū 2000). In March 2007, Jōyū Fumihiro, ex-spokesperson for Aum, left Aleph and set up a new religious organization called Hikari no Wa (literally "Circle of Light," and officially "The Circle of Rainbow Light"). The new group initially included around 40 *shukkesha*, a term used in Buddhism to indicate renunciants, and approximately 200 lay members. Despite Hikari no Wa's claims that it completely rejects Asahara and Aum, the Public Security Intelligence Agency (Kōan Chōsachō) decided that the organization would remain subject to surveillance under the so-called "Anti-Aum laws," two laws introduced in 1999 to keep Aum and its members under strict control.

Hikari no Wa launched an official website immediately after the foundation of the group and the leader, Jōyū, has become an active user of Mixi, the biggest social network website in Japan. In August 2010 he also started interacting with members and other users through a new Twitter account, and in February 2011 he joined Facebook.

Method

This case study is based on three years of online participant observation, which involved observing and gathering detailed field notes on Hikari no Wa's use of the Internet and interactions between members and non-members on social networking services. In particular, I have followed Jōyū's Mixi and Twitter accounts (http://twitter.com/#!/joyu_fumihiro) and actively participated in members' interactions and discussions on Mixi. I have also gained access to and participated in online public talks on Ustream and, from December 2010, online yoga practices. In addition, interviews were conducted with Hikari no Wa's leader and some of its members during two fieldwork periods (December 2008 to January 2009, and November 2010 to January 2011). Interview questions delved into such matters as the primary purposes of the webpages, whether people had become affiliated with the group as a result of contact online, and their views on what the leader defined as "Net Religion." During the fieldwork I actively participated in a three-day pilgrimage organized by the group, attended seminars, meetings, public events and *off kai*, offline meetings between Hikari no Wa's leader and members, and users who contacted the group online, in particular through Mixi and Twitter.

Findings relating to Hikari no Wa and *Netto Shūkyō* (Net Religion)

After the split with Aleph, the Internet was the only means available for Hikari no Wa to publicly present its opinions and the reasons for the disagreement with Aleph. Because of its relationship to Aum – which had had established media venues and resources, and, in the early 1990s, access to television shows and magazines, but had lost its status as an officially recognized religious movement – Hikari no Wa does not have access to media other than the Internet (in particular television and newspapers), and currently cannot afford to publish for itself.

As mentioned, Hikari no Wa launched an official website in May 2007, immediately after the announcement of the new group's establishment. The website was initially registered using the name of the leader (joyus.jp) and included, among other features, a leader's diary.

In 2008, the diary was moved to Jōyū's page on the social network service (SNS) Mixi. Mixi was launched in 2004 by Kenji Kasahara, initially as a job search and recruiting site (Billich 2007). Quickly converted to an invitation-only SNS, by June 2009 it had around 24 million members, up from 19 million only a year earlier. Mixi is only available in Japanese and its success is based on its particular features. First of all, Mixi emphasizes security and privacy more than most other SNS: joining Mixi requires an invitation from a current user and, because it is invitation-only, members' URLs are not indexed by Google (in contrast to, for example, Facebook accounts). Further, the *ashiato* (footprints) function allows users to see every visitor to their profile pages.

On Mixi, Jōyū immediately attracted a significant number of requests to be added to other users' "MyMIXI" lists (similar to friend lists on Facebook or MySpace), quickly reaching the 1000-friend limit allowed by the service. From the beginning, Jōyū invited viewers to send him questions and engaged in an interactive dialogue with them. The shift from a one-to-many communication style (which still characterizes the official website) to many-to-many interactions was reinforced through use of Twitter and the creation in October 2010 of a new blog (Jōyū 2010), used by the leader to reply to the numerous questions received on Twitter.

Users' participation is not yet part of the official website; instead it takes place on external sites, creating "interaction zones" (Helland 2005). These interactive features serve as an opportunity for Jōyū to spread his teachings, and also to promote the idea of a religious leader who is not untouchable, but instead is approachable and happy to answer questions. This includes very private and challenging questions, because, Jōyū claims, he doesn't have anything to hide.

Mixi, Twitter and blogging are indeed offering Jōyū and Hikari no Wa the possibility of presenting themselves as very different from their predecessors, Aum and its leader Asahara. In fact, the image of the group presented online is often consciously constructed as the opposite of Aum: they value openness over Aum's exclusivity, and privilege explanation over secrecy, as can be seen in the inclusion of members' detailed explanations of Aum Shinrikyō's activities. The fact that the website was created with the cooperation and input of the group's members clearly expresses the group's awareness of the potential of the Internet to effect a change in its image, and to improve the possibility of its being recognized as a group different from its predecessor.

During the fieldwork I was able to follow the development of the Net Dōjō (*dōjō* is the usual Japanese term for "training hall" or "meditation hall") and the beginning of *off kai* (literally, offline meetings), which are meetings between Hikari no Wa's members and users who have been in contact with the group and its leader through Mixi or Twitter. The *off kai* are usually held at public halls and create a "neutral" space where interested (or simply curious) people can meet and talk with the leader. Many declared that they preferred to use these outside venues as they still did not feel comfortable visiting the group's centers – either because of its "dangerous" image or because, especially in Tokyo, they didn't want to be stopped and questioned by the police officers standing outside the group's headquarters.

However, Hikari no Wa is not using the Internet only to rebuild its image or for the purposes of proselytism. During an interview I conducted in November 2010, Jōyū expressed his idea of the role of the Internet in what he called *Netto Shūkyō* (literally Net Religion) and defined as "the new religion of the twenty-first century." According to his vision of the development of religion in contemporary society, one does not necessarily have to attend religious rituals or practices in person, and one can participate in Hikari no Wa's activities without even joining the group. These ideas where expressed by Jōyū in group booklets and online (for example Jōyū 2011).

The idea of "Net Dōjō," a platform including different types of material and videos, was developed in 2007 in order to allow potential members to engage with the group in the privacy of their houses and without having to visit its centers. Beginning in September 2009, the group started online live broadcasting of Jōyū's Buddhist sermons (*seppō*) through Ustream. Hikari no Wa also has its own YouTube channel, which includes videos of the leader's public talks and the group's official press conferences. During the "end of the year seminar" in December 2010, other rituals and yoga sessions were streamed, and for the first time live comments and questions were allowed during the leader's talks.

So, what exactly is religion online in the case of Hikari no Wa? Is it the Internet helping to shape the group toward a new form of religion? It is still too early to understand clearly the effects that an online presence is having on the perception of Hikari no Wa in Japan, and on the group's practices and teachings. The group will face various issues in developing the Net Dōjō. First of all, interaction with the leader is still strictly regulated. Comments on blog posts or videos, for example, are not allowed. And the attempt to allow live comments during the leader's talks proved challenging because the chat facility was used by some to ask unrelated questions, and both online viewers and members attending the talk in person found this quite distracting.

Furthermore, the image of a "transparent" leader may create tensions between old members, and viewers and new members. If viewers feel free to ask Jōyū any question online and appear not to be wholly respectful of his role as a leader, older members may consider their behavior offensive, and may feel uncomfortable with those questions being publicly accessible online. Finally, the group still needs to elaborate the idea of "Net Religion," expanding the opportunities for online practice or, as intended by the leader, starting to organize interactive seminars and discussions online as part of the development of Net Shūkyō.

Conclusion: lessons on religion from Japanese new religions

The development of Internet-based interaction is vital for groups which, like Hikari no Wa, do not have access to other media. For them, the Internet can be an important means of spreading their teaching, communicating with members, attracting potential new followers and negotiating their new identity. Further, a well-planned strategy for the use of so-called "Web 2.0" applications (including blogs, social networking services and video sharing sites) may encourage the creation of a new type of online religious practice and a religious environment that users can interact with from the privacy of their homes.

Further, the Hikari no Wa example shows that religion online needs to be understood in relation to the history and development of the group. Indeed, Hikari no Wa was forced to create its Net Dōjō because of its specific circumstances and because of the group's need for credibility and legitimacy.

Finally, the Internet may affect the relationship between members and (charismatic) leaders in new religions. Indeed, Jōyū's use of social networking represents an adaptation of the traditional leader–members interaction and an attempt to recreate at least a perceived proximity between leader and members. In the case of Hikari no Wa this may shape a different image for a religious leader, as being open to dialogue and (mediated) interaction, and this may, in contrast to the findings of earlier studies on new religious movements online, reinforce his central authority.

The idea of "Net Religion," although still not completely developed by the group, has the potential to change not only how the group is perceived but also the group's teachings and its understanding of religious practice. First, the ability to participate in rituals and other religious practices (such as yoga) via the Internet may change the idea of "sacred space." Indeed, the training hall or sacred space may be expanded through the Internet to include the private space of members' houses. Second, the ability to attend training and study sessions online may transform Hikari no Wa's practice, causing it to move away from group-based activities (with members living, performing rituals, and training together) toward a more individual practice. More generally, the idea of Net Religion can challenge the idea – considered one of the reasons for Japanese new religions' cautious use of the Internet – that physical interaction is central to religious practice, by offering a form of religion in which the physical presence of participants is secondary to the achievement of spiritual goals.

Discussion questions

- On the Internet, we can talk about religion, read about religious groups, download religious texts, buy religious artifacts, and watch religious services and rituals ... but can we have a religious experience online?
- Is the Internet becoming a new and more effective means of recruiting members to religious groups, especially among small groups? If it is, what might be the implications for the future of new religious movements?
- How might the Internet affect the relationship between members and leaders in new religious movements?

References

Astley, T. (2006) "New Religions," in P. L. Swanson and C. Chilson (eds) *Nanzan Guide to Japanese Religions*, 91–114, Honolulu: University of Hawai'i Press.

Baffelli, E. (2010a) "Charismatic Blogger? Authority and New Religions on the Web 2.0," in E. Baffelli, I. Reader and B. Staemmler (eds) *Japanese Religions on the Internet: Innovation, Representation, and Authority*, 118–35, New York: Routledge.

——(2010b) "Japanese New Religions and the Internet: A Case Study," *Australian Religion Studies Review*, 10(3): 255–76.

Baffelli, E., I. Reader and B. Staemmler (2010) *Japanese Religions on the Internet: Innovation, Representation, and Authority*, New York: Routledge.

Barker, E (2004) "What Are We Studying? A Sociological Case for Keeping the 'Nova,'" *Nova Religio*, 8(1): 88–102.

Billich, C. (2007) *Mixi: A Case Study of Japan's Most Successful Social Networking*, Tokyo: Infinita Inc.

Dawson, L.L. and J. Hennebry (1999) "New Religions and the Internet: Recruiting in a New Public Space," *Journal of Contemporary Religion*, 14(1): 17–39.

Helland, C. (2005) "Online Religion as Lived Religion: Methodological Issues in the Study of Religious Participation on the Internet," *Online – Heidelberg Journal of Religions on the Internet*, 1(1). Online. Available: http://archiv.ub.uni-heidelberg.de/ojs/index.php/religions/article/view/380 (accessed June 4, 2012).

Hozak, K. and S. Stanina (n.d.) "Religion and the Internet." Online: www.und.nodak.edu/dept/philrel/Internet.html (accessed October 15, 2000).

Jōyū, F. (2000) "Outlook on the Aum-Related Incidents." Online. Available: http://english.aleph.to/pr/01.html (accessed February 27, 2011).

——(2010) *21seiki no shisō no sōzō*, weblog. Online. Available: http://ameblo.jp/joyufumihiro (accessed February 27, 2011).

——(2011) Twitter status, January 25, 2011, Twitter. Online. Available: http://twitter.com/#!/joyu_fumihiro/status/29684011404103680 (accessed February 27, 2011).

Kawabata, A. and T. Tamura (2007) "Online-Religion in Japan: Websites and Religious Counseling from a Comparative Cross-Cultural Perspective," *Journal of Computer-Mediated Communication*, 12(3): article 12. Online. Available: http://jcmc.indiana.edu/vol12/issue3/kawabata.html (accessed February 27, 2011).

Melton, G. (2004) "Toward a Definition of 'New Religion,'" *Nova Religio*, 8(1): 73–87.

Ministry of Internal Affairs and Communications (2008) *White Paper 2008: Report on the Current Status of Information and Communication*, Tokyo: Economic Research Office, General Policy Division, Information and Communications Policy Bureau. Online. Available: www.johotsusintokei.soumu.go.jp/whitepaper/eng/WP2008/contents.pdf (accessed April 18, 2011).

Reader, I. (1991) *Religion in Contemporary Japan*. London: MacMillan.

——(2000) *Religious Violence in Contemporary Japan: The Case of Aum Shinrikyō*, Honolulu: University of Hawai'i Press.

Robbins, T. (2005) "New Religions and Alternative Religions," *Nova Religio*, 8(3): 104–11.

Watanabe, M. (2005) "Aum Shinrikyo and its Use of the Media: Five Phases of Development," *Bulletin of the Nanzan Institute for Religion & Culture*, 29: 42–53.

Zaleski, J. (1997) *The Soul of Cyberspace: How New Technology is Changing Our Spiritual Lives*, New York: HarperCollins.

19 "'Go online!' said my guardian angel"

The Internet as a platform for religious negotiation

Nadja Miczek

Introduction to New Age on the Internet

Even with a superficial look into the history of religions, it becomes apparent that the voices to be heard in our source material belong to only a few religious individuals. The media used for religious communication are written and oral texts, images, and, in modern times, mass media such as television or movies. Most prominently transmitted in these media are statements and testimonies on religion and religious practice that are verbalized, written down, or otherwise transmitted by religious experts, meaning clerics, religious leaders, high-profile figures like the so-called "founders" of religions, or professionals in the performance of rituals. This situation has been changing dramatically since the 1990s, with the worldwide popularization of the Internet. With its low barriers to entry, the Web theoretically enables all people to actively participate in its discourses. With respect to religion, this means that for most likely the first time in religious history, "ordinary" people become visible and audible to a quantitatively large degree (see Radde-Antweiler 2006: 56f.). They can now present their religiosity online by setting up personal home pages and blogs, or communicate about religious topics on forums or on social networking websites. No matter what religious tradition they belong to, actors[1] increasingly construct dynamic and complex concepts of their religious identities and corresponding ritual practices on the Internet. Several new questions and perspectives arise for researchers in this regard: How can we deal with the vast plurality of online documents related to religious identity construction and its negotiation? How, if at all, is the use of the Internet embedded in actors' constructions of religiosity? How can we deal with the conflicts that inevitably arise in relation to the medium?

Besides actors belonging to "traditional" religions like Islam, Buddhism and Christianity, the Internet has also become a platform for historically younger movements and developments such as "New Religious Movements," or "the" New Age. What constitutes "New Age" has been debated in religious studies for several decades. New Age as a phenomenon was first recognized in the early 1970s in the US, with the term being used to describe new religious groups or charismatic individuals who proclaimed certain religious concepts as alternative ideas to existing mainstream, mostly Christian concepts. This includes, for example, a focus on individual and personal "spiritual" growth, metaphysical beings like angels or ascended masters, or the idea of holism (see Hanegraaff 1996). Over time New Age has transformed from a phenomenon on the edge of society to a very popular and widespread practice. Because the category of New Age encompasses a heterogeneous set of religious ideas and practices, much discussion has occurred in religious studies about how to arrive at a clear definition. Phenomenologically oriented approaches define "New Age" mainly through identifiable characteristics such as holism; though this can be problematic as not every New Age group or practioner displays these characteristics, or relates to them in the same way.

Thus, scholars such as Michael Bergunder suggest considering New Age – or "Esotericism," as Bergunder calls it[2] – as a discursive construction that is constantly changing (see Bergunder 2010). New Age (or Esotericism) can be seen as a "name" with which both religious actors and scholars label "a certain discourse related to religion and scholarship" (Bergunder 2010: 19). In this case study New Age is viewed as a dynamic and shifting religious field that is constantly being constructed through discursive negotiations by religious participants as well as by scholars, the media and other actors. Whereas in the 1980s topics like reincarnation and past life recovery, or the connection between New Age and modern physics, were frequently discussed themes, today angels, Reiki and the development of one's personal spirituality are often-debated topics. Much of the discursive negotiation about what constitutes New Age topics today takes place within modern media networks, primarily the Internet. It therefore seems important that researchers also turn their attention to the media usage of New Age actors.

In this case study, the focus is on two questions, in particular: What kind of statements do we find being made by religious actors in the field of New Age about their use of modern mass media, especially the Internet? And are there cases in which this media use implies any kind of conflict with other actors? The findings of this study allow me to propose that religious actors construct their narrations about media use alongside dominant negotiation patterns from the field of New Age; and that, because of the public nature and accessibility of constructions of individual religiosity on the Internet, conflict situations may occur.

Case study: going online – the Internet use of New Agers

Methodology

The following case study refers to a qualitative study that focused on the analysis of identity construction, rituals and media in the field of New Age, with a special focus on the Internet (see Miczek 2009). Over a period of three years (2006–9), parts of the German-speaking field of New Age were observed on the Internet, with a special focus on personal websites. On these websites, religious actors presented themselves using biographical notes, gave an overview of the main topics of their religiosity and, in many cases, offered certain ritual practices – for both online and offline performance – that they had invented or with which they had had positive experiences. From a vast potential field, 12 actors were chosen for qualitative interviews.[3] Because the nature of New Age is not clearly definable, the study sample included owners of home pages on which New Age elements like angels, Reiki or other spiritual healing techniques were present, and actors who identified themselves as participants of New Age (or Esotericism) in German-speaking areas. The interviews were conducted in Germany and Austria and consisted of a narrative interview in which the actors were asked to tell their religious biography, and a semi-structured interview consisting of two guided sections of questions on ritual habits and media usage. The aim of this qualitative approach was to analyze the construction of religious identity structures and interpretation patterns from the actors' point of view.

The examples provided here refer to a guided section of the semi-structured interview focusing on media usage, in which people were asked to talk about the personal home page each of them owned and their habits of Internet use. Based on findings from the interviews the following question is addressed: What do New Age actors say about their usage of the Internet? This is done first through discussing interviewees' religious motivations for Internet use and related New Age adaptations of their personal web pages. Next, the case study looks at whether the processes involved in media presence and communication bear any potential for conflict with actors in other religious fields. It concludes with reflections on the kinds of dynamics and shifts that may evolve within the media-related negotiations of religion in the New Age field.

Motives for the use of the Internet

The motives for going online that are explicitly mentioned by the interviewees indicate that the decision in favour of new media use was taken intentionally and on the basis of personal religiosity. However, in the interviewees' stories, the agency and the process of decision-making is often attributed to superhuman entities. In the field of New Age, several categories of such entities have gained popularity in recent years. Most important today are angels, followed by ascended masters, or other beings like fairies or power animals. In the interviewees' narrative constructions, these entities are positioned as playing a guiding part, leading the actor on his or her way into the Internet:

> And then, there was a time, when I thought I had to do something and then the angels told me they wanted to go on the Internet. ... And I said: "Great! I don't know anything about computers and I have no clue how this works! Now, how do I get a PC?" Then I said to a friend: "The angels want to go on the Internet, I think I need a PC."
>
> (Luca, personal interview, June 28, 2007)

Here, angels appear to be the guiding entities in Luca's going online. The use of the medium is clearly embedded in the religious setting of the field of

New Age. In a similar way, Toni tells her story about starting to use the Internet:

> The reason why I put my religious knowledge online is because the Being of Light who teaches me said: "Spread it [the knowledge] with the means of communication that are given to you on your planet earth."
> (personal interview, May 11, 2007)

Besides reference to superhuman entities, there are also other motives expressed for the use of the Internet in which the agency is not attributed to someone else. But in these cases, there are also religious factors leading the actors to use the medium: for example, the desire to share one's religious knowledge.

In sum, the interview examples support the idea that, in individuals' narratives, the use of the Internet is seen as something that fits with the construction and practice of their religiosity. The motives for going online are associated with religious topics by the actors themselves. Angels are named by interviewees as a legitimizing authority, or their own religious knowledge of the field of New Age provides motivation for using the Internet as a space for personal presentation.

Changes on the personal home page

In the narrative construction of individuals' religious identities, it becomes apparent that they see their presence on the Internet as corresponding to their personal development. A dominant narrative pattern in the field of New Age for the description of one's life is the use of the image of a "seeker" on a spiritual "path" along which the actor is moving (see Sutcliffe 2003). This path exhibits certain characteristics: it is seen as an ongoing process of learning and personal development, and actors have the authority and agency to decide which religious elements they want to integrate along the way; and it is seen as reaching beyond death into many subsequent lives that are expected to be lived following several rebirths. The concept of life as an individual pathway is also reflected in the composition of interviewees' personal websites and in the changes made therein:

> My website is structured to that effect – and this I think is quite uncommon for the Internet – so that certain stages of development I went through, I expressed them [the stages] right in the moment on the level of content and brought them to the Internet.
> (Maxi, personal interview, September 6, 2007)

In a similar way, the next interviewee also describes the connection between personal "spiritual" development and presentation on the Internet:

> And then, according to my personal development, I constantly added something [to the home page]. The website has been in existence since

2000 or 2001, and the site has expanded more and more, depending on what happened. I once participated in a class on angels, ... I met a lot of nice people, but, in sum, it was not the right thing for me, but I could write about it on my website. And bit by bit, my site grew.

(Michi, personal interview, July 1, 2007)

As these examples indicate, presence on the Internet in the form of a personal home page is seen as changing dynamically, depending on how individual religious constructions are developed. In some cases, the visitor to the home page sees only the religious topics that are of recent importance to the page's owner. In other cases the home page offers a diachronic perspective, a wide shot of the evolution of the owner's personal religiosity as it has developed over the last few years. As the Internet reflects both synchronic (fixed-point) and diachronic (through-time) perspectives on the dynamic development of personal religiosity, it can be assumed that it is also a place for active (self-)reflection. Writing down changes in personal religious views on home pages and adapting the design accordingly calls for deliberate processes of self-reflection.

Coming back to the main issue of this case study – what New Age individuals say about their use of the Internet – we can provisionally state that the motive for going online and the development of the online presentation (both in content and design) are deeply embedded in the personal construction of New Age religiosity. By using or applying certain explanatory statements or legitimizing comments, New Age individuals make (narrative and rhetorical) connections to dominant themes within the field of New Age spirituality, such as the "spiritual path" or the idea of "holism."

Clashing religiosities: media presence and conflicts

Individual religious concepts and interpretations are probably more visible on the Internet than they are in other mass media. Patchwork patterns incorporating, transforming and reorganizing various religious elements within one single biography stand side by side with more "traditional" ways of constructing personal religiosity, which follow the dominant discourses of churches or established religious traditions. It is not only the researcher who becomes aware of the complexity and dynamics of religious concepts, but also religious actors themselves. In many cases, this pluralism may not be a problem. Depending on actors' level of tolerance and sense of mission, other religious concepts might be noticed but not judged negatively. In other cases, we can see religious actors trying to persuade others, arguing that their religious belief is "false." This often leads to clashes within religious fields. In the field of New Age, this is illustrated by an example provided by the interviewee Nicki.

During the interview it became clear that Nicki, in a similar way to the other interviewees, constructs her religiosity more as a patchwork than in terms of exclusive membership of one religious tradition. Although she feels a strong connection with Jesus and his teachings, over the years she has become more and more critical of the Christian church and its practices. She describes herself as very interested in religious questions in general. This can be seen as the main reason for her interest in a contemporary understanding of angels and for her first coming into contact with Reiki. With her increasing interest in various religious matters, she not only used the Internet more and more frequently as a source for information, but also actively participated in it. She acted as an administrator for a Christian forum where she also performed several online rituals. In the interview, she said that she had regularly conducted a Christian prayer chat that ran for several hours online; people used this chat to pray for their hopes and needs. She rated herself as a person who was very popular with the participants of the prayer chat. Trouble began when Nicki published her own home page, which included her ideas about Reiki and angels. This brought her into conflict with the members of the Christian forum, particularly with the prayer chat participants:

> And then we used to have this prayer chat on Mondays from 8:00; sometimes it went on till midnight ... it was a really good thing ... and then I got my own home page and then big trouble started because they said I am of the devil because of Reiki and with ... because of my homepage ... , because of the angels and Reiki, because of the things I had on this page they said I had become estranged because of the things I used to write in the prayer chat, and because I used the name "Devotee of Jesus" – they said this wasn't right and in fact I was a sect member – after that incident I left all this behind [the chat and the Christian forum].
> (personal interview, February 7, 2007)

What exactly happened here and how did the conflict arise? Nicki describes herself as a person who has presented herself in the context of the Christian forum as an "orthodox" Christian believer. This position was made clear to the other participants through her nickname, "Devotee of Jesus," and her behavior during the online prayer meetings. But, as can be seen from the subsequent conflict, this position was only *one* of Nicki's religious interests. For her, it seems normal to be a Christian who also uses Reiki rituals and refers to (New Age) angels.[4] On her home page, she presents a Christian version of the legend of Usui – the "founder" of Reiki – and concludes with the following personal remarks:

> As a Reiki practitioner I am following the way of Jesus and his love with cheerfulness, confidence, honesty, thankfulness and freedom.
> (Nicki, personal interview, February 7, 2007)

As she points out in this statement, Nicki is able to integrate the Reiki healing system into her personal Christian beliefs. The conflict arose when her self-positioning (her religious identity construction and her ritual practice) and positioning as perceived by the members of the forum were in conflict. Following the publication of the home page, the forum members were no longer able to agree with Nicki's self-positioning, which they had previously thought of as "truly" Christian. They did not consider the Christian ritual practice and belief as conducted in the online prayers to be compatible with Reiki healing or New Age ideas of angels. Thus, they now needed to allot Nicki a new position that would make it clear that they strongly disagreed with her ideas of combining Christian ideas with Reiki rituals. However, the rhetoric they chose seems to have intensified the conflict. By linking Nicki with the "devil" and with "sects," they associated her with topics that usually carry negative connotations. Nicki could resolve the conflict only by leaving the situation and breaking completely with the forum and its members.

At a more abstract level of discussion, we can observe that various processes of identity construction and positioning are apparent in the presentation of religious and ritualistic identities on the Internet. The public character of the medium makes it possible to examine the complex negotiation processes occurring in the field of New Age. It is interesting that, in this case, conflict arose in relation to statements about an individual's religious background, especially her usage of rituals foreign to the tradition she belonged to. It is also important to notice the role of the medium in this case. The Internet works as a multilayered network that hosts a huge variety of information and communication. In Nicki's narrative, the lines of conflict ran between a forum, a chat and a home page. The co-action of these three structures and the specific discursive background of each provided the basis for the conflict. The complexity of the medium in which a conflict might take place is therefore significant.[5]

Conclusion: negotiating religiosity online

As the examples used in this case study indicate, the Internet is a dynamic and complex place in which New Age individuals present themselves and communicate with others on religious topics. The large number of New Age personal websites shows the importance of the Web for negotiating religiosity. But looking only at online presentations does not answer the question of whether and how media use is itself embedded in users' construction of religious identity. As we have seen, both motives for going online and changes to style and content on personal websites are intertwined with people's religiosity; this only becomes apparent when the researcher goes "back" offline and actually talks to people. The Internet has become an important space for building, negotiating, presenting and communicating religious identity constructions. In the field of New Age, we can state that the complexity of these construction processes on the Internet is – most likely for the first time, from a quantitative perspective – becoming apparent to researchers and religious actors alike. Instances of conflict may be the result for religious actors. For the researcher, such conflicts can be placed in the broader perspective provided by a detailed analysis of the negotiation of religiosity, both offline and online.

Discussion questions

- How do new media technologies and the opportunities they offer empower religious actors, especially those with New Age beliefs?
- To what extent does the Internet create opportunities for the construction of unique, personalized forms of religiosity not previously available to individuals?

Notes

1 The term "actor" or "agent" is used here in the sense originated by Pierre Bourdieu. It can be used for both individuals and groups. Following Bourdieu, "actors" are highly socially embedded beings. Their actions are strongly dependent on their "habitus," meaning incorporated schemes of acting, thinking and cognition which are generated in the "fields" the actors are part of.
2 Bergunder uses the word "esotericism" to refer to the European discourse in which the term is often used synonymously with "New Age."
3 The interviews used in this article have been translated from German into English by the author; all real names and places have been anonymized.
4 In New Age, angels have become beings from whom people ask personal support or healing, or help in "profane" things like finding a parking lot. They are often associated with certain energetic frequencies, a specific color and chakras. New Age angels don't need to be connected with God, as they are in the Christian view. They can exist and act on their own.
5 On rituals and conflict in Virtual Worlds, for example, see Heidbrink, Miczek and Radde-Antweiler 2011.

References

Bergunder, M. (2010) "What is Esotericism? Cultural Studies Approaches and the Problems of Definition in Religious Studies," *Method and Theory in the Study of Religion*, 22: 9–36.
Hanegraaff, W. (1996) *New Age and Western Culture: Esotericism in the Mirror of Secular Thought*, Leiden: Brill.
Heidbrink, S., Miczek, N. and Radde-Antweiler, K. (2011) "Contested Rituals in Virtual Worlds," in R. Grimes, U. Hüsken, U. Simon and E. Venbrux (eds) *Ritual, Media, and Conflict*, 165–87, Oxford: Oxford University Press.
Luca (June 28, 2007) personal interview (name anonymized).
Maxi (September 6, 2007) personal interview (name anonymized).
Michi (July 1, 2007) personal interview (name anonymized).
Miczek, N. (2009) "Identitäten – Rituale – Medien. Eine qualitative Studie zu Aushandlungen gegenwärtiger Religiosität," unpublished thesis, University of Heidelberg.
Nicki (February 7, 2007) personal interview (name anonymized).
Radde-Antweiler, K. (2006) "Rituals Online: Transferring and Designing Rituals," *Online – Heidelberg Journal of Religions on the Internet*, 2(1): 54–72. Online. Available: www.ub.uni-heidelberg.de/archiv/6957 (accessed 31 January 2011).
Sutcliffe, S. (2003) *Children of the New Age: A History of Spiritual Practices*, London: Routledge.
Toni (May 11, 2007) personal interview (name anonymized).

Part III
Reflections on studying religion and new media

20 Theoretical frameworks for approaching religion and new media

Knut Lundby

What are the dominant theoretical approaches employed in the study of religion and new media? How do these theories influence methods employed or questions explored in research? The aim of this chapter is to provide students and scholars with an overview of key theoretical approaches to the study of religion and media. This, it is hoped, may work as a lens for interpretation, especially for studies of new media engagement and interaction by religious users and communities.

Studies of religion and new media draw upon scholarly resources in religious studies as well as in media studies. The former includes a range of approaches rooted in different disciplines from the social sciences (sociology of religion, anthropology of religion, psychology of religion), the humanities (history of religions), and theology. Media studies also has roots in various social science and humanities traditions. Sociology, political science, economics, history, language, literature, music, and aesthetics all inform media studies as a field of communication. When it comes to "new media" or "digital media," media studies are also informed by computer science or informatics. These lists are not comprehensive and the naming of the different research traditions may vary from one country or academic context to another. There may also be other ways of organizing the various knowledge traditions in relation to studies of religion and new media. The above is meant only to demonstrate how interdisciplinary and complex the seemingly limited research area of religion and media actually is.

In principle, religious studies should be able to analyze religious expressions in various media using the interpretative (hermeneutic) and critical-historic approaches that dominate their written, text-oriented disciplines. Similarly, the social scientific traditions on religion may approach how people use media as a substitute or supplement in their religious practices. However, none of these aspects of religious studies can prosper without further insight into how media and communication processes work in contemporary society. Religious studies will benefit from an understanding of the production processes for media content, produced "texts" as also visual or multimodal documents and wider reception processes, as well as the role of such mediated communication in society. These approaches are part of media studies. Religious studies could learn from media studies in order to undertake proper research into religion and media. Similarly, media studies could approach religion in the same way as any symbolic field in the media. However, deeper analyses require greater understanding of religious traditions and their symbolic universes.

Religion is not just transmitted via particular media. The forms of mediation should actually be regarded as an integral part of the definition of religion. Religions are to a large extent shaped by their dominant means of communication. Whether they are mainly oral, codified in writing, or further distributed in print has significance. Printing technology was an "agent of change" in the Protestant Reformation in Europe (Eisenstein 1979), and likewise digital technologies are probably crucial to transformations of contemporary religion. These are ongoing processes, open for further research.

Throughout history, religious traditions have had to be translated (or "transmediated") for new generations in changing contexts of communication. The tradition, then, is put in a new form. New religions, for their part, relate to their contemporary context of mediated communication. Religion, the anthropologists Birgit Meyer and Annelies Moors argue, "cannot be analyzed outside the forms and practices of mediation that define it" (2006: 7). It then becomes paramount to explore how the transition from one mode of mediated communication to another contributes to reconfiguring a particular religious practice. The focus should be on the cultural practices of mediation rather than on the media themselves, as already suggested by the communication scholar Jesús Martín-Barbero (1993), based on his Latin American experiences. However, the extent to which media technologies are driving forces in transformations of religions is a key issue that distinguishes the theoretical approaches to be discussed in this chapter.

When such modern technological media as the telegraph and the printing press became part of industrialization and colonization, they were conceived of as vehicles of transportation, which, James Carey (1989) explains, had religious roots, and the moral meaning of this transportation of messages and ideas "was the establishment and extension of God's kingdom on earth" (p. 16). However, science and secularization removed the basis for such religious metaphors of communication and the media technologies themselves became the central concern, though Carey reminds us that the alternative model, a ritual view of communication, also has religious roots, being aimed at the representation and confirmation of shared beliefs (1989: 18–21).

By "new media," this book and this chapter points to the contemporary digitization of communication. Small-scale digital media give a ritual view of communication new energy, as these tools are woven into daily social interaction within a variety of communities. They invite "user-generated content" as symbolic sharing, although the transmission view still applies when religious actors use these new media to reach out via new forms of mediation. Further, it is clear that the theoretical approaches to be discussed below may have deeper roots in "old" than in "new" media.

My presentation of theoretical frameworks for approaching religion and (new) media will be limited by my own academic horizons. As a media scholar with a background in the sociology of religion, my work has emphasized Christian traditions in high modern Nordic societies. The context for the reflections in this chapter is, more generally, that of high or late modern media-saturated societies.

Discussion: five approaches to media and religion

I have selected five theoretical approaches to religion in "new media" that have proven prominent in this field. They may from the outset have been engaged with what in today's digital environment are "old" media. However, their proponents are taking these theories toward the digital realm. Due to space restrictions, I have limited myself to discussing one significant piece of work from one key scholar of religion and media within each approach (see the recommended reading at the end of the chapter). This is intended to provide some comparisons not just between media research approaches: the selected works also employ a variety of definitions of religion as well as scientific methodology. This will be explicated in the sections to come. The overview is shown in Table 20.1.

As with all such typologies, the categories simplify and leave out important nuances. To some extent there are also cross-linkages between the authors related to the five approaches (for example, on mediatization). Their much richer works will not be given the proper attention they deserve, but we may find points of comparison from which to begin further explorations of religion and new media.

Technological determinism – Marshall McLuhan

Marshall McLuhan (1911–80) early on (1964) envisioned "the global village" of electronic networking, but being a scholar of the television age, he had no knowledge of the contemporary digital media yet to come. His famous phrase that "the medium is the message" (1964) identifies him as a prominent scholar of "medium theory," a term coined after his death. Medium theory observes influences of communication technologies in addition to, and also separately from, the content they deliver. Medium theory focuses on the distinct characteristics and influences of each type of medium, for example, how print and television encourage different modes of thinking and different value systems (Meyrowitz 2008). Hence if Marshall McLuhan had lived to experience today's

Table 20.1 Approaches to studying religion in "new media"

Approach to the study of media and religion	Selected author	Definition of religion	Methodology
Technological determinism	M. McLuhan	G. K. Chesterton	Philosophical
Mediatization of religion	S. Hjarvard	P. Boyer	Survey
Mediation of meaning	S. M. Hoover	C. Geertz	Ethnography
Mediation of sacred forms	G. Lynch	E. Durkheim	Cultural sociology
Social shaping of technology	H. Campbell	C. Geertz	Case studies

Internet, smartphones and other small-scale digital media he would no doubt have theorized about the specific affordances of these new media.

McLuhan was a technological determinist in the sense that he asked about the effects of any technology upon people's lives, upon the "whole population," and the study of effects drove him to the study of causality (E. McLuhan 1999: xxii–xxiv). However, against accusations of determinism, media theorists have "a much subtler argument: about *tendencies* rather than absolutist mechanisms, about interactions between media and society rather than media wholly shaping society" (Meyrowitz 2008; emphasis in the original). Even McLuhan said that "There is absolutely no inevitability as long as there is a willingness to contemplate what is happening" (McLuhan and Fiore 1967: 25).

Jacques Ellul, the French sociologist, had opened this avenue of thinking about the dominance of technology in social life ten years before McLuhan. In *The Technological Society* (1964), Ellul argues that technology is laden with values that shape social and cultural practices. He suggests large-scale evolutionary thinking about how technology changes civilization, combined with a personal, Catholic view of how technical "disease" can be cured with Christian therapy (Wilkinson 1964: xx). McLuhan shares some of Ellul's visions but is careful to distinguish his theorizing on technology from his faith.

Although Marshall McLuhan mostly kept religion a private matter (E. McLuhan 1999: xviii–xix), he reflected on religion throughout most of his life (McLuhan 1999a) with a kind of loose philosophical methodology. McLuhan's first published academic article, in 1936, was on the English writer G. K. Chesterton (1874–1936) as a "practical mystic" rooted in Christianity. "The mysteries revealed by Mr. Chesterton are the daily miracles of sense and consciousness" (1999b: 4) which McLuhan came to explore through media as extensions of these senses and this human consciousness (1964). Although he did not openly allow his amateur religious reflections to shape his theories of the media, McLuhan saw many parallels.

McLuhan once remarked that his own approach to media was similar to the Formal Causality of the Catholic thinker Thomas Aquinas (1225–74). Eric McLuhan sees his father's ideas of media as extensions of Aquinas' thought, and of media as an environment as inspired by him (E. McLuhan 1999: xx). However, when it comes to religion, Marshall McLuhan may have been even more influenced by Chesterton and his practical and mystic Christianity. They both converted to the Catholic Church. McLuhan was a devout Catholic throughout his entire academic career and wanted to contribute reflections on "Discarnate Man and the Incarnate Church" (E. McLuhan 1999: xxviii).

Mediatization of religion – Stig Hjarvard

Stig Hjarvard, a Danish media sociologist, proposes a theory of the mediatization of religion (2008a) as part of a more general theory of the mediatization of society (2008b). This "theory of the media as agents of media change" (2008a) does not imply a technological determinism, although it is not far from a subtle "medium theory" (Hjarvard 2008b: 109–10). There are other conceptualizations of mediatization processes (Couldry 2008; Lundby 2009), but Hjarvard has provided a coherent argument that includes religion.

Mediatization, according to Hjarvard, is to be considered a two-sided process of late modernity "in which the media on the one hand emerge as an independent institution with a logic of its own that other institutions have to accommodate to. On the other hand, media simultaneously become an integrated part of other institutions" (2008b: 105). Religion is one of these institutions.

"Through the process of mediatization, religion is increasingly being subsumed under the logic of the media," Hjarvard holds (2008a: 11). He refers to the three metaphors advocated by the media theorist Joshua Meyrowitz (1993): media can be understood as conduits for the delivery of content, as languages with a certain "grammar" that format the output of a given medium, or as environments that establish a certain context or setting for the mediated communication.

Hjarvard (2008a) argues that media as conduits of communication in media-saturated societies have become the primary source of religious ideas, in terms of the bits and pieces of religious texts, symbols, and imageries that journalists and producers put together when they construct their media stories. "As a language the media mould religious imagination in accordance with the genres of popular culture, and as cultural environments the media have taken over many of the social functions of the institutionalized religions," Hjarvard adds (2008a: 9). He thinks that media provide both moral and spiritual guidance and a sense of community. Taken together, these processes imply a mediatization of religion. Much of Hjarvard's argument is related to popular media such as film and television. He submits survey evidence that people (in his case, Danes) engage in spiritual and religious issues much more via various media than by attending places of worship.

Hjarvard sticks to a substantive definition of religion, that is, religions as supernatural agencies of action that people relate to. He thinks of religion in terms of human evolution and applies a cognitive-anthropological approach (2008a, 2008c). Pascal Boyer's book *Religion Explained*, in which he elaborates on "the human instincts that fashion gods, spirits and ancestors" (2001), is a key reference.

Stig Hjarvard has not yet explicated his theory in the domain of the digital media. However, he includes them in general. More specific theorization on mediatization processes with digital media is needed (Krotz 2008, Schulz 2004), and it is likely that one will observe some continuity rather than a paradigmatic shift (Finnemann 2011), as old and new media are so closely intertwined in today's "mediatized worlds" (Krotz 2008).

Mediation of meaning – Stewart M. Hoover

Stewart M. Hoover takes a cultural approach to the study of media and religion. He is influenced by the culturalist turn in media studies of television and the press pioneered by James Carey (1988, 1989), and applies this cultural approach to new forms of digital communication.[1] However, "digital media" are only covered in passing in his 2006 book on *Religion in the Media Age*. They are included in the overall argument that takes theories about media, religion, and culture "[f]rom medium to meaning" (2006: 26).

Medium theory is laid aside; "a focus on meaning is both a contrast with other approaches, and a potential complement to them," Hoover holds (2006: 36). This approach looks for the social meanings that the media have for people and turns to the reception side of communication: how "the various media and messages that are accessible to individuals in the private sphere are received, understood, and potentially used in other spheres of social and cultural life" (Hoover 2006: 36). "Personal" digital media (Lüders 2008) are, to a growing extent, among those that are accessible to people in the meaning-making processes of everyday life.

However, the research that Hoover and his team undertook with a variety of American families centered mainly on the meaning-making processes around television. They asked people to give their "accounts" of the media: this meant that parents "were called upon to offer stories, or *accounts,* of how their family operated in relation to media" and to share how they as parents "felt *accountable*" (Alters and Clark 2004: 5; emphasis in the original). This ethnographic methodology offers rich insight into what meaning people make out of the media in various contexts of use.

Mobile and small-scale tools expand the repertoire of media that people use in the social interaction and meaning-making of everyday life. These on-the-move media demonstrate Hoover's understanding of "media" as *practices* (2006: 23–24). This goes beyond "media" as just institutions, texts or technological objects and turns toward mediated communication as it occurs in various social settings. Or, as Nick Couldry points out, to theorize media as practice is quite simply to ask what people are *doing* in relation to media across a whole range of situations and contexts (2004). As part of this, one can ask how people use the media in terms of meaning-making.

New digital media may in themselves change and shape our practices. However, this approach shifts focus *From the Media to Mediations* (Martín-Barbero 1993). The ongoing mediation of meaning catches the attention rather than the specific media that are applied in these mediation processes. The cultural context, however, has to be a key aspect. Mediation of meaning takes place within a larger matrix of communication, culture, and hegemony (Martín-Barbero 1993), while the specific role of media culture may deserve particular attention in relation to "meanings ... made through mediated sources" (Hoover 2006: 36). The conditions of these mediating practices in religious cultures may be so complex that the nature of religion and spirituality itself is fundamentally changed. Hence they should be considered processes of mediatization (Hoover 2009) rather than mediation.

Stewart Hoover thinks of religious meaning as a particular kind of cultural meaning (2006: 37). This resonates with his understanding of religion. He builds his approach on the definition submitted by the anthropologist Clifford Geertz, who sees religion as a system of symbols or a cultural system (Hoover 2006: 23).

Mediation of sacred forms – Gordon Lynch

Gordon Lynch, the British sociologist of religion, for his part, leans on the sociologist Émile Durkheim to frame his understanding of religion. Durkheim defines religion as a social phenomenon, "a unified system of beliefs and practices relative to sacred things … which unite into one single moral community … all those who adhere to them" (1995: 44). Lynch searches for a cultural sociology of the sacred to come "After Durkheim" (Lynch 2012: 30). Durkheim is himself within the cultural sociological tradition that regards the sacred through the "particular form of cultural signification in which symbols, objects, sentiments and practices are experienced as expressions of a normative, absolute reality" without assuming an "actual ontological referent lying behind sacred forms" (Lynch 2012: 15). Sacred experiences need not be related to religion's expressions. However, Lynch avoids the term "sacred secular," as sacred forms such as human rights or the care of children, in his view, have complex and implicit religious histories and may shape the lives of religious individuals and groups as much as secular ones. Hence, he finds thinking in terms of multiple sacred forms more useful than making distinctions along sacred and secular lines (Lynch 2012: 18).

Lynch lines up behind Edward Shils, Robert Bellah, and Jeffrey Alexander, who were all influenced by Durkheim but shaped further foundations for a cultural sociology of the sacred. Lynch (2012: 29) defines the sacred by what people "collectively experience as absolute, non-contingent realities which present normative claims over the meanings and conduct of social life." Sacred forms, then, are historically specific instances of the sacred. Lynch reformulates the profane in relation to the sacred: "The normative reality constituted by a sacred form simultaneously constructs the evil which might profane it, and the pollution of this sacred reality is experienced by its adherents as a painful wound" (Lynch 2012: 29).

Such painful experience of evil invites communication in order to establish some form of restitution of the sacred. I have elsewhere argued the other side of this coin: the sacred has to be continuously communicated to be held in awe, set apart from the mundane. "The sacred is to be found at the intersection of mediation processes, between the constructed representations of the potentially sacred, and the actual devotion of the audience" (Lundby 2006: 60). What is to be regarded as sacred is not just a matter of representation of certain objects but also of the reception of these representations.

All sacred forms are mediated, Lynch states: "The interaction of symbol, thought, feeling and action that characterizes sacred forms is only possible through media which give sacred forms material expression. Media enable communication about, and interaction with, those forms" (2012: 87). There are secret or closed circles that celebrate their specific sacred symbols. However, mediation with technological media usually makes it public. Representation and reception of the sacred as well as of evil occurs in relation to the media. "It is reasonable to argue that public media have become the primary structure for engaging with the sacred," Lynch notes (2012: 93). This leads into a mediatization of the sacred (Lynch 2012: 87–98).

Gordon Lynch applies his theoretical tools to empirical analyses of how sacred forms are mediatized. He looks at discourses in various examples of coverage, particularly from the BBC, of Middle East conflicts and of child suffering (2012: 98–113). Kim Knott and her team have also researched British "[m]edia portrayals of religion and the secular sacred" – they find the term "secular sacred" relevant, using quantitative and qualitative content analyses (Taira, Poole, and Knott 2012).

Lynch and Knott and her colleagues acknowledge how the new digital media, such as blogs and net news, interfere in the representation and reception of the religious sacred as well as the secular sacred in the main news media. Analysis of this interplay is just beginning. Knott and Mitchell (2012) find it useful to be reminded that, although the World Wide Web is just two decades old, "the way that the Internet is being used by both religious institutions and individuals is transforming the daily practices and expressions of religion not only in Britain but also around the world" (p. 260). However, actual studies of these transformations on a broader scale have still to emerge.

Social shaping of technology – Heidi Campbell

Heidi Campbell, the editor of this volume, turns straight to the new digital tools in her book *When Religion Meets New Media* (2010). She also turns the binoculars around and focuses on processes by which religious traditions help shape technology, instead of asking how the media shape religion.

Her theoretical base is the social shaping of technology (SST). This theory observes that technology is not just a given, but is shaped through choices made by designers as well as by users. The choices may not be deliberate or intentional, but are outcomes of social interaction with the technology. SST theorists look for different possible routes to establish new technologies, holding that different choices may create different paths, and lead to the adoption of different technologies (MacKenzie and Wajkman 1985; Williams and Edge 1996).

SST is one of the models in the field of science and technology studies (STS) aiming to grasp the relations between social patterns and technology. Under this umbrella one also finds the theories known by the acronyms SCOT and ANT, the social construction of technology (Bijker, Huges, and Pinch 1987) and actor-network theory (Callon and Latour 1981) respectively. This family of theories contrasts with technological determinism and linear thinking about innovations. They all stress the potential and role of human actors and, in the case of ANT, also of non-human elements in social networks (Latour 2005).

Campbell learns from all the aforementioned theories but sticks to SST and develops it into an approach she terms "the religious-social shaping of technology." She thinks that the specific sacred texts and theological positions of a religious tradition blend with its rituals and other social practices, or, in her own words: "a religious community's historical life practice, interpretive tradition, and the contemporary outworking of their values inform their choices about the adoption and adaptation of technology" (Campbell 2010: 41). Campbell thinks that the "moral economies" of religious communities make them unique in their negotiations with media (2010: 58).

These negotiations are studied from four perspectives. First, the specific history and traditions of the actual religious community; second, its core beliefs and patterns; third, how the negotiation process itself turns out in the face of new media; and, finally, the framing and discourse on the new media within the specific religious community.

Campbell (2010) applies a comparative methodology as she looks at Jewish, Christian, and Muslim communities to see how they shape their uses of new media technologies. She presents a series of case studies as evidence. To take one example for each of the four perspectives: *history and tradition* is certainly behind the avoidance of most visual and digital media among Orthodox Jews. When there are conflicts between Jewish law and technology, it is the latter that has to change. Creative technology solutions arise in order to be faithful to the Torah while managing everyday activities. *Core beliefs and patterns* shape Islamic responses to media, as when religiously defined communal values inform Muslim televangelism and its accompanying web presence. *Negotiating new media* is, for religious communities, a question of whether they should accept, reject, reconfigure, or possibly innovate with technological solutions. Evangelical Christians usually accept and appropriate in order to reach out. The Orthodox instead rejects and resists. But there are also groups that reconfigure and innovate to shape the technology for religious outcomes and needs, like the virtual Anglican cathedral in Second Life. *Framing and discourse on the new media* can be observed in how various Protestant groups argue for e-vangelism, how the Anglican or Catholic church establishments regard use of the Internet, or how the emerging church movement embraces countercultural uses of new media.

There is a great variation in how religious groups and institutions relate to new media technologies and these variations will, to a significant extent, be grounded in their theologies. Campbell, like Hoover, follows Geertz in understanding religion as a cultural or symbolic system. However, unlike Hoover, Campbell does not tackle religious uses of new media that are outside the tight control of religious organizations – where so much contemporary expression of spirituality and religiosity takes place.

Conclusion: patterns and uncovered topics

The approaches to research on religion and new media represented by these five scholars could be organized along two dimensions. One is the span from institutionalized religion to free-floating religiosity. The other dimension runs from traditional mass media to small-scale digital media.

It is striking how deeply embedded Hjarvard, Hoover, and Lynch all are in theories related to the mass media. All three are in the process of working their way towards addressing the impact of personal, digital media on religious or sacred practices. However, a lot remains to be done to really integrate an understanding of communication and interaction involving these new, small-scale media with the theories of mediatization of religion, mediation of meaning, and mediation of sacred forms.

While all three of these scholars relate to the institutions of mass communication in various ways, they all avoid a preoccupation with institutional religion. They all point to religious influences from popular culture and they all stress the individual agency of those who seek spiritual or religious meaning in a media-saturated late modernity. They are all aware of the power of institutions, but religious institutions are consigned to the background. When it comes to media institutions, Hjarvard and Hoover see them from the reception side, of people's media use, rather than from the production side, of media content. However, Lynch directs his analysis towards representations of the sacred in the media (Sumiala-Seppänen, Lundby, and Salokangas 2006).

Hjarvard, Hoover, and Lynch differ primarily in their definition and understanding of religion. Hence, they will grasp somewhat different aspects of religion and religiosity as social and cultural practices. Hjarvard observes the bits and pieces of "banal religion" (2008a: 14–16) that people pick up from the popular media. Hoover looks for the accounts people make of the media in the spiritual and religious meaning-making of everyday life, trying to make "plausible narratives of the self" (2006: 84). For Lynch, "sacred," and not "religion," is the main category. He defines this from a collective viewpoint, as the secular or religious sacred cultural forms that people relate to.

McLuhan and Campbell, in comparison, turn to the institutions of the main traditions when they try to grasp religion. McLuhan has an eye for the mystical but moves within a religious universe determined by his personal relation to the Catholic Church. Campbell traverses a wider spectrum of monotheistic religions, but her understanding of religious communities is limited to the traditions of Judaism, Islam, and Christianity. However, of these five scholars, it is Campbell who gets closest to the new digital media.

The differences between the theories influence the methods that are employed and the questions that are explored. The comparative, philosophical approaches used by McLuhan and Campbell, the two thinking in institutional terms about religion, help raise new questions about relation to technology. However, the three that approach religion through the "spiritual marketplace" (Roof 1999; Clark 2007) using empirical methods, Hjarvard, Hoover, and Lynch, may be in a better position to grasp changes in the overall picture of religion and new media, especially as they develop their theories to account for small-scale digital media.

This may be the biggest challenge for further research: Internet-based and personal media in new networks change the media landscape. People have new opportunities for participating and expressing themselves. These new media have not so far been addressed on a broader scale in research on media and religion. Approaching this task, the five authors selected for this chapter represent different viewpoints on the shaping role of the media in relation to religion. McLuhan will emphasize how the various media determine religious practices.

Campbell, at the other end of the scale, stresses the agency of religious collectives, how they contribute to shaping the technology. The remaining three take intermediate positions, all claiming that media turn into mediatization processes that shape religion and religiosity. Still, they think people and institutions influence the outcome. How will research on the mediatization of religion, on the mediation of meaning, and on the mediation of sacred forms approach the changing patterns of participation in "digital religion"? That remains to be seen.

Recommended reading

Technological determinism

McLuhan, M., ed. McLuhan, E. and Szklarek, J. (1999) *The Medium and the Light: Reflections on Religion*, Toronto: Stoddart.

A posthumous collection of Marshall McLuhan's public and private reflections on religion, related to his famous works on the media as extensions of the human senses, and the media as the message.

Mediatization of religion

Hjarvard, S. (2008) "The mediatization of religion: A theory of the media as agents of religious change," *Northern Lights: Film & Media Studies Yearbook*, 6: 9–26.

This article is a condensed version of Hjarvard's theory of the media as agents of religious change, framed within his more general theory of the mediatization of society. See also the discussion of Hjarvard's thesis in the special issue of the journal *Culture and Religion* on the mediatization of religion (2011, vol. 12, no. 2).

Mediation of meaning

Hoover, S. M. (2006) *Religion in the Media Age*, Oxon: Routledge.

The book captures much of the scholarly debate in the research community on media, religion, and culture, where Hoover has been and is a leading figure, with input from the ethnographic studies of Hoover and his team in which American families were asked to give an account of the media in their lives.

Mediation of sacred forms

Lynch, G. (2012) *The Sacred in the Modern World: A Cultural Sociological Approach*, Oxford: Oxford University Press.

This book explicates the relation between the media and what is sacred in society, be it secular or religious. It is based on a cultural-sociological approach developed from Durkheim's sacred–profane distinction.

Social shaping of technology

Campbell, H. (2010) *When Religion Meets New Media*, Oxon: Routledge.

This volume develops the theory of religious social shaping of technology and applies it to case studies within Jewish, Muslim, and Christian religious communities.

Note

1 For example, the conference on religion and digital media at the Center for Media, Religion, and Culture, University of Colorado Boulder, of which Hoover is director.

References

Alters, D. F. and Clark, L. S. (2004) "Introduction," in S. M. Hoover, L. S. Clark and D. F. Alters (eds) *Media, Home, and Family*, 3–17, New York: Routledge.
Bijker, W. E., Huges, T. P. and Pinch, T. (eds) (1987) *The Social Construction of Technological Systems: New Directions in the Sociology and History of Technology*, Cambridge, MA: MIT Press.
Boyer, P. (2001) *Religion Explained: The Human Instincts that Fashion Gods, Spirits and Ancestors*, London: Vintage.
Callon, M. and Latour, B. (1981) "Unscrewing the big leviathan: How actors macrostructure reality and how sociologists help them to do so," in K. D. Knorr-Cetina and A. V. Cicourel (eds) *Advances in Social Theory and Methodology: Toward an Integration of Micro- and Macro-Sociologies*, 277–303, Boston: Routledge and Kegan Paul.
Campbell, H. (2010) *When Religion Meets New Media*, Oxon: Routledge.
Carey, J. W. (ed.) (1988) *Media, Myths, and Narratives: Television and the Press*, Newbury Park: Sage.
——(1989) *Communication as Culture: Essays on Media and Society*, Boston: Unwin Hyman.
Clark, L. S. (ed.) (2007) *Religion, Media and the Marketplace*, New Brunswick: Rutgers University Press.
Couldry, N. (2004) "Theorising media as practice," *Social Semiotics*, 14(2): 115–32.
——(2008) "Mediatization or mediation? Alternative understandings of the emergent space of digital storytelling," *New Media & Society*, 10(3): 373–91.
Durkheim, E., trans. Fields, K. E. (1995; first published 1912 in French) *The Elementary Forms of Religious Life*, New York: The Free Press.
Eisenstein, E.L. (1979) *The Printing Press as an Agent of Change: Communication and Cultural Transformations in Early-Modern Europe*, 2 vols, Cambridge: Cambridge University Press.
Ellul, J. (1964; first published 1954 in French) *The Technological Society*, New York: Vintage.
Finnemann, N.O. (2011), "Mediatization theory and digital media," *Communications: The European Journal of Communication Research*, 36(1): 67–89.
Hjarvard, S. (2008a) "The mediatization of religion: A theory of the media as agents of religious change," *Northern Lights: Film & Media Studies Yearbook*, 6: 9–26.
——(2008b) "The mediatization of society: A theory of the media as agents of social and cultural change," *Nordicom Review*, 29: 105–34.
——(2008c) "Religionens medialisering: Fra kirkens tro til mediernes fortryllelse," in S. Hjarvard, *En verden af medier. Medialiseringen af politik, sprog, religion og leg*, 155–213, Fredriksberg: Samfundslitteratur.
Hoover, S.M. (2006) *Religion in the Media Age*, Oxon: Routledge.
——(2009) "Complexities: The case of religious cultures," in K. Lundby (ed.) *Mediatization: Concept, Changes, Consequences*, 123–38, New York: Peter Lang.

Knott, K. and Mitchell, J. (2012) "The changing faces of media and religion," in L. Woodhead and R. Catto (eds) *Religion and Change in Modern Britain*, 243–64, Oxon: Routledge.

Krotz, F. (2008) *Mediatized Worlds: Communication in the Medial and Social Change: Application to the DFG for Implementation of a Priority Program*, Memo, Bonn: Deutsche Forschungsgemeinshcaft.

Latour, B. (2005) *Reassembling the Social: An Introduction to Actor-Network-Theory*, Oxford: Oxford Universty Press.

Lüders, M. (2008) "Conceptualizing personal media," *New Media & Society*, 10(5): 683–702.

Lundby, K. (2006) "Contested communication: Mediating the sacred," in J. Sumiala-Seppänen, K. Lundby and R. Salokangas (eds) *Implications of the Sacred in (Post)Moderen Media*, 43–62, Gothenburg: Nordicom.

——(ed.) (2009) *Mediatization: Concept, Changes, Consequences*, New York: Peter Lang.

Lynch, G. (2012) *The Sacred in the Modern World: A Cultural Sociological Approach*, Oxford: Oxford University Press.

McLuhan, E. (1999) "Introduction," in M. McLuhan, ed. E. McLuhan and J. Szklarek, *The Medium and the Light: Reflections on Religion*, ix–xxviii, Toronto: Stoddart.

McLuhan, M. (1964) *Understanding Media: The Extensions of Man*, New York: McGraw Hill.

——, ed. McLuhan, E. and Szklarek, J. (1999a) *The Medium and the Light: Reflections on Religion*, Toronto: Stoddart.

——(1999b; first published 1936) "G. K. Chesterton: A practical mystic," in M. McLuhan, ed. E. McLuhan and J. Szklarek, *The Medium and the Light: Reflections on Religion*, Toronto: Stoddart.

McLuhan, M. and Fiore, Q. (1967) *The Medium is the Massage: An Inventory of Effects*, New York: Bantam Books.

MacKenzie, D. and Wajkman, J. (1985) *The Social Shaping of Technology: How the Refrigerator Got Its Hum*, Milton Keynes: Open University Press.

Martín-Barbero, J. (1993) *Communication, Culture and Hegemony: From the Media to Mediations*, London: Sage.

Meyer, B. and Moors, A. (2006) "Introduction," in B. Meyer and A. Moors (eds) *Religion, Media, and the Public Sphere*, 1–25, Bloomington: Indiana University Press.

Meyrowitz, J. (1993) "Images of media: Hidden ferment – and harmony – in the field," *Journal of Communication*, 43(3): 59–66.

——(2008) "Medium theory," in W. Donsbach (ed.) *International Encyclopedia of Communication*, vol. VII, 3055–61, Malden, MA: Blackwell.

Roof, W. C. (1999) *Spiritual Marketplace: Baby Boomers and the Remaking of American Religion*, Princeton: Princeton University Press.

Schulz, W. (2004) "Reconstructing mediatization as an analytical concept," *European Journal of Communication*, 19(1): 87–101.

Sumiala-Seppänen, J., Lundby, K. and Salokangas, R. (eds) (2006) *Implications of the Sacred in (Post)Modern Media*, Gothenburg: Nordicom.

Taira, T., Poole, E. and Knott, K. (2012) "Religion in the British media today," in O. Gower and J. Mitchell (eds) *Religion and the News*, Aldershot: Ashgate.

Wilkinson, J. (1964) "Translator's introduction," in J. Ellul, *The Technological Society*, v–xx, New York: Vintage.

Williams, R. and Edge, D. (1996) "The Social Shaping of Technology," *Research Policy*, 25 (6): 856–99.

21 Ethical issues in the study of religion and new media

Mark D. Johns

Scholars have used a variety of methods to study religious beliefs and practices. Sometimes they have employed tools of literary analysis to explore religious texts, such as the Christian Bible or the Muslim Quran. Tools of rhetorical analysis have been used to examine religious discourses, such as sermons or devotional materials. Sociologists of religion have used participant-observation studies to experience worship rituals or other community meetings. And other types of ethnographic studies have been utilized to better understand the thinking and behavior of individuals or groups in various religious traditions. In short, scholars of religion have employed the full range of methods used in the social sciences and the humanities to better understand religions and the practices of their adherents.

But religious expressions on the Internet are not precisely the same as those "in real life." That is, religious practices in the virtual or online realm are not available for study in the same way as those in the material world of unmediated experience. Religious ideas and meanings are always conveyed symbolically. But those who interact online often do so utilizing different symbol systems – using text, graphics, sound, video, or combinations of these (generally referred to as "hypertext") in place of vocal utterances or gestures. The addition of this hypertextual symbolic layer may add richness to the interaction, or conversely it may create distance between individuals. The difference depends on the technical context (the exact mode of communication technology being employed in the diverse array of Internet applications), and the social context (the nature and content of the communication taking place). Most frequently, it is precisely these differences that researchers are seeking to understand. That is, the ways in which the mediation of technology enhances, constrains, or modifies religious experience and interactions among religious persons are precisely the focus of study. But in any case, scholars who wish to study religion online must adjust their research methods to adapt to this new environment.

This chapter explores the unique challenges facing researchers in online contexts as they attempt to fulfill the essentials of determining what ethical standards apply in a given situation, ascertaining when informed consent is necessary and how it can be obtained, and assuring that privacy and anonymity can be maintained. It begins with a very brief overview of the background of the legal regulation of research ethical practice, and then raises a number of specific issues created by the formal features of computer-mediated communication. Finally, some approaches to ethical decision making are examined and some resources offered.

Ethics and legal issues in research

From a legal perspective, ethical decision making about research methods and practices is guided by measuring the benefits to society of gaining understanding about social phenomena as weighed against the risks to those whose behaviors are being studied. This equation has been established in Western culture fairly recently. It emerged from mid-twentieth-century experiences of grotesque medical experiments in the Nazi holocaust in Europe, and shocking disregard for human life in experiments such as the Tuskegee Study in the US. These events led to the production of documents such as the Nuremberg Code of 1949, and the Declaration of Helsinki adopted by the World Health Organization in 1964. Eventually, ethical concerns were encoded in law. In the United States, the National Research Act of 1974 created the National Commission for the Protection of Human Subjects of Biomedical and Behavioral Research. In accordance with its mandate, the Commission produced the "Belmont Report," published in 1979, which continues to serve as the foundation for the practice and regulation of research in the US. The report established informed consent of persons being studied as a central tenet, not only of biomedical research, but of research into human behaviors, as well. Also established was the requirement for institutional review boards (IRBs) to approve research projects at all institutions sponsoring research that receive any sort of federal funding (which would essentially be all educational and medical facilities in the nation). The Department of Health and Human Services in 1991 issued a second set of regulations, including a collection of guidelines known as the "Common Rule" (Buchanan 2010). These regulations ordered that research institutions must comply with the provisions of the Common Rule if funded by federal monies, and empowered the IRBs to approve, require modification, or disapprove research. According to the Common Rule, it is the task of the IRB to weigh the risk/benefit equation for any proposed study in order to assure the protection of research participants[1] (Johns, Hall, and Crowell 2004).

Such legal requirements are not limited to the US. The European Union also has regulations requiring the oversight of research for the purpose of protecting research participants. Guidelines adopted in 2005 direct EU member nations to establish conventions for research ethics committees (RECs) to govern various types of research. In the UK, for example, social research has generally enjoyed considerable freedom from oversight. But in 2005 the Department of Health revised the Research Governance Framework for Health and Social Care for England (RGF) to match the EU guidelines. This Framework establishes general principles for the governance of research, both clinical and social, and sets standards for research ethics, methods, informed consent, health and safety, and intellectual property issues. Although implementation of the EU guidelines varies from country to country, in many instances the regulations are more stringent than those in the US (Boddy, Boaz, Lupton, and Pahl 2006).

The mediation of technology may affect the risk/benefit ratio of a particular study. Those who study human behavior in any context must navigate the regulatory environment of IRBs, RECs, or equivalent panels that maintain strict oversight of research proposals. Those who conduct research on the Internet must further be concerned with the fact that this context and its special requirements are new territory not only to researchers themselves, but also to those who sit on ethics review boards, and to those who supervise research. Sometimes the adjustments to methods – and the difficult decisions that must be made concerning matters of privacy, consent, and/or presentation of data – raise issues that confound veteran researchers, as well as students and others just entering the field (Zimmer 2010). Thus, while all social researchers must adhere to the legal requirements of ethics review procedures, Internet researchers must navigate unfamiliar terrain, both in terms of ethical decision making, and in terms of satisfying ethics panels, which are similarly on unfamiliar ground in their review process. Hopefully, researchers will wish to take on this task out of ethical conscience and concern that supersedes the legal minimums.

Online research ethics

Conducting research online adds a new level of complexity to the research enterprise. Some of this complexity is simply due to the obvious fact that there are so many different contexts in which humans do things online. The Internet is not a single, monolithic environment, but serves as a framework supporting e-mail, mail lists, games, virtual worlds, social networks, blogs, web pages, synchronous chat, and more. Each of these types of computer-mediated communication has its own formal characteristics that shape the type of communication or interaction taking place. Further, within these categories are a multitude of venues with their own purposes, rules, and conventions. A mail list for a religious group may have a very different set of acceptable practices than a list for the discussion of football, for example, even though the technology used to convey the messages is identical. Looming above these specific differences is the not always so obvious complexity introduced by computer-mediated communication technology itself. The difficulties for researchers associated with this overarching reality can be boiled down to two central and interrelated issues: identity and privacy. Issues of identity are complex and are dealt with at some length elsewhere in this volume, but for this discussion it is sufficient to say that the technology challenges the researcher to understand precisely who or what she is studying in any given instance. This is frequently not as clear and simple as in more traditional types of social research. Privacy, too, is not as easily guaranteed in online contexts. Paradoxically, the same technology that clouds identity is capable of defeating the usual steps researchers take to maintain the anonymity of research participants. Thus, conducting research of religious activities online is complicated by the online environment itself.

The good news in this is that scholars of religion are not alone in dealing with these issues. All who study human behavior of any sort online are facing many of the same challenges, so there are others who have trod the path. The bad news is that the way is never going to be completely clear for any who do research online. Research methods are always tied to issues of theory and of ethics. These are impacted by the research questions being posed, the context of the research online, the context of the researcher in real life, and the interests of those who participate in the research. There may be easy answers concerning the ways to go about researching religion online, but the easy answers may not necessarily be the right answers. And in fact, there may be no totally right answers at all. What can be done here is to put the spotlight on some of the issues that may be faced by researchers new to online study of religion and to suggest some resources that may be helpful in addressing these. These include considering the basics of identity and privacy, as well as details related to accessibility of data, issues surrounding informed consent, and means of weighing the potential risks and benefits of research.

What or who is being studied?

Those who conduct research into religious beliefs and practices in traditional contexts generally have little difficulty grasping the focus of study and the level of analysis being employed. It is usually quite simple to discern that one is studying a religious text, for example, as opposed to studying the behavior of a religious group, or conducting an interview to learn about the beliefs and practices of a religious individual. However, in online contexts, human interactions are frequently conducted through the production of textual materials – e-mails, web pages, blog posts, audio or video clips, status updates, tweets, etc. (Herring 2004). One of the fundamental issues for Internet researchers is determining which of these texts are to be considered personal interactions, and which are to be considered publications. Different ethical guidelines apply in each case, and the distinctions are not always clear.

Consider, for example, the blog of a religious group, assembly, or congregation. In most cases, such a site is open and available for public viewing. The blog may contain information about meeting times and places, community events or activities, devotional reflections, and so forth. Often, such a blog is intended as a publication, much in the way a congregation or group might create a printed brochure to introduce itself to a newcomer or seeker, or a newsletter concerning upcoming activities. The safe assumption may be that this blog is intended in exactly this way, and is therefore open to study as a text, just as one might study a collection of printed materials produced by the same group. Because the focus of study is on public documents provided by the group, the fact that these documents have been disseminated electronically through the blog makes them no less available for study than if they had been printed on paper. However, one may ask if there are any copyright restrictions on the quoting of such a document in a scholarly paper or research report. If it is treated as a publication, what legal restrictions might apply? Should it be the copyright laws of the country in which the group is headquartered? Or would it rather be the copyright laws of the country in which the researcher will publish?

At the opposite end of the spectrum, imagine that the same blog is open to response posts, and in the electronic notes posted are comments from members of the group about the events that have taken place or are upcoming. Perhaps some of these express what was meaningful to them about the event, or how the event made them feel, or how it impacted their spiritual life. Perhaps other group members also posted comments agreeing with the first posters – or perhaps others had posted criticisms of the event of some sort. Multiple posts show a back-and-forth conversation, with various persons responding to one another. The blog is still open and publicly accessible on the Internet, but clearly there are group members exchanging ideas, beliefs, and opinions in this forum. Is it still a public text, available for study as a document? Or has it become a record of interaction among human subjects? If the latter, must the participants give their consent before a scholar may ethically study the blog? Must their identities be protected (Ess 2007)?

The cases presented here as examples may be extreme enough to suggest an easy decision, but online environments present an array of situations along the continuum between these extremes. Researchers must make sometimes difficult decisions concerning the nature of what they are studying. Behind every text is an author. Sometimes authors create a text for public distribution, and at other times they create texts that are directed specifically to certain other individuals. Even in the case of directed conversation, some have insisted that their notes be considered documents to be cited, and their authorship credited to them by name – while others have insisted on anonymity (Danet 2001). The researcher must, therefore, determine whether the level of analysis is focused on the text as a document, or on the thoughts and actions of the author as a human subject. In online contexts it is quite easy to convince oneself that a text exists apart from the person of the author because the text on screen hides the individual from view. At the same time, despite the firmly established development of the technology, there is often a tendency to discount the importance of a document that appears only on a screen and not on a printed page. Online researchers must avoid both of these fallacies.

The Internet researcher is sometimes exploring publications, similar to a book, magazine, or newspaper, which have certain copyright protections that vary from nation to nation around the globe. At other times, the Internet researcher is eavesdropping on written conversations, much like personal letters between individuals who have rights of privacy that also vary from place to place. More often the Internet researcher is confronted with an amalgam of the two, and must discern the type and level of protection to afford.

Public space or sacred ground?

Some online contexts are "members only," requiring registration, membership, permission, or some sort of password access for entry. Such areas automatically carry a caution sign for researchers. Conducting research within such restricted areas would suggest the necessity of permission from a controlling party, at a minimum. The owner, moderator, manager of passwords, or other gatekeeper must allow the researcher access to these restricted areas online. If a researcher requests permission to enter under false pretenses or without fully explaining to gatekeepers their intent, the ethical concerns are evident. Only when the benefits of a research project are extremely desirable can deception be justified (Bruckman 2002). However, even if a controlling authority agrees to allow research to be conducted within a particular online context, persons interacting within such a space may make assumptions about their privacy that are unwarranted if permission is granted without informing users or gaining their consent. Will the focus of the study be on the group generally? Or will the level of analysis focus on specific actors? Certainly, if individuals are singled out for interview or questioning, they ought to be informed of the reason and their consent should be sought. But if the focus is more general, are the interactions taking place within the space sufficiently innocuous that users will not be harmed by passive observations and published reports of a researcher? Similar issues are raised if the researcher happens to be a participant in a closed group, and then later decides to conduct research within it. In such a case, members who elect to become researchers should not assume permission to shift from participant to participant-observer.

Burning bushes are not always enclosed by fences, and, like Moses, researchers must sometimes be told to tread lightly. Some assume that any site that is available online without password or other protection is automatically fair game for research. After all, a long-standing rule of thumb among sociologists is that passive observations in public spaces are exempt from informed consent requirements, because the observer sees and hears nothing other than what member of the public might happen to see and hear in that time or place, and the observer does nothing to change the normal behavior of the persons being observed (Adler and Adler 1998). Yet context shapes these decisions greatly. Many contexts, online and offline, involve interactions that are not sensitive, with subject matter that would be of little concern. But passive observation in some spaces may yield data that is confidential or potentially damaging. Consider a medical office or hospital emergency room, for example, where sensitive information about a person's identity and medical condition might easily be overheard. Would patients consider this information publicly available to a researcher without their knowledge and consent? More than likely, they would find the appropriation of their personal information in this way to be highly offensive. A support group for persons struggling with some sort of addiction might be open to the public. Nothing would prevent a researcher from entering and participating. But would members of such a group consider what they share in such a setting to be public information for a scholar to include in a published research report? More than likely, they too would find such action to be highly offensive. Participants in open forums online may similarly be offended. Hall, Frederick, and Johns (2004) document one such instance, in which confidential and potentially damaging information was being shared in an open online space. In this case, participants reacted strongly against having their "private" interactions studied by a researcher, despite the lack of technology in place that might have ensured privacy. While it may not be wise for participants to engage in such activity openly, is it wise for researchers to conduct their work uninvited, or to call public attention to such communication? To determine whether permission or consent must be gained requires more subtlety in weighing the content and circumstances than merely determining that an online venue is accessible without a password.

What harm may be done?

Certainly the horrors of Nazi medical experiments and the Tuskegee syphilis experiment will not be duplicated in an online context. But just because invasive medical procedures are not possible over the Internet (at least with current technology) it does not follow that no harm may be done. The National Research Act of 1974 added oversight of social and behavioral research to that of biomedical research precisely because of the risks involved in asking people to reveal details of their personal thoughts and actions. Social stigma may be attached to a wide assortment of human activities, including association with certain religious groups or engaging in certain religious practices. To reveal these associations and practices online carries no less stigma. Stories are legion in the popular press of lost jobs, or lost economic opportunities, because of words posted on the Internet. Relationships and marriages have ended as a result of conflicts over online interactions. These are real-life consequences of online activities.

Behavioral researchers have long masked the identities of research participants in their research reports in order to avoid such unpleasant consequences. This remains standard practice for online researchers, as well. But there is one huge caveat: much of what is written on the Internet is searchable – even a good bit that occurs behind password protection – and most of what is posted online is archived somewhere for long periods of time. Thus, a brief quote in a research report, even if attributed to a participant labeled as anonymous or pseudonymous by the researcher, might be quickly traced by an online search, defeating the researcher's effort to keep the participant's identity secure. Many social networking sites, blogs, discussion groups, and even some synchronous chat venues maintain searchable archives of the activity taking place, and these are, in many instances, fully catalogued by Google or other search engines. Qualitative research often involves the reporting of significant quotes, which raises the possibility that the original post may be discovered. Even if the research method employed is largely quantitative it may be possible, in some instances, to trace the identity of certain individuals in a data set (Zimmer 2010).

The fact that some use pseudonyms in their online interactions is also not a guarantee of anonymity. Often, sufficient information is revealed over time that the pseudonymous identity can be linked to the actual author with some simple searching. Further, many participants in online activities spend huge amounts of time, energy, and resources to build up a pseudonymous persona over months or even years. This is particularly true in multi-user online game environments, such as World of Warcraft, and virtual worlds, such as Second Life. Religious ritual and symbolism has been the subject of research in both of these environments (Radde-Antweiler 2008). Thus, in some cases, damage to the reputation of the online persona may be nearly as harmful as damage to the reputation of the real person controlling that persona. Identity is not a simple matter and is possibly even more complicated by the technology than it is offline, as noted in previous chapters in this volume.

Some participants in online religious activities are more vulnerable than others. Certainly children and teens are almost universally considered persons whose data must be carefully protected in any circumstance. Researchers should consider how religious groups are viewed in various cultural situations. Study of an online Christian group, for example, is not generally controversial in North America or Europe, but if participants in such a group are situated in the Middle East or parts of Asia, what are the risks in those contexts? Any group that may be considered unusual or exotic in a culture is open to possibilities of stigma or persecution.

Therefore, researchers must ask themselves about the possible risks to reputation or personal credibility that may be associated with their work. But more importantly, they must be willing to allow their research participants to assess these risks from their own perspective. A researcher may not always be able to anticipate what may or may not be harmful information to be revealed about someone online. Are there risks that only the participant can ascertain for herself or himself? This is the essential foundation of the requirement for informed consent.

Who speaks for whom?

Informed consent in the traditional sense is often difficult, if not impossible, in online venues. A lengthy informed consent statement often cannot be posted in the space available on a social network. Twitter, for example, limits all posts to 140 characters. Debriefing one-on-one is generally not practical online. It is often impossible to know who all of the users of a particular online venue may be, or even to know how many there might be. The larger the number of participants involved in an online venue, the more difficult gaining consent from all of them will be. Certainly it is impossible to obtain contact information that would allow sending each user a traditional printed information statement and consent form. To do so would require gathering even more personal information than otherwise necessary – just the opposite of the goal of most ethical research practices. As discussed above, it is frequently impossible even to know if the users really are the people they represent themselves to be. Is the consent granted by a person, or by the persona representing the person? All of these issues surrounding informed consent have been major sticking points for review boards and ethics committees, particularly those who are insistent upon doing things the way they've always been done before.

But things aren't as they've been before. New technologies have changed the way many everyday activities are conducted. Bank accounts are no longer managed with paper checks and signatures, but more often with plastic cards and PINs. Many very personal transactions are conducted online using a login and password. It is routine to gain legal assent to terms of service, user agreements, or other contractual obligations with a simple click of a mouse, which qualifies as a digital signature. If such measures are considered legally adequate in banking, finance, and other corporate matters, they should be equally adequate in fulfilling the requirements of an ethics panel. Thus, while consent in the traditional manner may be difficult or impossible, with some creativity it should be possible, when necessary, to inform participants that they are being researched, explain known risks, and gain an electronic acknowledgment of willingness to proceed.

There certainly are cases in which persons are involved in religious actions or discussions openly online, and for which no permissions or consents are necessary for passive observation. As mentioned previously, it is sometimes adequate to gain consent only from a controlling authority, such as the moderator of a discussion or the password manager of a virtual environment, if other protections for individual users are adequate. But when it is necessary to gain informed consent from an individual, there are ways to completely fulfill the requirements online, without the need to gather more personal information that would otherwise be necessary, and without the need for a signature in ink on paper.

What good may come of it?

If risks are weighed against benefits, how are benefits to be determined, and by whom? Most researchers feel their research is important, or they wouldn't be putting the time and energy into it that they do. Certainly successful research is beneficial to a scholar's career, reputation, and sense of accomplishment. But actually measuring the benefit of a particular research project to society as a whole is a difficult calculation. Unfortunately, at least in the US, some IRBs have quantified risk and benefit entirely in terms of dollars – if the risk of a lawsuit seems too great, the amount of the external research grant must exceed the cost of the potential litigation. Rather than protecting human participants, protecting the institution's corporate backside is the only consideration. The horror stories told among graduate students about unreasonable demands by IRBs are usually rooted in this sort of abuse of the ethics protection system.

Researchers may often take their cue from research participants themselves. Many members of stigmatized religious groups would be happy to have research published about them that is fair, objective, and unbiased. When a researcher can develop the trust of a community, the research may be seen as an apologetic that can help alleviate misunderstanding and prejudice in the wider community. This is no less true of religious groups online than it is in non-mediated settings. A communitarian approach understands those whose activities are being studied to be partners in the research effort, rather than mere subjects to be studied. With such an approach, participants not only consent to being part of the study, but are consulted about the general approach to be used and important issues to be investigated. The researcher also makes a continuing effort to check conclusions with the participants in order to see if perceptions are correct or if inappropriate assumptions have been made. This does not mean that participants necessarily have veto power over what is included in the final research report (unless that has been promised to them). The researcher should remain the final arbiter of the finished product. But it does offer the participants an opportunity to have their say in how the story of their lives and community is being presented to the wider world (Hall, Frederick, and Johns 2004).

How shall these things be weighed?

In Western cultures there are two major philosophies of ethics that have dominated ethical decision making for at least the past two centuries. Utilitarianism, the calculation of the greatest good for the greatest number, put forward by British economists Jeremy Bentham and John Stewart Mill, suggests that significant public benefits of research may outweigh the rights of individuals, such as privacy, copyright, or consent. A deontological ethical philosophy, rooted in the thinking of Danish philosopher Immanuel Kant, suggests that there are certain individual rights that are inviolable regardless of benefit to others, and that researchers have an absolute duty to safeguard these rights (Ess 2007).

It should be noted that research along the lines of the infamous Tuskegee Study may be perfectly justifiable using utilitarian reasoning – a relative few were sacrificed for the sake of knowledge that might benefit many. Despite the outrage which resulted from Tuskegee, it should be further noted that the entire IRB system in the US tends to assume a utilitarian model of weighing risks against benefits. So long as the benefits are clear, it is only necessary to minimize the risks to "human subjects." European systems – and more recent application of ethical principles by IRBs in the US – have tended to lean more toward the deontological model. It is common for ethics panels today to insist that research be modified, complicated, or even abandoned altogether in order to preserve essential rights. The communitarian model suggested above carries the deontological philosophy further yet, not only suggesting that research participants deserve essential protections, but allowing them to have a say for themselves in the parameters and levels of those protections (Ess 2007; Hall, Frederick, and Johns 2004).

A few scholarly organizations have created ethical guidelines for their members, some specifically addressing the ethics of online research. Many of these are specific to a particular discipline or nation. The Association of Internet Researchers (AoIR) is an organization that has developed a set of ethics guidelines that may be helpful to researchers of all disciplines and all nationalities as they design their studies. This document does not offer rules, but rather raises questions that should be considered and discussed as a particular research project is contemplated. It can also be most helpful in assisting ethics committees to understand that proposals which seem esoteric are actually accepted practice in the realm of online research (Ess and AoIR ethics working group 2002). This document is under considerable revision as of this writing, and a newer edition may soon be available to the reader. This newer version will take into account the rapid technological changes of the past decade, as well as the experiences of researchers developed as Internet research has matured.

Conclusion

Those who would undertake the study of religious groups and activities online have a number of unique opportunities. The gap between how people behave online in virtual worlds and how they behave offline "in real life" is quickly closing. As the Internet has become mainstream, and a part of everyday life for a large proportion of the world's population, online activities have *become* real life. As more and more religious groups create an online presence, more religious practices are taking place in online contexts, and as a wider variety of religious ideas are discussed in online environments, the possibilities for researchers to discover rich treasures of insight are increased. However, the Internet also provides new challenges in terms of method and preserving the integrity of ethical practices in research. Words on a screen may be more than they initially appear to be, identities may be even more complicated online than in face-to-face encounters, and the ability to gain access may not guarantee that an assumption of public openness is valid. The ability to search Internet archives creates difficulties for researchers who seek to preserve the privacy of research participants. Because of the wide variety of venues, the diverse research methods that may be employed, and the multifarious nature of the possible risks involved, there can be no hard and simple rules concerning what is or is not ethical research. A communitarian approach suggests that research participants themselves are the ideal guide, if a relationship of trust can be established by the researcher early in the process. Ultimately, however, the researcher must make the difficult decisions and take responsibility for his or her work.

This chapter began by briefly describing the background to the legal regulation of the ethical practice of research, and has explored some of the unique challenges facing researchers in online contexts as they attempt to determine what ethical standards apply in a particular situation. These have been reduced to basic principles of identity (which is complex) and privacy (which is difficult to ensure). Some suggestions have been made concerning when informed consent is necessary and how it can be obtained. Finally, some approaches to ethical decision making were examined. Following is a brief list of some of the more important and significant books and resources currently available as guides to researchers seeking to practice their craft ethically. While there can be no simple formula for ethical research, the study of religion online can be conducted fruitfully if researchers are committed to the welfare of participants and willing to be creative in meeting the challenges presented by the technology.

Recommended reading

Buchanan, Elizabeth A., (ed.) (2004). *Readings in Virtual Research Ethics: Issues and Controversies.* Hershey, PA: Information Science Publishing.

This is a relatively early edited collection of essays about ethical issues which includes both North American and European perspectives. It focuses primarily on the use of e-mail and e-mail list communities as foci of study. Though somewhat dated now, it serves as an excellent introduction to the basic ethical issues encountered in online research.

Ess, Charles (2009). *Digital Media Ethics.* Boston: Polity Press.

The most thorough and up-to-date treatment of the fundamental philosophy of ethics as applied to Internet research. Ess takes a more theoretical approach to the essential issues facing researchers today, incorporating US, EU, and Asian perspectives.

Ess, Charles and the Association of Internet Researchers ethics working group (2002). *Ethical Decision-Making and Internet Research: Recommendations from the AoIR Ethics Working Committee.* Available at: http://aoir.org/reports/ethics.pdf

As described in the text of this chapter, this document is invaluable to researchers as they design their studies and to ethics panels as they consider research proposals. Currently under extensive revision by the AoIR ethics working group.

Johns, Mark D., Chen, Shing-Ling, and Hall, G. Jon, (eds) (2004). *Online Social Research: Methods, Issues, and Ethics.* New York: Peter Lang.

Another early and now somewhat dated collection of essays that takes a more applied and empirical approach by providing case studies of actual research in venues that include e-mail lists, and MUDs, MOOs, and other environments, employing several ethnographic models. Practical advice for dealing with ethics panels is also included in several chapters.

Markham, Annette N. and Baym, Nancy K., (eds) (2008). *Internet Inquiry: Conversations about Method.* Thousand Oaks, CA: Sage Publications.

This is a collection of reflections by researchers about their studies and the ethical and methodological issues they faced. Each is followed by responses by other scholars who point out both pros and cons of the decisions made by the researcher. An excellent teaching text for beginning researchers, or those just entering the online realm.

McKee, Heidi A. and Porter, James E. (2009). *The Ethics of Internet Research: A Rhetorical, Case-Based Process.* New York: Peter Lang.

As the title implies, this is a practical book based on case study analysis. It is more up to date than some of the earlier such books on this list, and it goes further by suggesting ways in which cases can be helpful in teaching researchers how to weigh the various factors and make the difficult choices necessary to doing ethical projects.

Note

1 Throughout this essay, humans involved in behavioral studies will be referred to as "participants" rather than as "subjects" of research. This conforms to the communitarian idea that human beings are not research "subjects," but individuals with rights, feelings, and volition.

References

Adler, Patricia and Adler, Peter (1998). Observational Techniques. In Norman K. Denzin and Yvonne S. Lincoln, (eds), *Collecting and Interpreting Qualitative Materials*, 79–109. Sage Publications: Thousand Oaks.

Boddy, Janet, Boaz, Annette, Lupton, Carol, and Pahl, Jan. (2006). What Counts as Research? The Implications for Research Governance in Social Care. *International Journal of Social Research Methodology*, 9(4): 317–30

Bruckman, Amy (2002). Ethical Guidelines for Research Online: A Strict Interpretation. Available: www.cc.gatech.edu/~asb/ethics (accessed June 8, 2011).

Buchanan, Elizabeth A. (2010). Internet Research Ethics: Past, Present, Future. In Mia Consalvo and Charles Ess, (eds), *The Blackwell Handbook of Internet Studies*, 83–108. Oxford: Wiley-Blackwell.

Danet, Brenda (2001). *Cyberpl@y: Communicating Online*. Oxford, UK: Berg.

Ess, Charles (2007). Internet Research Ethics. In A. N. Joinson, K. Y. A. McKenna, T. Postmes, and U.-D. Reips, (eds), *The Oxford Handbook of Internet Psychology*, 487–502. Oxford, UK: Oxford University Press.

Ess, Charles and the Association of Internet Researchers ethics working group (2002). *Ethical Decision-Making and Internet Research: Recommendations from the AoIR Ethics Working Committee*. Available: http://aoir.org/reports/ethics.pdf

Hall, G. Jon, Frederick, Douglas, and Johns, Mark D. (2004). "NEED HELP ASAP!!!": A Feminist Communitarian Approach to Online Research Ethics. In Mark D. Johns, Shing-Ling Chen, and G. Jon Hall, (eds), *Online Social Research: Methods, Issues, and Ethics*, 239–52. New York: Peter Lang.

Herring, Susan C. (2004). Computer-Mediated Discourse Analysis: An Approach to Researching Online Behavior. In Sasha A. Barab, Rob Kling, and James H. Gray, (eds), *Designing for Virtual Communities in the Service of Learning*, 338–76. New York: Cambridge University Press.

Johns, Mark, Hall, G. Jon, and Crowell, Tara Lynn (2004). Surviving the IRB Review: Institutional Guidelines and Research Strategies. In Mark D. Johns, Shing-Ling Chen, and G. Jon Hall, (eds), *Online Social Research: Methods, Issues, and Ethics*, 105–24. New York: Peter Lang.

Radde-Antweiler, Kerstin, (ed.) (2008). Being Virtually Real: Virtual Worlds from a Cultural Studies Perspective. *Online – Heidelberg Journal of Religions on the Internet*, 3(1). Online. Available: http://archiv.ub.uni-heidelberg.de/volltextserver/volltexte/2008/8294/pdf/Radde.pdf (accessed July 8, 2011).

Zimmer, Michael (2010). "But the Data is Already Public": On the Ethics of Research in Facebook. *Ethics and Information Technology*, 12(4): 313–25.

22 Theology and the new media

Stephen Garner

Around the beginning of the third century CE the Christian author Tertullian, writing in his treatise *De praescriptione hereticorum*, posed the question "What has Athens to do with Jerusalem?" Tertullian's conclusion was that human philosophical constructions had little to offer to a Christian faith rooted in sacred revelation. While ultimately futile, Tertullian's separation of these two things into two mutually exclusive categories is not uncommon, with similar "catch cries" calling for the separation of church and state, science and religion, and social action versus care of the soul running through Christian history. Perhaps too, we see a similar separation in the question asked in some quarters about what the Internet has to do with a faith founded on the life, death and resurrection of a first-century Palestinian Jew. For some, the Internet has no connection with a faith tradition rooted in identification with a physical community and a God who became flesh and blood and relocated to the physical world, but for others, the Internet represents a new location for theological reflection and exploration.

Theology brings a different perspective from other disciplines to its engagement with the Internet. While informed by scholarship from fields such as religion and media (e.g. Helland 2000; Dawson and Cowan 2004; Campbell 2010), theological reflection is primarily sourced from the religious tradition the theological scholars and practitioners participate in. As such, Christian theology about the Internet is set within a broad framework that sees the online world through the life, death and resurrection of Jesus Christ. Through this lens, attitudes and questions towards technology evolve regarding how Christians should live in relationship to the Internet, and intersect with the wider world with respect to social justice, identity, and ethics.

Theology asserts that being sourced in certain truth claims about God and the world, it has something to contribute to public and scholarly discussion about the Internet. Christian theology is cautiously optimistic about technologies like the Internet, with the caveat that all technology is open to being used oppressively, and seeks to bring insight drawn from its tradition on how to live well with the Internet. In this chapter, theology within the Christian tradition and its key approaches to technology are defined, leading into an examination of how theology has started to address concerns of interest within the church and the wider world.

What is theology?

Etymologically, the term "theology" is derived from the Greek *theos* ("god") and *logos* ("word," "teaching," "study"), meaning that theology literally means "words about god(s)" or "the teaching about or study of god(s)." Traditionally, theology has been linked to a systematic study of ideas and concepts within a religious tradition; broadly it can be described as "thinking about questions raised by and about the religions" (Ford 1999). That said, this chapter focuses particularly upon theological reflection upon the Internet from the Christian tradition.

One common definition of Christian theology is that of Anselm of Canterbury (c. 1033–1109), who saw it as "faith seeking understanding" (Latin: *fides querens intellectum*). Anselm's description was rooted in his own medieval context, and every generation rearticulates what theology is in relation to the socio-cultural situation of their day. For example, "faith seeking understanding" might be tied to a sense of "faith seeking intelligent action" in the world, which by necessity demands an understanding of that world. Paul Tillich's (1886–1965) approach saw the wider world as raising existential questions to be addressed by the interpretation of key Christian symbols, while Rudolph Bultmann (1884–1976) drew upon philosophies from outside Christianity, such as existentialism, to provide new interpretative lenses for understanding the Bible (Ford 1999). Therefore, the ways in which theology and the Internet might engage each other form part of a diverse theological landscape, where questions similar to the one posed by Lutheran theologian Ted Peters are grappled with:

> [H]ow can the Christian faith, first experienced and symbolically articulated in an ancient culture now long out-of-date, speak meaningfully to human existence today as we experience it amid a worldview dominated by natural science, secular self-understanding, and the worldwide cry for freedom?
>
> (Peters 2000: 7)

If, as Kathryn Tanner asserts, Christian theology must be comprehensive because all aspects of the universe are in some form of a relationship with God, then theology must nevertheless grapple with the Internet. In order to do that kind of theologizing, Tanner argues the theologian should not attempt to become an expert in all things, but rather draw from the knowledge and wisdom of others who are already steeped in that field (Tanner 1994). Thus theological reflection on technology, and by implication the Internet, is often a kind of contextual theology, which locates itself as a theological endeavor seeking to articulate and critique a practical theology rooted in the experience of the individual or community, through an explicit dialog between the past (represented by scripture and tradition) and the present (represented particularly by personal and community experience) (Bevans 2002). In doing so, theology responds to voices like theologian and bioethicist Ronald Cole-Turner, when he asks:

> Can theology – that communal process by which the church's faith seeks to understand – can theology aim at understanding technology? Can we

put the words *God* and *technology* together in any kind of meaningful sentence? Can theology guess what God is doing in today's technology? Or by our silence do we leave it utterly godless? Can we have a theology of technology that comprehends, gives meaning to, dares to influence the direction and set limits to this explosion of new powers?

(Cole-Turner 2000: 101; italics in original)

Some, such as sociologist Brenda Brasher (2004), think that institutional Christianity, with its dependence on pastoral and agrarian imagery and symbols found in religious texts, will struggle with this task, though examples later in this chapter highlight communities that are working to address the heart of Cole-Turner's charge to them.

Theology and technology

On the whole, technology is seen within the Christian tradition in a cautiously positive light, in which God-given human reason is expressed creatively in ways that improve the human condition and impart material mercies. In particular, the affirmation by medieval Benedictine monasticism of the "practical arts," as well as the influence of Francis Bacon (1561–1626), provides a theological foundation based on the virtue of charity that has often been used to argue the case for technology (Noble 1997; Mitcham and Grote 1984). In the contemporary context, this can be seen in articulations which identify technology as a human cultural activity, in which humans are called by God to responsibly transform the natural world through the application of their freedom and ingenuity (Monsma 1986).

This theological reflection on technology recognizes that technology is more than simply created artifacts, and embraces both human relationships with technology and wider societal values underpinning technological development (White 1994), as highlighted in Ian Barbour's broad definition of technology as "the application of organized knowledge to practical tasks by ordered systems of people and machines" (Barbour 1993: 3–4). Engagement with this broad vision of technology is seen in sociological analyses, such as those of Jacques Ellul (1964, 1980), as well as in anthropological and epistemological investigations of technology from Christian perspectives (Tillich 1953; Hefner 1993). While Christian perspectives tend to be cautiously optimistic and pragmatic about technology, Barbour (1993) argues that some do see it in overly negative terms. Barbour offers a scheme for classifying theological responses to technology as *liberator*, *oppressor* or *instrument*, while recognizing that some responses do not always fit neatly into this broad framework (Stahl *et al.* 2002).

Technology as liberator

Optimistic responses associate technology with a liberating force with the potential to overcome hunger, disease, and poverty, and to produce economic growth resulting in an overall improvement of the human condition. Within the context of theological reflection upon the Internet, optimism makes itself known particularly in the contexts of mission and the church. The Internet, with its potential to reach people with the gospel or "good news" of God, provides evangelists with tools and opportunities to use in conjunction with existing media channels. The instructions in the Gospel of Matthew (Matt. 20:18–20) to go and make disciples of all nations and in the Book of Acts to similarly witness to "the ends of the earth" (Acts 1:7–8) are transformed to support evangelism in the physical world supported by the Internet, as well as in the new online environment (Internet Evangelism Coalition 2011). Similarly, the Internet is seen as having a positive impact upon the nature and function of the church, with the Internet aiding the attraction of new church members and the retention of existing churchgoers, especially youth, and serving as a force for the maintenance and/or reformation of existing institutional structures.

Technology as oppressor

Of course, an overly optimistic view of technology tends to downplay problems that are presented by technological developments, especially in their interaction with economic, political, and social institutions (Barbour 1993). Questions about who can afford and access technology, the disproportionate consumption of resources in the industrialized world, and the nature of relationships of power maintained by technology are picked up by technological pessimists who see technology threatening what is truly human. For some, the pervasive nature of technology in modern society is a significantly bad thing, while others would argue that not all of technology is bad, it is just that the negatives outweigh the positives (Ellul 1964, 1980). Here, the pursuit of goals such as efficiency through mass production, influence of mass media, and production of products for consumption lead to the suppression of individuality and creativity within society. Furthermore, these developments often appear to be imposed upon society by some external force, a technological determinism which drives people to adapt to technology or be left on the margins of society (Pullinger 2001).

For theological advocates of this kind of approach, the Internet tends to accentuate problems perceived as inherent within humanity and its societal structures. Emphases upon the breakdown of flesh-and-blood, face-to-face relationships; disconnection from a physical worshipping community (Wynne-Jones 2009); access to different religious ideas and teachings; the supplanting of the religious and spiritual life; and social justice issues – not to mention concerns over pornography (Gardner 2001), and a common basis for ethics and morality – tend to dominate theological comment here.

Technology as instrument

Sitting between these positive and negative poles is the view that the Internet is an ambiguous instrument of power. Here technology is presented as value neutral until it is applied in some way, and the consequences of that application demonstrate whether it was used positively or negatively. For example, the Vatican recognizes the positive potential of the Internet for teaching, evangelism and supporting the community of the faithful, but at the same time its potential to diminish physical, face-to-face community and provide access to material damaging to the faith of individuals and the wider church is described in strikingly negative terms (Pontifical Council for Social Communications 2002b).

However, as Barbour contends, technology is not value neutral, but neither is it inherently wholly good or wholly evil. Theologizing about the Internet in this ambiguous context recognizes technology does not occur in a vacuum, but rather technologies are social constructions, created and used in response to guiding social and institutional values. Barbour describes this reality, reflected in Christian communities as they struggle to work out what it means to be followers of Christ in modern technoculture, saying:

> The biblical understanding of human nature is realistic about the abuses of power and the institutionalization of self-interest. But it also is idealistic in its demands for social justice in the distribution of the fruits of technology. It brings together celebration of human creativity and suspicion of human power.
>
> (Barbour 1993: 19)

It is this celebration of human creativity combined with a suspicion of human power that drives the cautiously optimistic response to the Internet, and leads Ronald Cole-Turner to comment that, "technology, for all its good, is constantly on the edge of sin, exploitation, and greed. It is, after all, *human* technology, beset by our weaknesses" (Cole-Turner 1993: 102; italics in original). Moreover, theological reflection also identifies that, in the Western world at least, technology has had more than just an effect on our environment – it has become our environment. As Monsma puts it:

> Technology and its results are so much with us that, like the air we breathe, their presence and effects go unnoticed and unanalyzed. As a result modern technology and all it entails are often accepted by default, with few questioning what life would be like if humankind performed tasks and attained goals by other means.
>
> (Monsma 1986: 1)

This all-embracing technological environment can obscure thinking, including theological thinking, about the Internet. The question being asked by some (Borgmann 2003) is whether technology can be passed through and removed to a secondary supporting role on the margins, where it can be met with neither submissiveness nor total rejection. The following section looks at how theology embraces this challenge.

Theology and the Internet

Christian theological engagement with the Internet has tended to see the Internet as an everyday reality created by natural human agency, with Christian believers called to live responsibly in that environment. Moreover, believers are also called to work to transform wider society, given that God is concerned with the entire world. Thus, theological engagement with the Internet is targeted in two different, but overlapping, directions: towards Christians, in other words the church; and towards wider society.

Firstly, theological reflection is focused upon the Internet in relation to the nature and purpose of the church, the proclamation of the teachings of Jesus Christ, Christian agency and identity, and wise living in the world. It is theology for the church by the church. The second direction, often called "public theology," is theology for society first, and the church second (Forrester 2004). Here the church engages with the Internet in relation to the wider public world, participating in public dialog and policy shaping from its own unique theological position.

The Internet initially made its presence felt in theological circles in the 1980s, with a particular flurry of activity in the 1990s as the World Wide Web pushed the Internet into the mainstream. For instance, when Jason Baker (1995) describes a variety of online Christian resources, his book is divided between those offered on Christian bulletin board services, and other resources becoming available through the Internet, including the World Wide Web. This echoes Hutchings (2007), who identifies embryonic theological engagement arising as both individual Christians and church denominations began to use the dial-up bulletin boards of the mid-1980s. These developments followed two key trends: first, resources for supporting members within church communities and particularly clergy, such as online bulletin boards with pastoral and teaching resources; and second, ventures into the emerging Internet world for the purposes of evangelism and mission.

Around the late 1980s the term "cyberchurch" entered into theologically related discussion of the Internet, where it was seen as both "[t]he body of all Christians who interact using global computer networks," and "[a]n electronically linked group of believers, aiming to reproduce in cyberspace some aspects of conventional church life" (Dixon 1997: 17). Then, in the mid-1990s, denominations and wider groupings of churches began to produce reports examining the Internet and its potential impact upon the world and religious life in particular. For example, in 1996, the Church of England formed a working group to draft a report designed to set out some ethical guidelines for and identify spiritual implications of the emerging Internet world (Church of England Board for Social Responsibility 1999). The World Council of Churches set out similar responses in the mid-to-late 1990s (Lochhead 1997; Arthur 1998). These kinds of publications tended to focus on the Internet's impact upon individuals in Western society (e.g. the Church of England publication has a section looking at potential issues surrounding relationships in cyberspace), as well as the implications of these technologies and media within the global context with respect to economics, justice, and religion. In the early 2000s, the Vatican also started to publish official documents about the Internet and reflect on its impact upon the wider world as well as the Church (Pontifical Council for Social Communications 2002a, 2002b).

After an initial burst of activity through the 1990s, this kind of institutional theological exercise tended to decline or to be redirected into how particular Internet technologies might be used pragmatically in ministry, or into the development of an Internet presence for particular institutions. The Vatican website is a good example of the latter, while the former might be characterized by the blending of theology with a commercial focus highlighted in Catholic web designer Brother M. Aquinas Woodworth's comment:

> People spend time online, and commercial companies want as much of their attention as possible … . The Church should capture that attention by providing a rich spiritual environment. We need to offer all the services people are seeking, but our objective is not just to sell stuff but to give it a spiritual sense.
>
> (Allen 1998: 7)

Furthermore, those who would have been involved in the task of theologizing about technology were often diverted into other areas, such as biotechnology in the 2000s. The rapid development and impact of the Internet also rendered the traditional methodical pace of institutional theological reflection ineffective as regards responding in a timely fashion. For example, as part of its ongoing reflections on how the Catholic Church might engage pastorally with the Internet, bloggers were invited recently to contribute to a conversation on that topic (Kerr 2011). However, it is now ten years after blogging emerged online, and maybe a better conversation to have would be about the current impact of social media.

Since the end of the 1990s the bulk of theologizing about the Internet has been marked by pragmatism, emphasizing the Internet in instrumental terms and also as a sign of a culture shift toward postmodernity in the Western world. As such, much published with a theological slant about the Internet has been written by practitioners, both academic and non-academic, working in pastoral and/or information technology contexts and wanting to provide the church with practical insights into this new online world. Thus, while theology recognized the impact of the Internet on wider society, its focus tended to be more on how to live as Christians on the Internet, and how the Internet might reshape and challenge the church. Often writing in this area followed a particular formula: (a) there is a culture shift towards postmodernity in the West; (b) the Internet is part of this shift; (c) the Internet contains both perils and promises; (d) to pastor, communicate and evangelize a new generation means the church needs to be present on the Internet; and (e) here are some possible ways to do that (Dixon 1997; Careaga 2001; Veith and Stamper 2000; Hipps 2009; Estes 2009).

This demonstrates an emphasis upon what Christopher Helland (2000) termed "religion-online," where particular religious communities replicate the traditional religious organization or structure in the online context, for example in creation of denominational websites. Moreover, the creation of various "cyberchurches" in the 1990s and 2000s, such as Church of Fools (later St Pixels), i-Church (sponsored by the Anglican Diocese of Oxford, in the UK), and more recently LifeChurch.tv, initially fell within this category of religion-online, replicating to a certain extent the experience of attending church physically. Over time these communities have continued to adapt to new Internet developments, as well as developing offline groups to supplement or augment the online experience and content (Hutchings 2007).

The nature and purpose of the church

The kinds of ventures described above reflect theologizing about the nature and purpose of the church on the Internet. For example, one issue that is wrestled with is whether flesh-and-blood presence is needed for true Christian community. Theologically, this discussion draws upon several core strands within the Christian tradition. First, human beings were intentionally created to be physical creatures, and rejection of this physical nature in favor of a spiritual or virtual world (e.g. Gnosticism) is to be resisted. Second, human beings were created to be social beings, and third, and perhaps most importantly, God became flesh and blood in the form of Jesus so as to provide a fuller revelation of God. Moreover, parts of Christianity also require the physicality of sacraments (e.g. baptism, holy communion) as integral parts of their community identity. Thus, the onus is on online forms of church to justify theologically to the wider church community their continuity with the Christian tradition.

This tension between online and offline communities can be seen in cases such as that of LifeChurch.tv, which encourages members to also participate in local groups for the purposes of discipleship, indicating that a fuller religious life might be found in a mix of online and physical relationships. Going further, the Vatican states religious experience online may be possible by the grace of God, but that true community and the sacraments are only present in physical community (Pontifical Council for Social Communications 2002b). That said, many people see online churches as their primary community of faith (Hutchings 2007), offering challenges to traditional institutions and their practices; a challenge recognized by reports such as the Church of England's *Mission-shaped Church* (Mission and Public Affairs Council 2004), which contends that the Internet cannot be ignored when considering new forms of mission activity and church practice. Taking up this challenge pushes the church toward Helland's other category, of "online-religion" (Helland 2000), where the online environment generates further questions about the purpose and nature of the church, its authority structures, and what it means to participate in worship and community.

Contemplation of the networked structure of the Internet, and in particular social networking, in relation to authority structures within the church is a frequent example of this. For example, Dwight Friesen (2009) argues that pastors should become "network ecologists," seeing the church as a network of people and resources, and building sustainable relational links between people both inside and outside their particular communities of faith. Likewise, Kester Brewin (2004) argues for contemporary church life being oriented around an adaptive network model that connects people, ideas and knowledge, with built-in feedback loops that allow that organization to learn and renew itself. The decentralization of authority structures, moving away from more traditional "top-down" models, will, he argues, allow better information sharing and increased collaboration in theological tasks such as the interpretation of scripture.

In both of these cases, the repositioning of authority and influence within the church challenges existing church structures and hierarchies that provide core identity and differentiation from other faith communities (e.g. Presbyterianism vs. Episcopalianism). Katharine Moody (2009) identifies that this perceived anti-authoritarian streak might be seen in terms of socialization in the Christian community taking precedence over any conformance to a particular doctrinal structure or content. Theology is done by all who draw upon their experience of the community, dialoging with others outside of the established theological "guilds," while also drawing upon the wider Christian tradition as desired. As blogger Tim Bednar puts it, "[w]e are not convinced that pastors know more about following Christ than we do. We tire of having their vision delegated to us and instead are looking for the church to embrace our visions and dreams" (Bednar 2004: 28).

The significance of these discussions should not be downplayed, for they go to the very heart of Christian identity. The church, in its various forms, sees itself as a special community in relationship with God through Jesus Christ, possessing hope and good news for the world manifested by acting as God's agents in the world. The challenges to this community presented by the Internet are met with both anxiety and anticipation, driving what Horsfield and Teusner (2007) identify as concrete examples of contextual theology – the dialog between the past (represented by scripture and tradition), and the personal and community experience of the Internet. Ultimately, what the church should be producing here is an understanding, sourced in its theology and experience, of how to live authentically, wisely and justly in a world connected to the Internet.

Embodiment and ethics

Overlapping with discussions about the church community are more general questions about the relationship between mediated communication found online and the nature of embodiment. The historic Christian tradition holds that God became flesh and blood in Jesus Christ and moved into the local neighborhood in order to reveal God more fully. Moreover, the tradition contains biblical concepts of humanity being intentionally created as embodied and offered new life through a physical resurrection. Therefore, the place and depth of mediated, non-flesh-and-blood relationships raises intriguing theological questions.

Christian sociologist David Lyon (2001) asks whether being "wrapped in media" adds or detracts from the human capacity for relationships. In one sense, it extends the abilities of human beings to network and communicate with others in new and powerful ways, but it may remove a level of meaning from that interaction, making communication dependent upon voluntary self-disclosure brought about by relationships of trust harder to sustain. Lyon is not denying the power of the Internet to facilitate communication, but use of the Internet requires care and control at both personal and corporate levels (e.g. surveillance). For him, the virtues of love and trust must guide this, a concern echoed by the Vatican, which sees the fundamental guiding principle for social communications media as being its use "by persons to persons for the integral development of persons" (Pontifical Council for Social Communications 2002a).

This spills over into theological discussions about the nature of personhood, community and human relationships with each other and the wider world. At its most pragmatic level, grassroots theological reflection is often tied to the welfare and practice of the Christian community and how the Internet might threaten that. So, for example, we see books and articles published about keeping young people safe on the Internet (David 2007), and reflections upon Internet pornography and pastoral ministry (Gardner 2001) and how a church's use of the Internet needs to align with their faith commitments (Baab 2008).

Academically, theological ethical reflection tends to focus upon issues of identity, intent, experience, and effects on individuals and communities. For example, as online worlds became more prevalent, questions about how virtual entities should be treated in those worlds began to surface in theological deliberations (Meadows 1995). Similarly, questions about whether ethics are "a function of our experience or reality" concern Graham Houston (1998: 59) in his consideration of whether the online world creates the true postmodern world of ethical relativism where individuals can be free of moral responsibility to God and fellow humans.

Both Houston and Meadows would reject this proposition, with Meadows arguing that a Christian understanding of God rejects that there are places able to be created that are "private" from God. Houston goes further, developing what he calls a "virtual morality" that draws on a moral order based on created order, freedom in Christ resisting technological determinism, and normative principles extracted from divine love. In this scheme, Houston argues that a participant's subjective experience in the online environment is primary, with ethical guidance principally engaging with the intention and desire of the participant and with the effects of those intentions as a secondary factor. Moreover, Houston offers this scheme not just to Christian believers for application in their personal lives, but also to the wider public, arguing that in a pluralistic society his theologizing can contribute to the wider ethical conversation about digital technologies.

Theology, such as Houston's, that is advanced into the public sphere reflects a concern about societal structures and processes, and the declaration that theology has something constructive to contribute to issues in that area. For example,

Eric Stoddart (2008) argues that the contemporary practice of surveillance, of increasing significance in Internet societies, can be addressed through the theme of truthful speech rooted in the biblical tradition. In particular, he argues that the relational responsibility to the other and the critical examination of the role of centralized control of surveillance are essential to maintaining human dignity in a society increasingly under digital surveillance. This approach resonates strongly with Paul Tillich's (1953) description of theology providing resources to address existential questions of the age.

A range of other, wider issues related to the Internet is also the target of theological engagement, from the perception that the Internet generates an unhealthy emphasis upon "cyberlibertarianism" (Clough 2000) through to issues centered on information poverty and the marginalization of individuals and communities in an increasingly digital world. Whether it is a Roman Catholic understanding of social concern, stemming from human dignity and the call for the faithful transformation of all aspects of the world, or a Protestant one, linked particularly to biblical injunctions to be just and compassionate, Christianity brings these frameworks into its reflections on the Internet. In particular, "digital divides," the potential objectification of persons, and the Internet becoming an end in its own right rather than a means to an end are concerns theology seeks to investigate and comment critically on in the public sphere (Caritas Aotearoa New Zealand 2000; Pontifical Council for Social Communications 2002a; Ottmar 2005).

Theological language

Finally, in addition to theology resourcing thinking about the Internet for the life of its own community and the wider public, it also contributes through others outside of the church using its theological themes, metaphors and language to construct their own visions of the Internet. A classic example of this is the appropriation of the work of Jesuit Pierre Teilhard de Chardin (1881–1955), who described an evolving world, shaped by science and technology, where individual human consciousness will transcend itself, becoming a communal unity of mind – the "noosphere." This world will converge to the final destination where love is in its fullness, that is, the Omega Point expressed in Christ (Teilhard de Chardin 1970). It is this idea of communal unity of mind that proponents of the Internet pick up, connecting the Internet to the next evolutionary step for humanity and the world, creating visions of individual and communal destiny.

For instance, Jennifer Cobb claims that the Internet's worldwide communications network is the incarnation of Teilhard's vision, representing both a spiritual energy that allows an individual's thoughts and ideas to interpenetrate with other individuals' to create a wider consciousness, and the structures of *organization* that give birth to and support the emergence of this noosphere (Cobb 1998). Futurist Mark Pesce, who links technology with neo-paganism, sees a similar connection to Cobb's, arguing that it feels like the Internet fulfills Teilhard's prophecy and, if it does, then perhaps cyberspace forms part of our evolution as human beings, in much the same way as the development of our eyes, hands and brains (Pesce 2000).

Conclusion

For all of its claims of looking to the future, most theological reflection upon the Internet has looked back. Scholars and practitioners within theological communities have had to learn about the different forms of technology, media, and communications involved, to bring them into dialog with their historic religious traditions. There is a danger that, by the time such reflection is done, the Internet will have moved on and the theology developed – at least in its expression – may have been rendered obsolete. Thus, theologizing about the Internet needs to engage with all aspects of it, from "older" technologies such as email and the World Wide Web, through to contemporary social media developments, while also keeping an eye firmly on any emerging trends. Moreover, this work must be done in partnership with others from a broad range of disciplines and experiences.

The late Baptist theologian Stanley Grenz (1950–2005) ventured that the theologian should be a poet who "crafts meaningful pictures about our world and our relationship to the transcendent" (Grenz 2001: 8), and it is this kind of theological "word painting" that theology invites all contemplating something like the Internet to enter into. For its own community, theology looks at how the Internet might shape religious life and wise living for individuals and the church. Some of the insights gleaned there, such as the need for authentic human relationships and ethical practice, can then be taken to the wider world, as theology seeks to take the truth claims it represents and connect them to issues that affect wider society, thus offering its own counter-narratives about the Internet. Furthermore, it also provides the language for others, who are seeking to articulate their visions of the Internet, to move beyond a purely pragmatic description of the Internet to something that connects to various levels of human being. In doing all of this, theology offers its "faith seeking understanding" to the world of the Internet.

Recommended reading

Horsfield, P. G. and Teusner, P. (2007) "A Mediated Religion: Historical Perspectives on Christianity and the Internet," *Studies in World Christianity*, 13(3): 278–95.

This article highlights the history of Christianity as a mediated religion and in light of the Internet considers how the separation of mediated experience from physical experience has become an artificial distinction.

Hutchings, T. (2007) "Creating Church Online: A Case-study Approach to Religious Experience," *Studies in World Christianity*, 13(3): 243–60.

This article provides a set of useful case studies describing how a number of online Christian church communities are using the Internet to provide immersive experiences for churchgoers, producing emotional commitment and experiences of sacred space.

Pontifical Council for Social Communications (2002) *Ethics in Internet*, Vatican City: Pontifical Council for Social Communications.

Pontifical Council for Social Communications (2002) *The Church and Internet*, Vatican City: Pontifical Council for Social Communications.

These publications by the Roman Catholic Church demonstrate how a major Christian tradition is attempting at an institutional level to frame how the Internet fits into the life of faith shaped by its historical theological tradition.

References

Allen, J.L. Jr. (1998) "Monk Targets Catholic Slice of On-line Market," *National Catholic Reporter*, 34(24): 7.

Arthur, C. (1998) *The Globalization of Communications: Some Religious Implications*, Geneva: WCC Publications; London: World Association for Christian Communication.

Baab, L.M. (2008) *Reaching Out in a Networked World: Expressing Your Congregation's Heart and Soul*, Herndon: Alban Institute.

Baker, J.D. (1995) *Christian Cyberspace Companion: A Guide to the Internet and Christian Online Resources*, Grand Rapids: Baker Books.

Barbour, I.G. (1993) *Ethics in an Age of Technology: The Gifford Lectures 1989–1991*, San Francisco: HarperSanFrancisco.

Bednar, T. (2004) "Blogging: Report from a Grassroots Revival," *Stimulus*, 12(3): 24–30.

Bevans, S.B. (2002) *Models of Contextual Theology*, Maryknoll: Orbis Books.

Borgmann, A. (2003) *Power Failure: Christianity in the Culture of Technology*, Grand Rapids: Brazos Press.

Brasher, B.E. (2004) *Give Me That Online Religion*, New Brunswick: Rutgers University Press.

Brewin, K. (2004) *The Complex Christ: Signs of Emergence in the Urban Church*, London: SPCK.

Campbell, H.A. (2010) *When Religion Meets New Media*, Oxon: Routledge.

Careaga, A. (2001) *eMinistry: Connecting with the Net Generation*, Grand Rapids: Kregel Publications.

Caritas Aotearoa New Zealand (2000) *The Digital Divide: Poverty and Wealth in the Information Age*, Wellington: Caritas Aotearoa New Zealand.

Church of England Board for Social Responsibility (1999) *Cybernauts Awake! Ethical and Spiritual Implications of Computers, Information Technology and the Internet*, London: Church House.

Clough, D. (2000) "The Message of the Medium: The Challenge of the Internet to the Church and Other Communities," *Studies in Christian Ethics*, 13(2): 91–100.

Cobb, J.J. (1998) *CyberGrace: The Search for God in the Digital World*, New York: Crown.

Cole-Turner, R. (1993) *The New Genesis: Theology and the Genetic Revolution*, Louisville: Westminster John Knox Press.

——(2000) "Science, Technology and Mission," in Stackhouse, M.L., Dearborn, T. and Paeth, S. (eds.) *The Local Church in a Global Era: Reflections for a New Century*. Grand Rapids: Eerdmans.

David, N. (2007) *Staying Safe Online*, Cambridge: Grove Books.

Dawson, L.L. and Cowan, D.E. (2004) *Religion Online: Finding Faith on the Internet*, New York: Routledge.

Dixon, P. (1997) *Cyberchurch: Christianity and the Internet*, Eastbourne: Kingsway.

Ellul, J. (1964) *The Technological Society*, New York: Vintage Books.

——(1980) *The Technological System*, New York: Continuum.

Estes, D. (2009) *SimChurch: Being the Church in the Virtual World*, Grand Rapids: Zondervan.

Ford, D. (1999) *Theology*, Oxford: Oxford University Press.

Forrester, D.B. (2004) "The Scope of Public Theology," *Studies in Christian Ethics*, 17(2): 5–19.

Friesen, D.J. (2009) *Thy Kingdom Connected: What the Church Can Learn from Facebook, the Internet, and Other Networks*, Grand Rapids: Baker Books.

Gardner, C.J. (2001) "Tangled in the Worst of the Web: What Internet Porn Did to One Pastor, His Wife, His Ministry, Their Life," *Christianity Today*, 45(4): 42–49.

Grenz, S.J. (2001) *The Social God and the Relational Self: A Trinitarian Theology of the Imago Dei*, Louisville: Westminster John Knox Press.

Hefner, P. (1993) *The Human Factor: Evolution, Culture and Religion*, Minneapolis: Fortress Press.

Helland, C. (2000) "Online-Religion/Religion-Online and Virtual Communitas," in Cowan, D.E. and Hadden, J.K. (eds) *Religion on the Internet: Research Prospects and Promises*, New York: JAI.

Hipps, S. (2009) *Flickering Pixels: How Technology Shapes Your Faith*, Grand Rapids: Zondervan.

Horsfield, P.G. and Teusner, P. (2007) "A Mediated Religion: Historical Perspectives on Christianity and the Internet," *Studies in World Christianity*, 13(3): 278–95.

Houston, G. (1998) *Virtual Morality: Christian Ethics in the Computer Age*, Leicester: Apollos.

Hutchings, T. (2007) "Creating Church Online: A Case-Study Approach to Religious Experience," *Studies in World Christianity*, 13(3): 243–60.

Internet Evangelism Coalition (2011) "Internet Evangelism Day." Online. Available: www.internetevangelismday.com (accessed May 10, 2011).

Kerr, D. (2011) "Vatican Gathering of Bloggers Hailed as a Success," *Catholic News Agency*. Online. Available: www.catholicnewsagency.com/news/vatican-gathering-of-bloggers-hailed-as-a-success (accessed May 31, 2012).

Lochhead, D. (1997) *Shifting Realities: Information Technology and the Church*, Geneva: WCC Publications.

Lyon, D. (2001) "Would God Use Email?" *Zadok Perspectives*, 71: 20–23.

Meadows, P.R. (1995) "The Gospel in Cyberspace: Reflections on Virtual Reality," *Epworth Review*, 22: 53–73.

Mission and Public Affairs Council (2004) *Mission-Shaped Church: Church Planting and Fresh Expressions of Church in a Changing Context*, London: Church House.

Mitcham, C. and Grote, J. (1984) "Aspects of Christian Exegesis: Hermeneutics, the Theological Virtues, and Technology," in Mitcham, C. and Grote, J. (eds) *Theology and Technology: Essays in Christian Analysis and Exegesis*, Lanham: University Press of America.

Monsma, S.V. (1986) *Responsible Technology: A Christian Perspective*, Grand Rapids: Eerdmans.

Moody, K.S. (2009) "Researching Theo(b)logy: Emerging Christian Communities and the Internet," in Deacy, C. and Arweck, E. (eds) *Exploring Religion and the Sacred in a Media Age*, Farnham: Ashgate.

Noble, D.F. (1997) *The Religion of Technology: The Divinity of Man and the Spirit of Invention*, New York: Alfred A. Knopf.

Ottmar, J. (2005) "Cyberethics: New Challenges or Old Problems," *Concilium*, 1: 15–26.

Pesce, M. (2000) *The Playful World: How Technology is Transforming Our Imagination*, New York: Ballantine Books.

Peters, T. (2000) *God – The World's Future: Systematic Theology for a New Era*, Minneapolis: Fortress Press.

Pontifical Council for Social Communications (2002a) *Ethics in Internet*, Vatican City: Pontifical Council for Social Communications. Online. Available: www.vatican.va/roman_curia/pontifical_councils/pccs/documents/rc_pc_pccs_doc_20020228_church-Internet_en.html (accessed Februrary 20, 2011).

——(2002b) *The Church and Internet*, Vatican City: Pontifical Council for Social Communications. Online. Available: www.vatican.va/roman_curia/pontifical_councils/pccs/documents/rc_pc_pccs_doc_20020228_church-Internet_en.html (accessed Februrary 20, 2011).

Pullinger, D. (2001) *Information Technology and Cyberspace: Extra-Connected Living*, London: Darton, Longman and Todd.

Stahl, W.A., Campbell, R.A., Petry, Y. and Diver, G. (2002) *Webs of Reality: Social Perspectives on Science and Religion*, New Brunswick: Rutgers University Press.

Stoddart, E. (2008) "Who Watches the Watchers? Towards an Ethic of Surveillance in a Digital Age," *Studies in Christian Ethics*, 21(3): 362–81.

Tanner, K. (1994) "The Difference Theological Anthropology Makes," *Theology Today*, 50(4): 567–79.

Teilhard de Chardin, P. (1970) *The Phenomenon of Man*, London: Collins.

Tillich, P. (1953) *Systematic Theology*, Welwyn: James Nisbet & Co.

Veith, G.E. Jr. and Stamper, C.L. (2000) *Christians in a .com World: Getting Connected Without Being Consumed*, Wheaton: Crossway.

White, S. (1994) *Christian Worship and Technological Change*, Nashville: Abingdon Press.

Wynne-Jones, J. (2009) "Facebook and MySpace Can Lead Children to Commit Suicide, Warns Archbishop Nichols," *The Telegraph*, August 1. Online. Available: www.telegraph.co.uk/news/religion/5956719/Facebook-and-MySpace-can-lead-children-to-commit-suicide-warns-Archbishop-Nichols.html (accessed May 11, 2011).

23 Concluding thoughts

Imagining the religious in and through the digital

Stewart M. Hoover

Within a few weeks of first encountering the chapters in this volume, I attended the Doha International Conference on Interfaith Dialogue in Qatar. The theme was digital religion, occasioned by the events of what had come to be called the "Arab Spring" uprisings of early 2011. The main presentations at the conference were by scholarly and clerical leaders from the three Abrahamic traditions. Interestingly and tellingly, the typical talk started, "You know, I really don't know anything about digital culture or social media so I asked my kids." Each then proceeded to offer a thorough evaluation of how digital media are affecting religion. It was a fascinating disconnect that caused me to reflect, especially in relation to these chapters, on the question of how we talk about the digital and how we should think about it.

The chapters and case studies in this book raise important questions about the frames we use when we encounter and respond to the changed realities resulting from the digitalization of religion and spirituality. In contrast to the arguments and information presented here, it occurs to me that there is a tendency for people who don't know much about the intersection of religion and the Internet, but want to talk about it, to either essentialize or particularize the digital.

First, by "essentializing," I mean that some tend to evaluate the digital and digital practice in relation to what it does, what it stands for, or whom it effectively stands in for. This means some see the digital as a pundit or poor substitute for the actual and authentic role played by religion. The second response, to "particularize" the digital, means "instrumentalizing" it and thinking about how digital culture and practice might serve or stand in for prior means of mediation and other previous forms of practice.

What the writings in this book illustrate is both the need for and the value of a more nuanced view of the digital. We have to understand that it is not just a question of authenticity in the broad sense, or a response which simply trivializes the digital or the social into a merely instrumentalist frame. It is actually a much more complex and layered approach or negotiation that we must undertake. The problem is that without this larger perspective it is not possible for us to consider whether there really is something truly unique produced by engagement with the digital. For me, some key ideas emerge out of these explorations, indicating that our understanding of the digitalization of the religious and spiritual is indeed moving forward to a more nuanced understanding.

One of the very interesting implications of this work is that there is a truly different relationship to authority being articulated due to the nature of the digital. The question is not so much, "How is the digital authoritative?" which is an important issue, or "How is it authentic?" which is also important. The more significant issue is how this range of practices online tends to particularize and relativize and thus challenge religious authority. There are new instantiations of authority emerging. Authority itself is very much, to use a Texas metaphor, "in the cross hairs." Many religious authorities do not fully understand this and are often in full panic mode when it comes to the implications of the digital, instead of carefully considering what they are actually up against. The real issue is not the digital media themselves; part of the problem is the particularization of those media.

The digital practices explored in these writings show how online religious and spiritual practice actually identifies and engages with real religious material by drawing on accepted symbols, icons and other meanings found in traditional religious contexts. It is possible for authorities that are related to those symbols and icons to be confused by these new online representations into focusing on the persistence of the symbols and other resources. They may believe that there are some consistent narratives online that they themselves actually have a piece of, when in fact what's going on is the practice is particularizing and relativizing those things and subsuming them into a broader, horizontal marketplace of choice. They aren't aware of how serious a challenge this is.

The issue of practice is central to this; it is a kind of meta-response to changes at work in our understanding of religion. What is new and what is different about the digital is the extent to which it encourages new modes of practice, and that it is practice that defines what is going on and not the symbols, not the history, not the authority. We need to explore the *generativity* of digital religion, of how "it" becomes a complex expression of nuance and constantly layered practice of interacting with tradition, quoting religion, particularizing religions, coming up with new and elastic forms of tradition. We need to explore more how the digital serves as a generative space for religion, and how we can actually generate meaning from online engagement and interaction.

Thus it seems to me that there are several lessons that come out of reflections on religion and the Internet. The first concerns the ways we think about the digital and its locus of generation as a new space, as a "third space." We use this term in our work at the Center for Media, Religion, and Culture (recognizing that others, such as the Pew Internet and American Life Project, have also taken on this concept) to consider the space which the digital creates. It is important to understand that constitution of the third space does not grow out of the logic of the technology, but out of the logic of digital practice. In other words, it grows out of various "as-ifs" generated by diverse practitioners and audiences who flexibly engage in actions within this new space that they inhabit, which is one that they create in their aspiration and their self-understanding and their subjectivity.

Second is the issue of how these third spaces act and are understood. Rather than being framed as vast spheres of discourse in which various religious symbols and values are linked to religious institutions with which they are in conflict, third spaces are in a way small sphericals of focused interactions. They are not a large public sphere, but small sphericals of action and practice that operate as their own spaces. Social action can be generated out of these logics. One concern of leaders of the Abrahamic faiths at the Doha conference was how digital space can be generative of social action. The assumption there was that these media are probably more distractions from actual social involvement than paths toward it. This is an important question, but we shouldn't be confused into thinking that it is always the instrumentalization of the digital or equating it with an implied or desired social action that is the central concern. Questions must be asked about what is entirely new in the sort of space the digital creates, and what sorts of things it produces.

Finally, let me point to the related issue of the ways that the digital and digital religion are treated, at least in public and journalistic discourse. Attention and discussion given to digital religion is usually focused on what it produces in the digital space. Yet we have to keep in mind that at some fundamental level digital religion is essentially about religion and spirituality. It is not about changing the world and politics; it is about people using technologies to live out the spiritual. We must see digital religion as being about the generation of models of practice and the ability to produce meaning in the world that relates to the religious. A colleague of mine has remarked that in many ways what really defines much of online practice is the aesthetic rather than the cognitive and perceptive logic of the digital. What do technologies hail us into because of the abilities that they have for us in terms of aesthetic purposes and qualities? This question and these related issues are the questions we must continue to ask and explore. The chapters here are a valuable and generative start.

Index

Abu Isa's Quest for Knowledge 137–39, 141, 144–45
Alt-Muslim 16, 191–94
apps 1, 11, 16, 199, 200, 201, 202–4, 205
authenticity 3, 9–10, 12, 15–16, 26, 30, 48, 51, 80, 88–99, 131, 133, 196–97, 199–5, 266
authority 3, 6–10, 12, 14–17, 25, 31, 48, 62, 72–84, 94, 99, 105, 112–13, 128, 177, 179, 182–88, 190, 193, 195, 199, 201–5, 208, 213, 218, 243, 246, 259, 267, 270

Baffelli, Erica 16, 18, 207–14
Bellah, Robert 231
blogs 12, 15, 44, 48, 60, 79, 81, 91, 98, 158, 166–68, 170, 182–88, 209, 213, 215, 233, 240, 244
Buddha 10, 32, 59, 81, 128–34
Buddhism 12–13, 128–30, 132–34, 208–9, 215

Campbell, Heidi 1, 7–10, 18, 29–31, 48, 57–71, 73, 77, 79, 90, 92, 104, 111–13, 147, 158, 165, 201–4, 232–35
cell phone 12, 15, 48, 64, 173–79, 202; mobile phone 10, 42; 3G 174–75, 177–79
Chabad 14, 155–61
Cheong, Pauline 3, 9, 14, 18, 48, 72–87, 113, 183
Christianity 12, 48, 73, 77, 215, 228, 234, 252–53, 258, 261
church 1, 5, 14–15, 31, 34, 48–49, 59, 67, 75, 78–80, 82, 93, 98, 104, 106, 148–53, 164–70, 183–88, 199–201, 203–4, 207, 219–20, 228, 233–34, 251–52, 254–62
Clark, Lynn 14, 18, 45–46, 49–51, 111 147–54, 199, 203, 232, 234

clergy 6, 73, 81, 83, 184–85, 187, 256
community 2–3, 5, 7–9, 12, 14–17, 26, 28–30, 36, 45, 47, 51, 58–68, 73, 75–79, 83, 95–96, 110–13, 128–29, 143–45, 147–50, 152–53, 155–62, 164–70, 173–79, 184, 201, 204, 209, 229, 231–33, 238, 241, 246–47, 252, 253–55, 258–62
computer games 44, 48, 108, 114 *see also* video games
conflict 28, 82, 144, 215–16, 218–21, 232–33, 244, 268
Connelly, Louise 10, 13, 18, 128–35
cyberchurch 1, 59, 80, 256, 258

darshan 122–24, 126
Dawson, Lorne 2, 9, 18, 46, 48, 51–52, 90, 99, 104, 111–12, 207–8, 252
digital 1–5, 7–18, 34, 41–46, 48–52, 57, 67, 72–74, 77, 80–81, 83–84, 88, 91, 93, 96–97, 104–5, 107–15, 141, 145, 147–53, 157, 164, 170, 174, 200–5, 225–30, 232–35, 246, 260–61, 267–68; digital media 1, 3, 7, 11, 13–14, 16, 41–42, 44–45, 48–52, 67, 72–74, 77, 80, 96–97, 104–5, 107–15, 147, 200, 202, 225–30, 233–34, 266–67
digital religion 1–5, 7, 11–12, 16–18, 104–5, 108–10, 113–15, 235, 266, 268
digital storytelling 14, 45, 49, 147–48, 150–53
Dierberg, Jill 14, 147–54

Echchaibi, Nabil 4, 16, 18, 190–98
ELCA 148
Eliade, Mercea 127
Enlightenment 128, 130, 133–34, 203
Enlightenment, The 104–7

270   Index

emerging church 15, 48, 98, 182–88, 233
ethics 239–1, 244, 246, 247–48, 251, 254, 259–60
Europe 96, 104–5, 107, 173, 193, 226, 239, 246

Facebook 1, 10, 36, 44, 60, 80, 83, 113–14, 161, 165, 167–70, 200, 210, 211
forum 1, 5, 16, 47–48, 58, 60–61, 76–78, 97, 114, 164, 166–68, 170, 183, 191, 196, 209, 215, 220–21, 242–43

Garner, Stephen 17, 251–65
gender 43, 49, 51, 80, 90–91, 95, 138, 145, 196
Golan, Oren 9, 14, 155–63
Grieve, Greg 4, 10, 16, 18, 93–94, 104–18, 128–29

Helland, Chris 2–3, 5, 9, 12, 18, 25–40, 45, 49, 58, 77, 111, 121, 211, 251, 258
hierarchy 5, 15, 72–73, 77, 79, 97, 179, 194, 207, 259
Hikari no Wa 16, 207, 209–13
Hinduism 12–13, 107, 121–22, 125–26
homepages 31, 37, 43, 215, 217, 219
Hoover, Stewart 4–5, 17–18, 46, 49–51, 67, 112, 165, 203, 228, 229–30, 233–34, 266–68
Hutchings, Tim 14, 67, 92, 164–72, 256, 258

identity 6–14, 16–17, 26, 42–52, 58, 60, 63, 67–68, 73, 77, 81, 93, 95, 98, 111–13, 128–29, 136–39, 141, 144–45, 147–53, 157, 179, 183, 191–92, 196, 199, 202–5, 212, 215–17, 220–21, 240–41, 243–45, 248, 251, 256, 258–60
Internet 1–18, 25–26, 29, 31–37, 41–52, 57–67, 72, 74–80, 82–83, 88–95, 96–97, 104, 110–14, 121–24, 126, 128, 155–61, 165–66, 173–74, 183–86, 190–91, 201–3, 207–13, 215–21, 228, 232–34, 238, 240–42, 244, 247–48, 251–52, 254–62, 266–67
Islam 7, 12–13, 16, 36, 47, 49, 61–62, 73, 76, 80, 112–13, 136–39, 141, 143–45, 190–94, 196, 215, 234
Israel 15, 79, 140–41, 156–58, 160, 173–74, 177–79

Japan 16, 76, 130, 144, 207–13
Jewish 5, 14–15, 58, 63, 79, 139, 148, 155–59, 173, 175–76, 178, 233
Jewish media 5, 14–15, 63, 79, 156–59 174–75, 178, 233
Johns, Mark 17, 107, 239–50
Judaism 5, 12, 73, 107, 155, 158–59, 234

late modernity 16, 43, 50, 105, 109–10, 161, 173, 229, 234
legitimacy 15, 31, 73, 75, 80, 83, 105, 159, 197, 213
Lovheim, Mia 9–10, 13, 18, 41–56, 90, 98, 113, 148, 183, 203
Lundby, Knut 17–18, 45, 49, 96–97, 148, 225–337
Lynch, Gordon 17, 231–34

media 1, 3–5, 7–18, 25, 27–28, 35, 37, 41–45, 48–52, 57, 63–64, 66–67, 72–84, 88, 92, 94, 96–99, 104–5, 107–15, 136, 139–41, 144–45, 147, 153, 156, 159, 161, 164–65, 170, 173, 175, 177–79, 182–85, 187, 190–94, 200, 202–5, 207–9, 212, 215–19, 221, 225–30, 232–35, 238, 252, 254, 257, 260, 262
media studies 3, 4–5, 10–13, 16–18, 44, 49, 52, 73, 88, 191, 225–27, 229
meditation 13, 81, 93, 109–10, 128–34, 201, 209, 211
mediation of meaning 17, 229–30, 234–35
mediation of sacred forms 17, 231, 234–35
mediatization 17, 96–97, 228–30, 232, 234–35; mediatization of religion 17, 229, 234–35
megachurch 167, 184
metanarrative 104, 106–7, 110, 113–14
Miczek, Nadja 16, 35–36, 91, 93, 164, 215–22
Mixi 210–11
mobile 10, 16, 18, 34, 42, 44, 67, 83, 97, 114–15, 192, 199–205, 230
mobile devices 44, 67, 115, 199, 201–3, 205; mobile technologies 97
Muslim video games 13, 136, 144–45

net religion 16, 58, 207, 210, 212–13
New Age 16–17, 51, 57, 66, 215–19, 221
new media 3–5, 7–19, 35, 37, 41, 43–45, 48, 51–52, 57, 63–64, 66–67, 72, 74, 78–79, 82, 84, 98, 105, 108–10, 113–15,

156, 179, 184, 191–92, 209, 217, 226–29, 232–34, 238, 251
new religious movements 12, 16, 75, 207–8, 213, 215

O'Leary, Stephen 29–30, 34, 46, 75, 112–14, 121
online–offline 1, 6, 14, 25, 63, 81, 89, 92, 94, 111, 113, 134; offline–online 48, 81, 90, 93–94
online churches 5, 14, 67, 165–70, 258
online community 5, 7, 14, 30, 57–68, 112, 156–61, 164–65, 169–70, 184, 204, 259
online forum 5, 16, 48, 58, 61, 77,
online *puja* 13, 78, 108, 122–26
online religion 2–4, 75, 94, 109–11, 123, 241
online rituals 13, 25, 28–29, 31–37, 88, 128, 133, 220

pagan 41–42, 47, 112, 142–44, 262
performance 2, 13–14, 26–28, 35, 47, 49, 51–52, 89–92, 95, 99, 107, 121, 169, 182, 199–200, 202, 204–5, 217
personalization 16, 42, 48, 147
prayer 1, 6, 29, 33, 46, 60, 92, 106, 128, 132–33, 139, 164, 166–67, 169, 195, 199–202, 220–21
priest 73, 76–78, 80–83, 107, 122, 130, 132
puja 13, 36, 77–78, 121–26
purity concerns 124–25

Quraish 141–45

Radde-Antweiler, Kerstin 15, 88–103, 245
Rashi, Tsuriel 15, 173–81
relationship 3, 10, 14, 37–38, 57, 59–60, 63, 65–67, 72, 74, 78, 80–81, 83–84, 89–90, 92–96, 98–99, 145, 148–51, 159, 165, 167, 169–70, 183, 185–86, 190, 192, 196, 204–5, 210, 213, 244, 248, 251–54, 256, 258–60, 262, 267
religion 1–18, 25–26, 31–32, 35–37, 41, 45–52, 58, 60–62, 67–68, 75, 76, 79, 82, 89, 94, 96–99 104–15, 121, 123, 133–34, 144, 147, 165, 179, 183–86, 188, 190, 196, 199, 202, 205, 207–13, 215–21, 225–35, 238, 241, 248, 251–52, 257–58, 266–68
religion online 2–4, 6, 8–12, 16, 36, 46, 50, 52, 60, 62, 75, 98, 112, 128, 182, 207–9, 212–13, 241, 258

religious communication 2, 8, 14–15, 29, 45, 47, 57, 60–68, 73, 75, 112, 155–61, 164–70, 179, 201, 232–33, 258
religious identity 6, 9–10, 13–14, 16, 41, 45–52, 67, 141, 145, 147–49, 152–53, 183, 215, 221
religious social shaping of technology 232
religious studies 10–11, 17–18, 26, 89, 99, 104, 115, 215–16, 225
ritual 2, 4, 6, 8–13, 16, 25–37, 41, 47, 49, 51, 61–62, 64, 77–78, 80–81, 88, 92–93, 95, 105–7, 111, 113–14, 121–22, 124–26, 128–34, 136, 156, 164–65, 184, 199–205, 212–13, 215, 217, 220–21, 226, 232, 238, 247

Scheifinger, Heinz 13, 73, 77, 121–27
Second Life 1, 12–13, 34–35, 60, 88, 91–92, 95, 109, 113–14, 128–34, 164, 166, 169, 233, 245
self 42–43, 45, 50–51, 90, 95, 136, 144, 147, 151, 199, 202–5, 231, 234
Sisler, Vit 13, 136–46
Smith, Jonathan Z. 30, 33–34, 42, 60, 62, 66, 88, 107, 126, 152
social construction 29, 38, 232, 255,
social media 3, 10, 45, 74, 80, 82, 113–14, 185, 191, 200, 202, 204, 257, 262, 266
social networking 16, 36, 44, 60, 67, 113, 161, 183, 209–10, 213, 215, 244, 258
social shaping of technology (SST) 17, 63, 232
spiritual 2–3, 6, 10, 14, 17, 25, 28, 30, 32, 45, 47–48, 60, 68, 75–77, 79, 81, 111, 133, 147, 177, 179, 185, 196, 199–200, 204, 207–8, 213, 216–19, 229, 234, 242, 254, 256–58, 262, 266–68
spirituality 5–6, 8, 10, 17, 110, 216, 219, 230, 233, 266, 268

technological determinism 17, 227–28, 232, 254, 261
Teusner, Paul 15, 48, 67, 98, 182–89, 260
theology 10, 17, 75, 89, 98, 165, 167, 170, 183–84, 187, 225, 251–53, 256–57, 259–62
Twitter 67, 82, 168, 200, 210–11, 245

ultra-Orthodox 14–15, 63, 79, 156–58, 160, 173–79; ultra-Orthodox media 173, 179
Under Siege 139–41, 145

video 13–14, 33, 37, 44, 108, 115, 148, 149–52, 164, 166, 168–70, 187, 190–91, 201–2, 209, 212, 238, 240

video games 13, 104, 136, 140, 144–45 *see also* computer games
virtual 1–2, 5–7, 10, 13, 15, 25, 29–30, 32–37, 45, 58–61, 67, 75, 83, 88–96, 98–99, 109–10, 114, 124, 126, 128–34, 136, 139, 144–45, 157, 164, 169, 200, 233, 238, 240, 245, 246, 248, 259, 261
virtual world 1, 10, 13, 33–35, 59–60, 88, 90–91, 93–96, 110, 114, 128, 139, 164, 240, 245, 248, 258

Wagner, Rachel 16, 199–206
website 1, 5–6, 16, 31–33, 36–37, 45, 47, 59, 61, 77, 79, 104–8, 114–15, 122–23, 155, 157–61, 164–67, 169, 188, 190, 194, 203, 207–11, 215–16, 218–19, 221, 256, 258
Web 2.0 36
World Wide Web 26, 36, 111, 232, 256, 262

Zen 129–30, 132, 201

Taylor & Francis

eBooks

FOR LIBRARIES

ORDER YOUR FREE 30 DAY INSTITUTIONAL TRIAL TODAY!

Over 23,000 eBook titles in the Humanities, Social Sciences, STM and Law from some of the world's leading imprints.

Choose from a range of subject packages or create your own!

Benefits for you
- Free MARC records
- COUNTER-compliant usage statistics
- Flexible purchase and pricing options

Benefits for your user
- Off-site, anytime access via Athens or referring URL
- Print or copy pages or chapters
- Full content search
- Bookmark, highlight and annotate text
- Access to thousands of pages of quality research at the click of a button

For more information, pricing enquiries or to order a free trial, contact your local online sales team.

UK and Rest of World: online.sales@tandf.co.uk
US, Canada and Latin America:
e-reference@taylorandfrancis.com

www.ebooksubscriptions.com

ALPSP Award for BEST eBOOK PUBLISHER 2009 Finalist

Taylor & Francis eBooks
Taylor & Francis Group

A flexible and dynamic resource for teaching, learning and research.